RED SONJA®

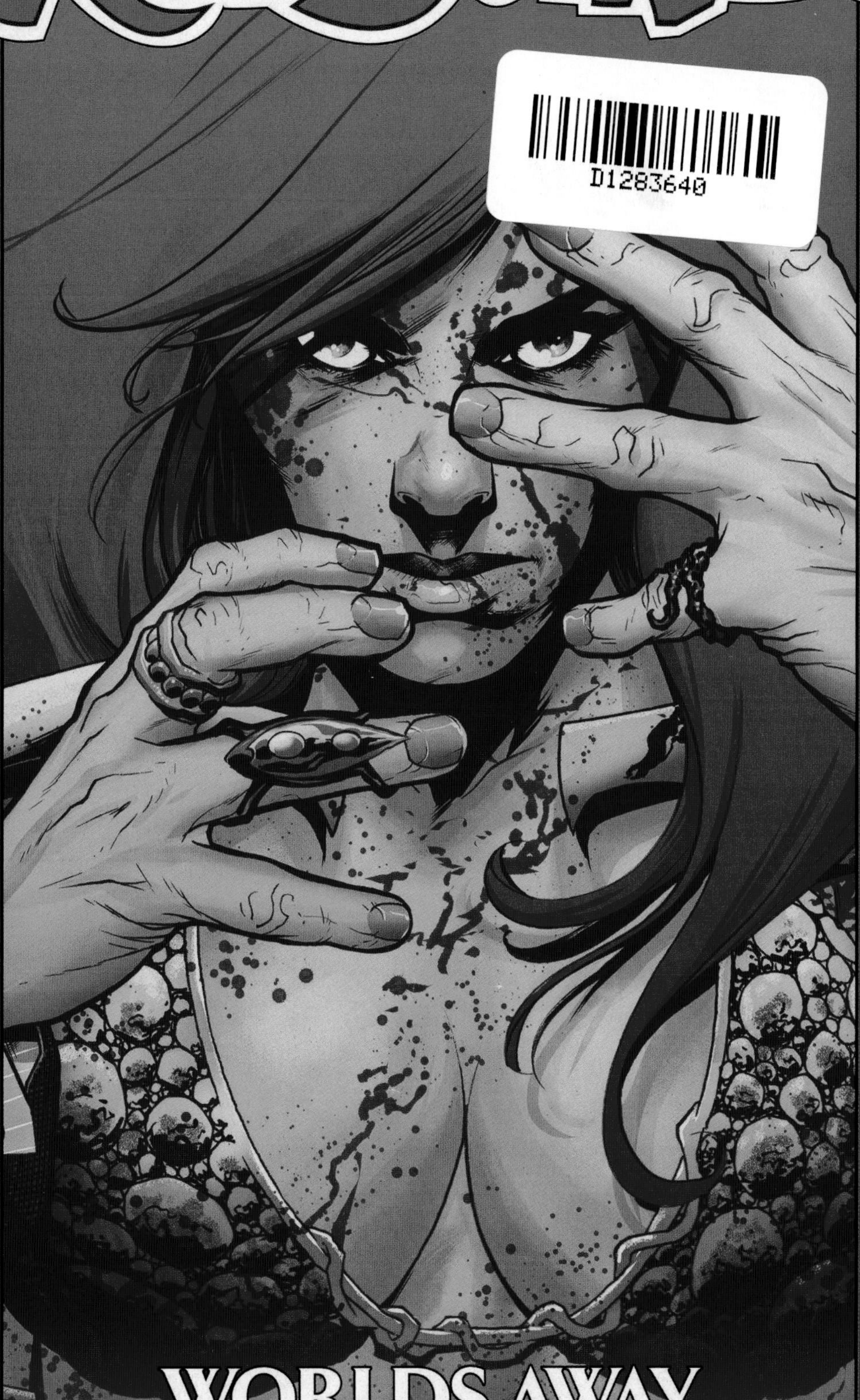

WORLDS AWAY
VOLUME 1

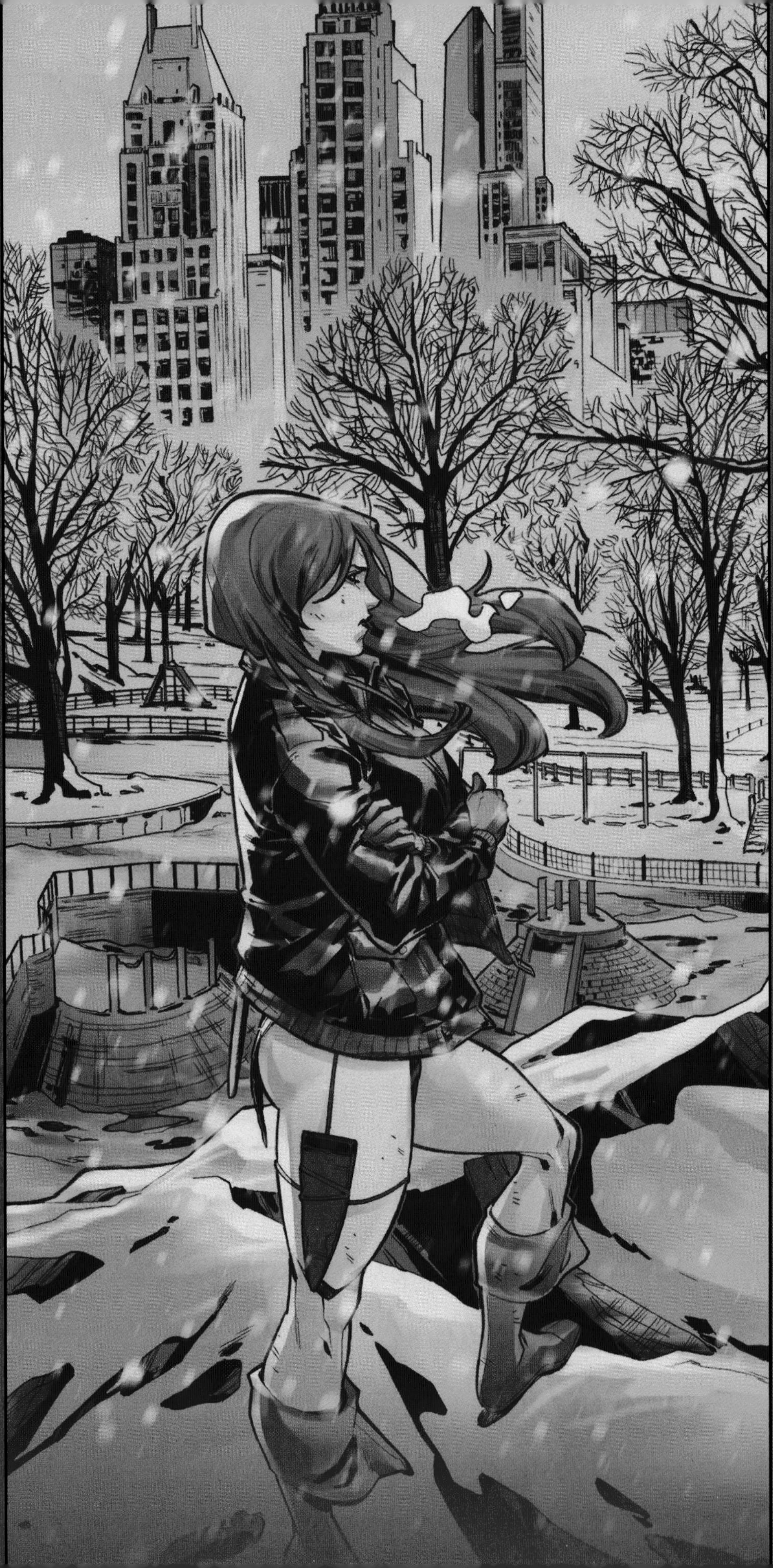

written by
AMY CHU

issues 0-4 & 6 illustrated by
CARLOS GOMEZ

issue 5 illustrated by
MARCIO FIORITO & CARLOS GOMEZ

colored by
MOHAN

issues 0-3 & 5-6 lettered by
SIMON BOWLAND

issue 4 lettered by
TOM NAPOLITANO

cover art by
NICK BRADSHAW

cover colors by
PETE PANTAZIS

co-executive editors **JOSEPH RYBANDT & LUKE LIEBERMAN**
associate editor **ANTHONY MARQUES**
book design by **CATHLEEN HEARD**

based on the heroine created by
ROBERT E. HOWARD

in memory of
ARTHUR LIEBERMAN

special thanks to
SHANNON KINGSTON

DYNAMITE®

Online at www.DYNAMITE.com
On Facebook /Dynamitecomics
On Instagram /Dynamitecomics
On Tumblr dynamitecomics.tumblr.com
On Twitter @dynamitecomics
On YouTube /Dynamitecomics

Nick Barrucci, CEO / Publisher
Juan Collado, President / COO

Joe Rybandt, Executive Editor
Matt Idelson, Senior Editor
Anthony Marques, Associate Editor
Matt Humphreys, Assistant Editor
Kevin Ketner, Assistant Editor

Jason Ullmeyer, Art Director
Geoff Harkins, Senior Graphic Designer
Cathleen Heard, Graphic Designer
Alexis Persson, Graphic Designer

Chris Caniano, Digital Associate
Rachel Kilbury, Digital Assistant

Brandon Dante Primavera, V.P. of IT and Operations
Rich Young, Director of Business Development

Alan Payne, V.P. of Sales and Marketing
Keith Davidsen, Marketing Director
Pat O'Connell, Sales Manager

ISBN13: 978-1-5241-0376-7
First Printing 10 9 8 7 6 5 4 3 2 1

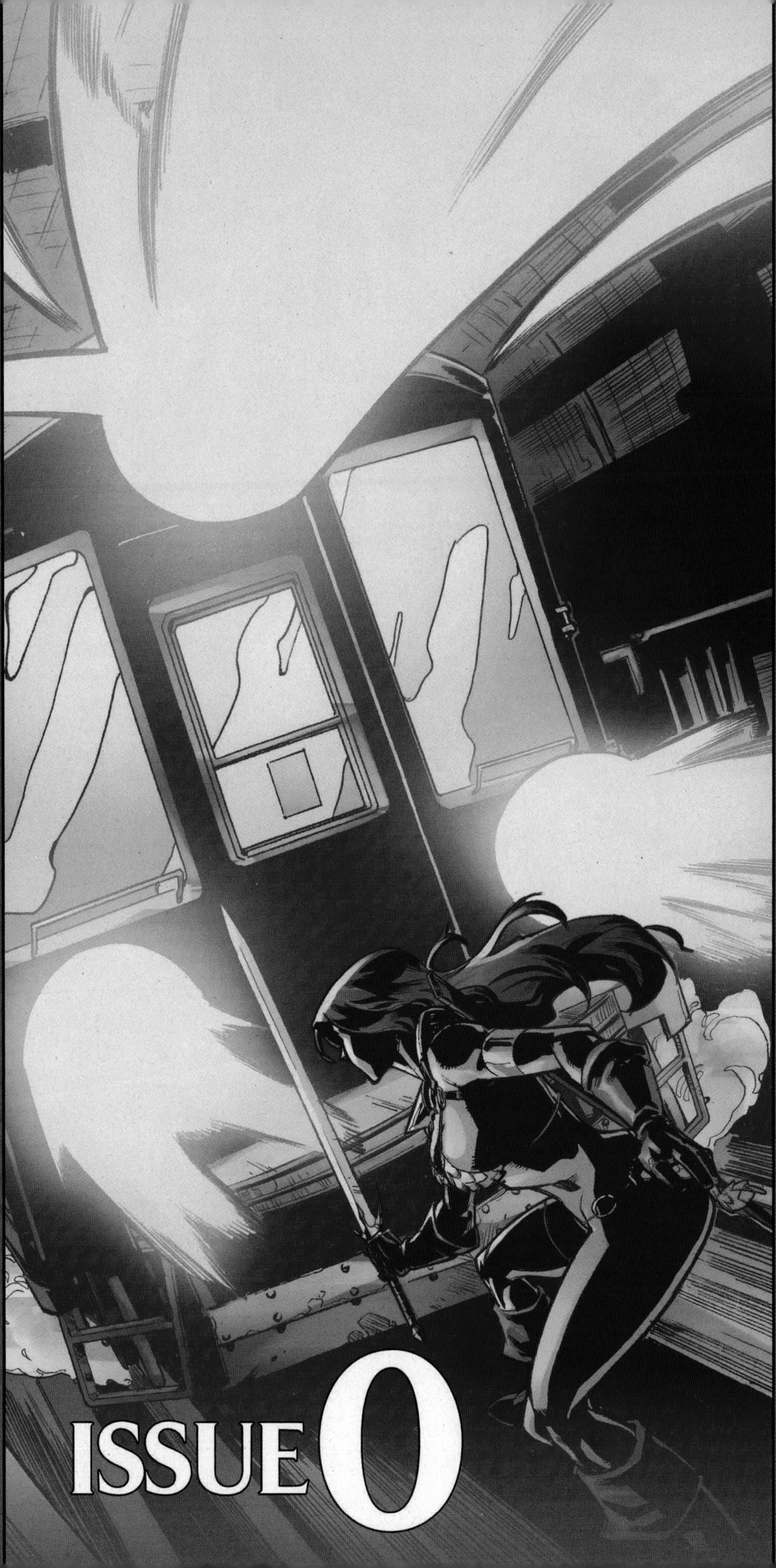
ISSUE 0

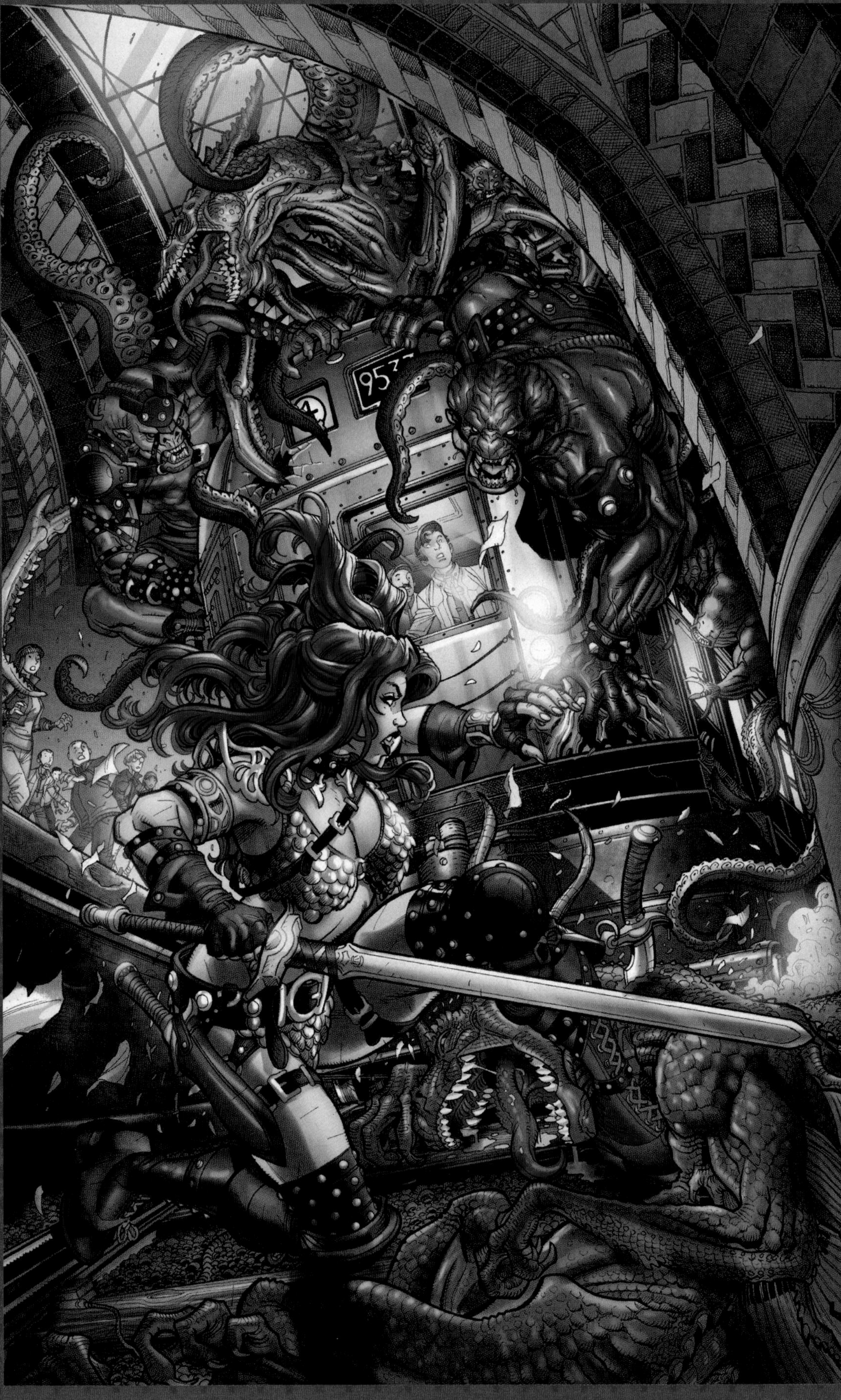

ISSUE #0: COVER ART BY **NICK BRADSHAW**, COLORS BY **PETE PANTAZIS**

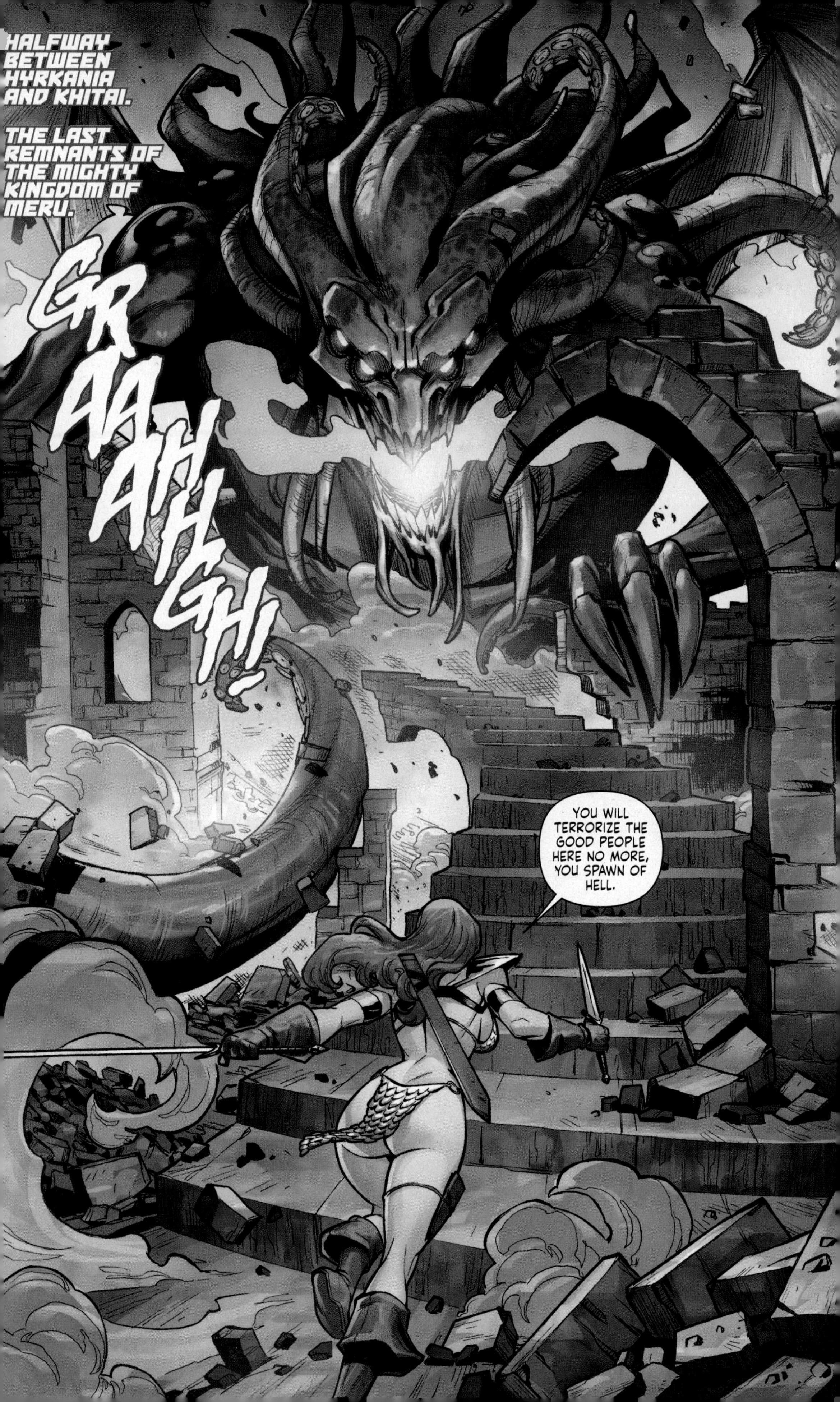
HALFWAY BETWEEN HYRKANIA AND KHITAI.
THE LAST REMNANTS OF THE MIGHTY KINGDOM OF MERU.
GRAAAHHGH!
YOU WILL TERRORIZE THE GOOD PEOPLE HERE NO MORE, YOU SPAWN OF HELL.

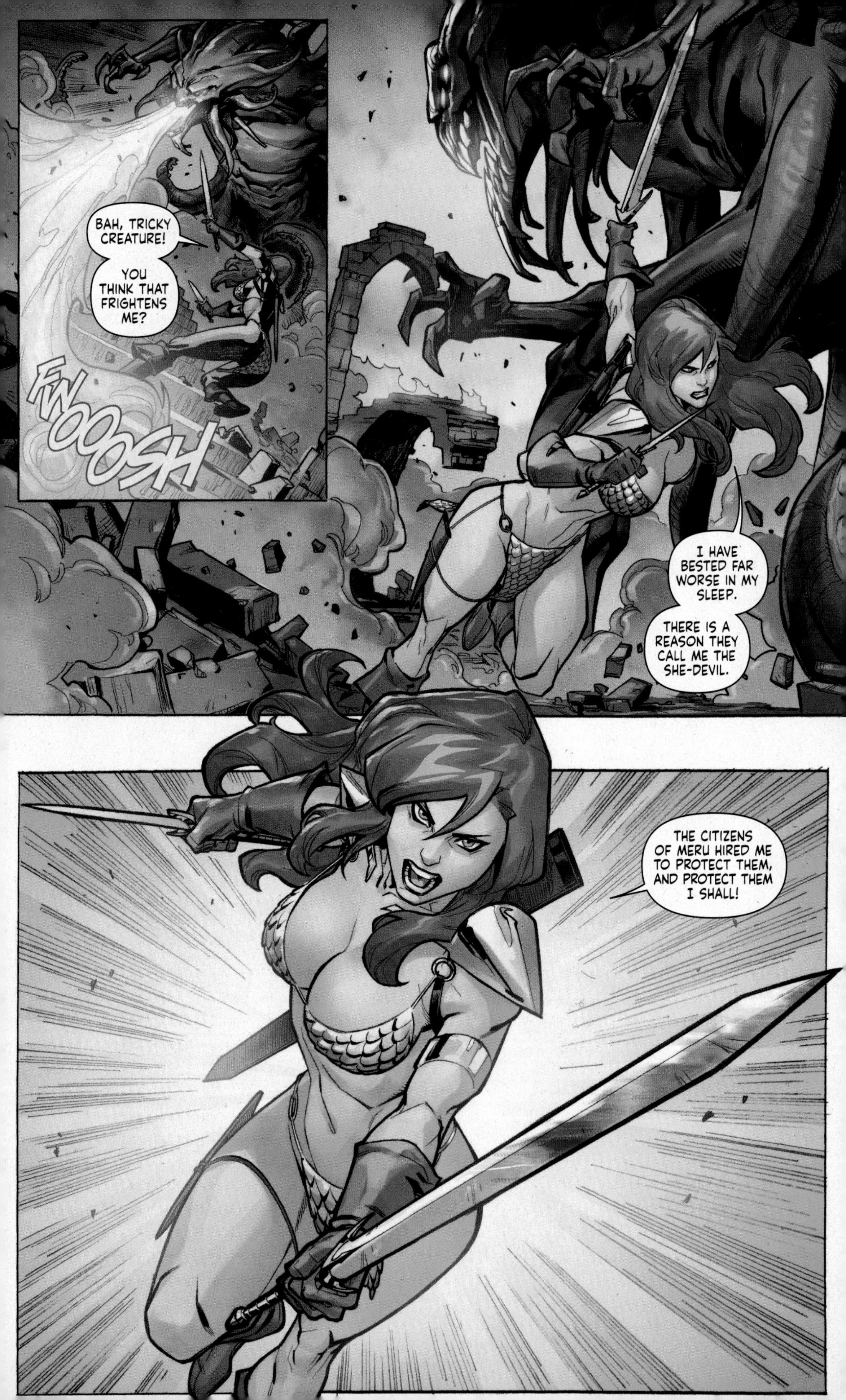
BAH, TRICKY CREATURE!
YOU THINK THAT FRIGHTENS ME?
FWOOOSH
I HAVE BESTED FAR WORSE IN MY SLEEP.
THERE IS A REASON THEY CALL ME THE SHE-DEVIL.
THE CITIZENS OF MERU HIRED ME TO PROTECT THEM, AND PROTECT THEM I SHALL!

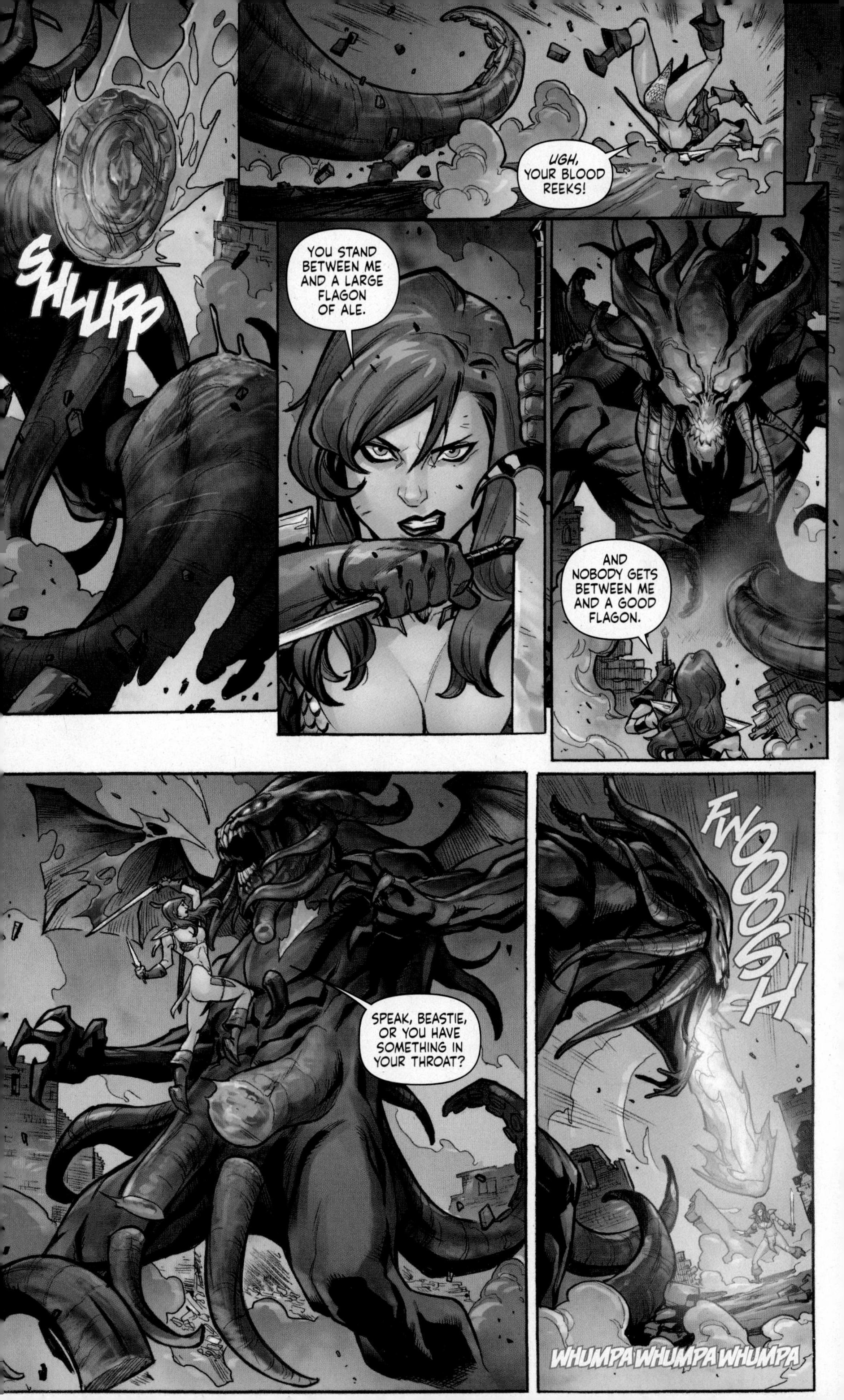
UGH, YOUR BLOOD REEKS!
SHLURP
YOU STAND BETWEEN ME AND A LARGE FLAGON OF ALE.
AND NOBODY GETS BETWEEN ME AND A GOOD FLAGON.
SPEAK, BEASTIE, OR YOU HAVE SOMETHING IN YOUR THROAT?
FWOOOOSH
WHUMPA WHUMPA WHUMPA

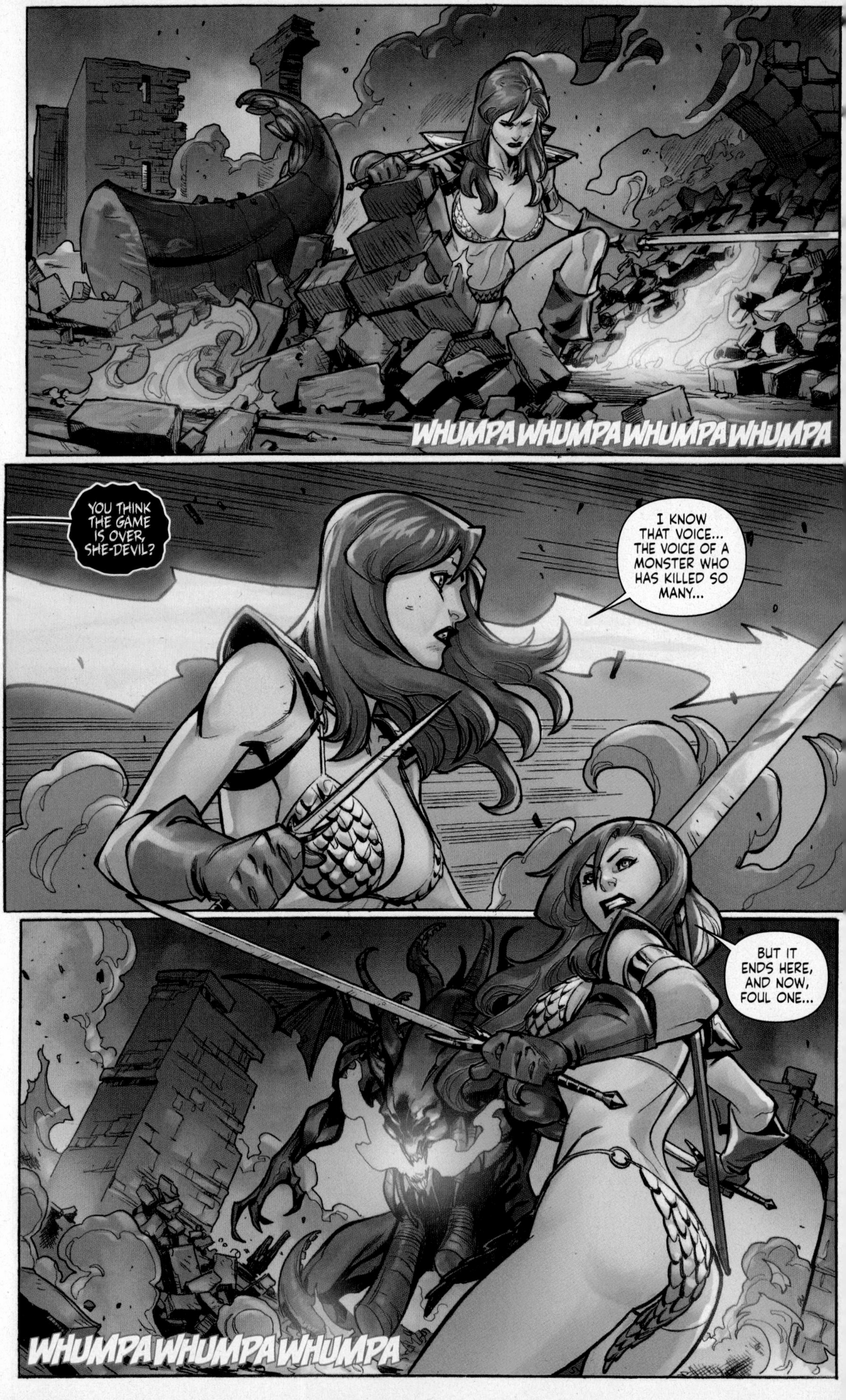
WHUMPA WHUMPA WHUMPA WHUMPA
YOU THINK THE GAME IS OVER, SHE-DEVIL?
I KNOW THAT VOICE... THE VOICE OF A MONSTER WHO HAS KILLED SO MANY...
BUT IT ENDS HERE, AND NOW, FOUL ONE...
WHUMPA WHUMPA WHUMPA

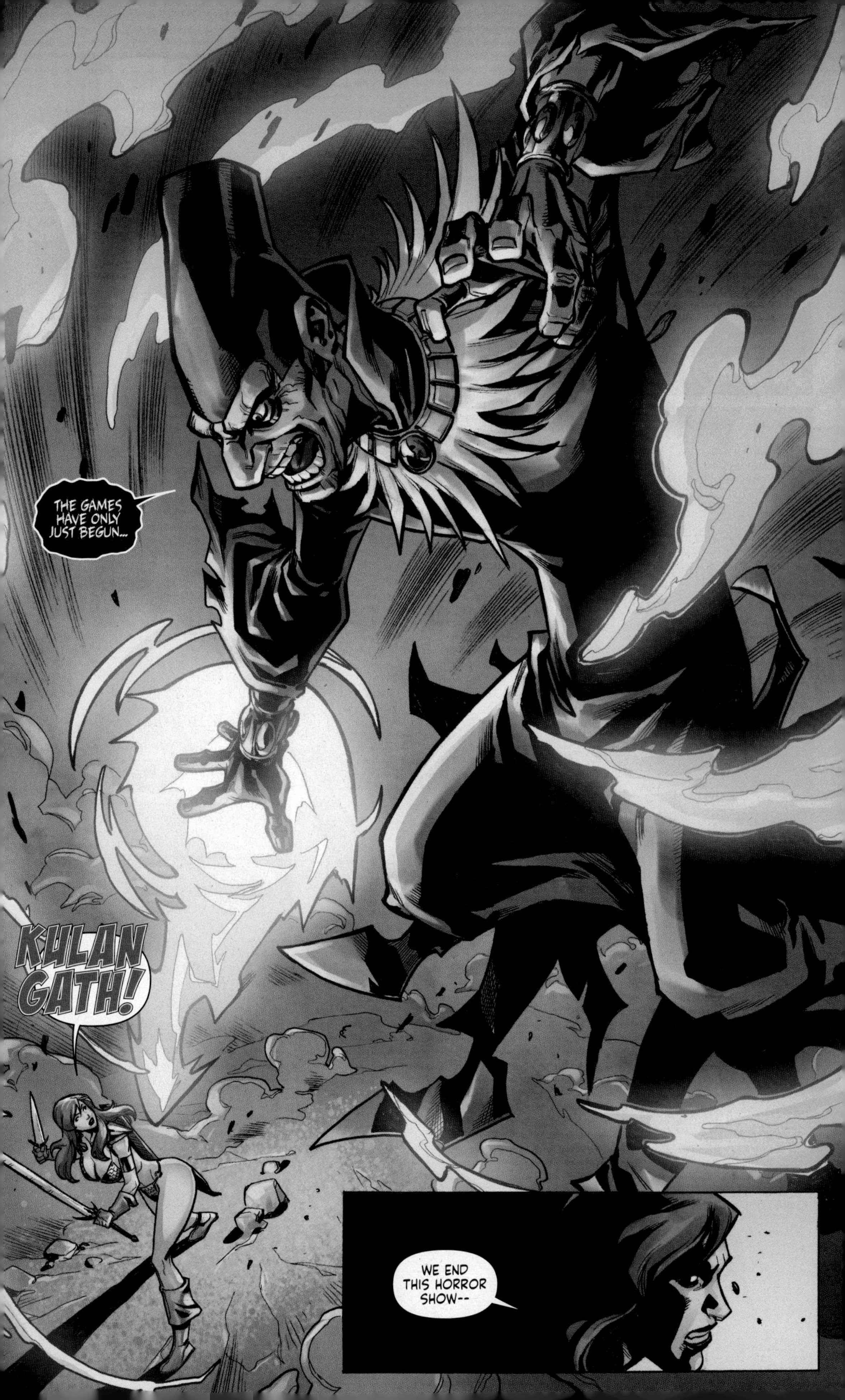

THE GAMES HAVE ONLY JUST BEGUN...
KULAN GATH!
WE END THIS HORROR SHOW--

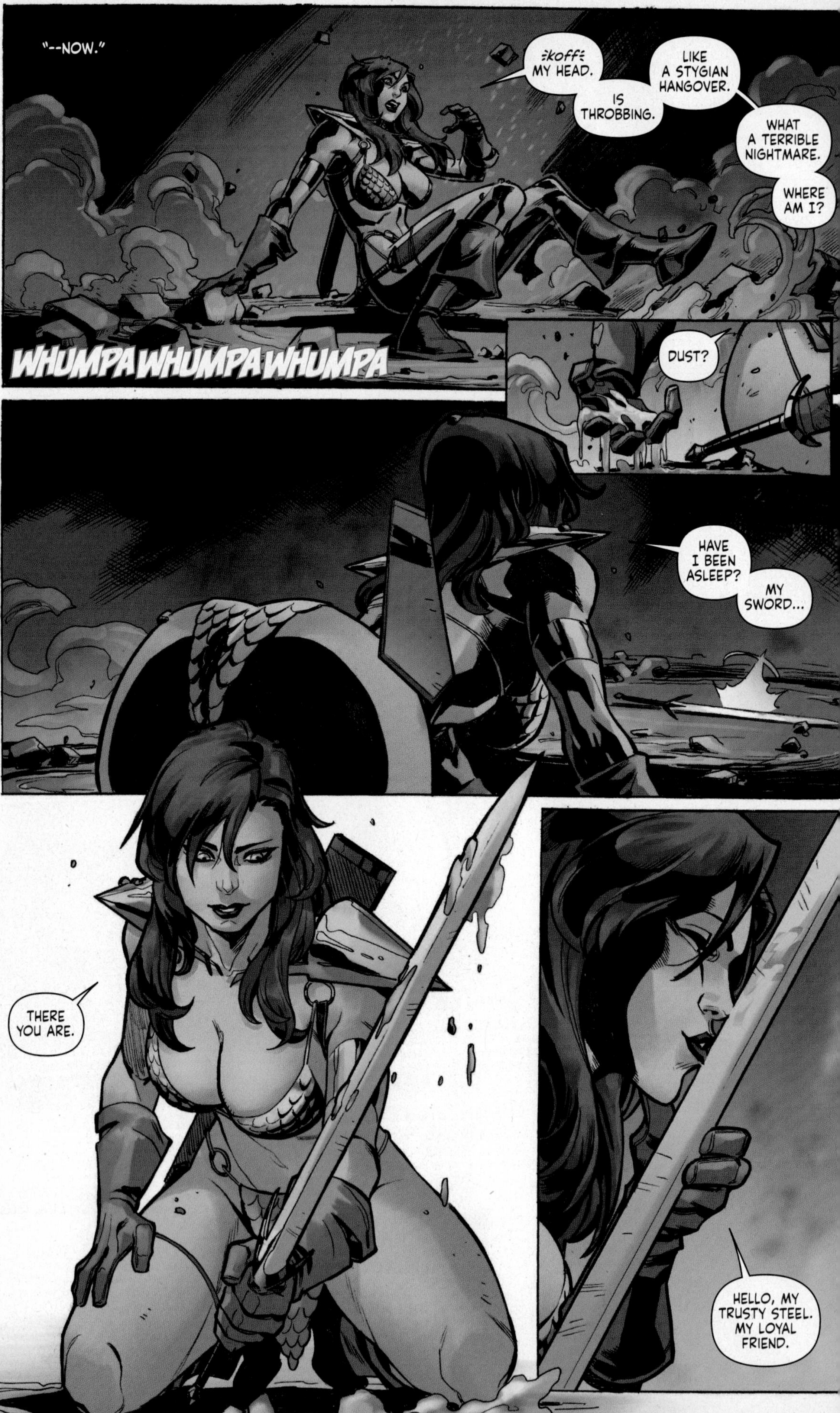
"--NOW."
≈koff≈ MY HEAD.
IS THROBBING.
LIKE A STYGIAN HANGOVER.
WHAT A TERRIBLE NIGHTMARE.
WHERE AM I?
WHUMPA WHUMPA WHUMPA
DUST?
HAVE I BEEN ASLEEP?
MY SWORD...
THERE YOU ARE.
HELLO, MY TRUSTY STEEL. MY LOYAL FRIEND.

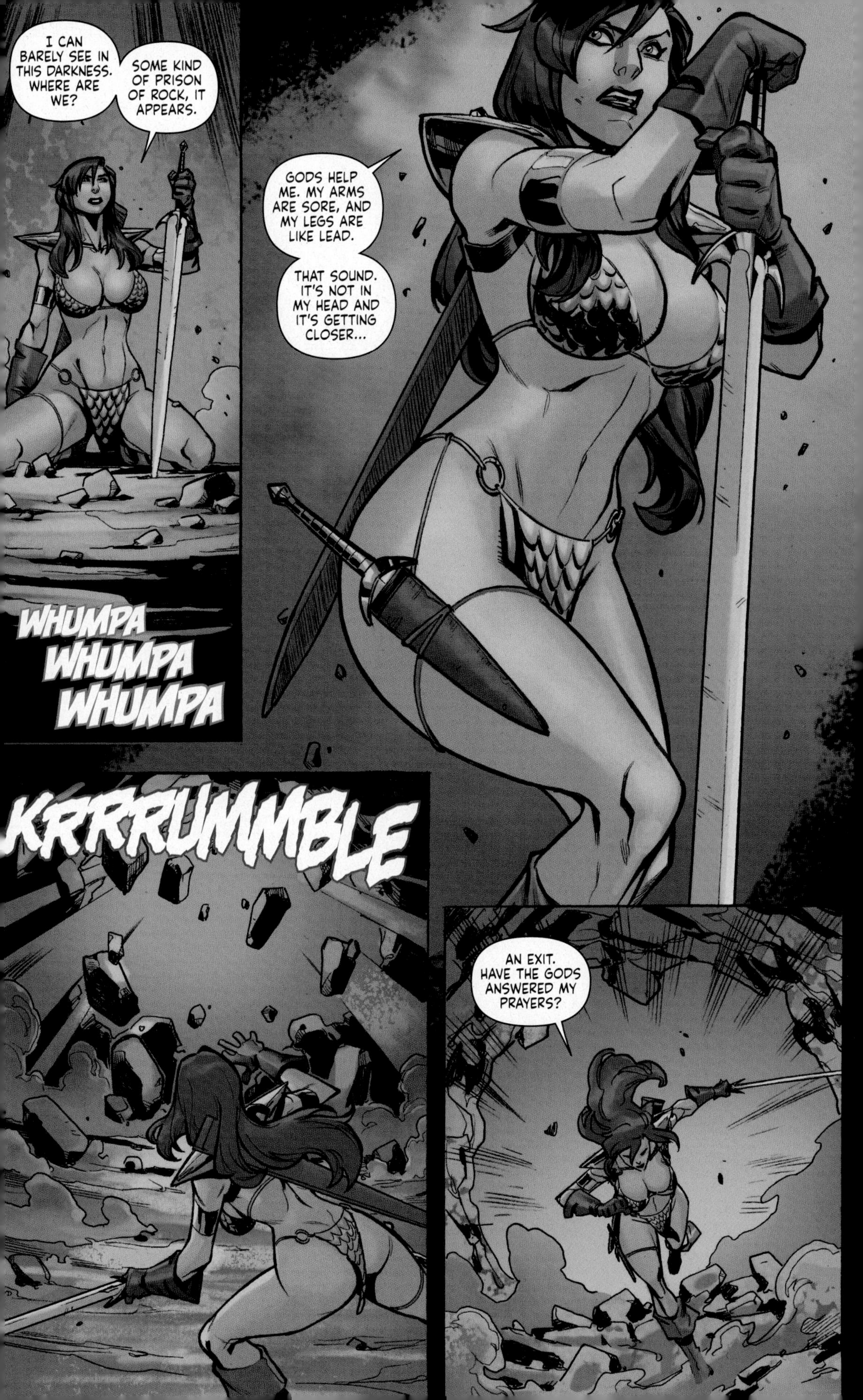
I CAN BARELY SEE IN THIS DARKNESS. WHERE ARE WE?
SOME KIND OF PRISON OF ROCK, IT APPEARS.
WHUMPA WHUMPA WHUMPA
GODS HELP ME. MY ARMS ARE SORE, AND MY LEGS ARE LIKE LEAD.
THAT SOUND. IT'S NOT IN MY HEAD AND IT'S GETTING CLOSER...
KRRRUMMBLE
AN EXIT. HAVE THE GODS ANSWERED MY PRAYERS?

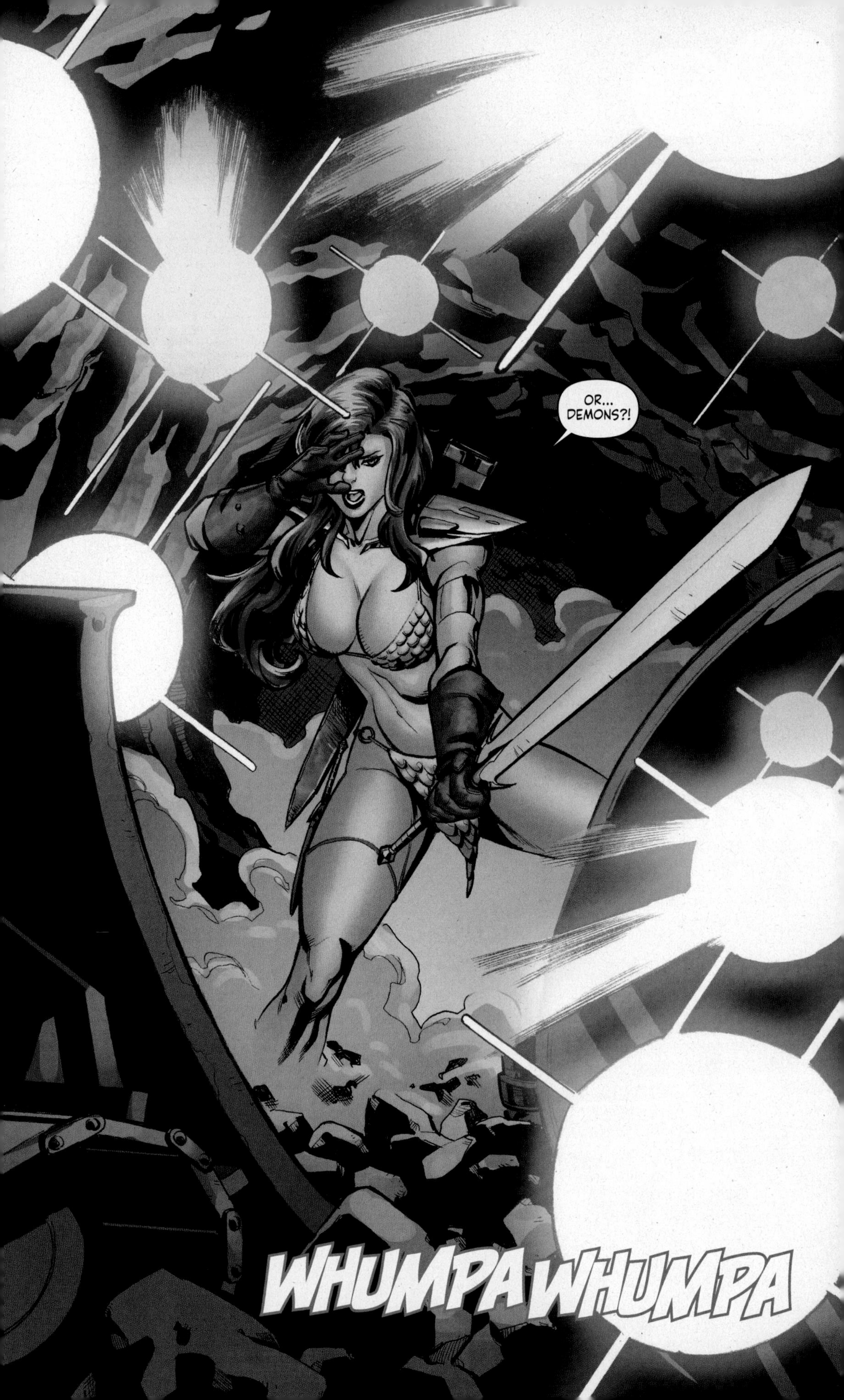
OR... DEMONS?!
WHUMPA WHUMPA

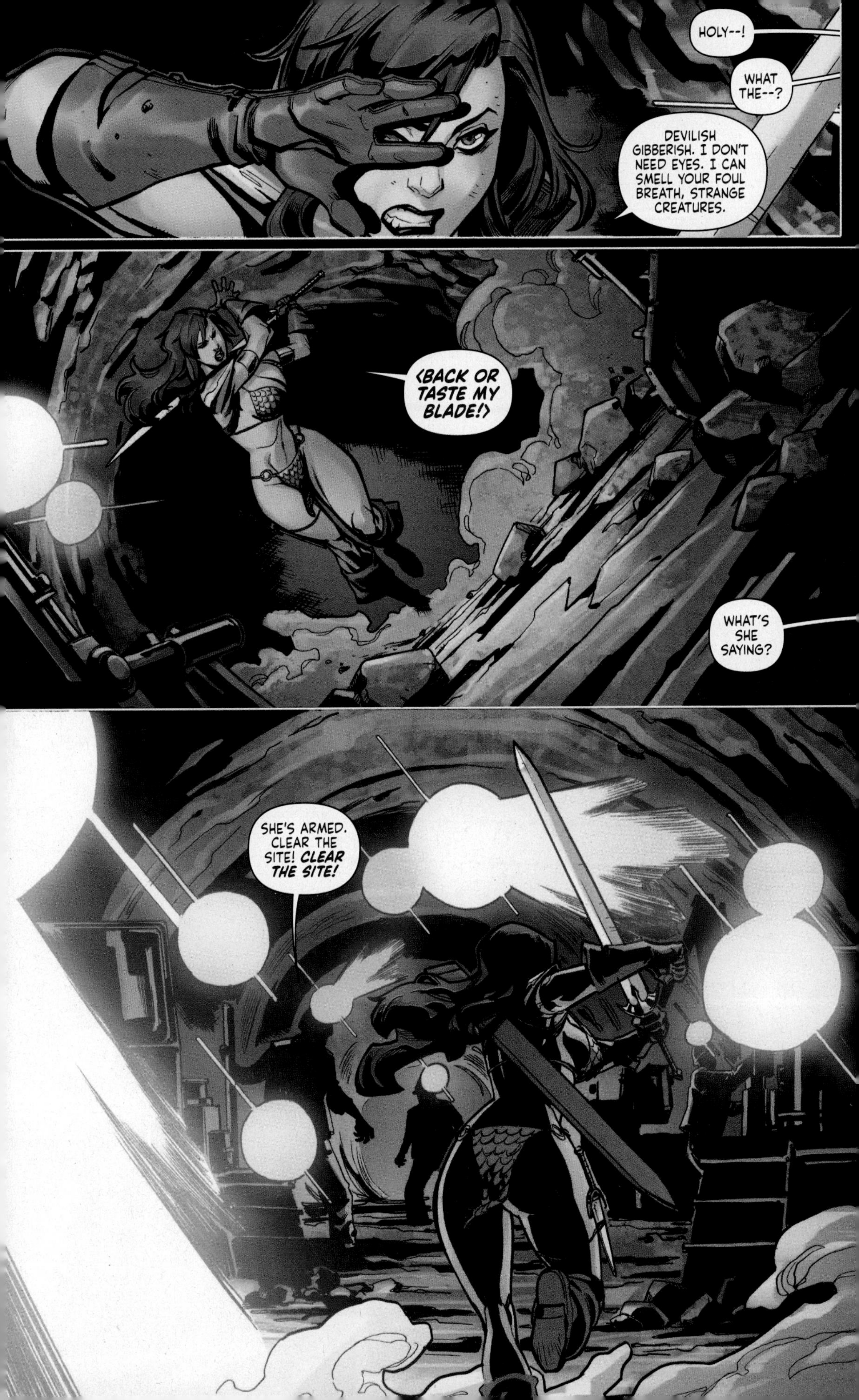
HOLY--!
WHAT THE--?
DEVILISH GIBBERISH. I DON'T NEED EYES. I CAN SMELL YOUR FOUL BREATH, STRANGE CREATURES.
<BACK OR TASTE MY BLADE!>
WHAT'S SHE SAYING?
SHE'S ARMED. CLEAR THE SITE! CLEAR THE SITE!

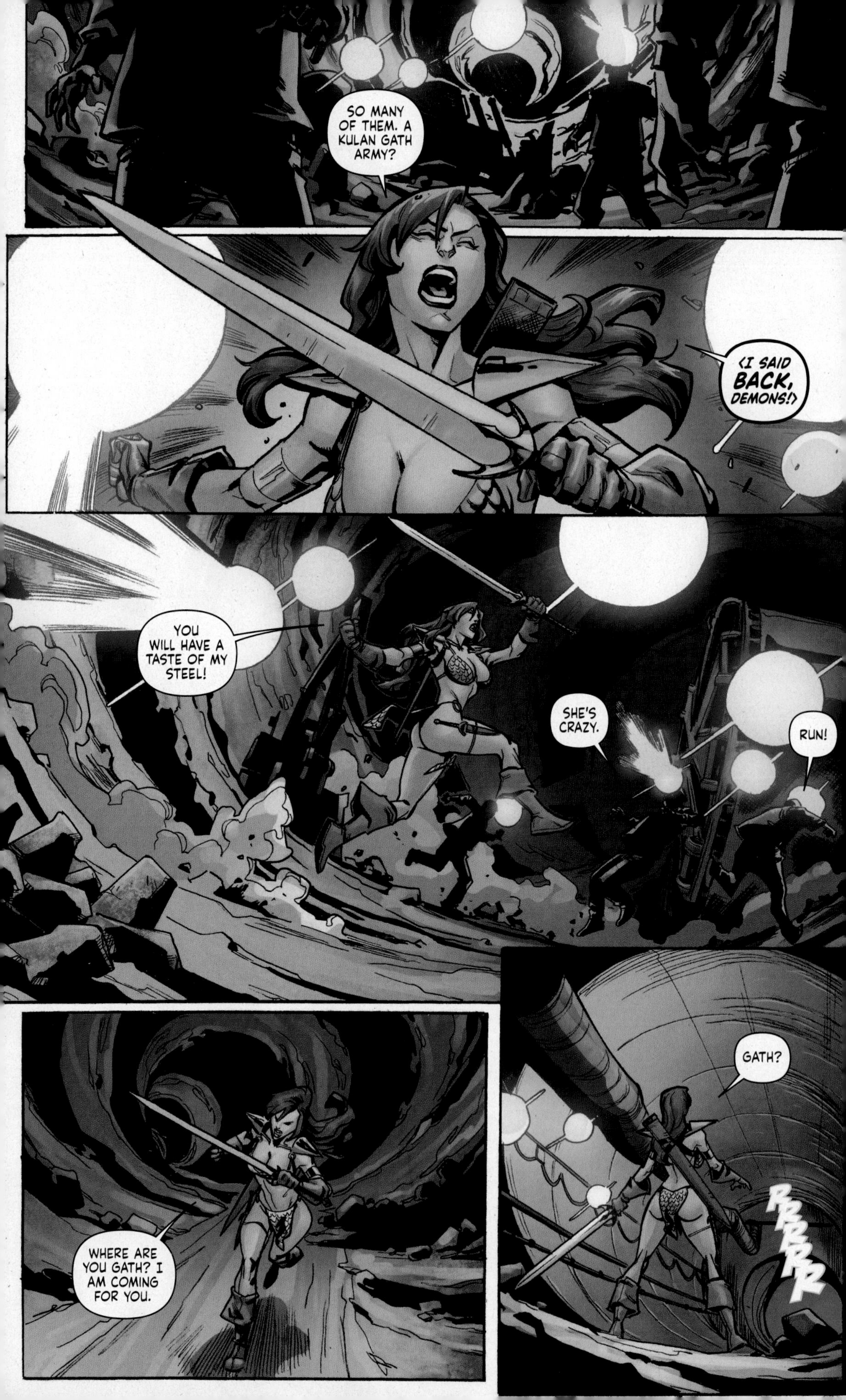
SO MANY OF THEM. A KULAN GATH ARMY?
<I SAID BACK, DEMONS!>
YOU WILL HAVE A TASTE OF MY STEEL!
SHE'S CRAZY.
RUN!
WHERE ARE YOU GATH? I AM COMING FOR YOU.
GATH?
RRRRR

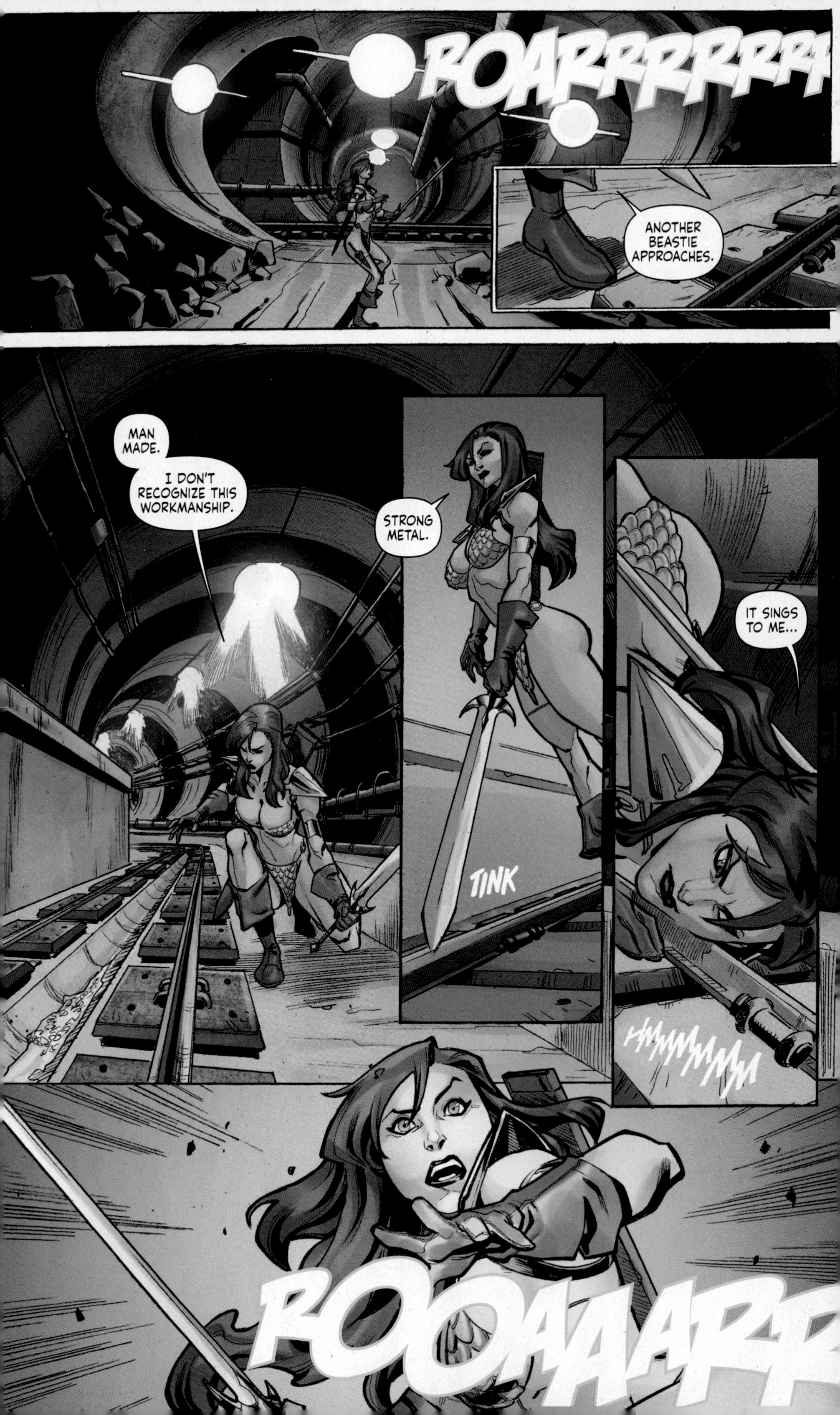
ROARRRRRR
ANOTHER BEASTIE APPROACHES.
MAN MADE.
I DON'T RECOGNIZE THIS WORKMANSHIP.
STRONG METAL.
TINK
IT SINGS TO ME...
HMMMMMM
ROOAAARR

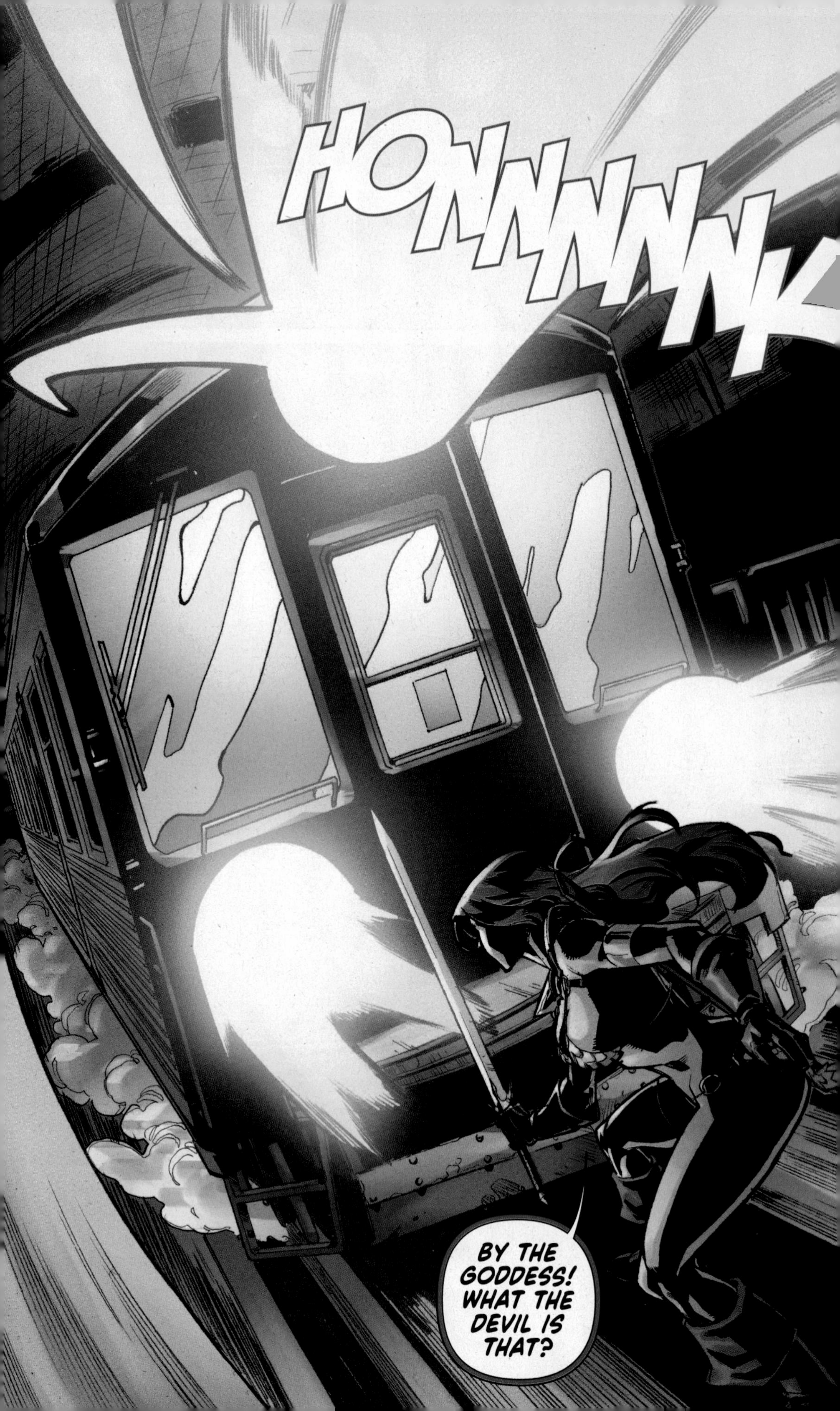
HONNNNNK
BY THE GODDESS! WHAT THE DEVIL IS THAT?

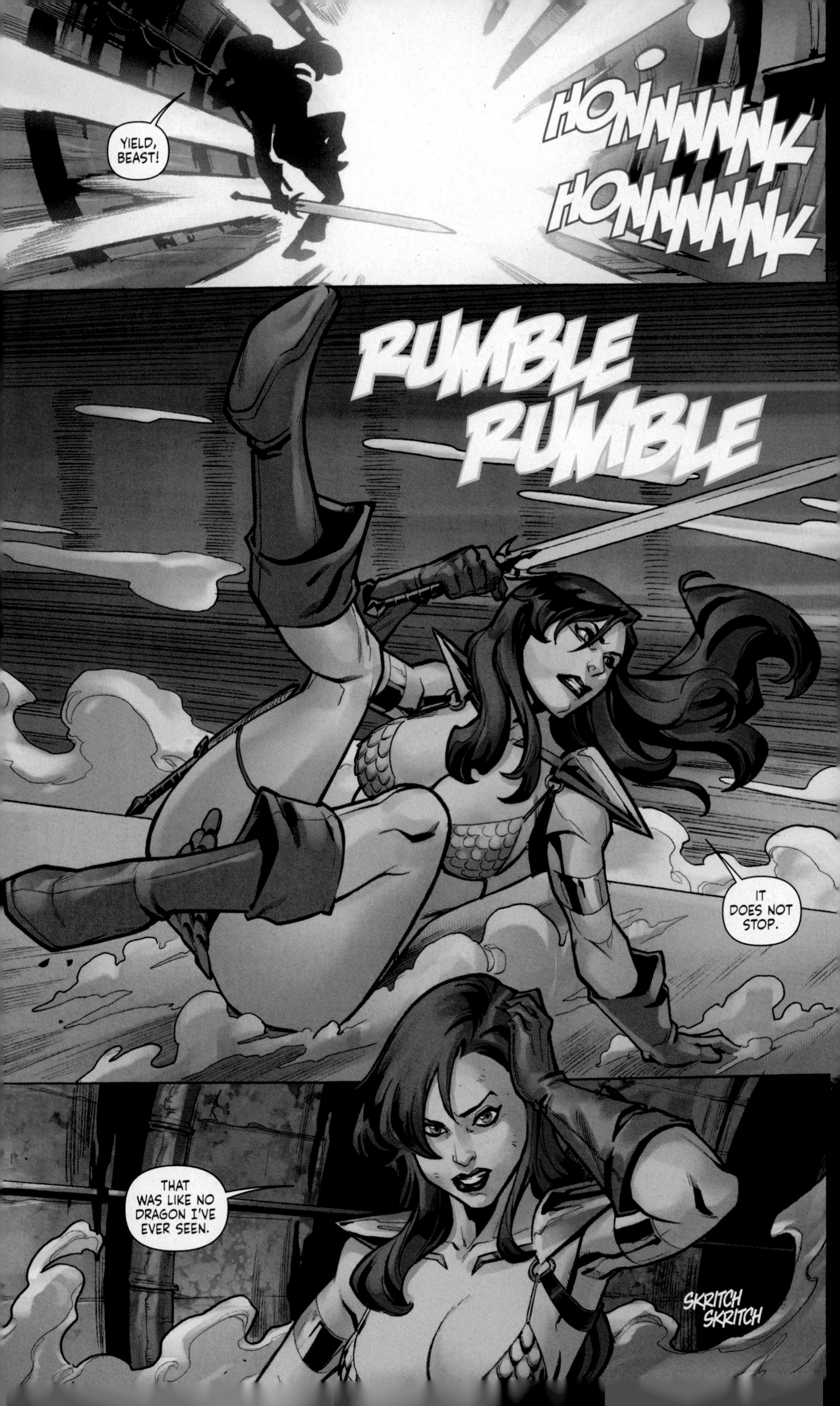
YIELD, BEAST!
HONNNNNK HONNNNNK
RUMBLE RUMBLE
IT DOES NOT STOP.
THAT WAS LIKE NO DRAGON I'VE EVER SEEN.
SKRITCH SKRITCH

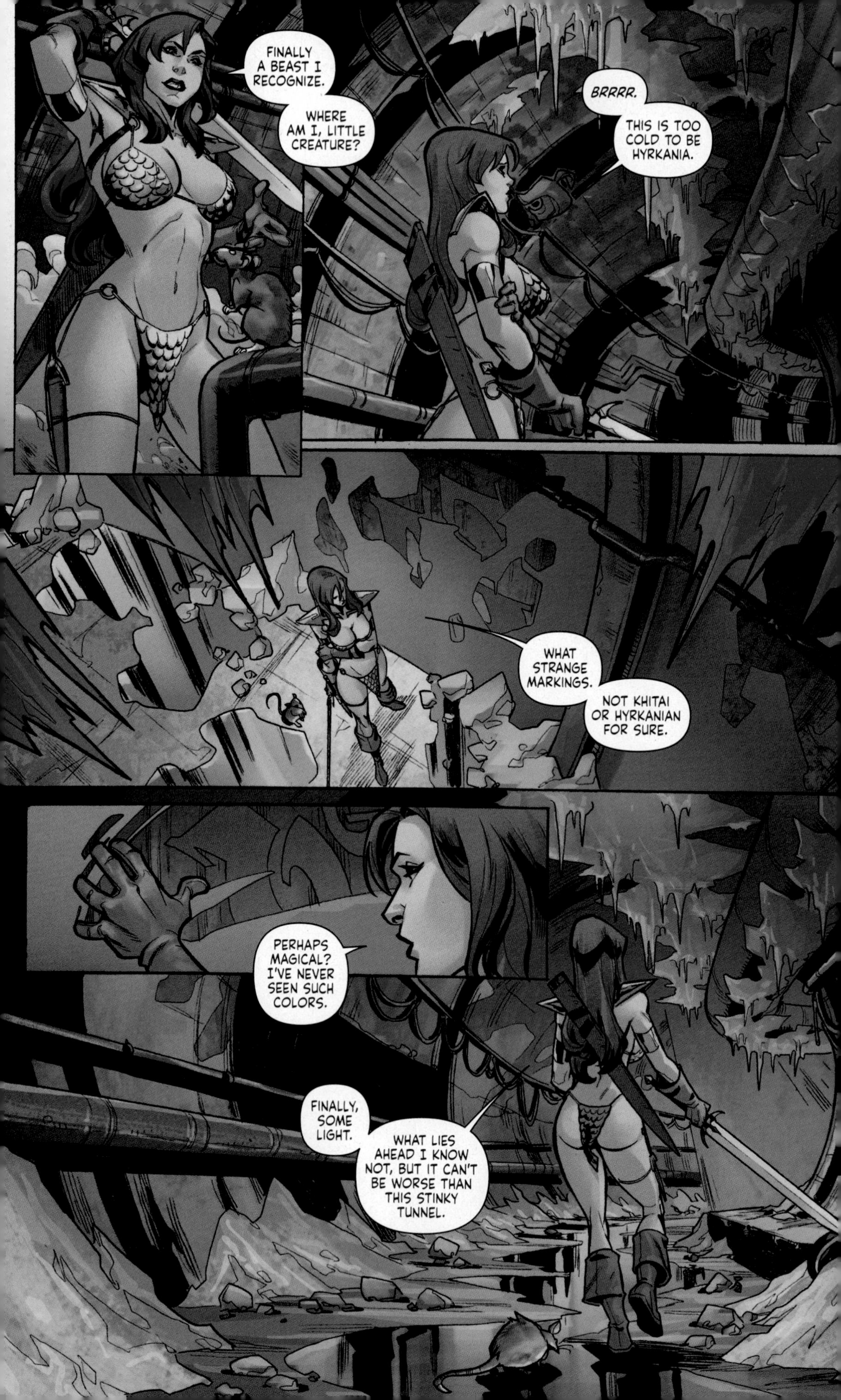
FINALLY A BEAST I RECOGNIZE.
WHERE AM I, LITTLE CREATURE?
BRRRR.
THIS IS TOO COLD TO BE HYRKANIA.
WHAT STRANGE MARKINGS.
NOT KHITAI OR HYRKANIAN FOR SURE.
PERHAPS MAGICAL? I'VE NEVER SEEN SUCH COLORS.
FINALLY, SOME LIGHT.
WHAT LIES AHEAD I KNOW NOT, BUT IT CAN'T BE WORSE THAN THIS STINKY TUNNEL.

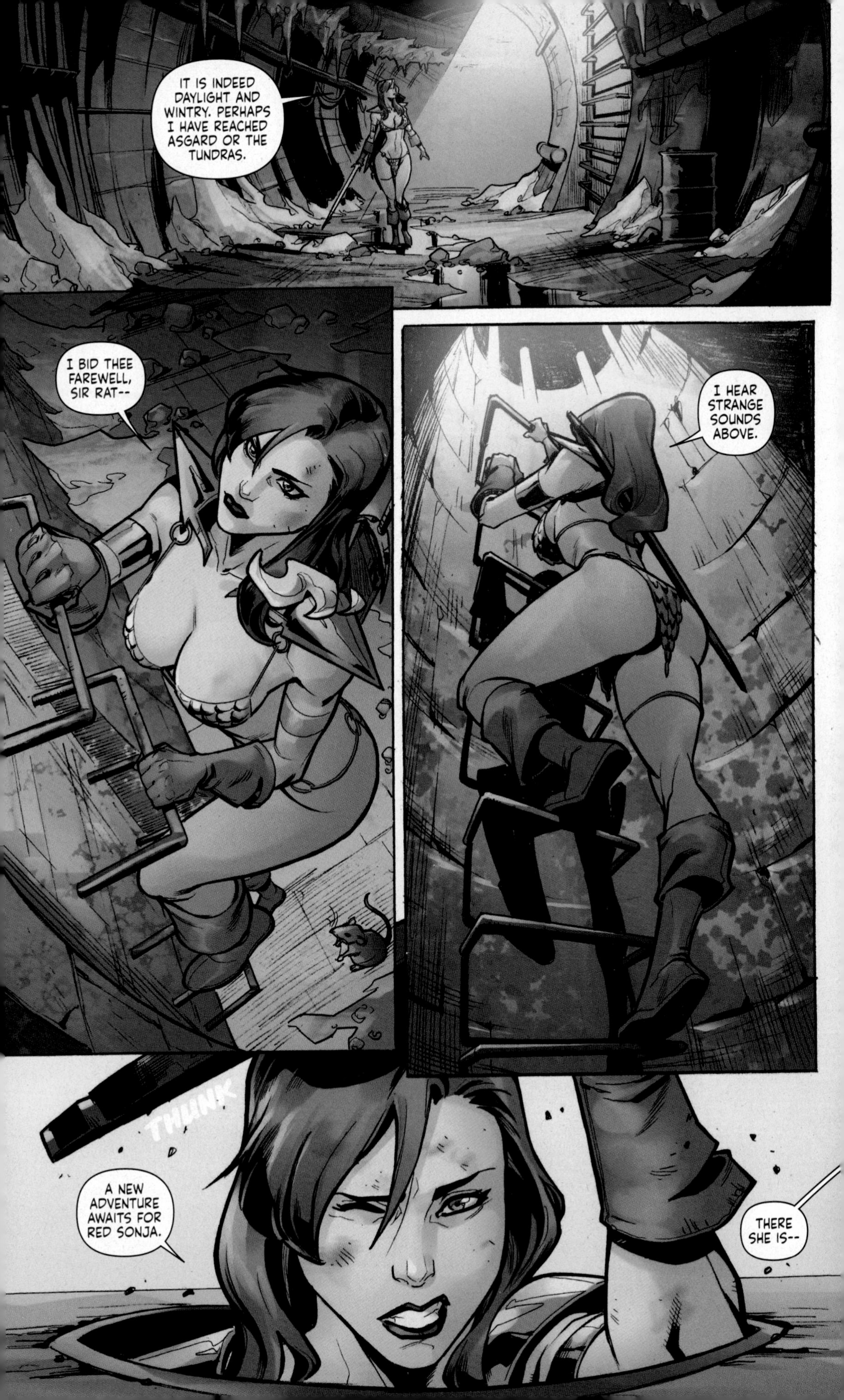
IT IS INDEED DAYLIGHT AND WINTRY. PERHAPS I HAVE REACHED ASGARD OR THE TUNDRAS.
I BID THEE FAREWELL, SIR RAT--
I HEAR STRANGE SOUNDS ABOVE.
THUNK
A NEW ADVENTURE AWAITS FOR RED SONJA.
THERE SHE IS--

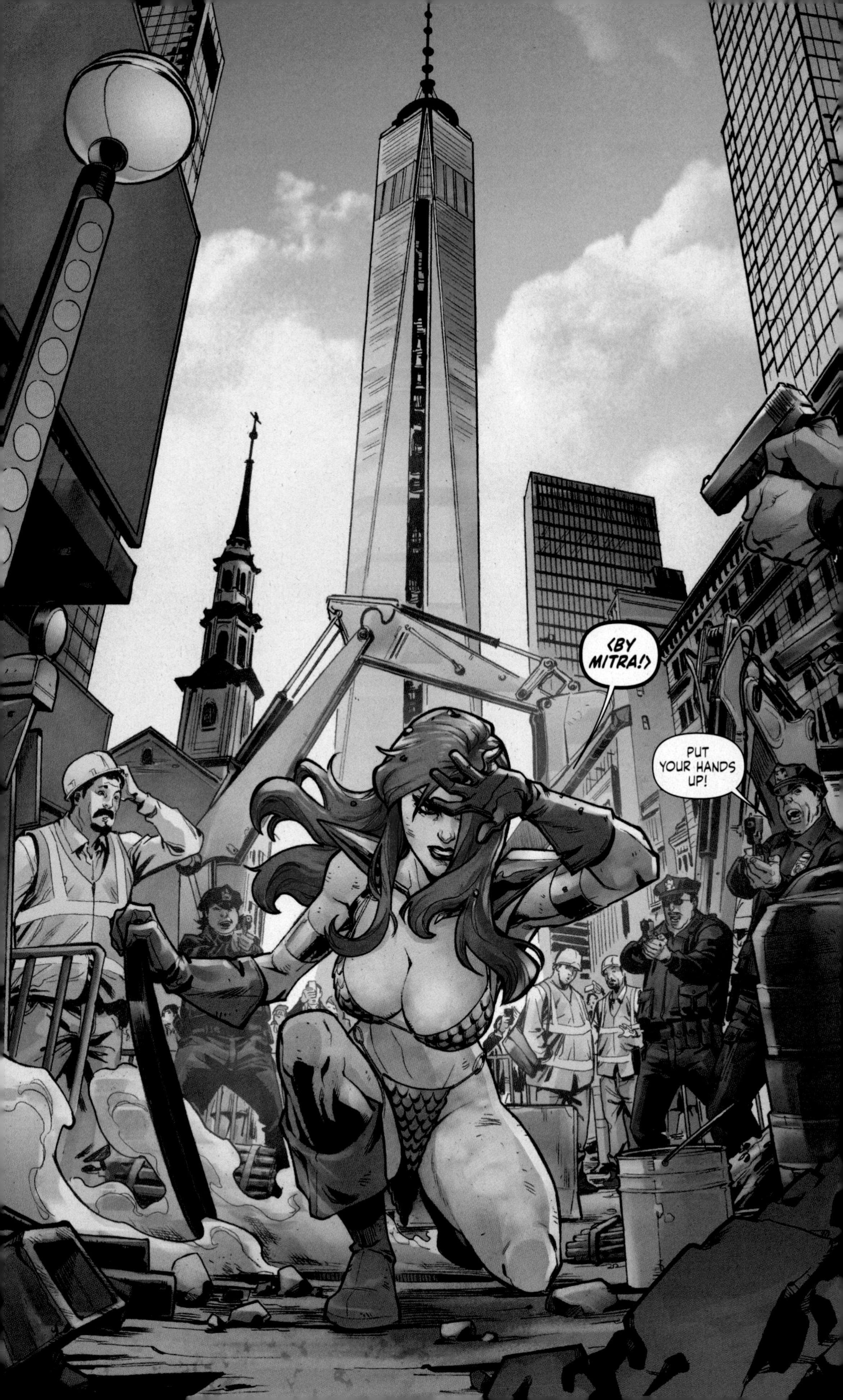
‹BY MITRA!›
PUT YOUR HANDS UP!

ISSUE #1

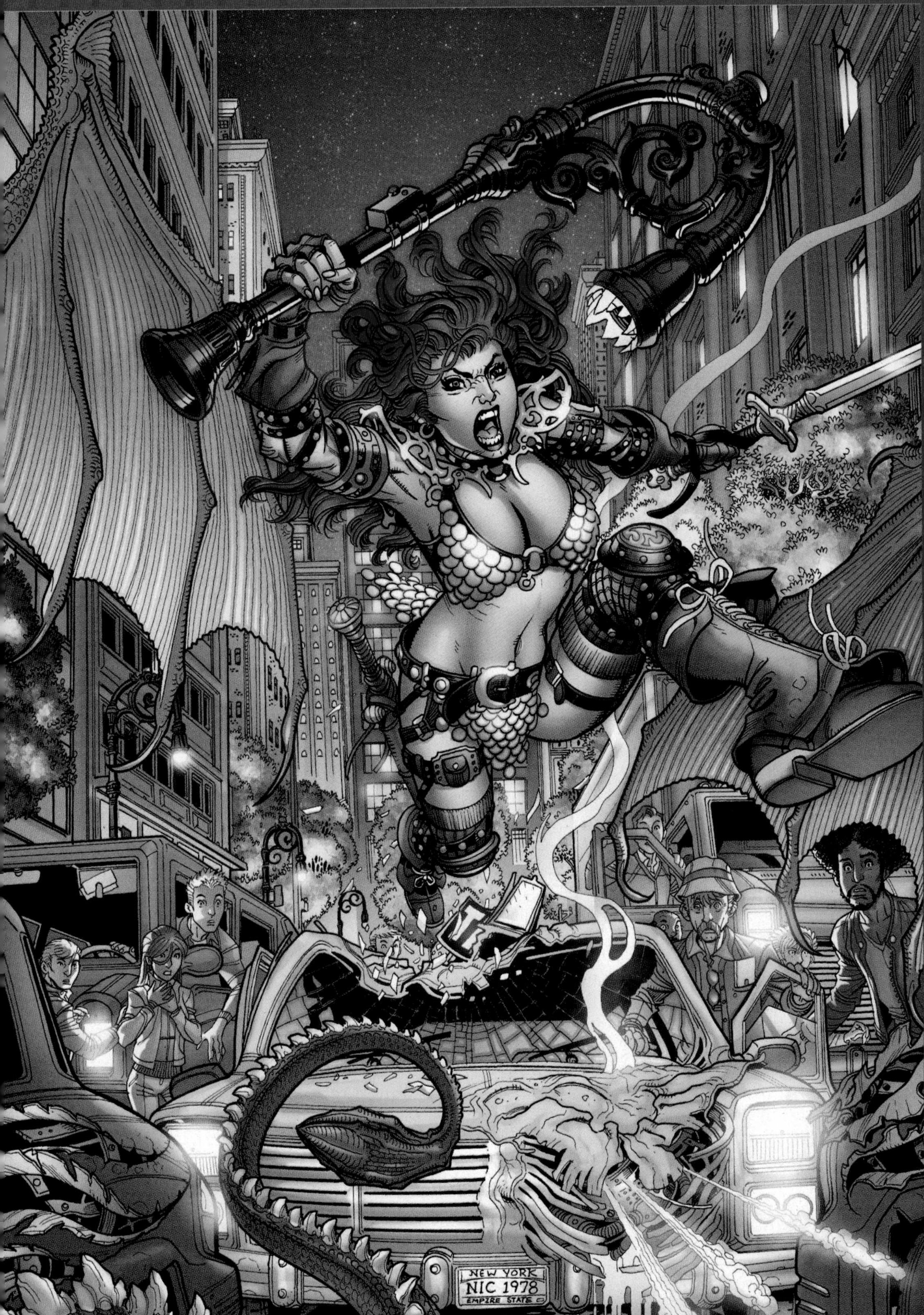
NEW YORK
NIC 1978
EMPIRE STATE

SSUE #1: COVER ART BY **NICK BRADSHAW,** COLORS BY **PETE PANTAZIS**

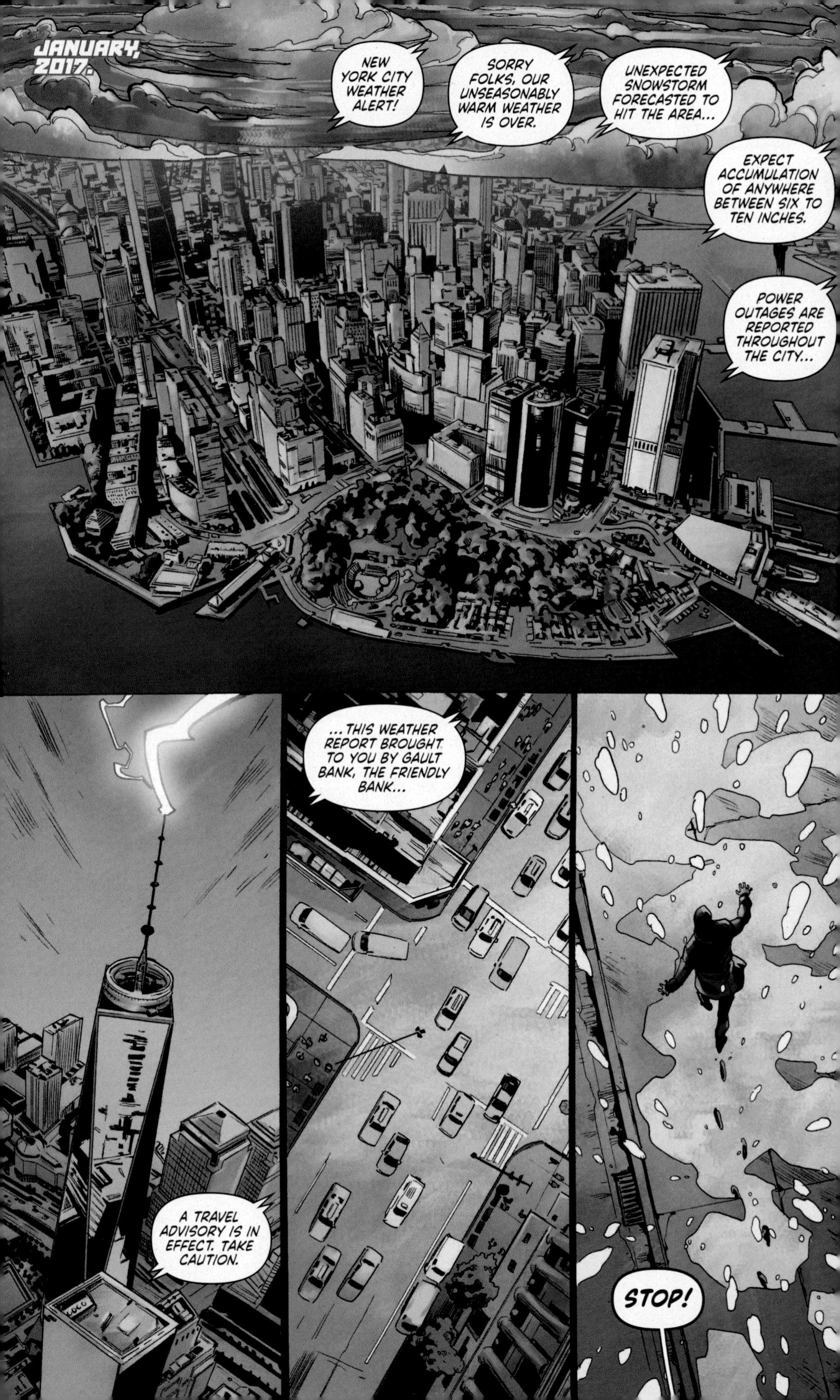

JANUARY, 2017.
NEW YORK CITY WEATHER ALERT!
SORRY FOLKS, OUR UNSEASONABLY WARM WEATHER IS OVER.
UNEXPECTED SNOWSTORM FORECASTED TO HIT THE AREA...
EXPECT ACCUMULATION OF ANYWHERE BETWEEN SIX TO TEN INCHES.
POWER OUTAGES ARE REPORTED THROUGHOUT THE CITY...
A TRAVEL ADVISORY IS IN EFFECT. TAKE CAUTION.
...THIS WEATHER REPORT BROUGHT TO YOU BY GAULT BANK, THE FRIENDLY BANK...
STOP!

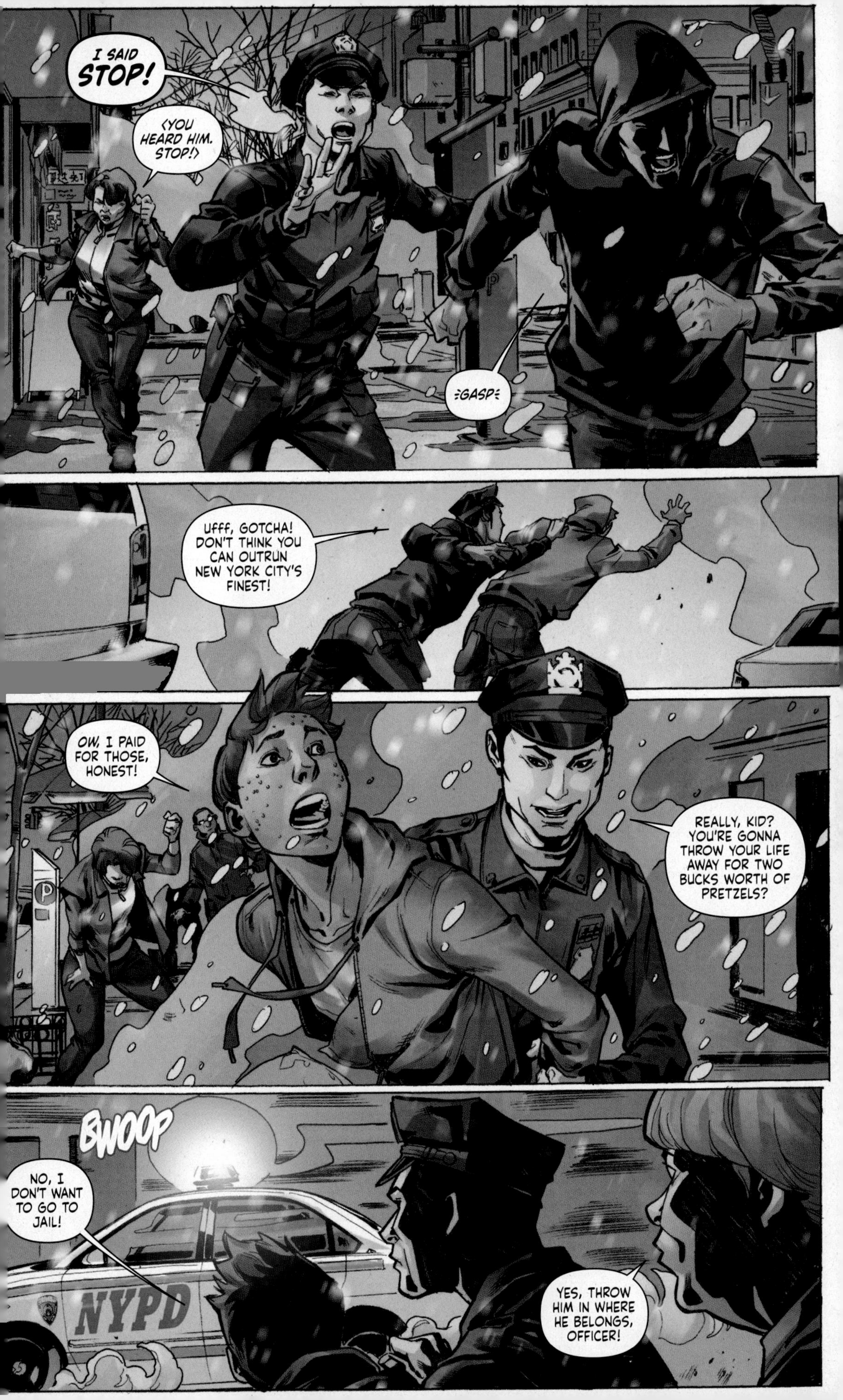
I SAID STOP!
<YOU HEARD HIM. STOP!>
GASP
UFFF, GOTCHA! DON'T THINK YOU CAN OUTRUN NEW YORK CITY'S FINEST!
OW, I PAID FOR THOSE, HONEST!
REALLY, KID? YOU'RE GONNA THROW YOUR LIFE AWAY FOR TWO BUCKS WORTH OF PRETZELS?
BWOOP
NO, I DON'T WANT TO GO TO JAIL!
NYPD
YES, THROW HIM IN WHERE HE BELONGS, OFFICER!

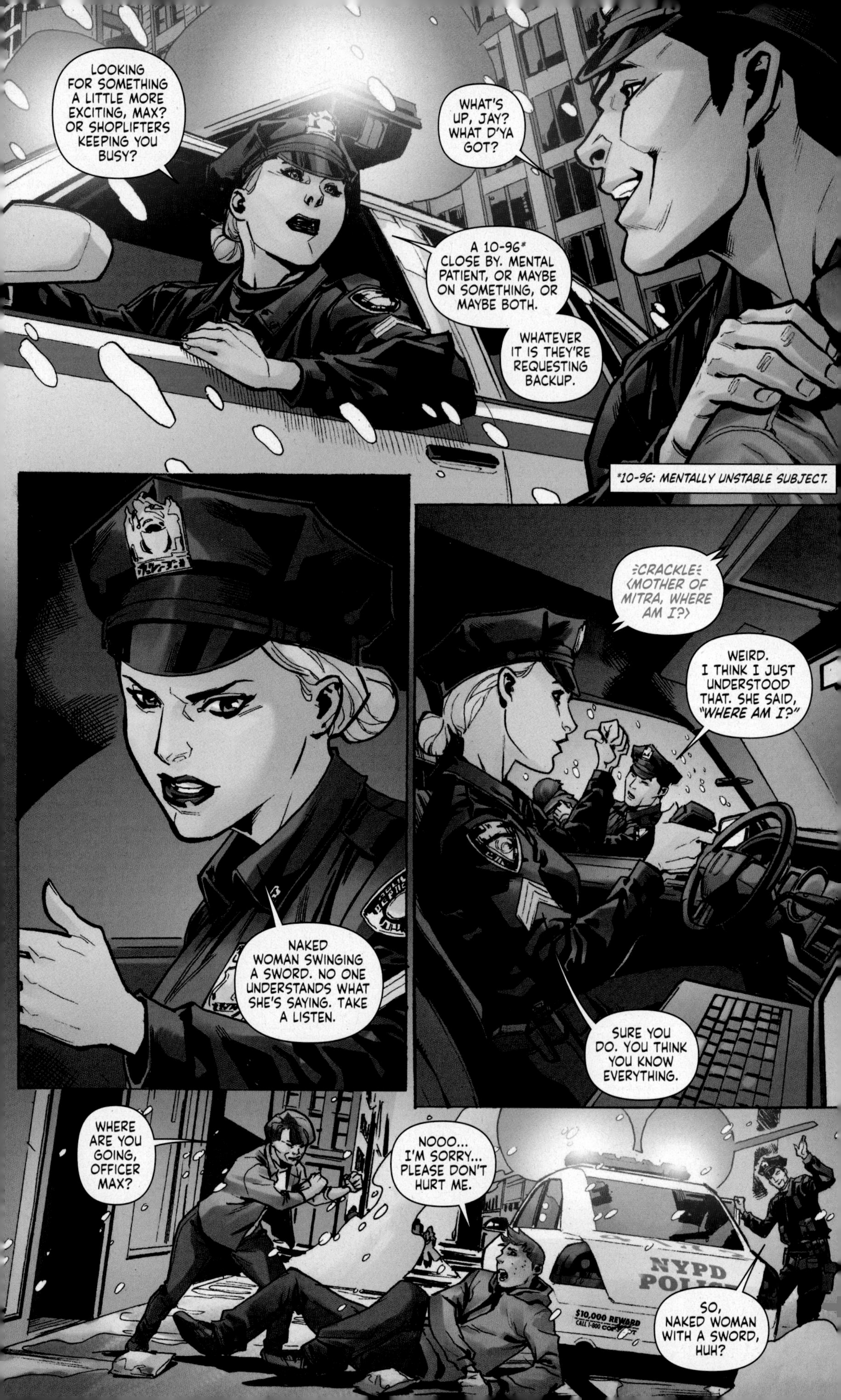

LOOKING FOR SOMETHING A LITTLE MORE EXCITING, MAX? OR SHOPLIFTERS KEEPING YOU BUSY?
WHAT'S UP, JAY? WHAT D'YA GOT?
A 10-96* CLOSE BY. MENTAL PATIENT, OR MAYBE ON SOMETHING, OR MAYBE BOTH.
WHATEVER IT IS THEY'RE REQUESTING BACKUP.
*10-96: MENTALLY UNSTABLE SUBJECT.
NAKED WOMAN SWINGING A SWORD. NO ONE UNDERSTANDS WHAT SHE'S SAYING. TAKE A LISTEN.
=CRACKLE= <MOTHER OF MITRA, WHERE AM I?>
WEIRD. I THINK I JUST UNDERSTOOD THAT. SHE SAID, "WHERE AM I?"
SURE YOU DO. YOU THINK YOU KNOW EVERYTHING.
WHERE ARE YOU GOING, OFFICER MAX?
NOOO... I'M SORRY... PLEASE DON'T HURT ME.
NYPD POLICE
$10,000 REWARD
SO, NAKED WOMAN WITH A SWORD, HUH?

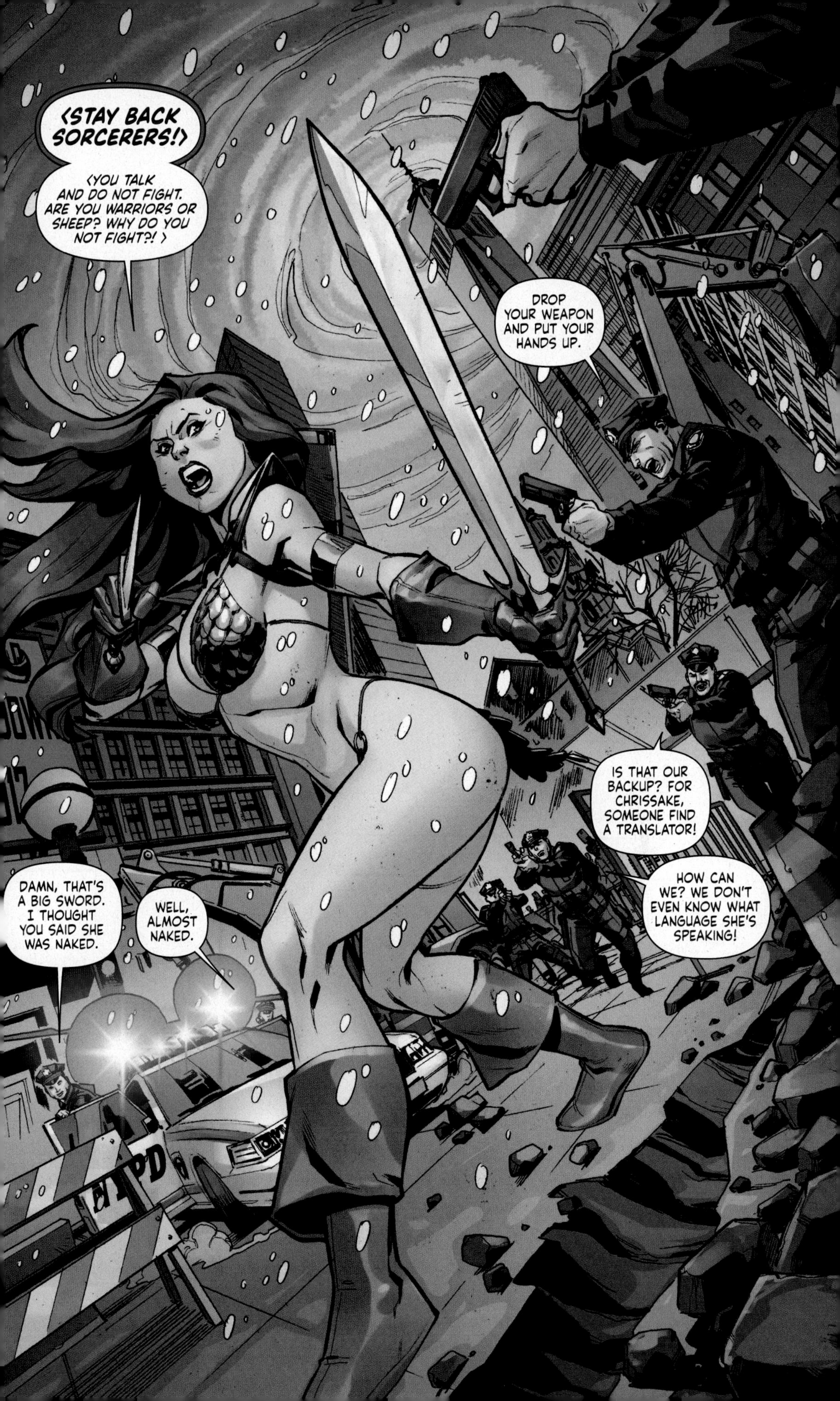

<STAY BACK SORCERERS!>
<YOU TALK AND DO NOT FIGHT. ARE YOU WARRIORS OR SHEEP? WHY DO YOU NOT FIGHT?! >
DROP YOUR WEAPON AND PUT YOUR HANDS UP.
IS THAT OUR BACKUP? FOR CHRISSAKE, SOMEONE FIND A TRANSLATOR!
HOW CAN WE? WE DON'T EVEN KNOW WHAT LANGUAGE SHE'S SPEAKING!
DAMN, THAT'S A BIG SWORD. I THOUGHT YOU SAID SHE WAS NAKED.
WELL, ALMOST NAKED.
NYPD

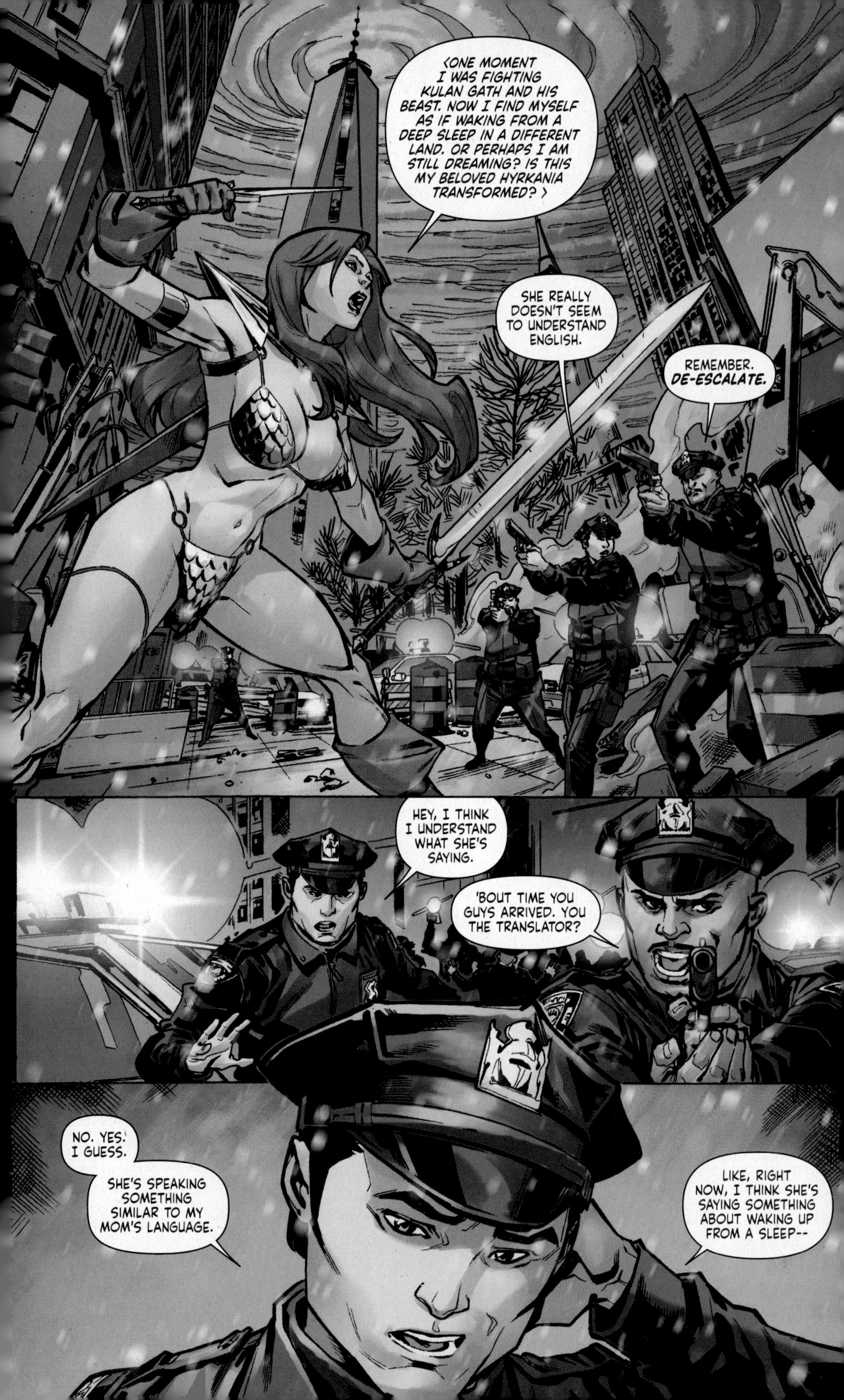
<ONE MOMENT I WAS FIGHTING KULAN GATH AND HIS BEAST. NOW I FIND MYSELF AS IF WAKING FROM A DEEP SLEEP IN A DIFFERENT LAND. OR PERHAPS I AM STILL DREAMING? IS THIS MY BELOVED HYRKANIA TRANSFORMED?>
SHE REALLY DOESN'T SEEM TO UNDERSTAND ENGLISH.
REMEMBER. DE-ESCALATE.
HEY, I THINK I UNDERSTAND WHAT SHE'S SAYING.
'BOUT TIME YOU GUYS ARRIVED. YOU THE TRANSLATOR?
NO. YES. I GUESS.
SHE'S SPEAKING SOMETHING SIMILAR TO MY MOM'S LANGUAGE.
LIKE, RIGHT NOW, I THINK SHE'S SAYING SOMETHING ABOUT WAKING UP FROM A SLEEP--

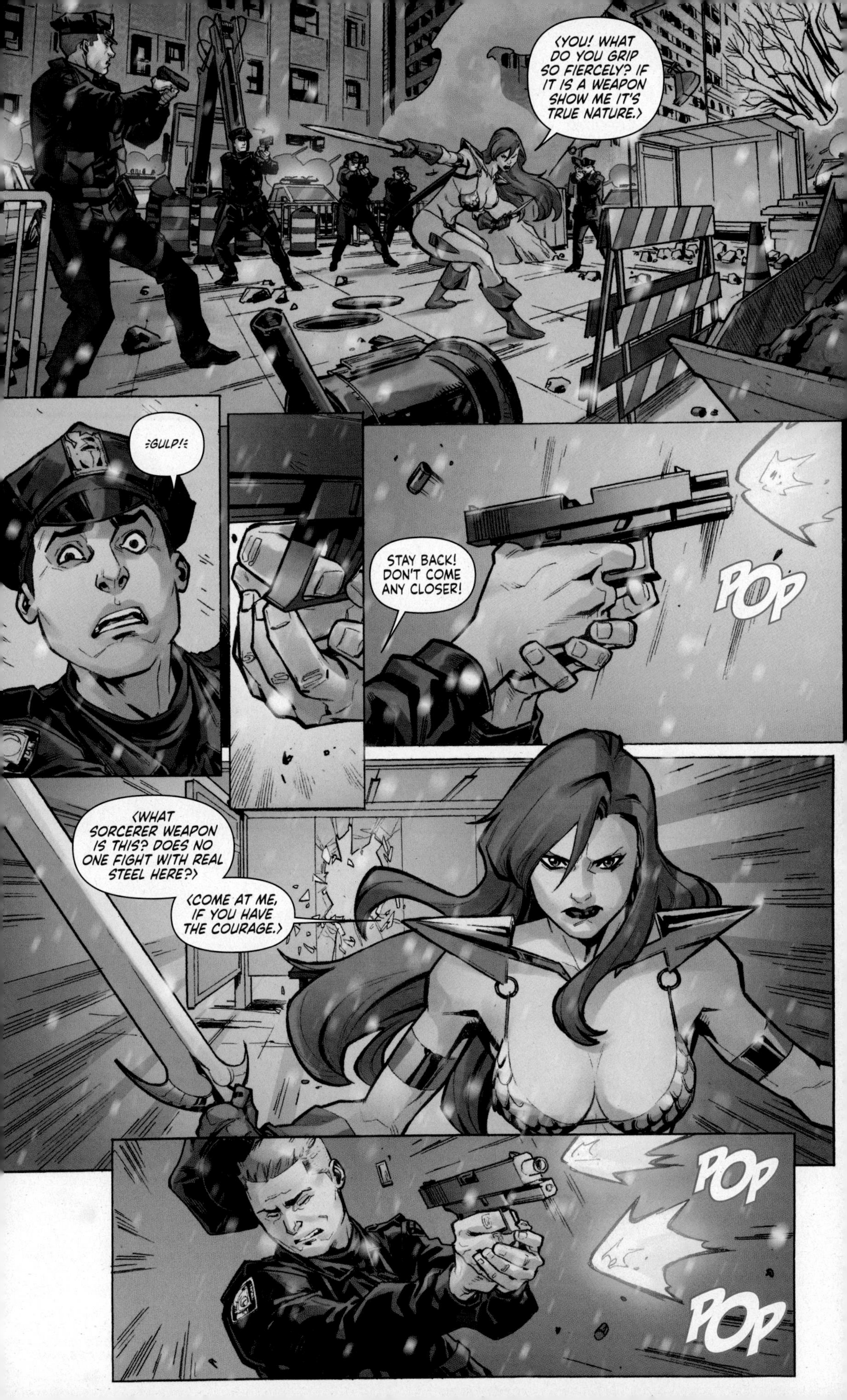

‹YOU! WHAT DO YOU GRIP SO FIERCELY? IF IT IS A WEAPON SHOW ME IT'S TRUE NATURE.›
GULP!
STAY BACK! DON'T COME ANY CLOSER!
POP
‹WHAT SORCERER WEAPON IS THIS? DOES NO ONE FIGHT WITH REAL STEEL HERE?›
‹COME AT ME, IF YOU HAVE THE COURAGE.›
POP
POP

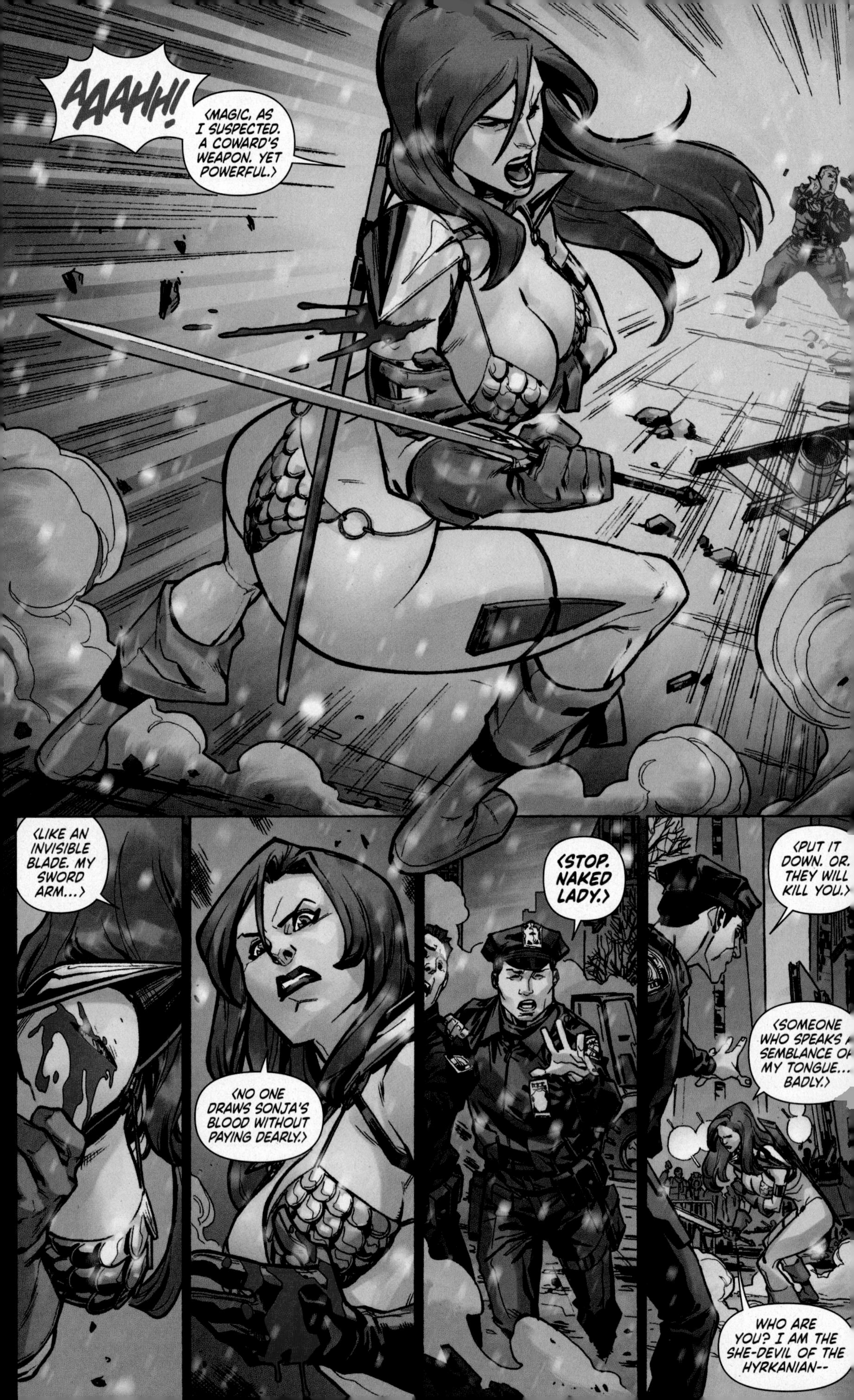
AAAHH!
<MAGIC, AS I SUSPECTED. A COWARD'S WEAPON. YET POWERFUL.>
<LIKE AN INVISIBLE BLADE. MY SWORD ARM...>
<NO ONE DRAWS SONJA'S BLOOD WITHOUT PAYING DEARLY.>
<STOP. NAKED LADY.>
<PUT IT DOWN. OR. THEY WILL KILL YOU.>
<SOMEONE WHO SPEAKS A SEMBLANCE OF MY TONGUE... BADLY.>
WHO ARE YOU? I AM THE SHE-DEVIL OF THE HYRKANIAN--

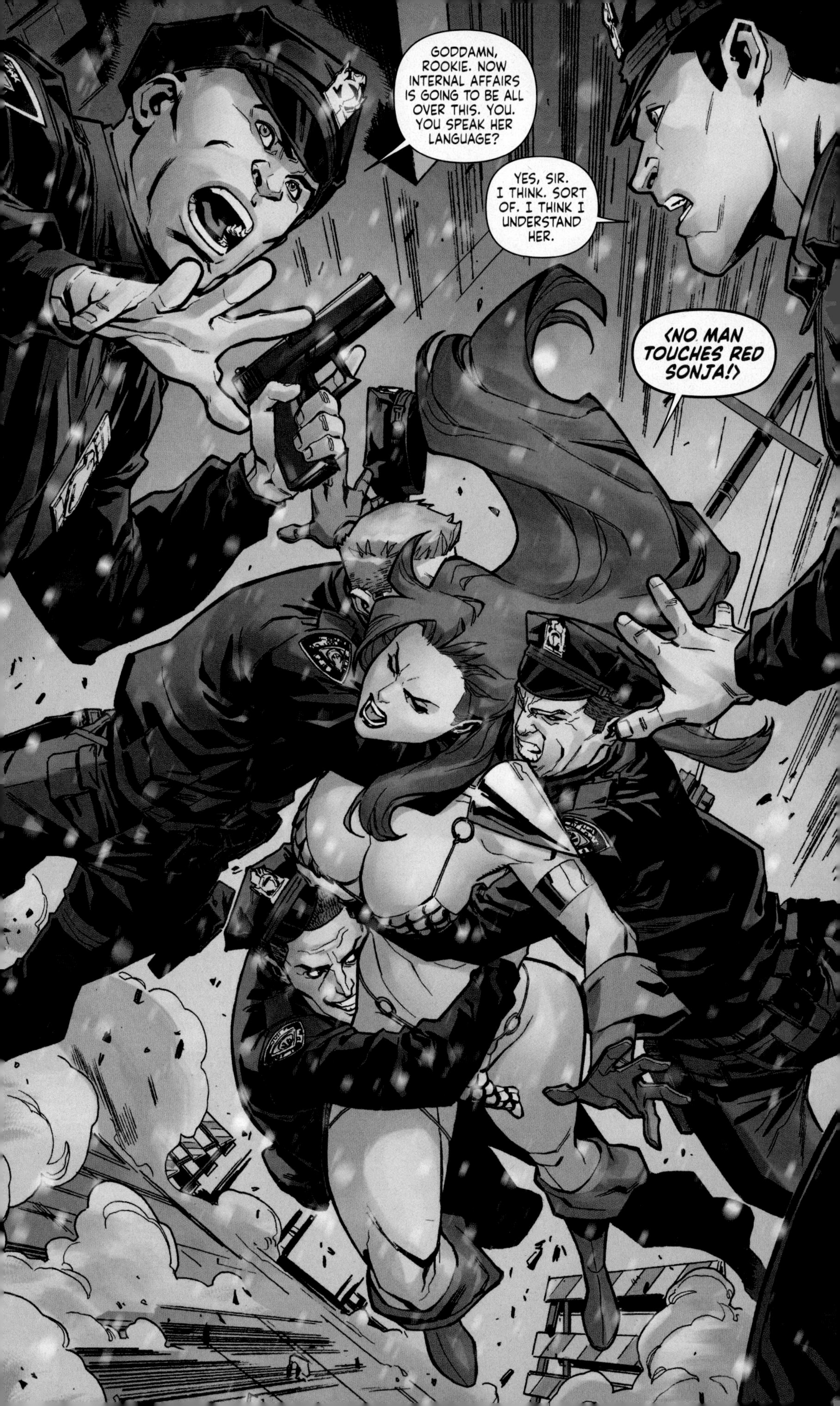
GODDAMN, ROOKIE. NOW INTERNAL AFFAIRS IS GOING TO BE ALL OVER THIS. YOU. YOU SPEAK HER LANGUAGE?
YES, SIR. I THINK. SORT OF. I THINK I UNDERSTAND HER.
<NO MAN TOUCHES RED SONJA!>

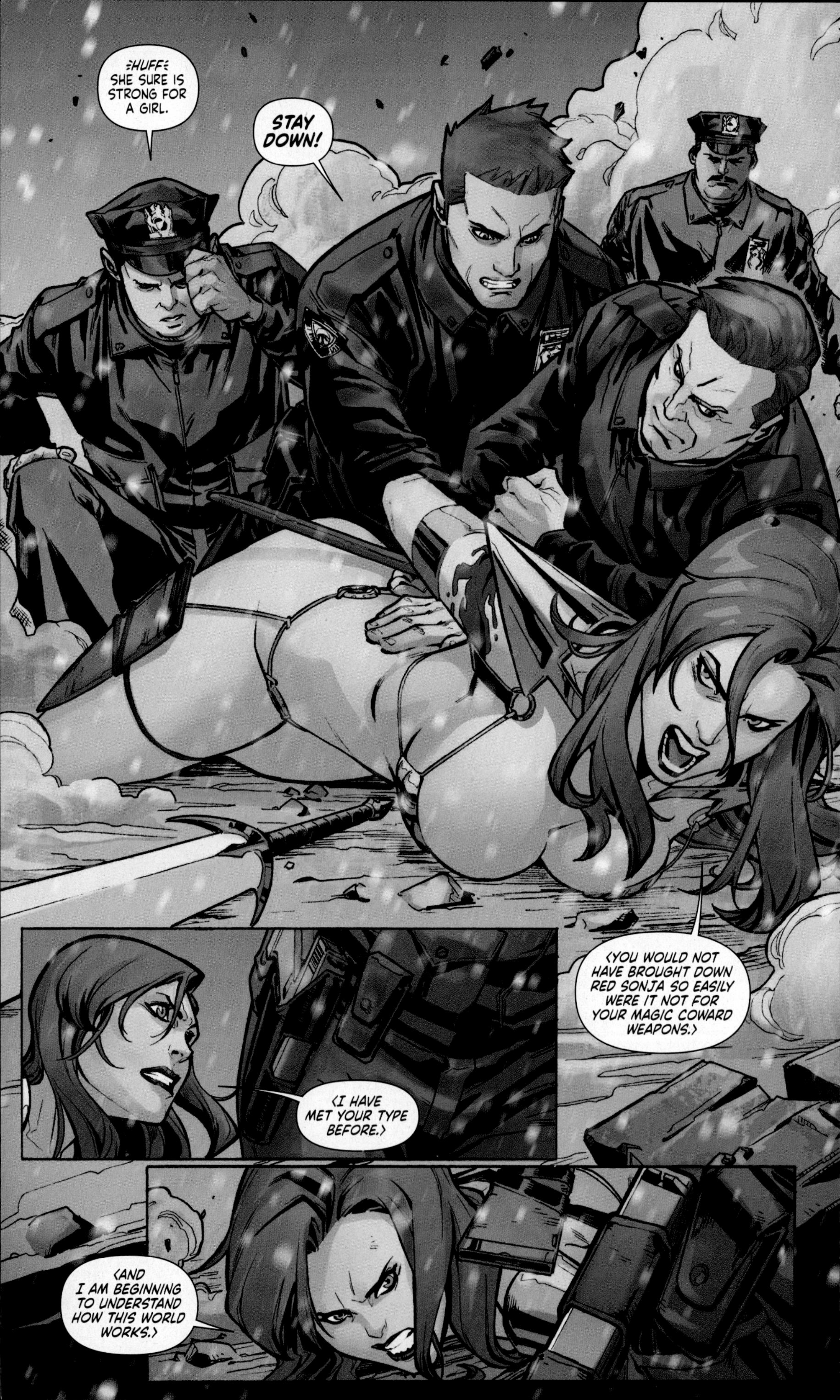

HUFF
SHE SURE IS STRONG FOR A GIRL.
STAY DOWN!
‹YOU WOULD NOT HAVE BROUGHT DOWN RED SONJA SO EASILY WERE IT NOT FOR YOUR MAGIC COWARD WEAPONS.›
‹I HAVE MET YOUR TYPE BEFORE.›
‹AND I AM BEGINNING TO UNDERSTAND HOW THIS WORLD WORKS.›

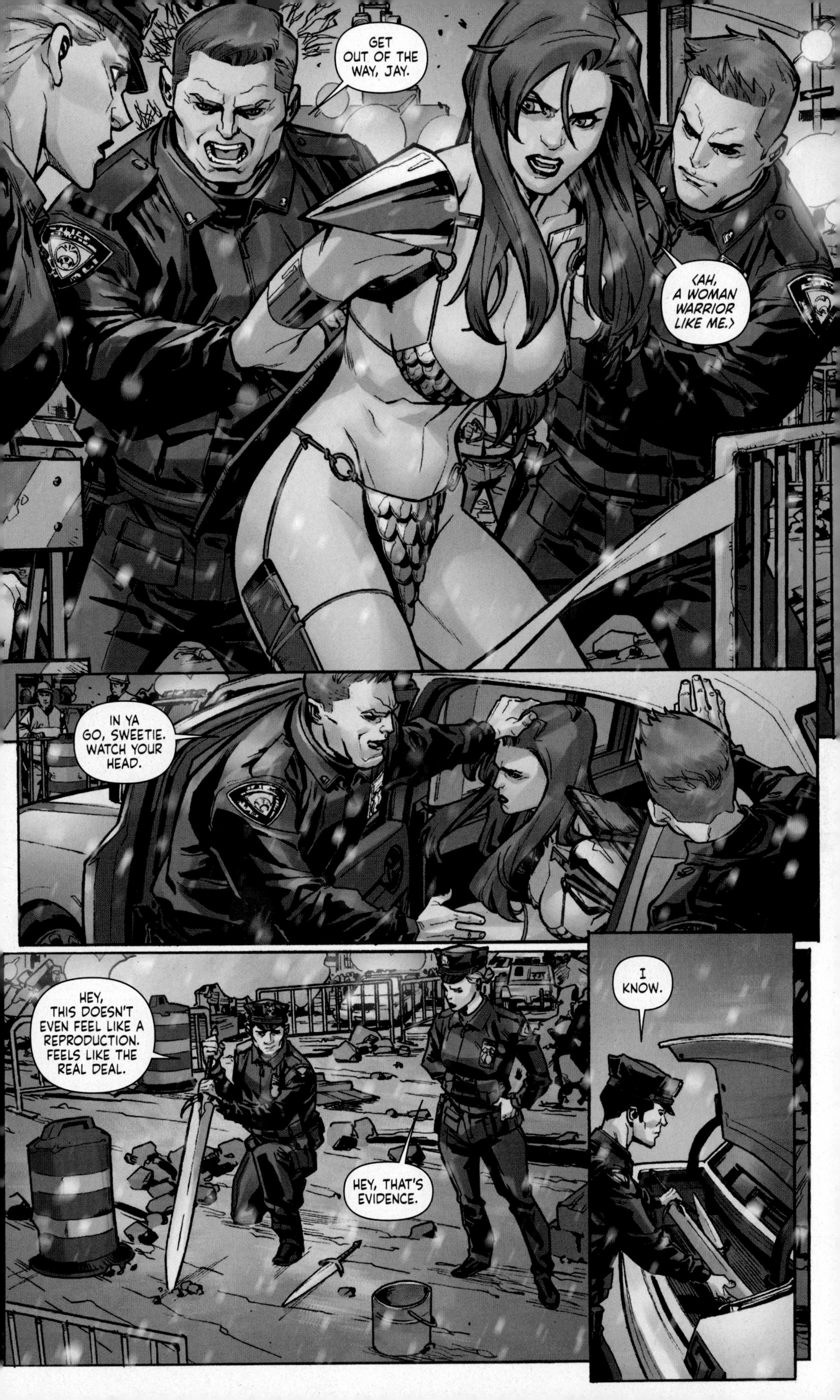
GET OUT OF THE WAY, JAY.
⟨AH, A WOMAN WARRIOR LIKE ME.⟩
IN YA GO, SWEETIE. WATCH YOUR HEAD.
HEY, THIS DOESN'T EVEN FEEL LIKE A REPRODUCTION. FEELS LIKE THE REAL DEAL.
HEY, THAT'S EVIDENCE.
I KNOW.

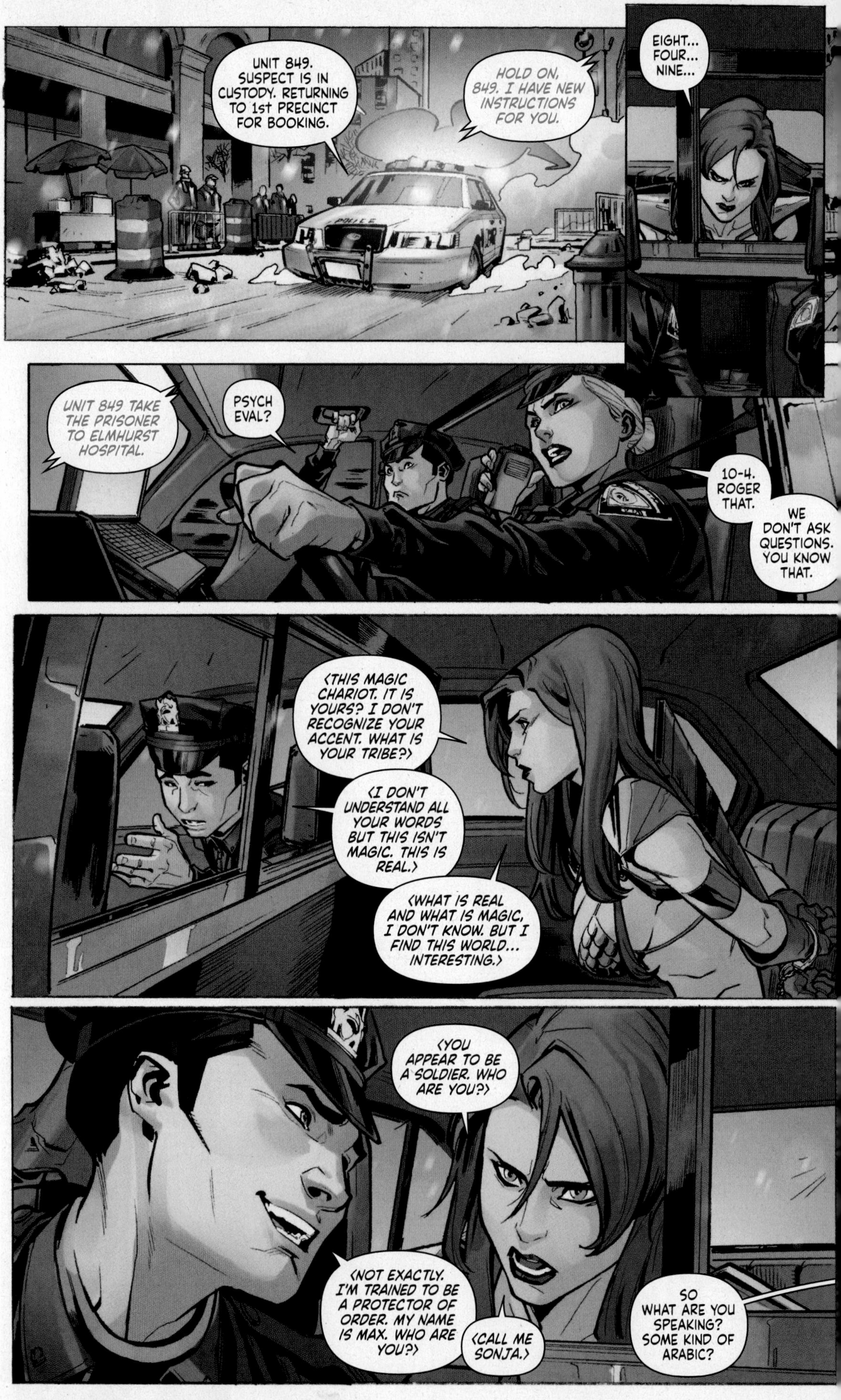
UNIT 849. SUSPECT IS IN CUSTODY. RETURNING TO 1st PRECINCT FOR BOOKING.
HOLD ON, 849. I HAVE NEW INSTRUCTIONS FOR YOU.
EIGHT... FOUR... NINE...
UNIT 849 TAKE THE PRISONER TO ELMHURST HOSPITAL.
PSYCH EVAL?
10-4. ROGER THAT.
WE DON'T ASK QUESTIONS. YOU KNOW THAT.
<THIS MAGIC CHARIOT. IT IS YOURS? I DON'T RECOGNIZE YOUR ACCENT. WHAT IS YOUR TRIBE?>
<I DON'T UNDERSTAND ALL YOUR WORDS BUT THIS ISN'T MAGIC. THIS IS REAL.>
<WHAT IS REAL AND WHAT IS MAGIC, I DON'T KNOW. BUT I FIND THIS WORLD... INTERESTING.>
<YOU APPEAR TO BE A SOLDIER. WHO ARE YOU?>
<NOT EXACTLY. I'M TRAINED TO BE A PROTECTOR OF ORDER. MY NAME IS MAX. WHO ARE YOU?>
<CALL ME SONJA.>
SO WHAT ARE YOU SPEAKING? SOME KIND OF ARABIC?

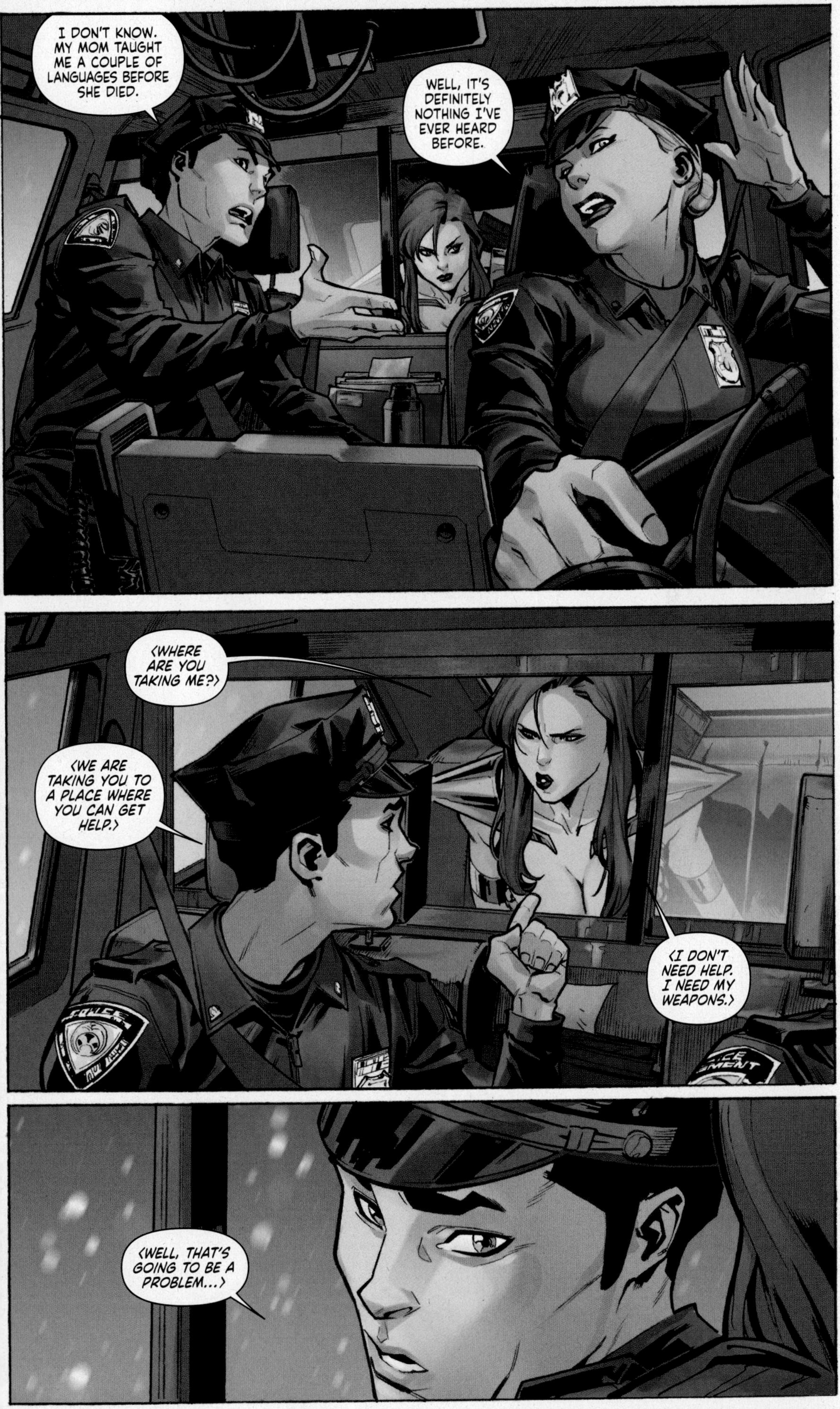
I DON'T KNOW. MY MOM TAUGHT ME A COUPLE OF LANGUAGES BEFORE SHE DIED.
WELL, IT'S DEFINITELY NOTHING I'VE EVER HEARD BEFORE.
<WHERE ARE YOU TAKING ME?>
<WE ARE TAKING YOU TO A PLACE WHERE YOU CAN GET HELP.>
<I DON'T NEED HELP. I NEED MY WEAPONS.>
<WELL, THAT'S GOING TO BE A PROBLEM...>

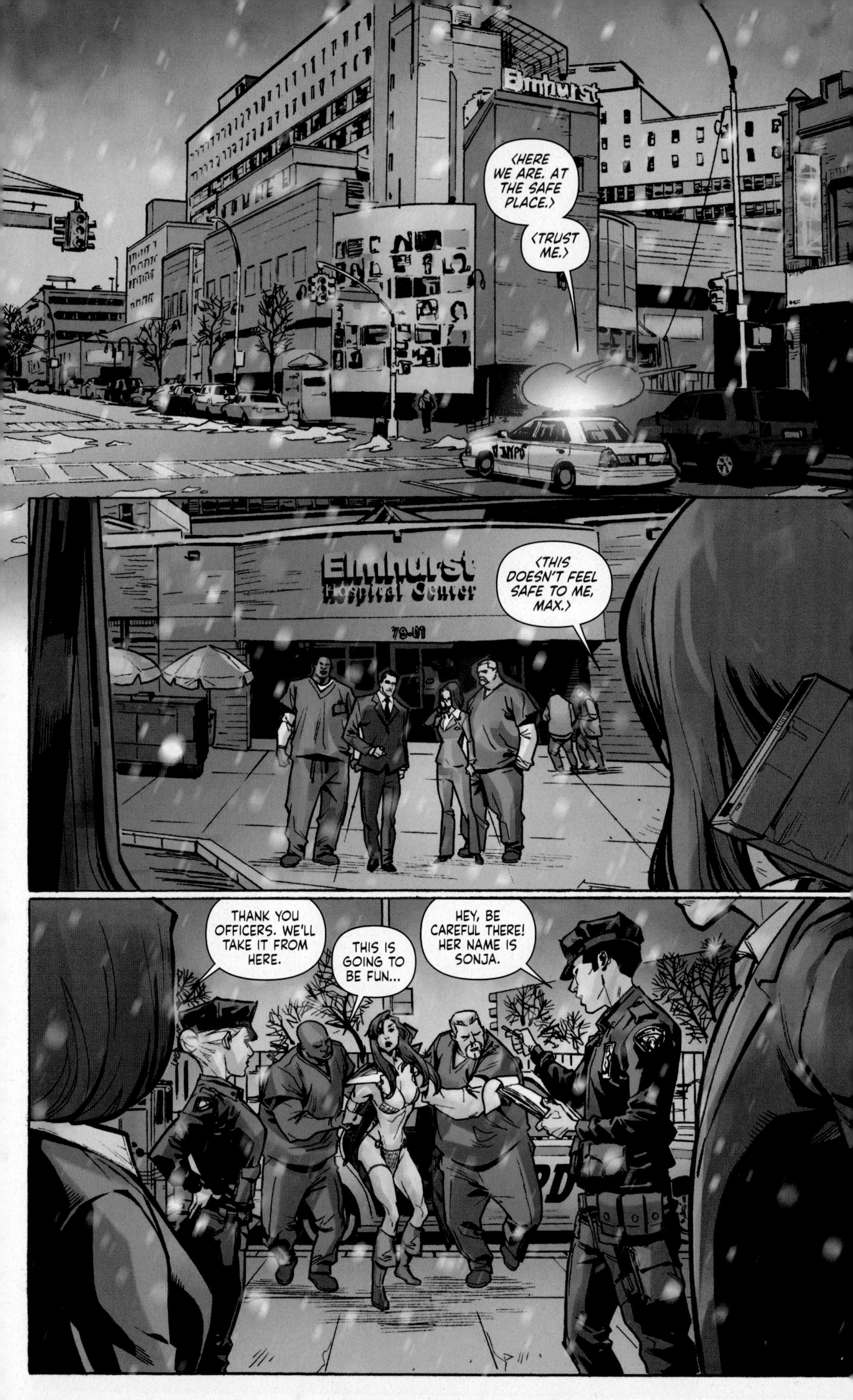
Elmhurst
‹HERE WE ARE. AT THE SAFE PLACE.›
‹TRUST ME.›
Elmhurst Hospital Center
79-01
‹THIS DOESN'T FEEL SAFE TO ME, MAX.›
THANK YOU OFFICERS. WE'LL TAKE IT FROM HERE.
THIS IS GOING TO BE FUN...
HEY, BE CAREFUL THERE! HER NAME IS SONJA.

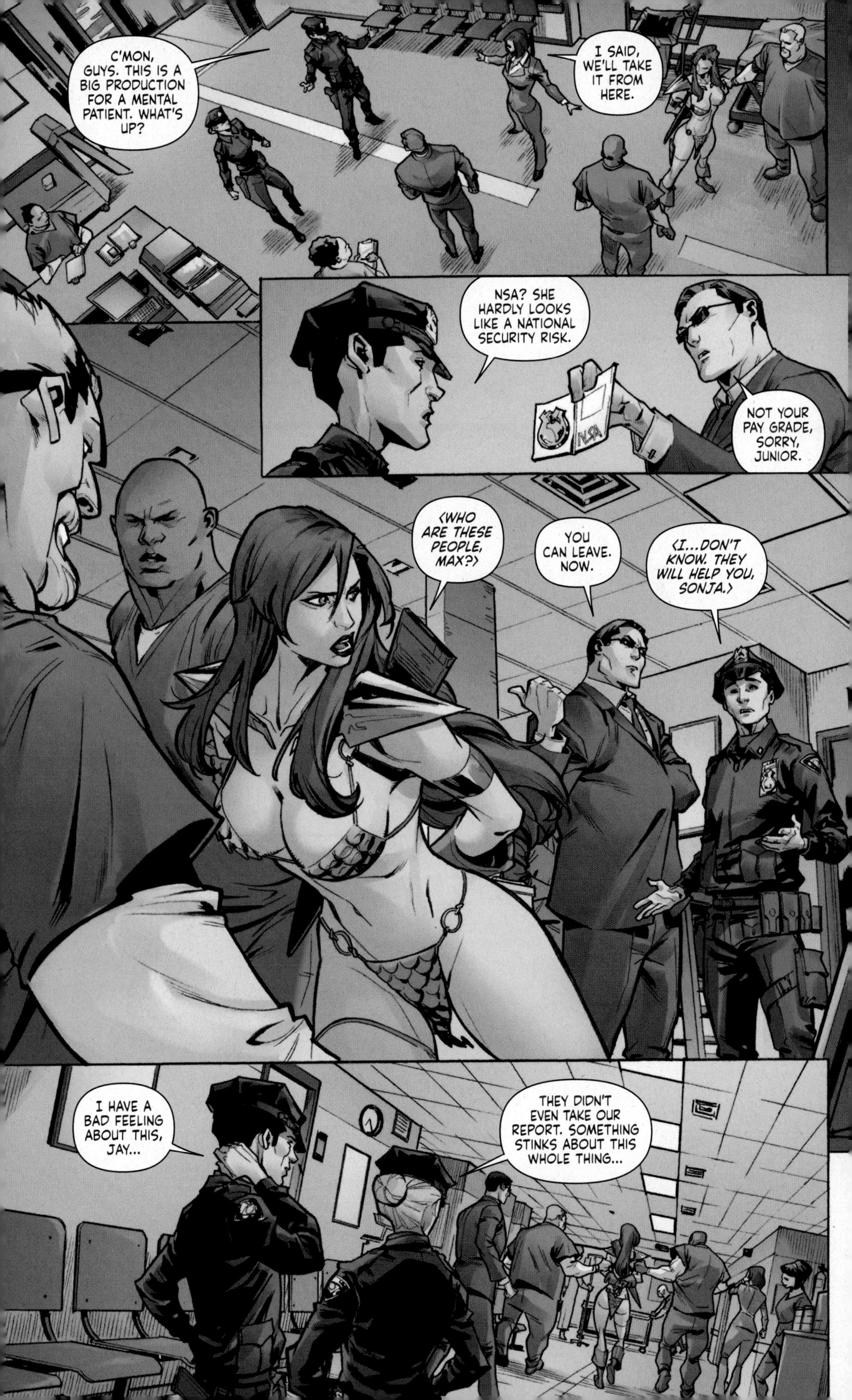
C'MON, GUYS. THIS IS A BIG PRODUCTION FOR A MENTAL PATIENT. WHAT'S UP?
I SAID, WE'LL TAKE IT FROM HERE.
NSA? SHE HARDLY LOOKS LIKE A NATIONAL SECURITY RISK.
NOT YOUR PAY GRADE, SORRY, JUNIOR.
NSA
<WHO ARE THESE PEOPLE, MAX?>
YOU CAN LEAVE. NOW.
<I...DON'T KNOW. THEY WILL HELP YOU, SONJA.>
I HAVE A BAD FEELING ABOUT THIS, JAY...
THEY DIDN'T EVEN TAKE OUR REPORT. SOMETHING STINKS ABOUT THIS WHOLE THING...

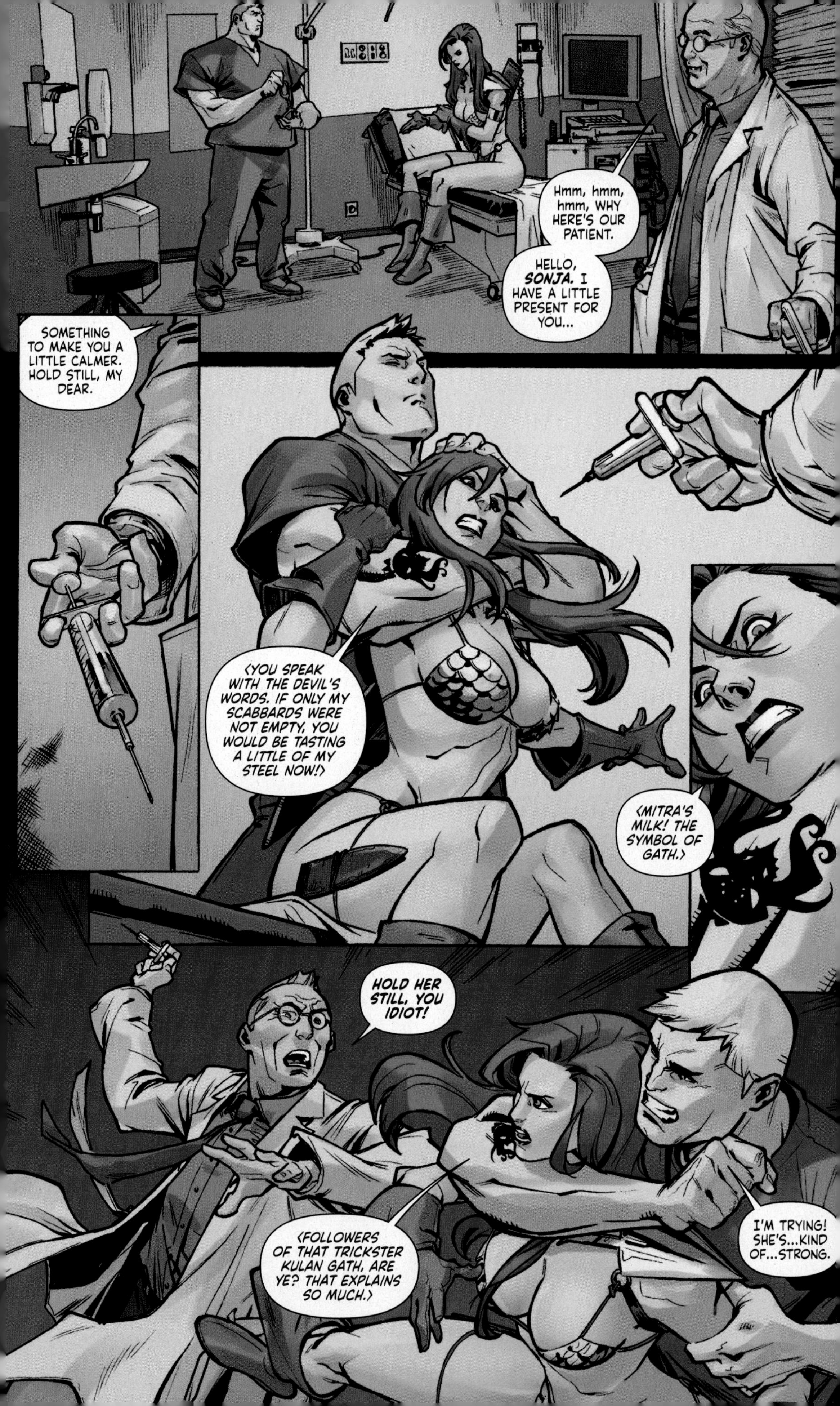
Hmm, hmm, hmm, WHY HERE'S OUR PATIENT.
HELLO, SONJA. I HAVE A LITTLE PRESENT FOR YOU...
SOMETHING TO MAKE YOU A LITTLE CALMER. HOLD STILL, MY DEAR.
<YOU SPEAK WITH THE DEVIL'S WORDS. IF ONLY MY SCABBARDS WERE NOT EMPTY, YOU WOULD BE TASTING A LITTLE OF MY STEEL NOW!>
<MITRA'S MILK! THE SYMBOL OF GATH.>
HOLD HER STILL, YOU IDIOT!
<FOLLOWERS OF THAT TRICKSTER KULAN GATH, ARE YE? THAT EXPLAINS SO MUCH.>
I'M TRYING! SHE'S...KIND OF...STRONG.

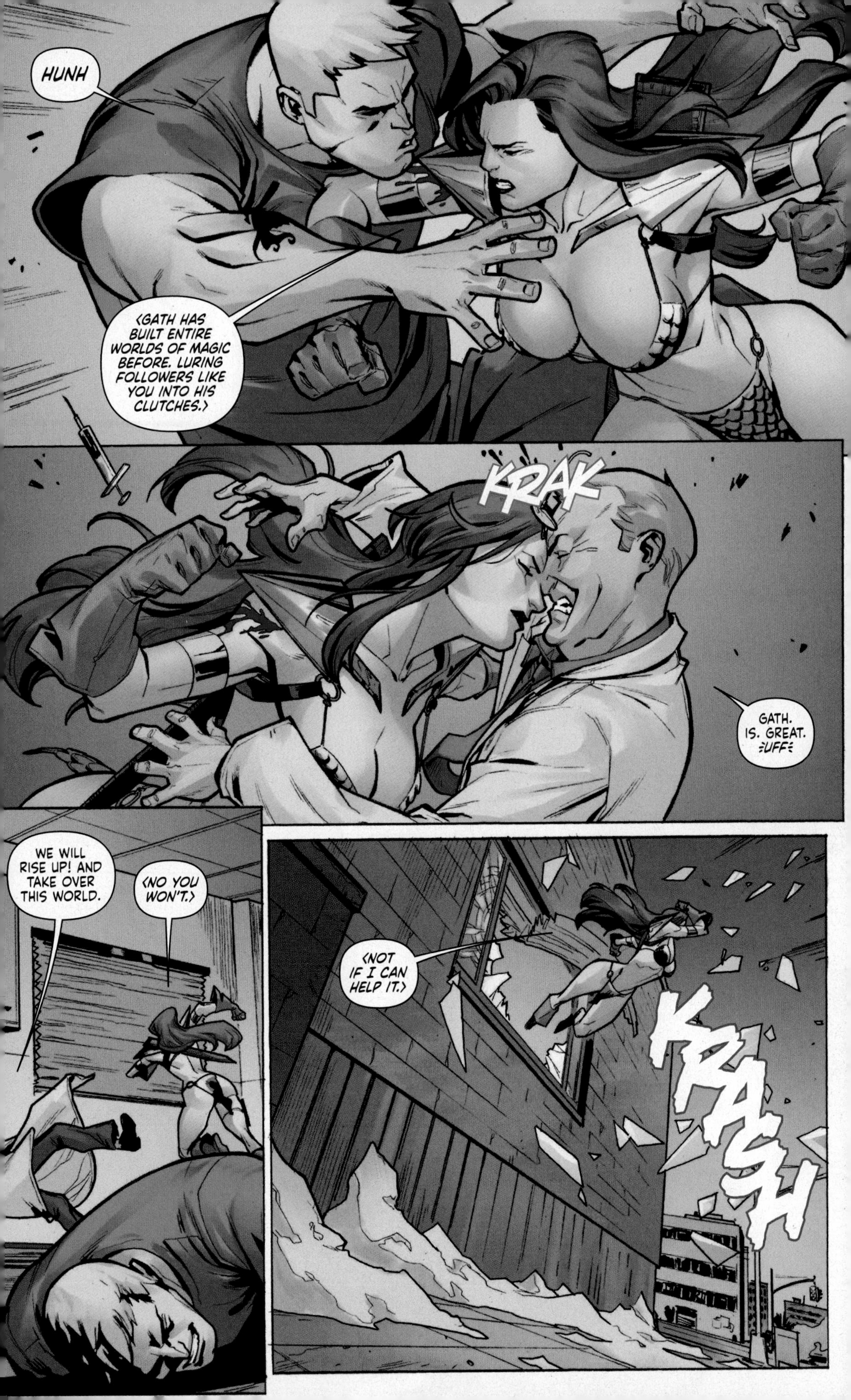
HUNH
<GATH HAS BUILT ENTIRE WORLDS OF MAGIC BEFORE. LURING FOLLOWERS LIKE YOU INTO HIS CLUTCHES.>
KRAK
GATH. IS. GREAT. UFF
WE WILL RISE UP! AND TAKE OVER THIS WORLD.
<NO YOU WON'T.>
<NOT IF I CAN HELP IT.>
KRASH

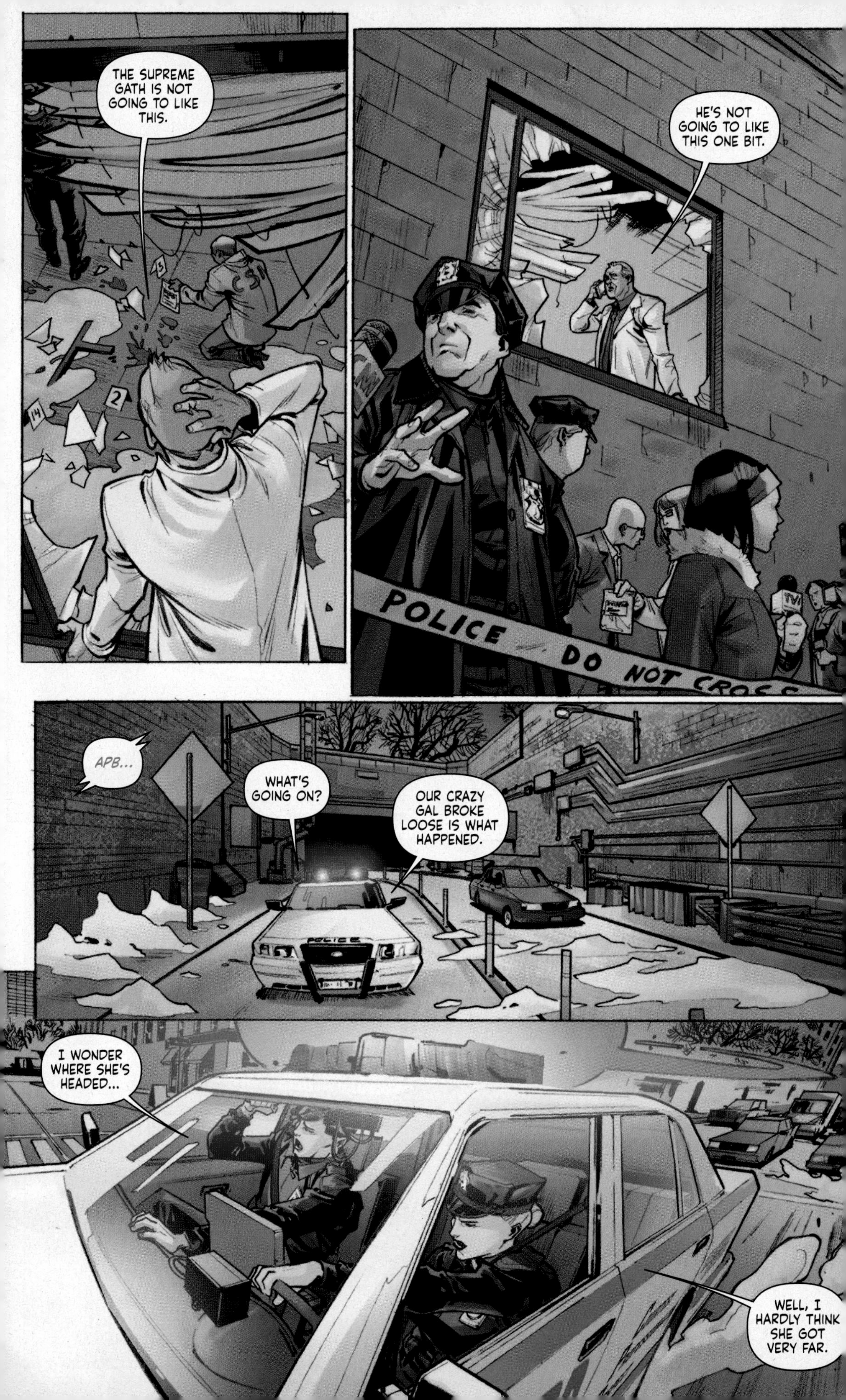
THE SUPREME GATH IS NOT GOING TO LIKE THIS.
HE'S NOT GOING TO LIKE THIS ONE BIT.
POLICE DO NOT CROSS
APB...
WHAT'S GOING ON?
OUR CRAZY GAL BROKE LOOSE IS WHAT HAPPENED.
I WONDER WHERE SHE'S HEADED...
WELL, I HARDLY THINK SHE GOT VERY FAR.

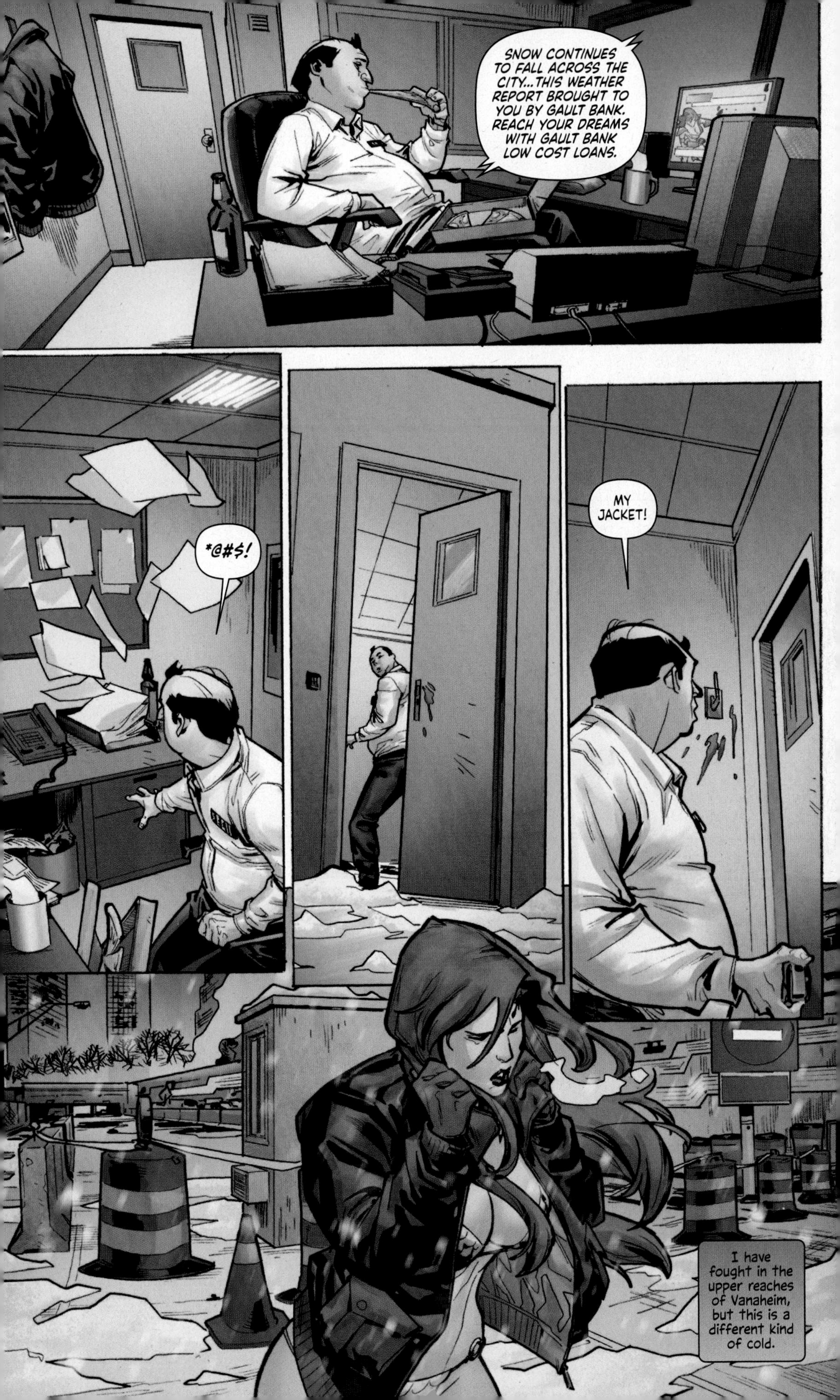

SNOW CONTINUES TO FALL ACROSS THE CITY...THIS WEATHER REPORT BROUGHT TO YOU BY GAULT BANK. REACH YOUR DREAMS WITH GAULT BANK LOW COST LOANS.
*@#$!
MY JACKET!
I have fought in the upper reaches of Vanaheim, but this is a different kind of cold.

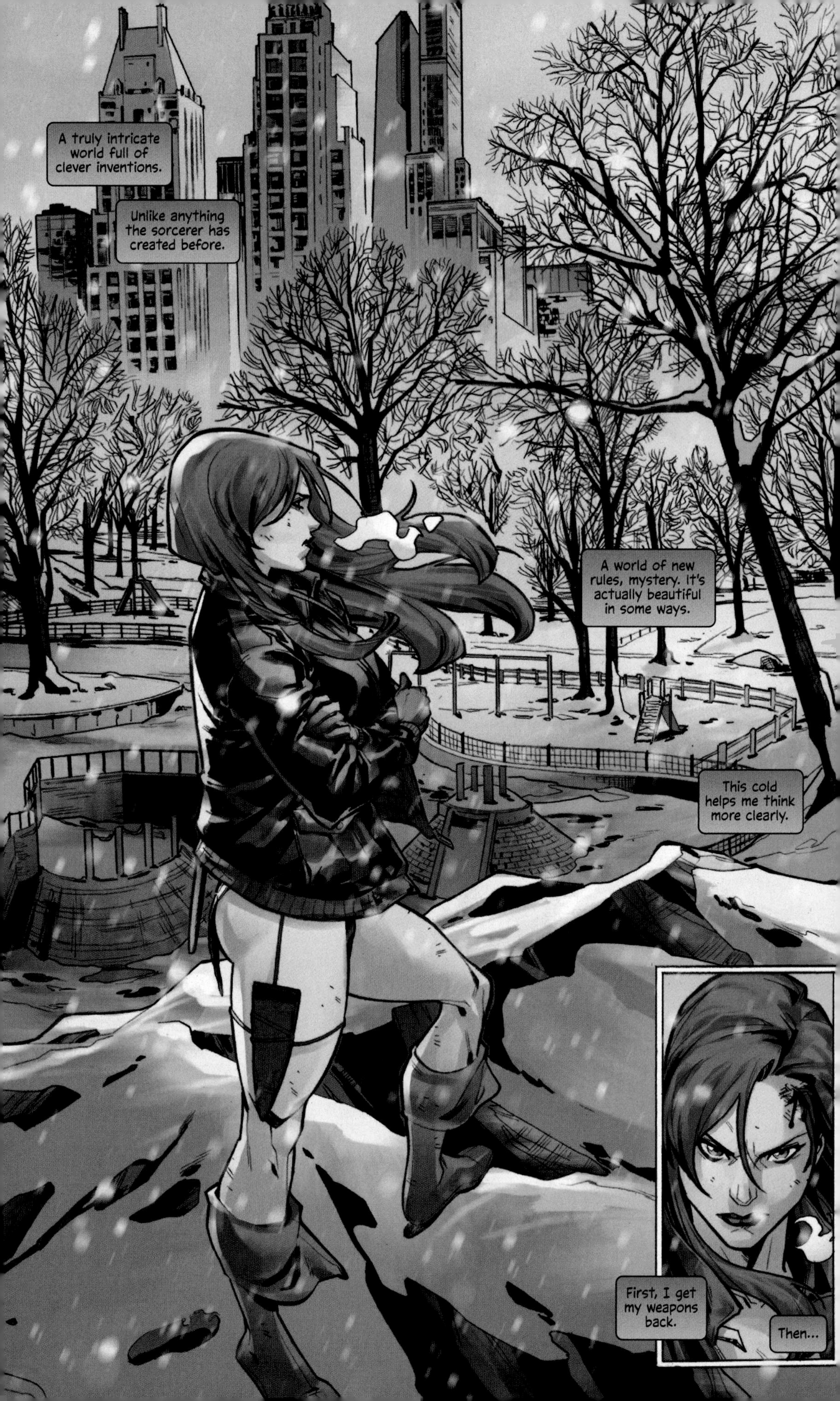

A truly intricate world full of clever inventions.
Unlike anything the sorcerer has created before.
A world of new rules, mystery. It's actually beautiful in some ways.
This cold helps me think more clearly.
First, I get my weapons back.
Then...

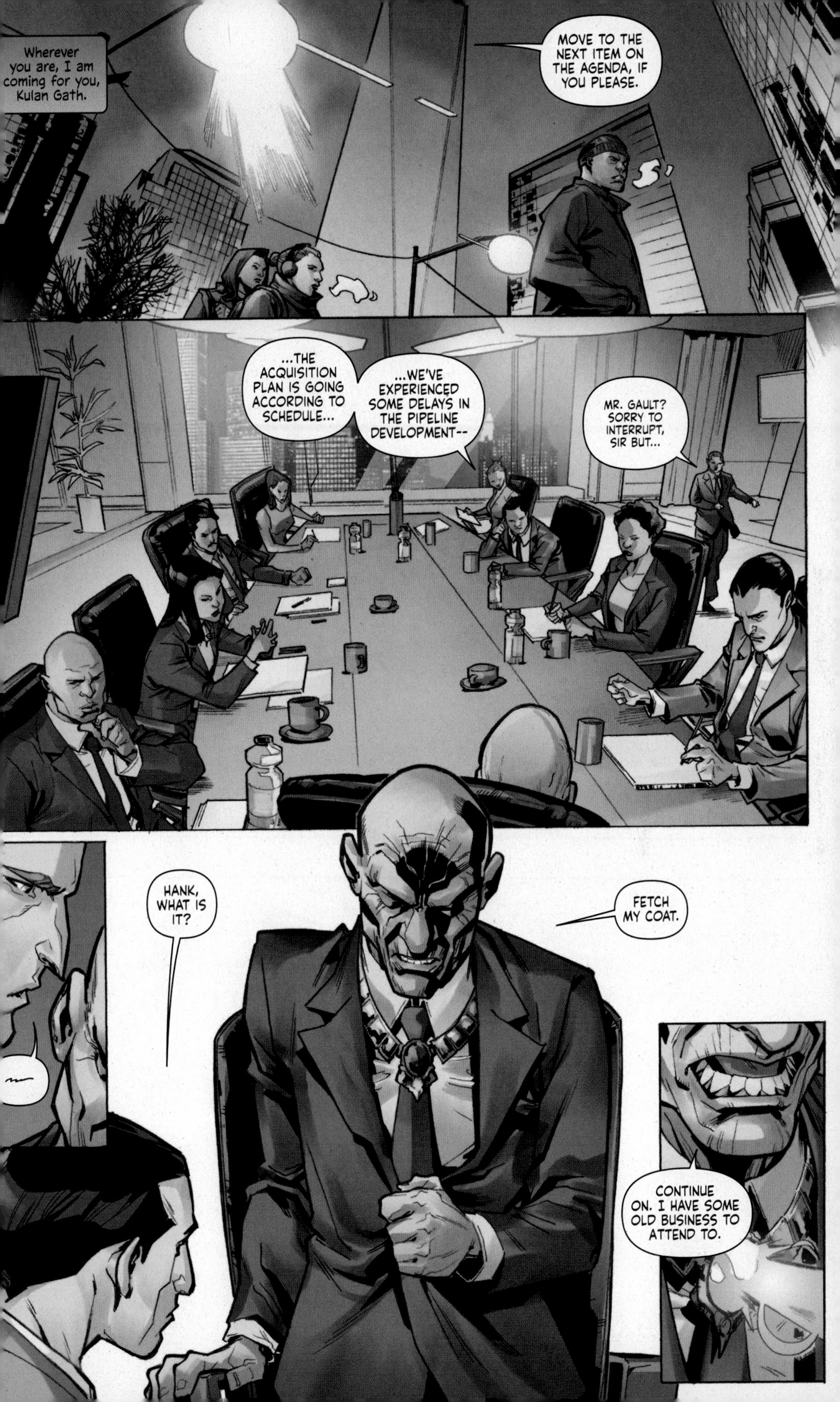

Wherever you are, I am coming for you, Kulan Gath.
MOVE TO THE NEXT ITEM ON THE AGENDA, IF YOU PLEASE.
...THE ACQUISITION PLAN IS GOING ACCORDING TO SCHEDULE...
...WE'VE EXPERIENCED SOME DELAYS IN THE PIPELINE DEVELOPMENT--
MR. GAULT? SORRY TO INTERRUPT, SIR BUT...
HANK, WHAT IS IT?
FETCH MY COAT.
CONTINUE ON. I HAVE SOME OLD BUSINESS TO ATTEND TO.

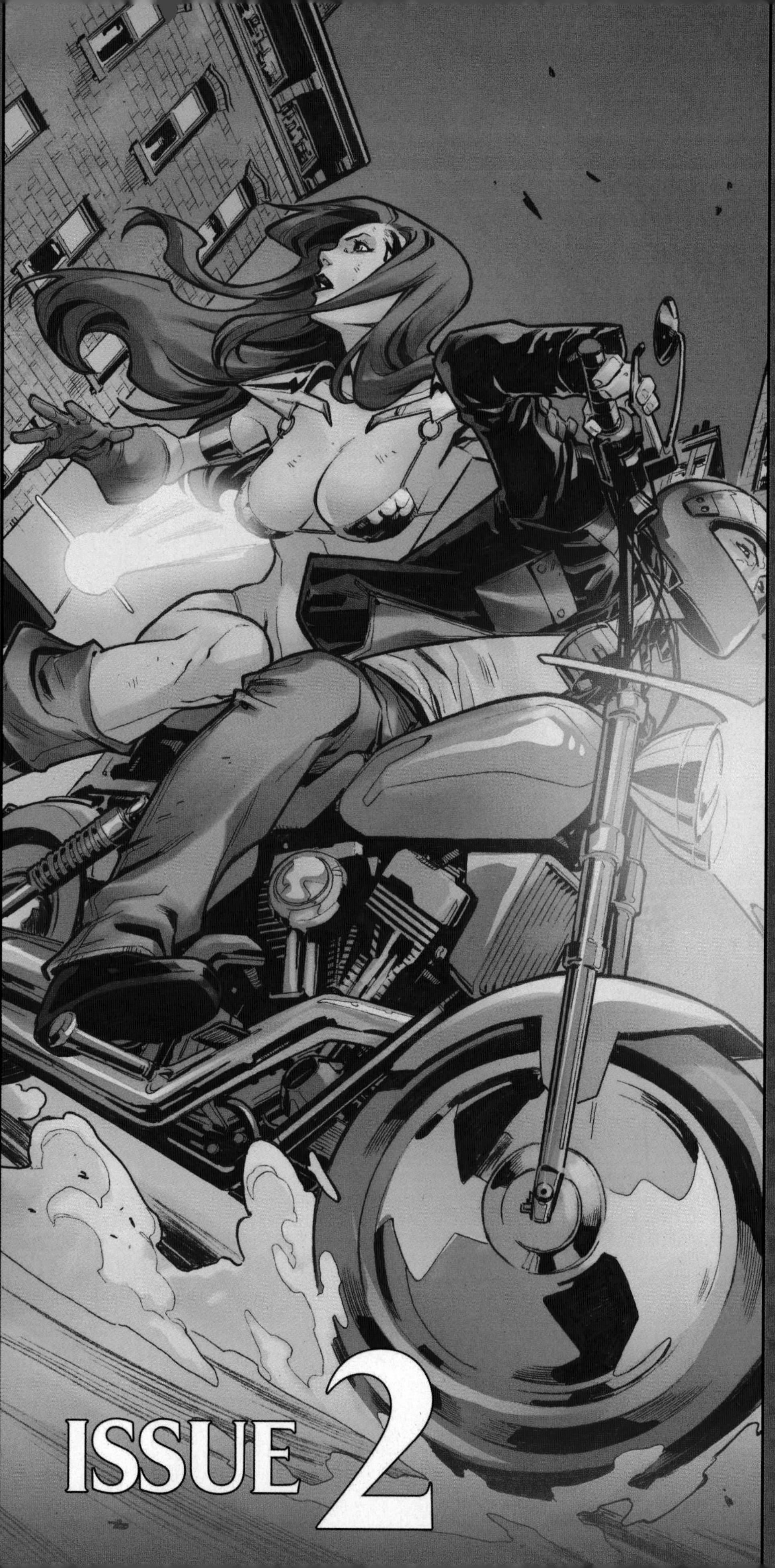
ISSUE 2

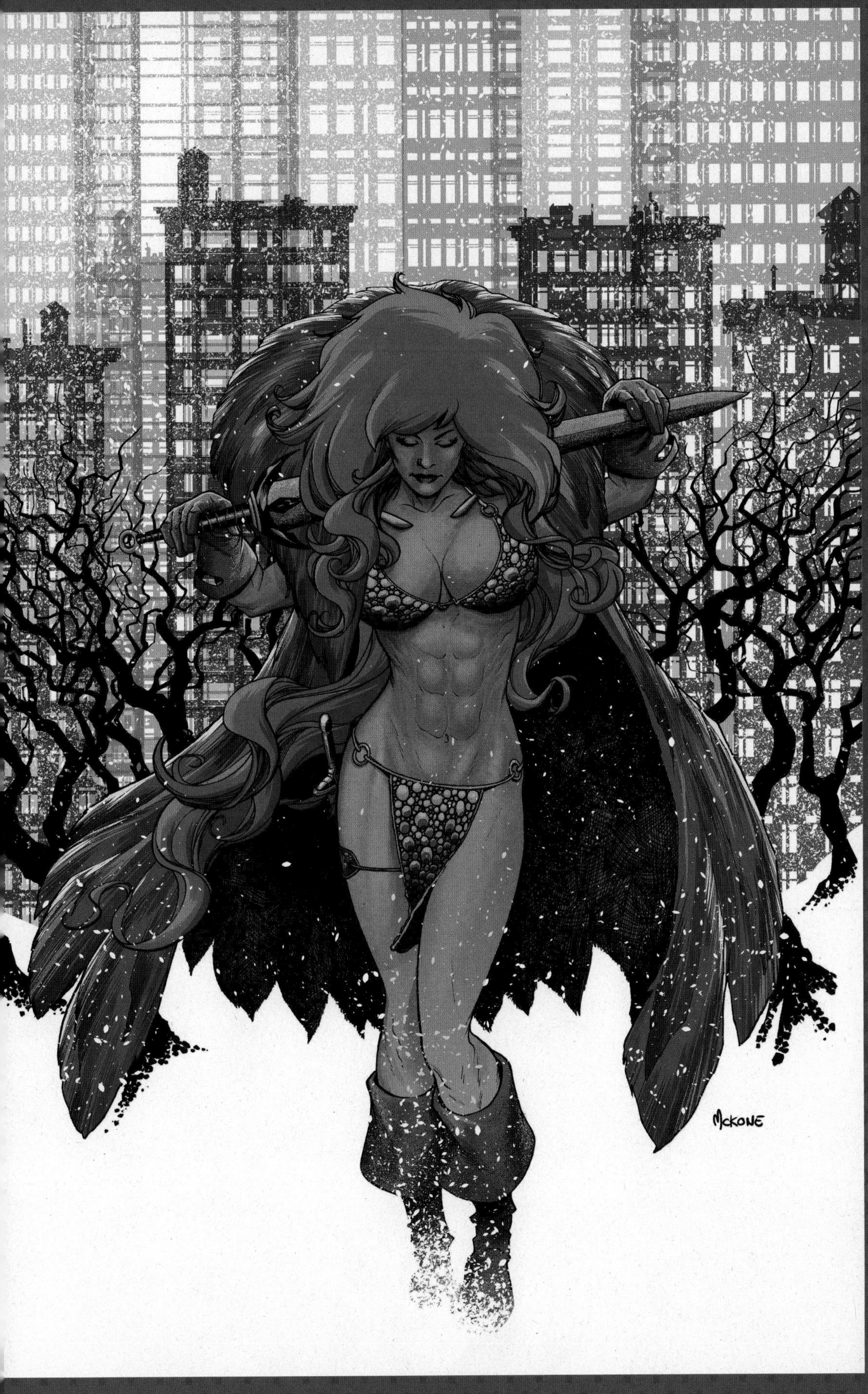
MCKONE

ISSUE #2: COVER ART BY **MIKE MCKONE**

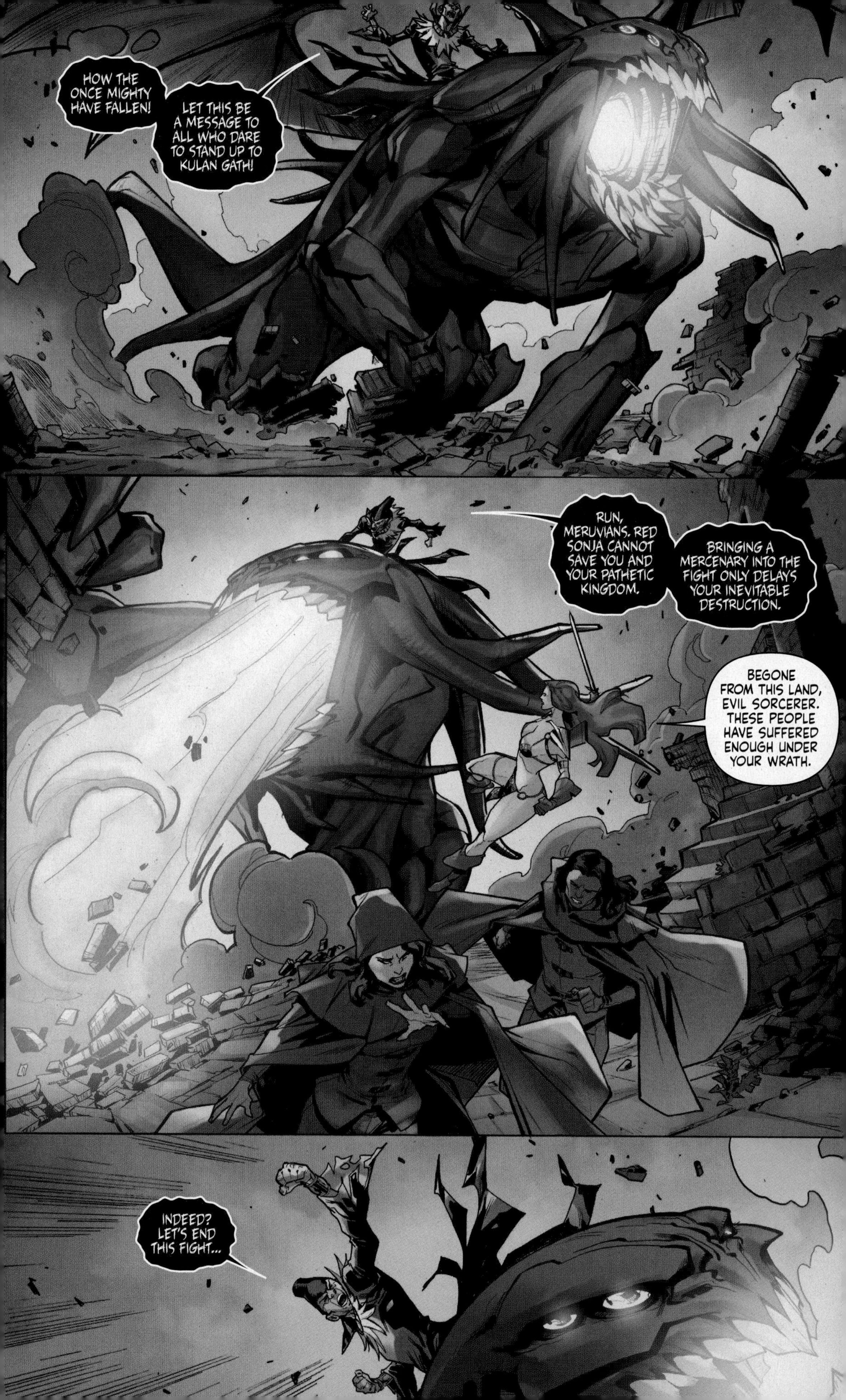
HOW THE ONCE MIGHTY HAVE FALLEN!
LET THIS BE A MESSAGE TO ALL WHO DARE TO STAND UP TO KULAN GATH!
RUN, MERUVIANS. RED SONJA CANNOT SAVE YOU AND YOUR PATHETIC KINGDOM.
BRINGING A MERCENARY INTO THE FIGHT ONLY DELAYS YOUR INEVITABLE DESTRUCTION.
BEGONE FROM THIS LAND, EVIL SORCERER. THESE PEOPLE HAVE SUFFERED ENOUGH UNDER YOUR WRATH.
INDEED? LET'S END THIS FIGHT...

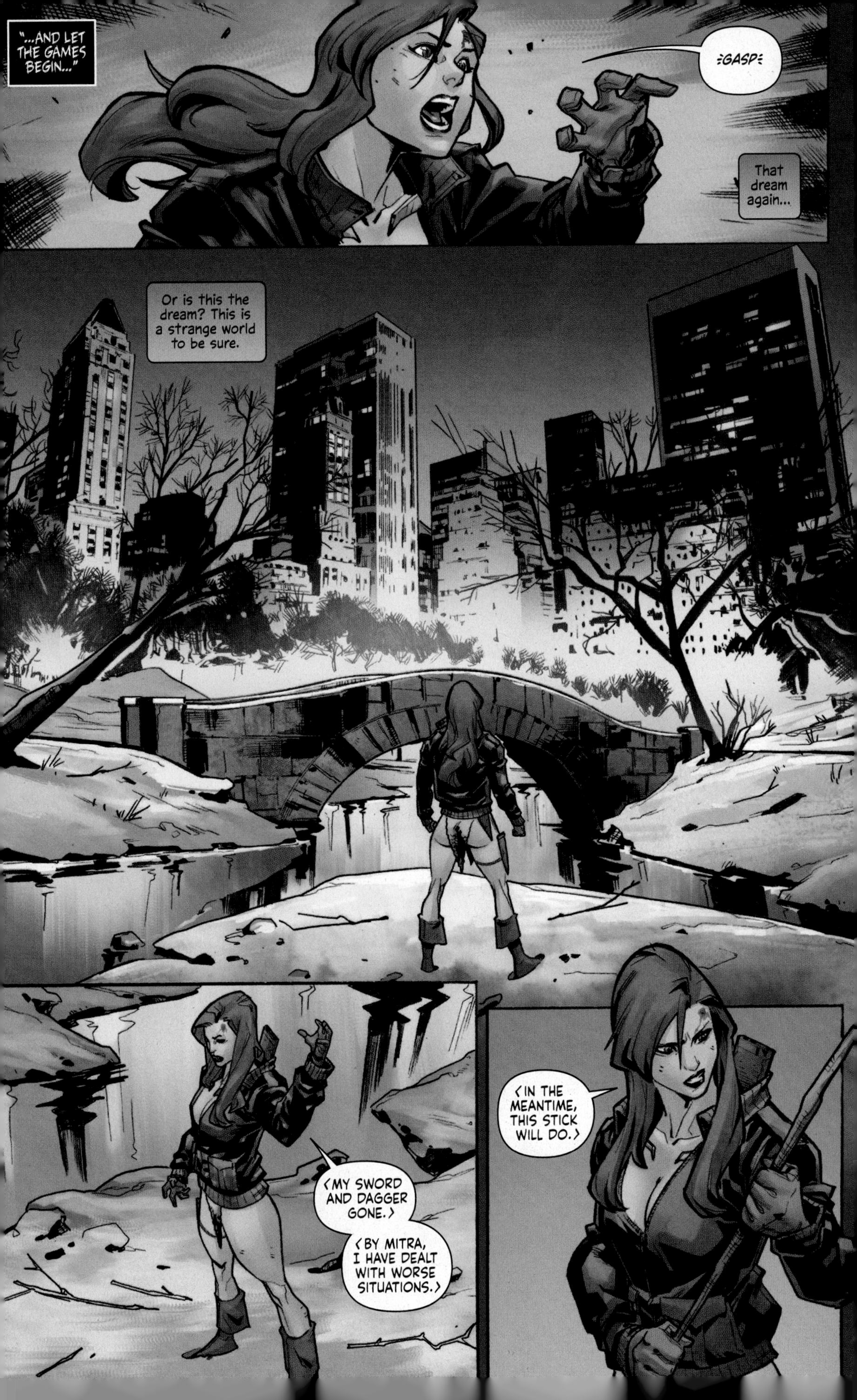
"...AND LET THE GAMES BEGIN..."
GASP
That dream again...
Or is this the dream? This is a strange world to be sure.
‹MY SWORD AND DAGGER GONE.›
‹BY MITRA, I HAVE DEALT WITH WORSE SITUATIONS.›
‹IN THE MEANTIME, THIS STICK WILL DO.›

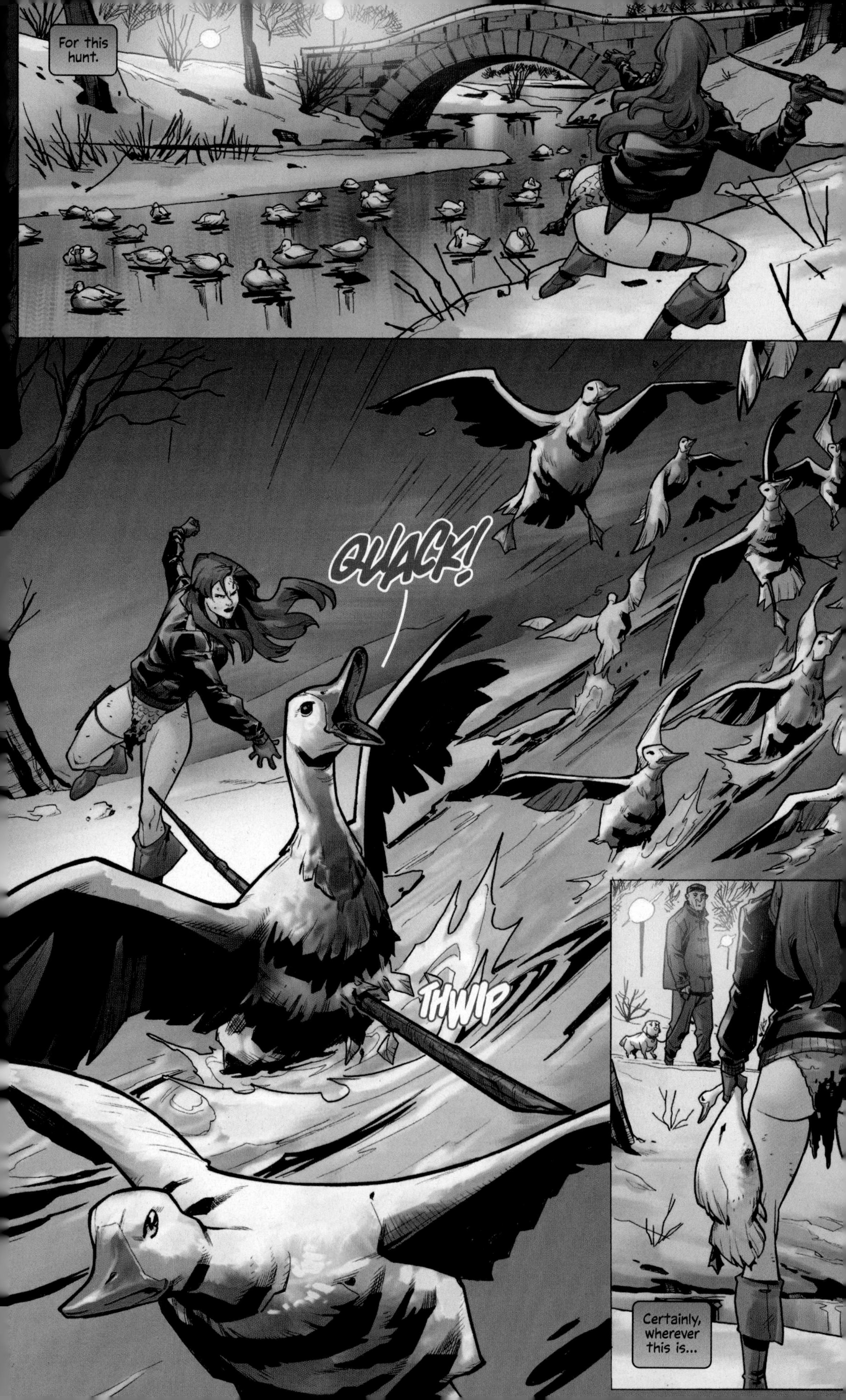
For this hunt.
QUACK!
THWIP
Certainly, wherever this is...

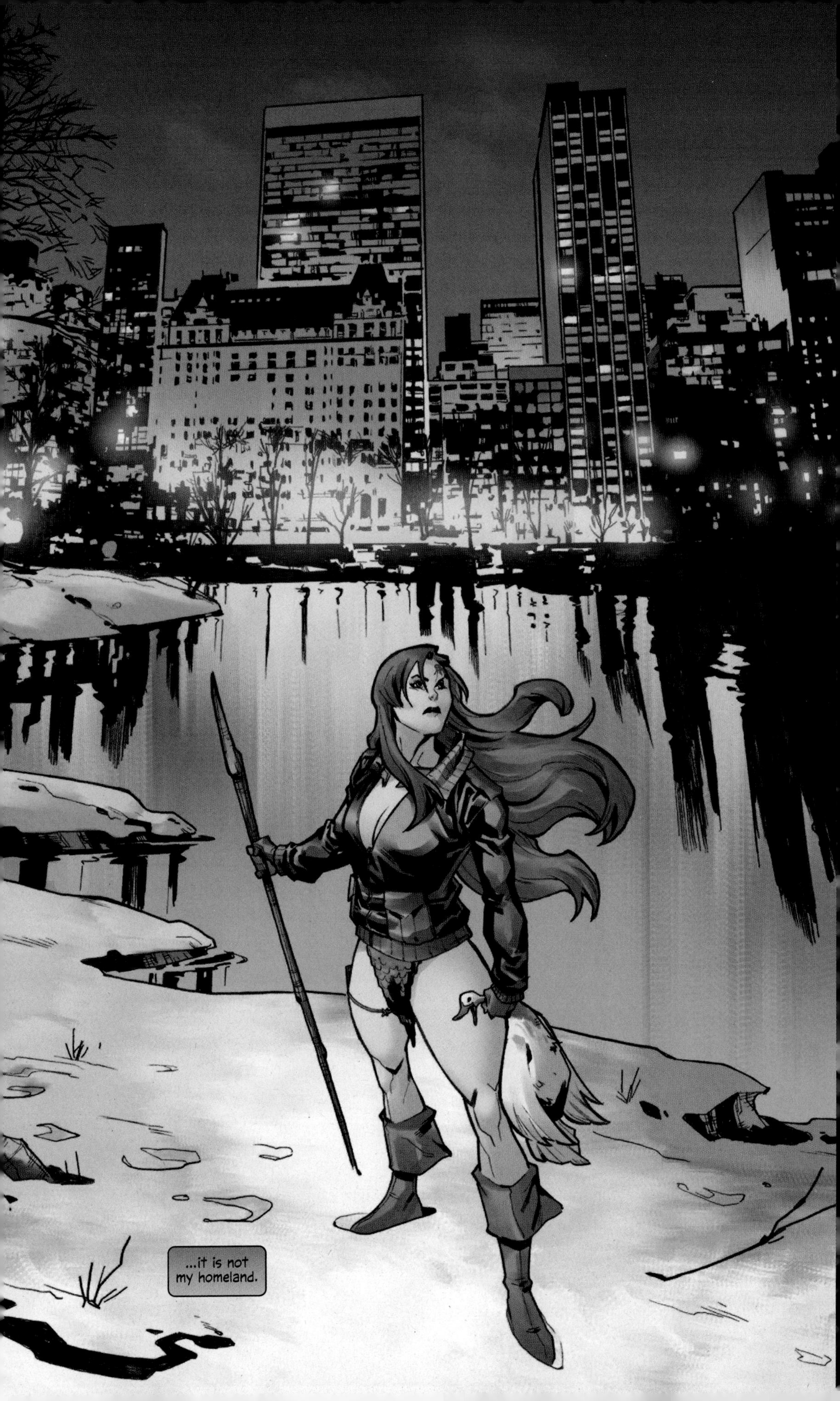
...it is not
my homeland.

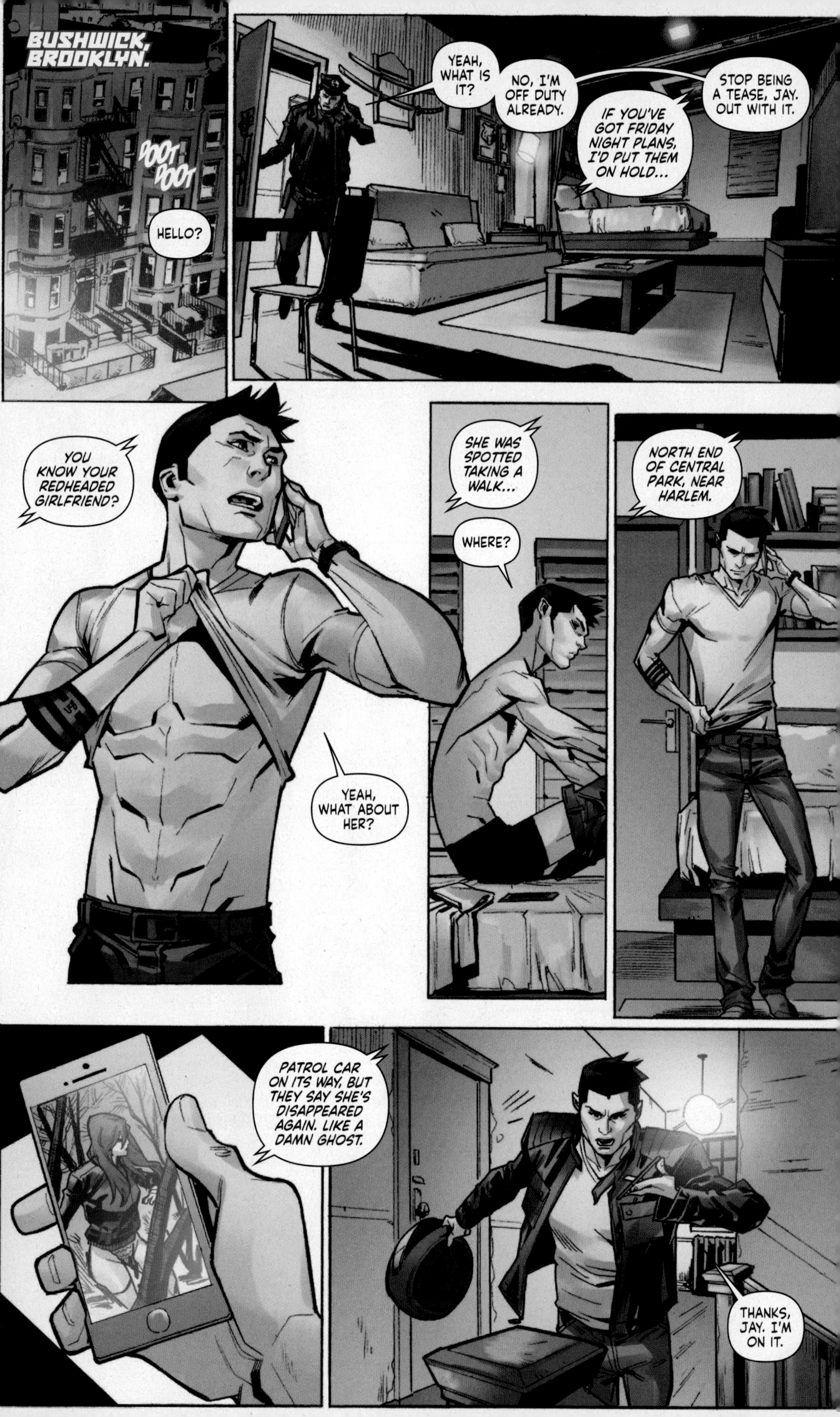

BUSHWICK, BROOKLYN.
DOOT DOOT
HELLO?
YEAH, WHAT IS IT?
NO, I'M OFF DUTY ALREADY.
STOP BEING A TEASE, JAY. OUT WITH IT.
IF YOU'VE GOT FRIDAY NIGHT PLANS, I'D PUT THEM ON HOLD...
YOU KNOW YOUR REDHEADED GIRLFRIEND?
YEAH, WHAT ABOUT HER?
SHE WAS SPOTTED TAKING A WALK...
WHERE?
NORTH END OF CENTRAL PARK, NEAR HARLEM.
PATROL CAR ON ITS WAY, BUT THEY SAY SHE'S DISAPPEARED AGAIN. LIKE A DAMN GHOST.
THANKS, JAY. I'M ON IT.

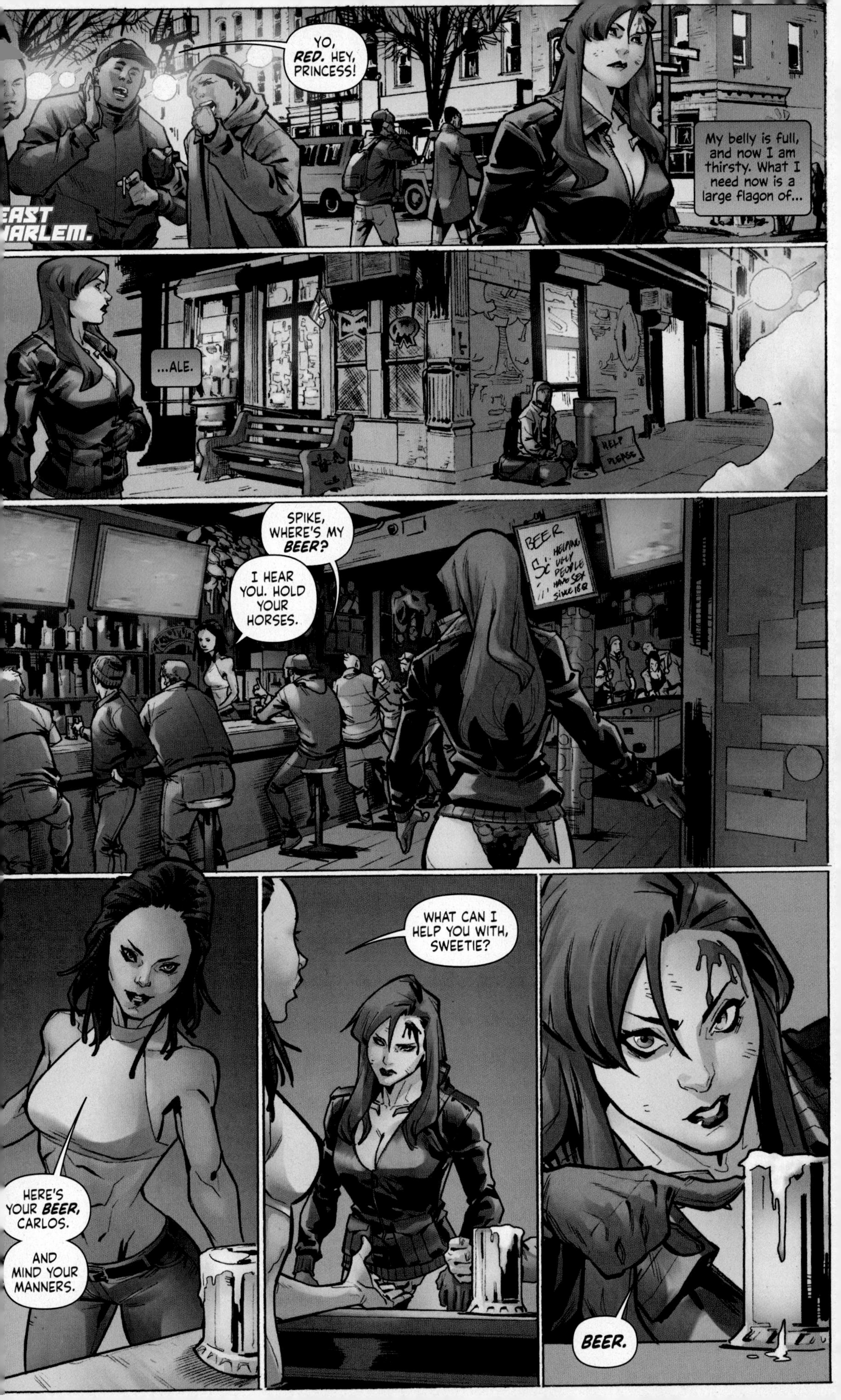
YO, RED. HEY, PRINCESS!
EAST HARLEM.
My belly is full, and now I am thirsty. What I need now is a large flagon of...
...ALE.
HELP PLEASE
SPIKE, WHERE'S MY BEER?
I HEAR YOU. HOLD YOUR HORSES.
BEER
HERE'S YOUR BEER, CARLOS.
AND MIND YOUR MANNERS.
WHAT CAN I HELP YOU WITH, SWEETIE?
BEER.

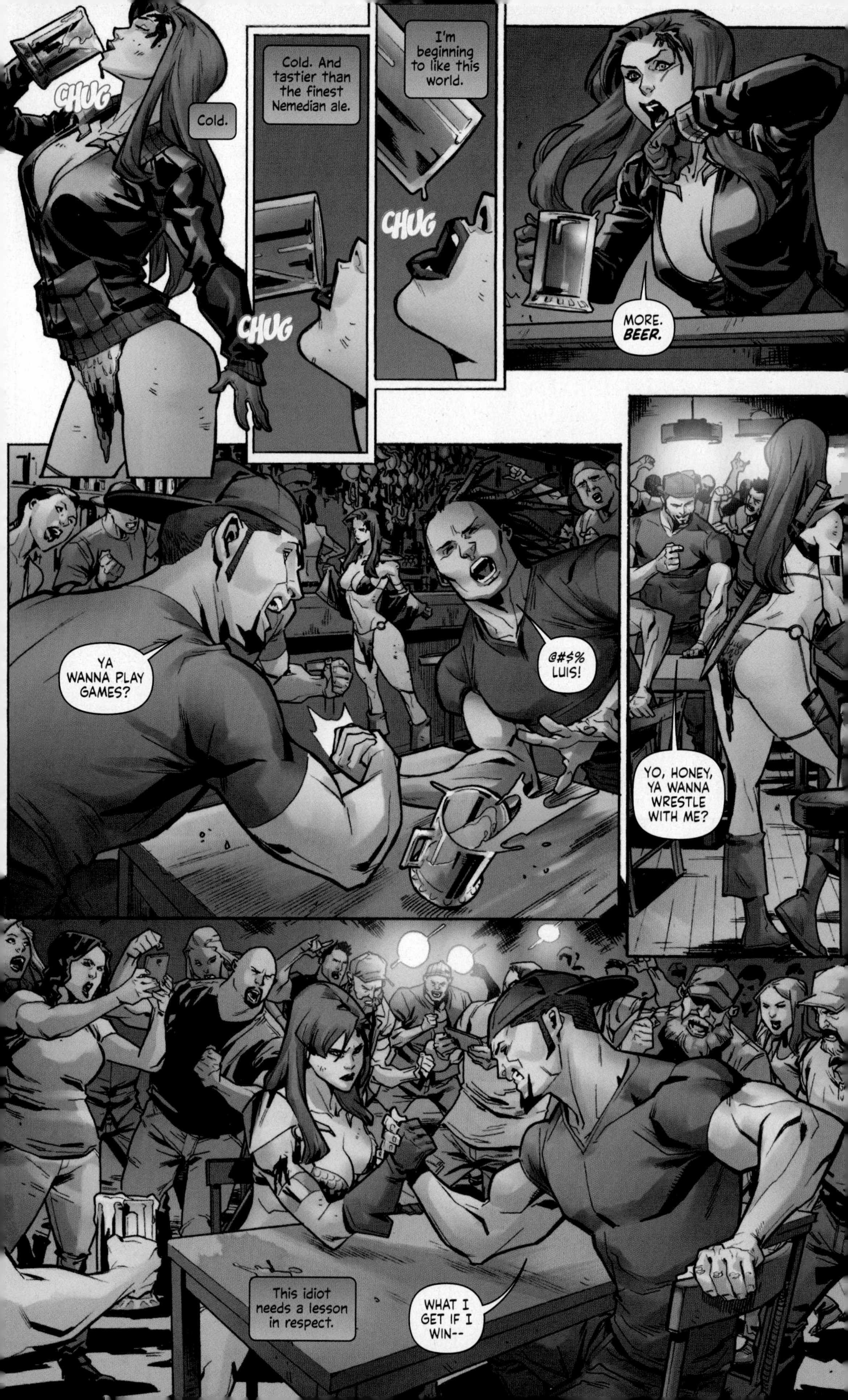
CHUG
Cold.
Cold. And tastier than the finest Nemedian ale.
CHUG
I'm beginning to like this world.
CHUG
MORE. BEER.
YA WANNA PLAY GAMES?
@#$% LUIS!
YO, HONEY, YA WANNA WRESTLE WITH ME?
This idiot needs a lesson in respect.
WHAT I GET IF I WIN--

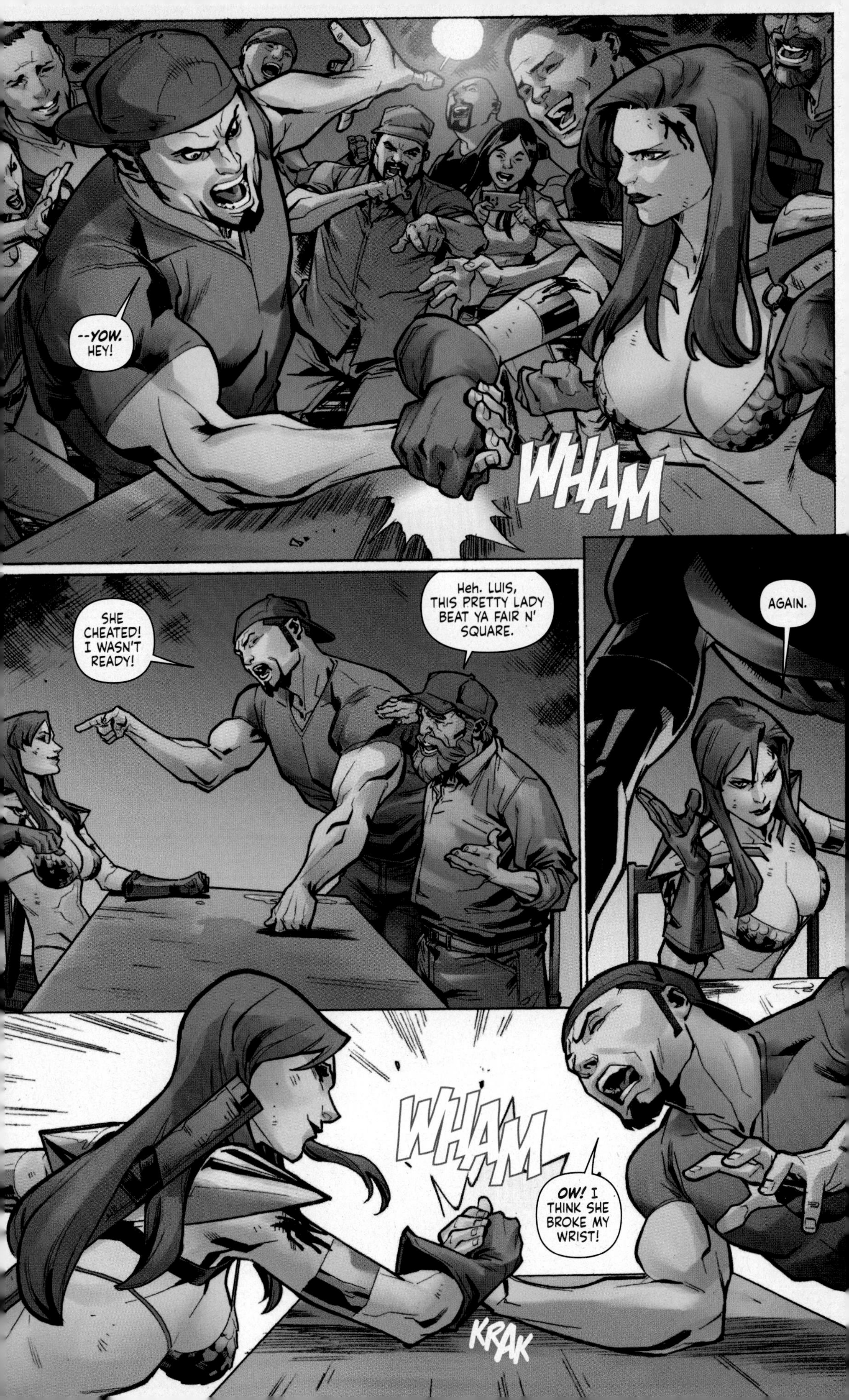
--YOW. HEY!
WHAM
SHE CHEATED! I WASN'T READY!
Heh. LUIS, THIS PRETTY LADY BEAT YA FAIR N' SQUARE.
AGAIN.
WHAM
OW! I THINK SHE BROKE MY WRIST!
KRAK

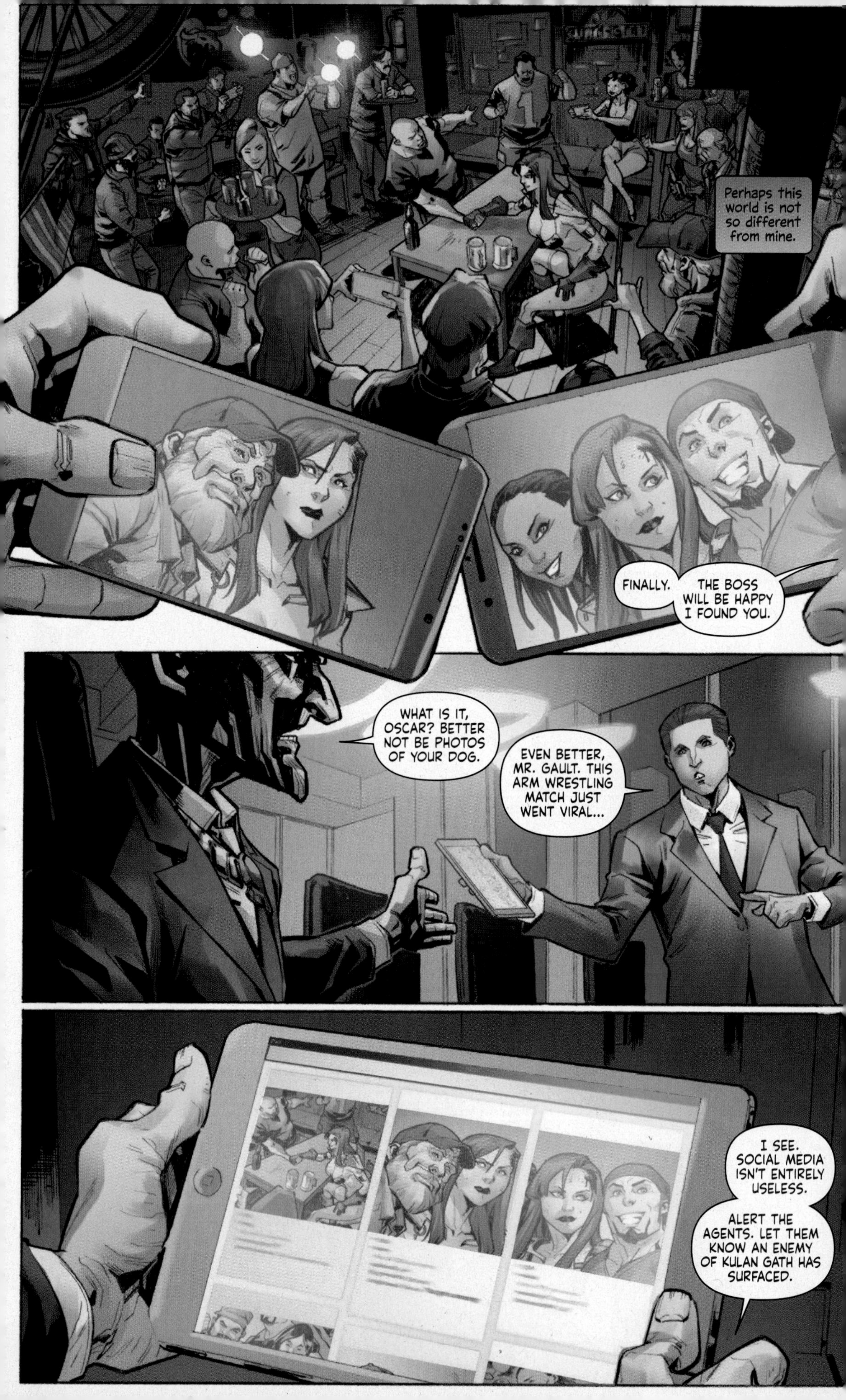
Perhaps this world is not so different from mine.
FINALLY.
THE BOSS WILL BE HAPPY I FOUND YOU.
WHAT IS IT, OSCAR? BETTER NOT BE PHOTOS OF YOUR DOG.
EVEN BETTER, MR. GAULT. THIS ARM WRESTLING MATCH JUST WENT VIRAL...
I SEE. SOCIAL MEDIA ISN'T ENTIRELY USELESS.
ALERT THE AGENTS. LET THEM KNOW AN ENEMY OF KULAN GATH HAS SURFACED.

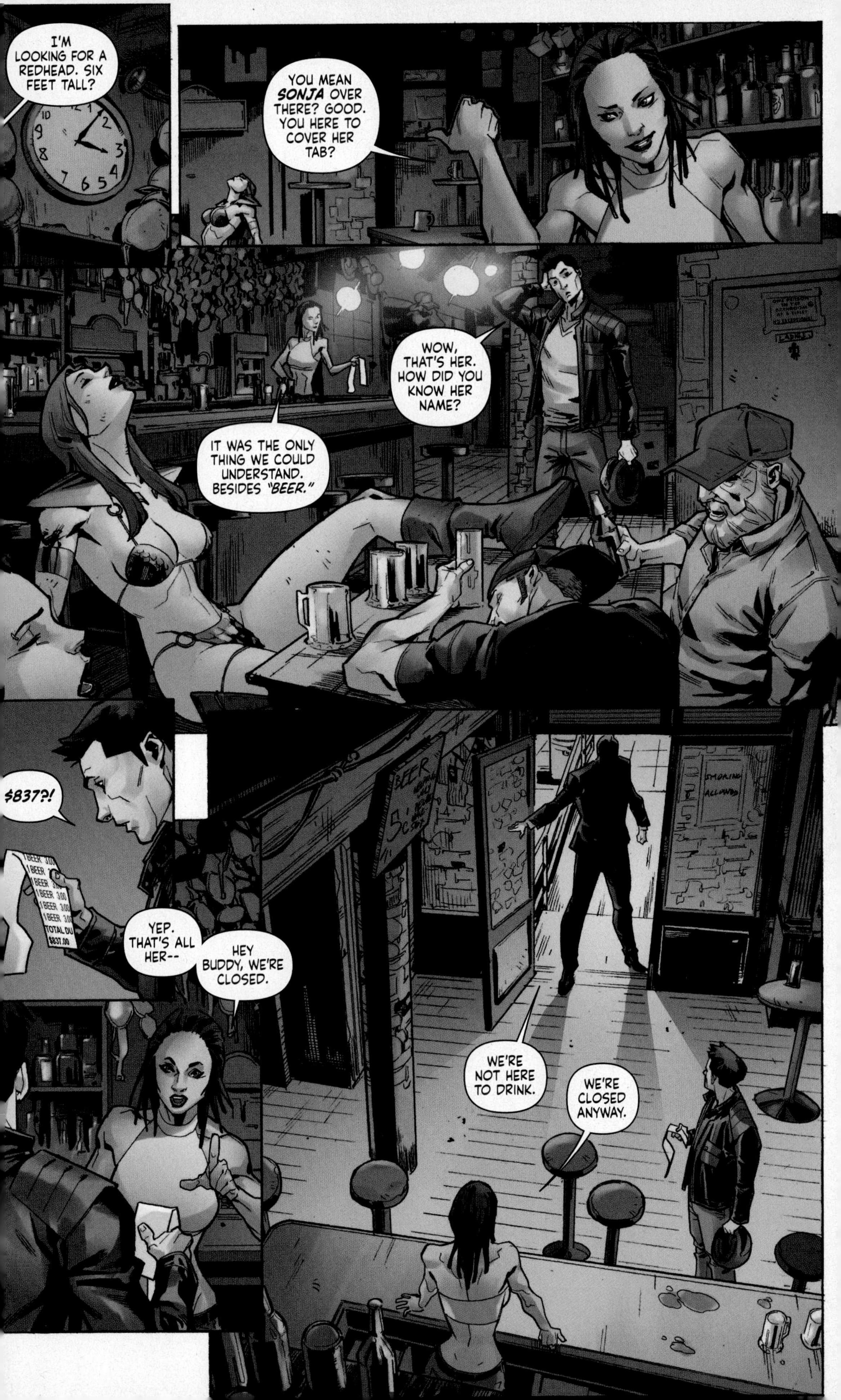

I'M LOOKING FOR A REDHEAD. SIX FEET TALL?
YOU MEAN SONJA OVER THERE? GOOD. YOU HERE TO COVER HER TAB?
WOW, THAT'S HER. HOW DID YOU KNOW HER NAME?
IT WAS THE ONLY THING WE COULD UNDERSTAND. BESIDES "BEER."
$837?!
YEP. THAT'S ALL HER--
HEY BUDDY, WE'RE CLOSED.
WE'RE NOT HERE TO DRINK.
WE'RE CLOSED ANYWAY.

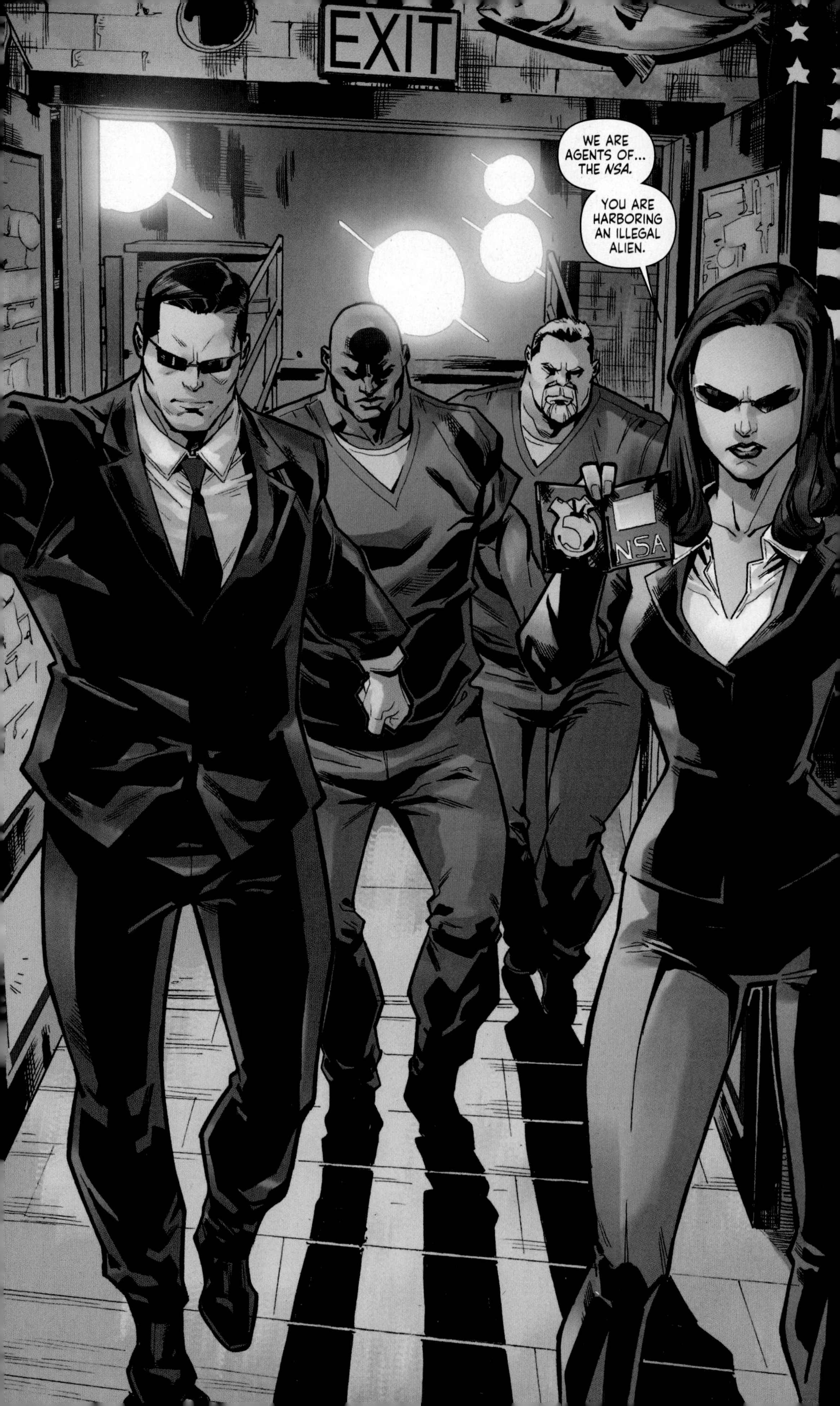
EXIT
WE ARE AGENTS OF... THE NSA.
YOU ARE HARBORING AN ILLEGAL ALIEN.
NSA

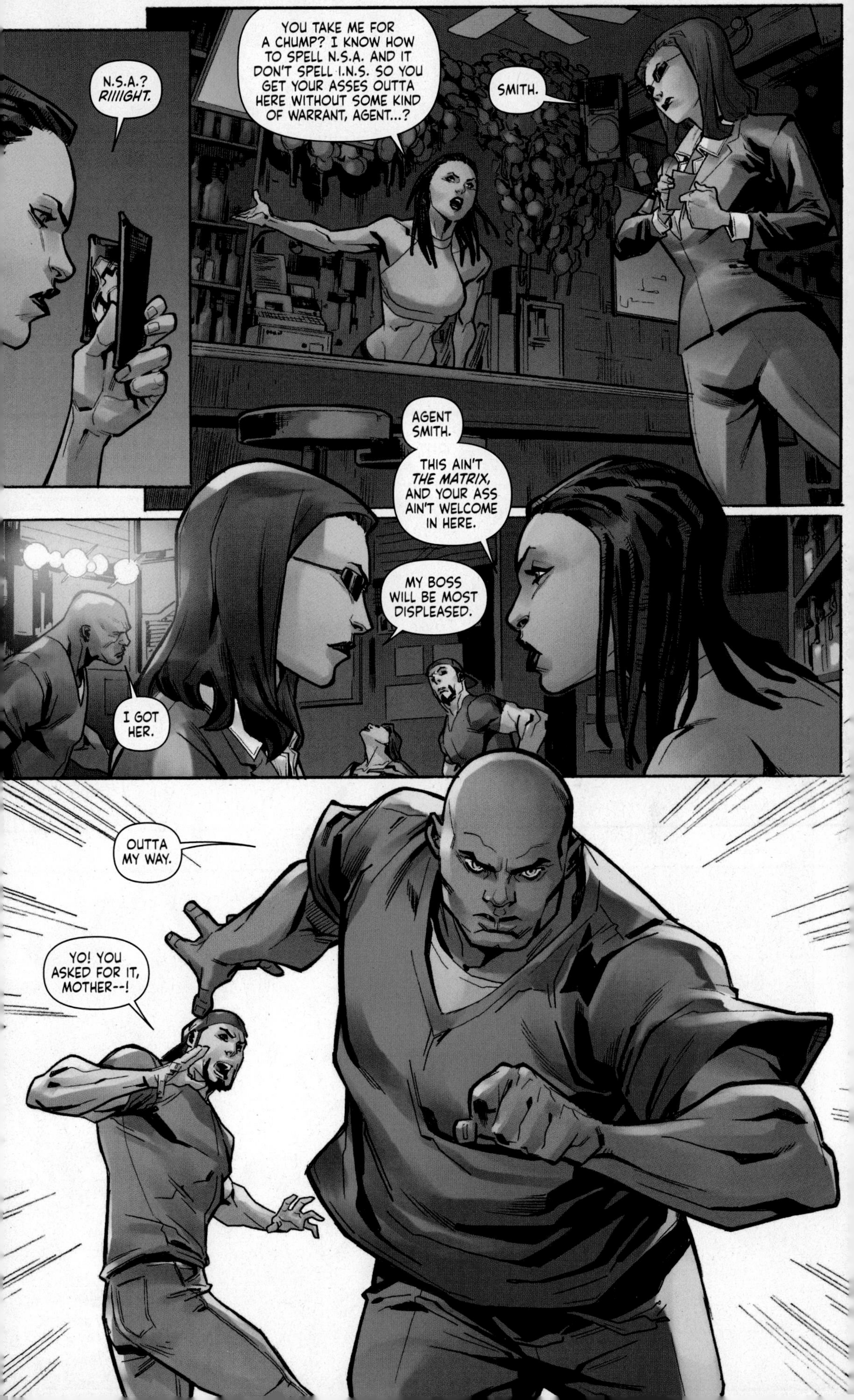

N.S.A.? *RIIIIGHT.*
YOU TAKE ME FOR A CHUMP? I KNOW HOW TO SPELL N.S.A. AND IT DON'T SPELL I.N.S. SO YOU GET YOUR ASSES OUTTA HERE WITHOUT SOME KIND OF WARRANT, AGENT...?
SMITH.
AGENT SMITH.
THIS AIN'T *THE MATRIX*, AND YOUR ASS AIN'T WELCOME IN HERE.
MY BOSS WILL BE MOST DISPLEASED.
I GOT HER.
OUTTA MY WAY.
YO! YOU ASKED FOR IT, MOTHER--!

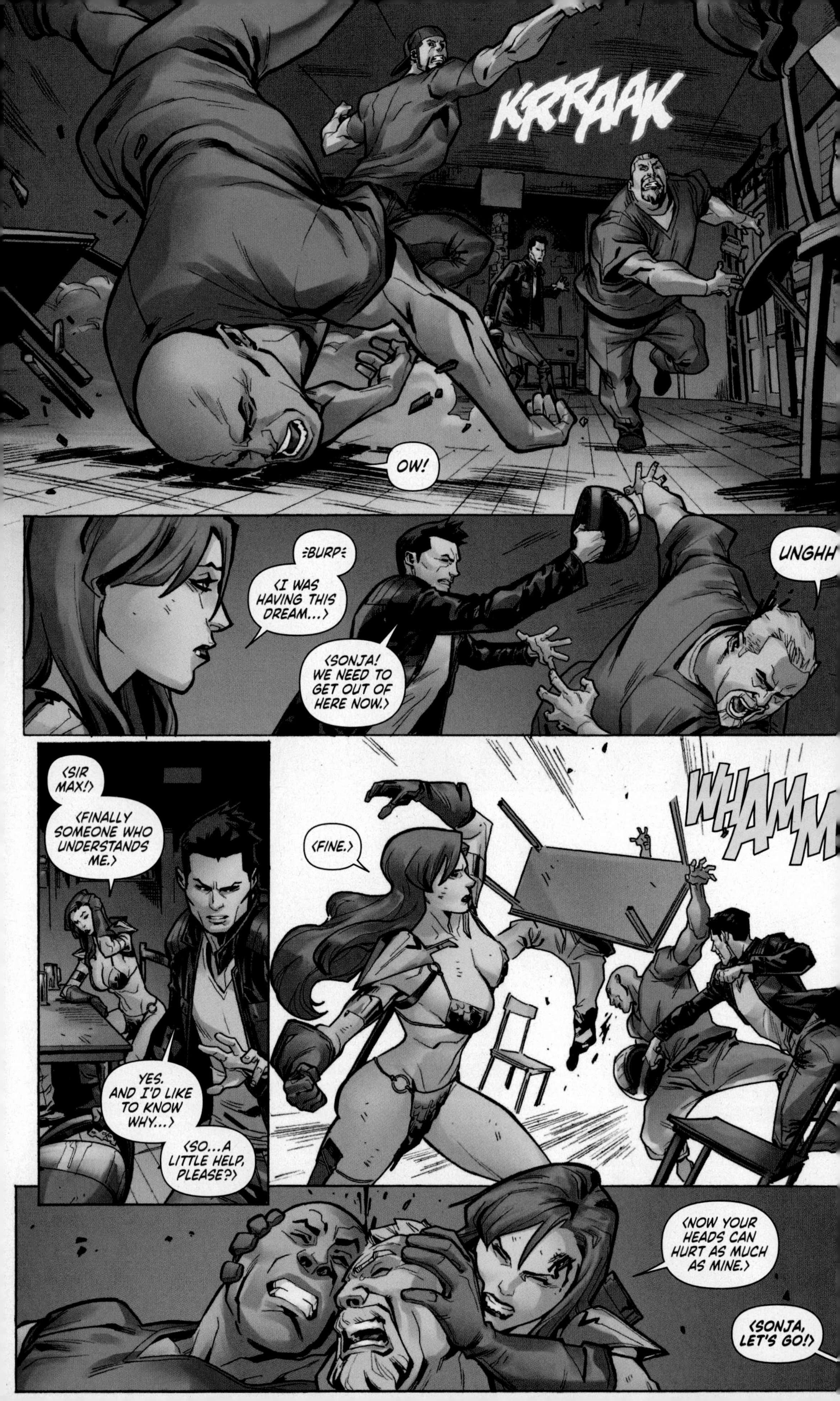
KRRAAK
OW!
=BURP=
‹I WAS HAVING THIS DREAM...›
‹SONJA! WE NEED TO GET OUT OF HERE NOW.›
UNGHH
‹SIR MAX!›
‹FINALLY SOMEONE WHO UNDERSTANDS ME.›
YES. AND I'D LIKE TO KNOW WHY...›
‹SO...A LITTLE HELP, PLEASE?›
‹FINE.›
WHAMM
‹NOW YOUR HEADS CAN HURT AS MUCH AS MINE.›
‹SONJA, LET'S GO!›

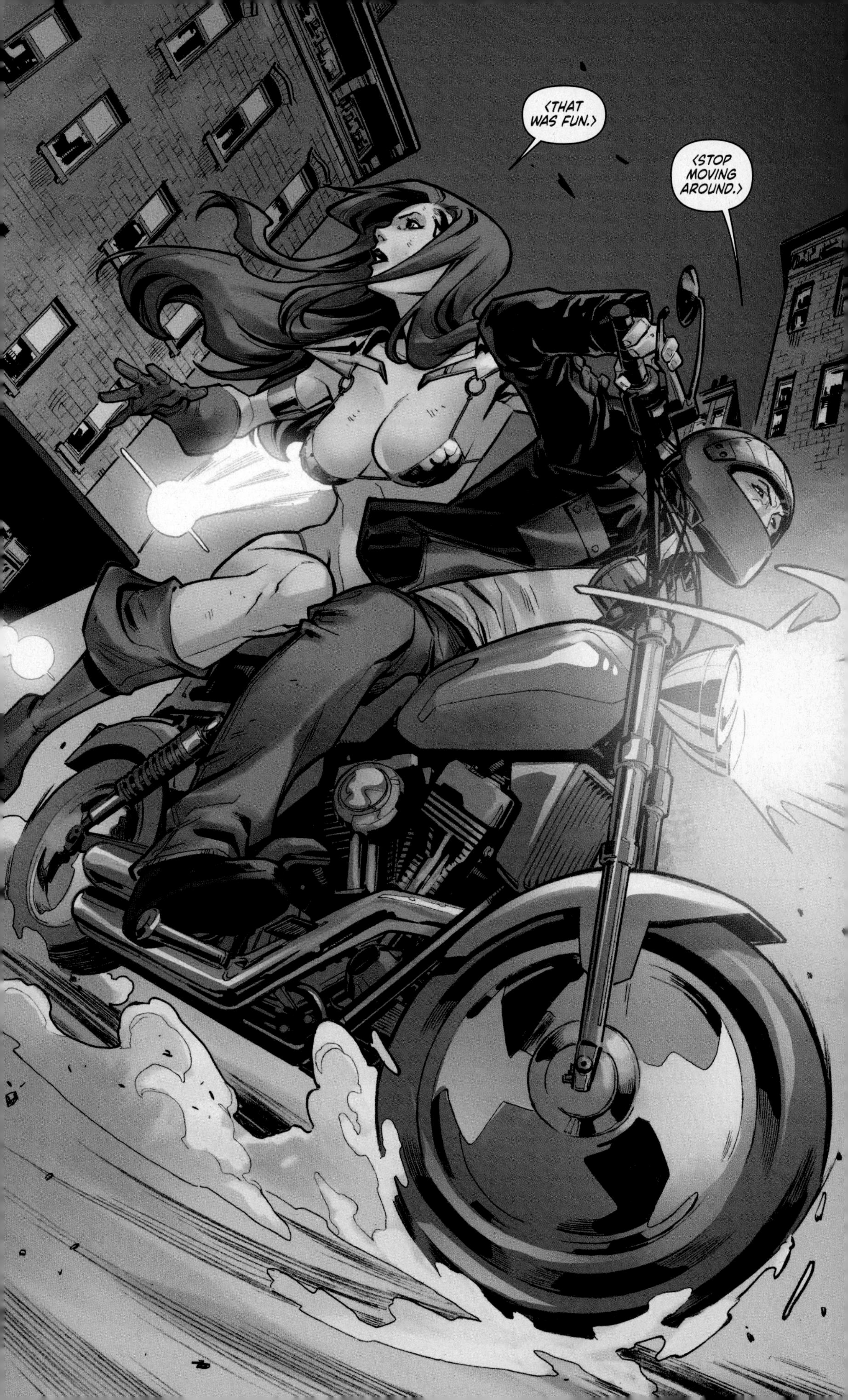

<THAT WAS FUN.>
<STOP MOVING AROUND.>

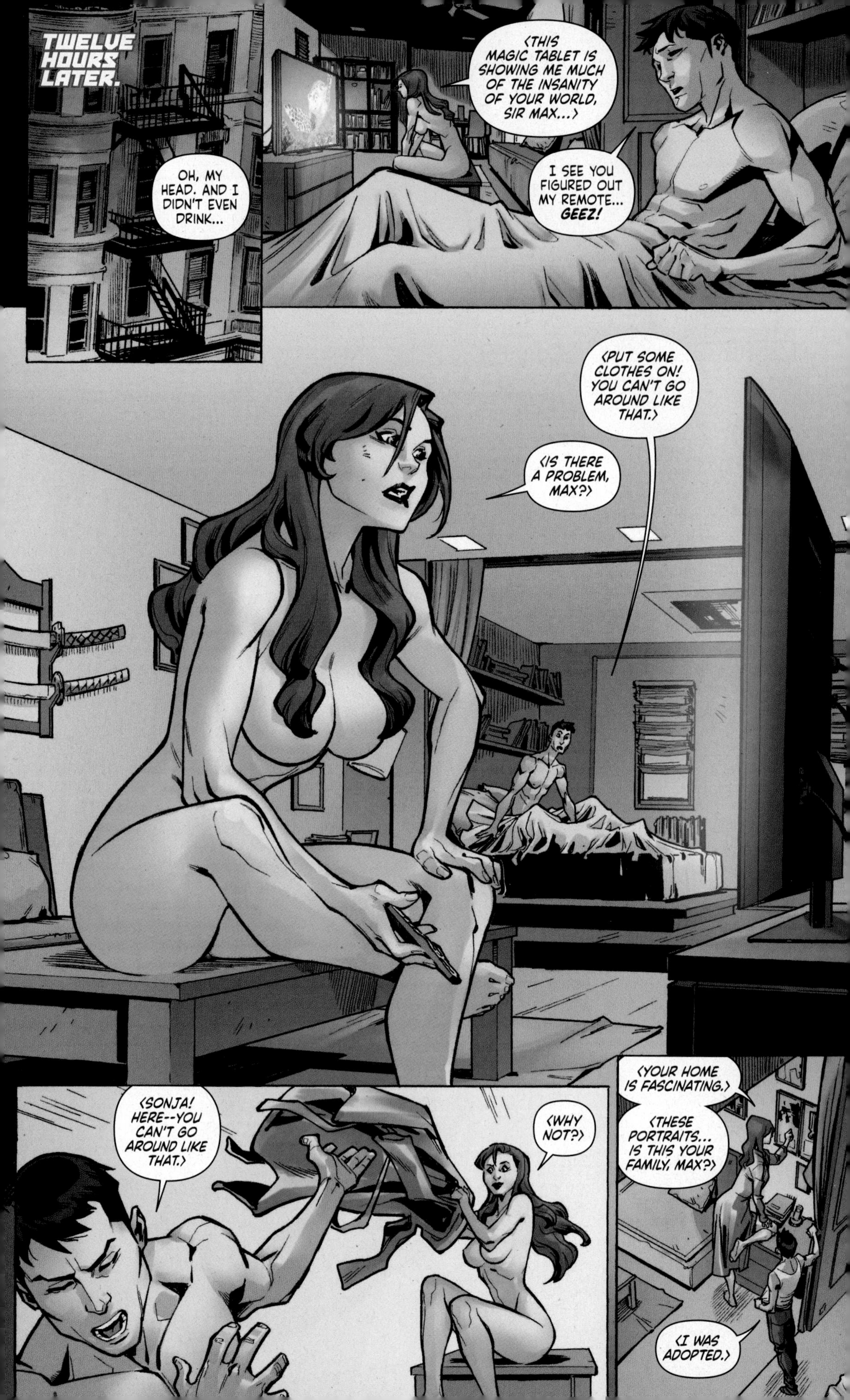
TWELVE HOURS LATER.
OH, MY HEAD. AND I DIDN'T EVEN DRINK...
‹THIS MAGIC TABLET IS SHOWING ME MUCH OF THE INSANITY OF YOUR WORLD, SIR MAX...›
I SEE YOU FIGURED OUT MY REMOTE... GEEZ!
‹PUT SOME CLOTHES ON! YOU CAN'T GO AROUND LIKE THAT.›
‹IS THERE A PROBLEM, MAX?›
‹SONJA! HERE--YOU CAN'T GO AROUND LIKE THAT.›
‹WHY NOT?›
‹YOUR HOME IS FASCINATING.›
‹THESE PORTRAITS... IS THIS YOUR FAMILY, MAX?›
‹I WAS ADOPTED.›

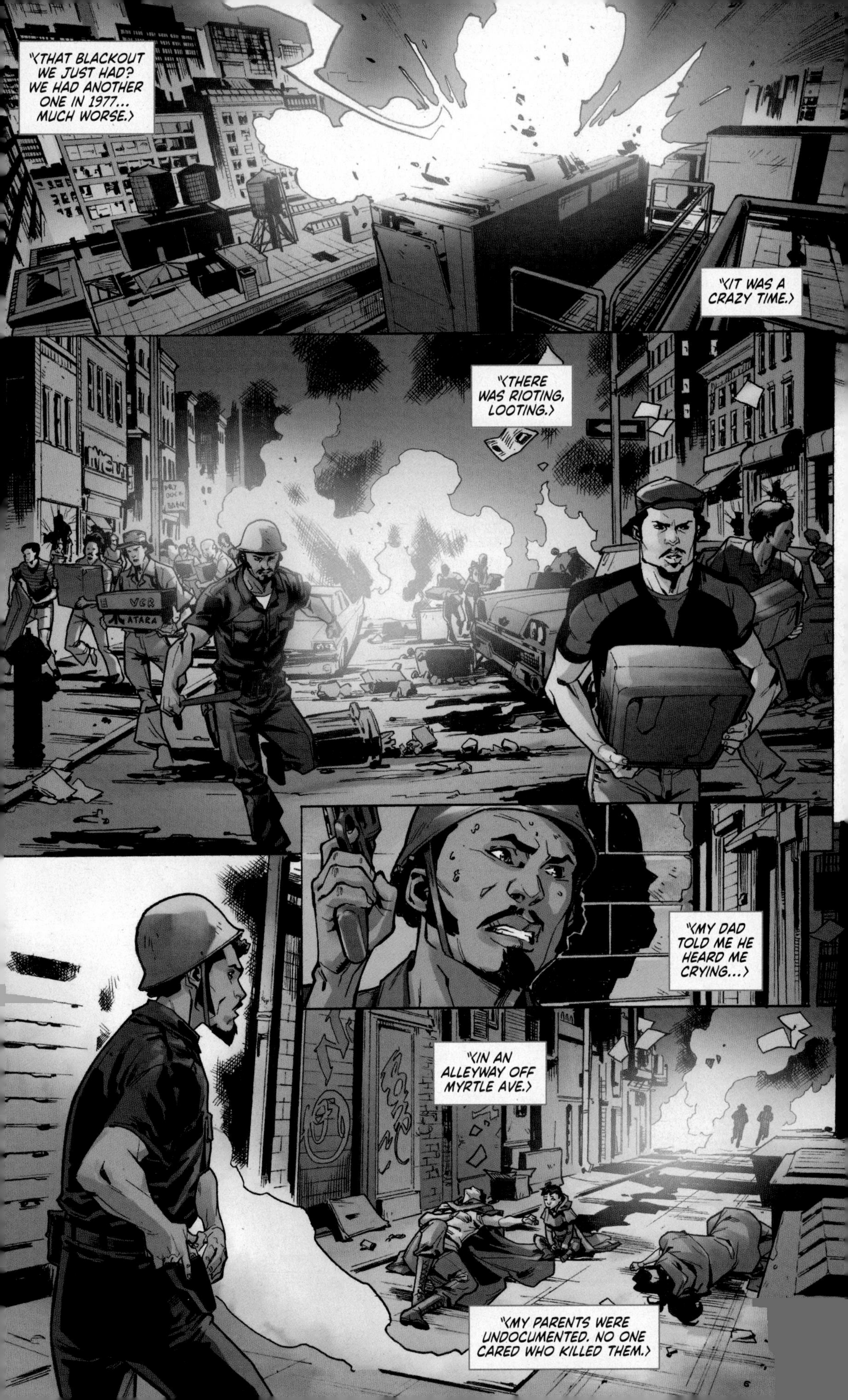
"‹THAT BLACKOUT WE JUST HAD? WE HAD ANOTHER ONE IN 1977... MUCH WORSE.›
"‹IT WAS A CRAZY TIME.›
"‹THERE WAS RIOTING, LOOTING.›
VCR
"‹MY DAD TOLD ME HE HEARD ME CRYING...›
"‹IN AN ALLEYWAY OFF MYRTLE AVE.›
"‹MY PARENTS WERE UNDOCUMENTED. NO ONE CARED WHO KILLED THEM.›

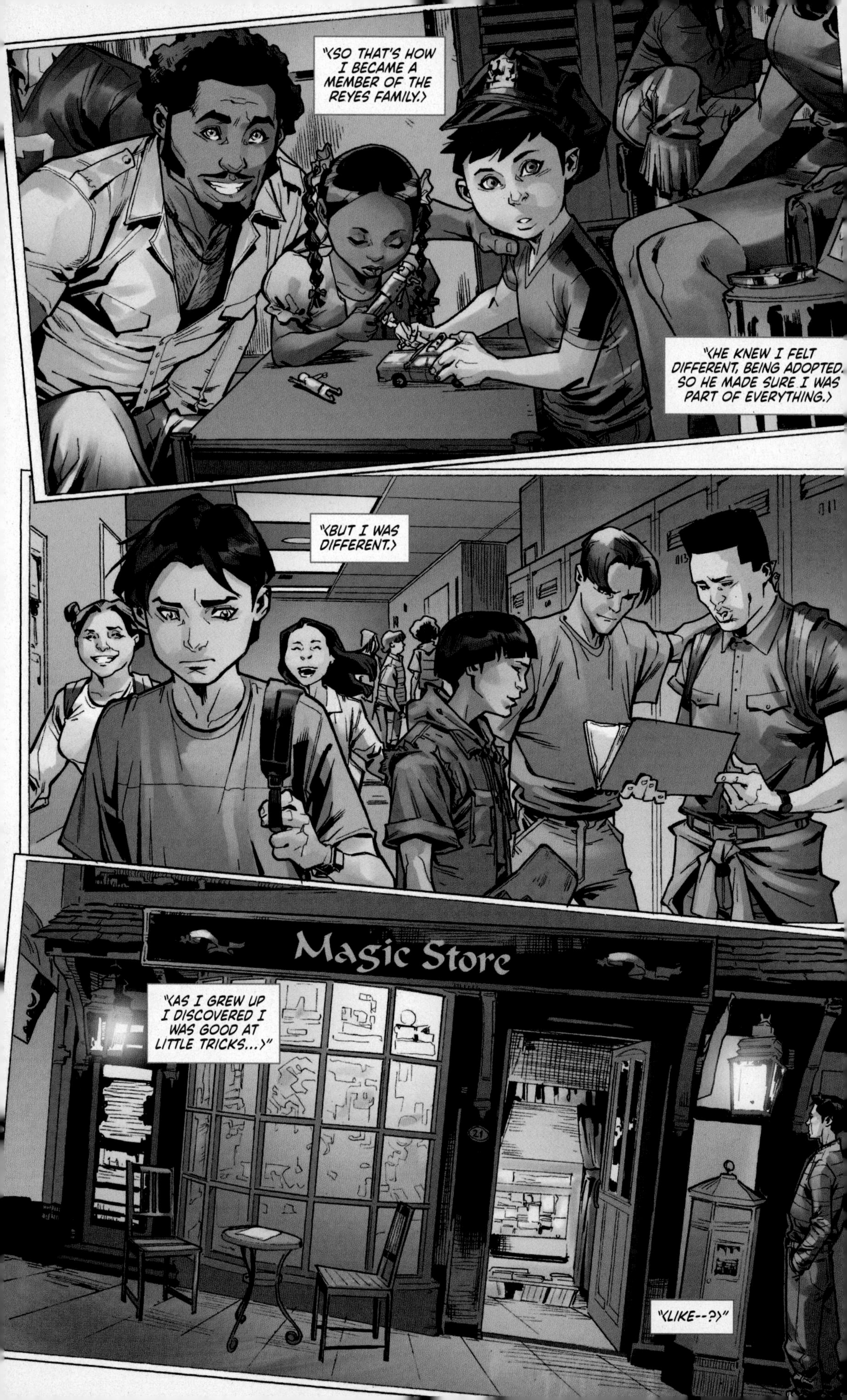
"<SO THAT'S HOW I BECAME A MEMBER OF THE REYES FAMILY.>
"<HE KNEW I FELT DIFFERENT, BEING ADOPTED. SO HE MADE SURE I WAS PART OF EVERYTHING.>
"<BUT I WAS DIFFERENT.>
Magic Store
"<AS I GREW UP I DISCOVERED I WAS GOOD AT LITTLE TRICKS...>"
"<LIKE--?>"

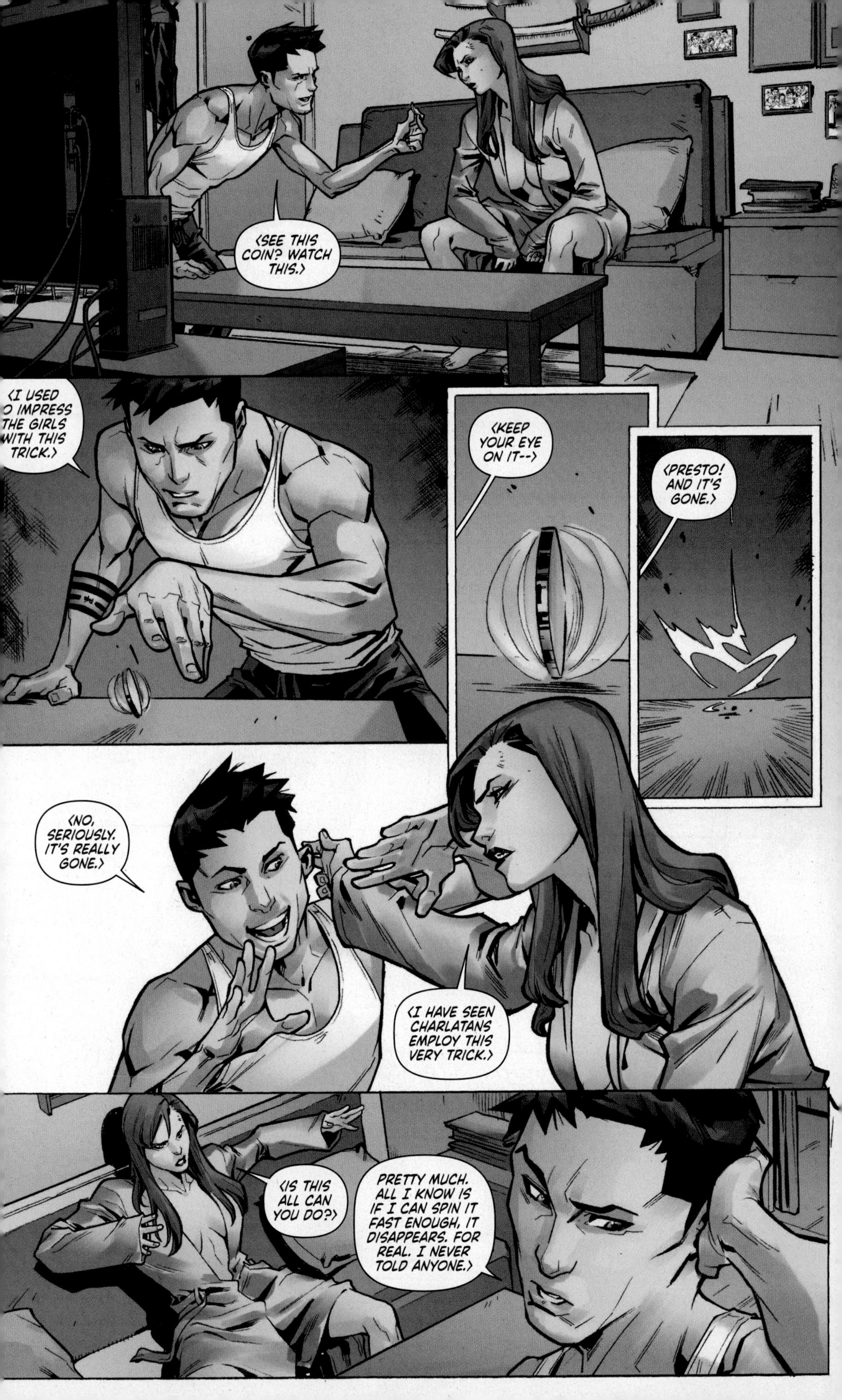

‹SEE THIS COIN? WATCH THIS.›
‹I USED TO IMPRESS THE GIRLS WITH THIS TRICK.›
‹KEEP YOUR EYE ON IT--›
‹PRESTO! AND IT'S GONE.›
‹NO, SERIOUSLY. IT'S REALLY GONE.›
‹I HAVE SEEN CHARLATANS EMPLOY THIS VERY TRICK.›
‹IS THIS ALL CAN YOU DO?›
PRETTY MUCH. ALL I KNOW IS IF I CAN SPIN IT FAST ENOUGH, IT DISAPPEARS. FOR REAL. I NEVER TOLD ANYONE.›

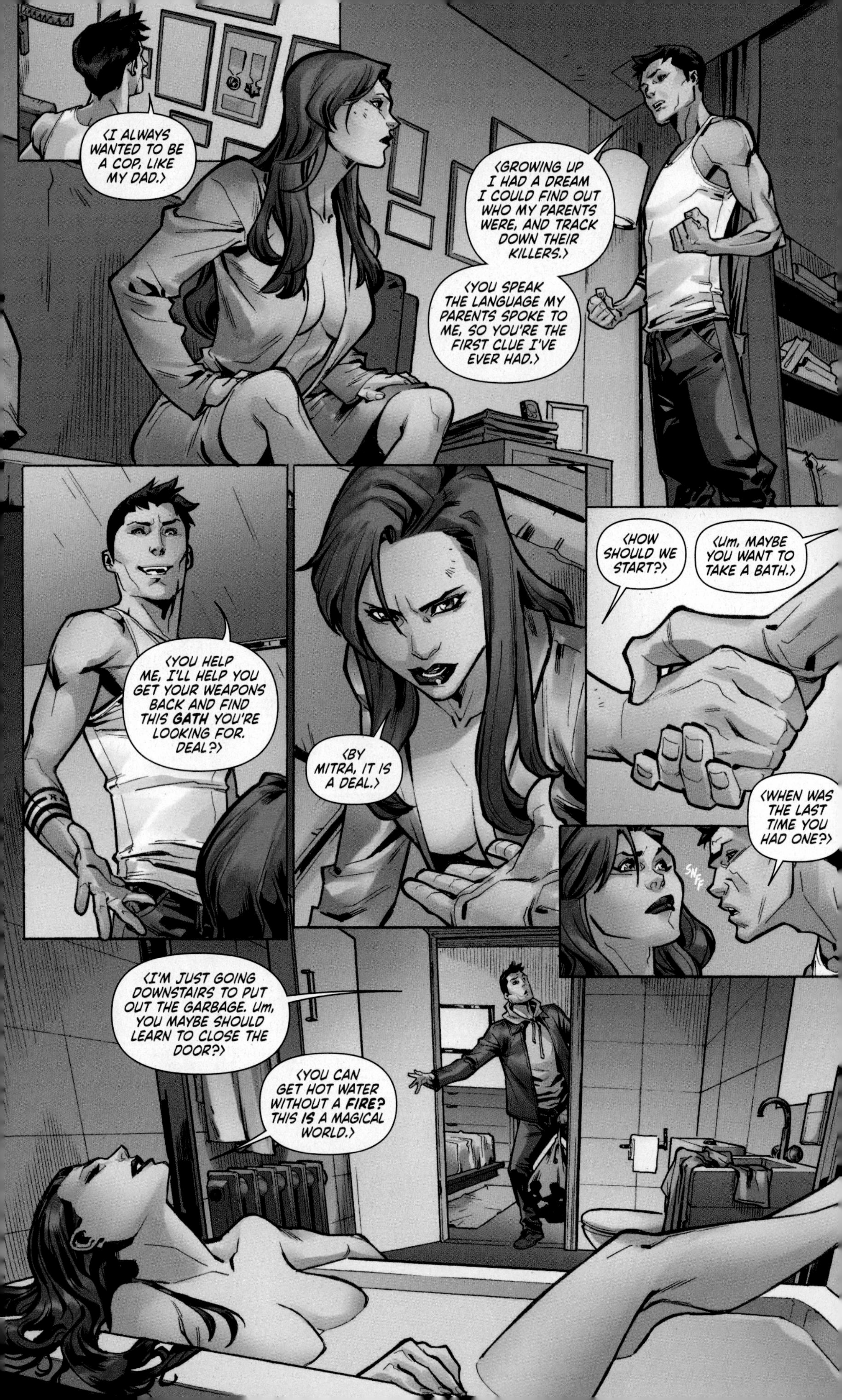

<I ALWAYS WANTED TO BE A COP, LIKE MY DAD.>
<GROWING UP I HAD A DREAM I COULD FIND OUT WHO MY PARENTS WERE, AND TRACK DOWN THEIR KILLERS.>
<YOU SPEAK THE LANGUAGE MY PARENTS SPOKE TO ME, SO YOU'RE THE FIRST CLUE I'VE EVER HAD.>
<YOU HELP ME, I'LL HELP YOU GET YOUR WEAPONS BACK AND FIND THIS GATH YOU'RE LOOKING FOR. DEAL?>
<BY MITRA, IT IS A DEAL.>
<HOW SHOULD WE START?>
<Um, MAYBE YOU WANT TO TAKE A BATH.>
<WHEN WAS THE LAST TIME YOU HAD ONE?>
SNFF
<I'M JUST GOING DOWNSTAIRS TO PUT OUT THE GARBAGE. Um, YOU MAYBE SHOULD LEARN TO CLOSE THE DOOR?>
<YOU CAN GET HOT WATER WITHOUT A FIRE? THIS IS A MAGICAL WORLD.>

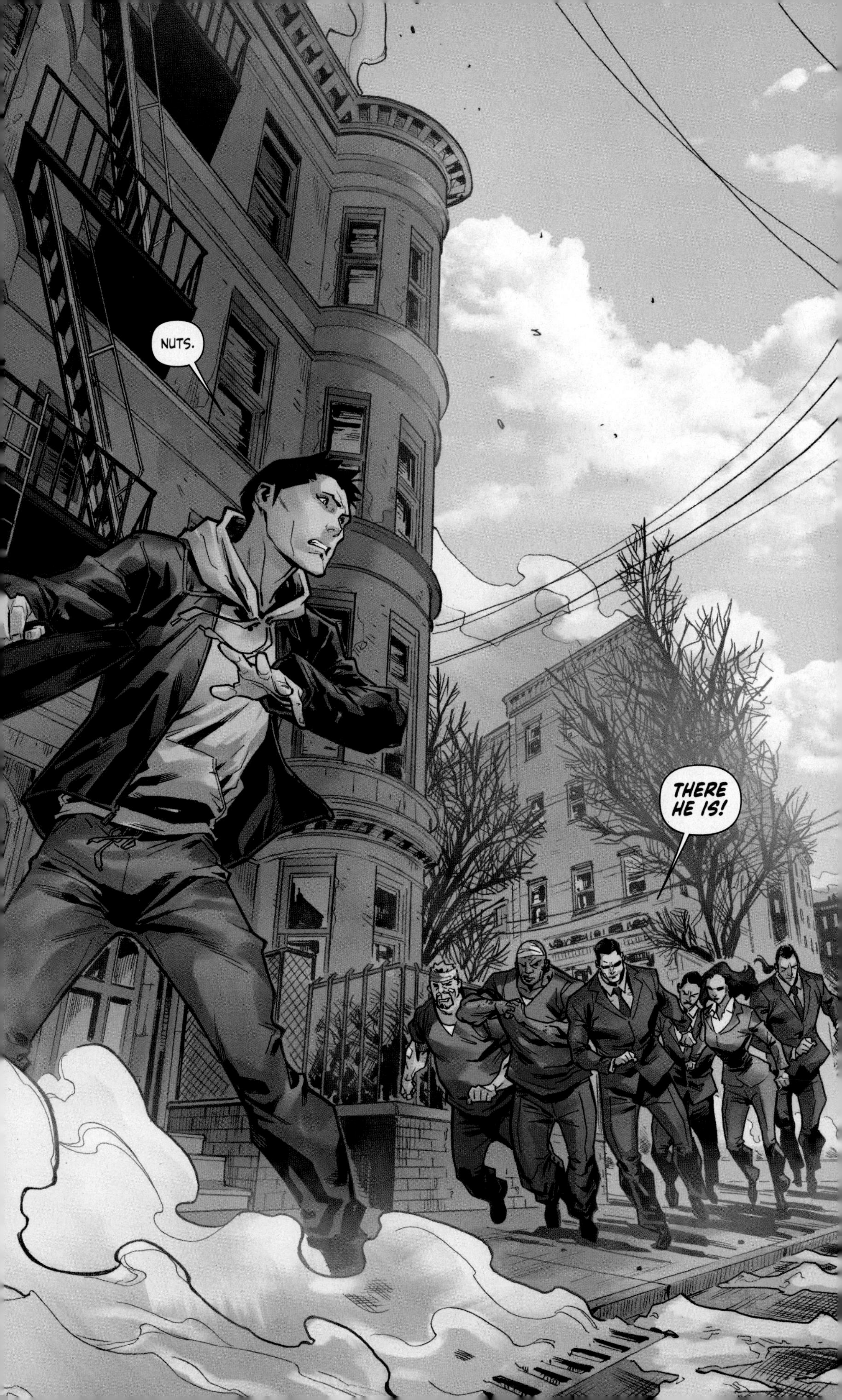
NUTS.
THERE HE IS!

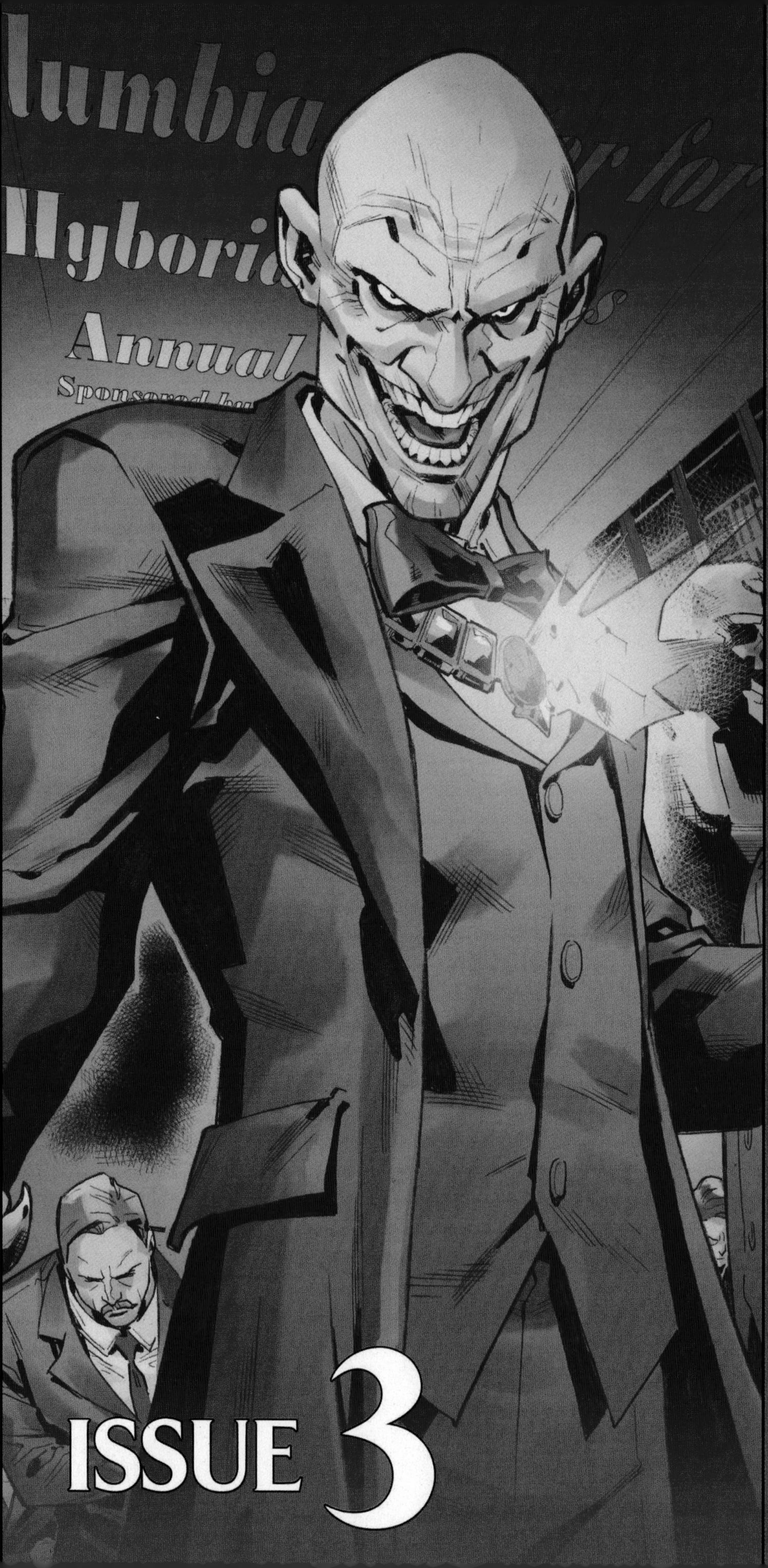
Annual

ISSUE 3

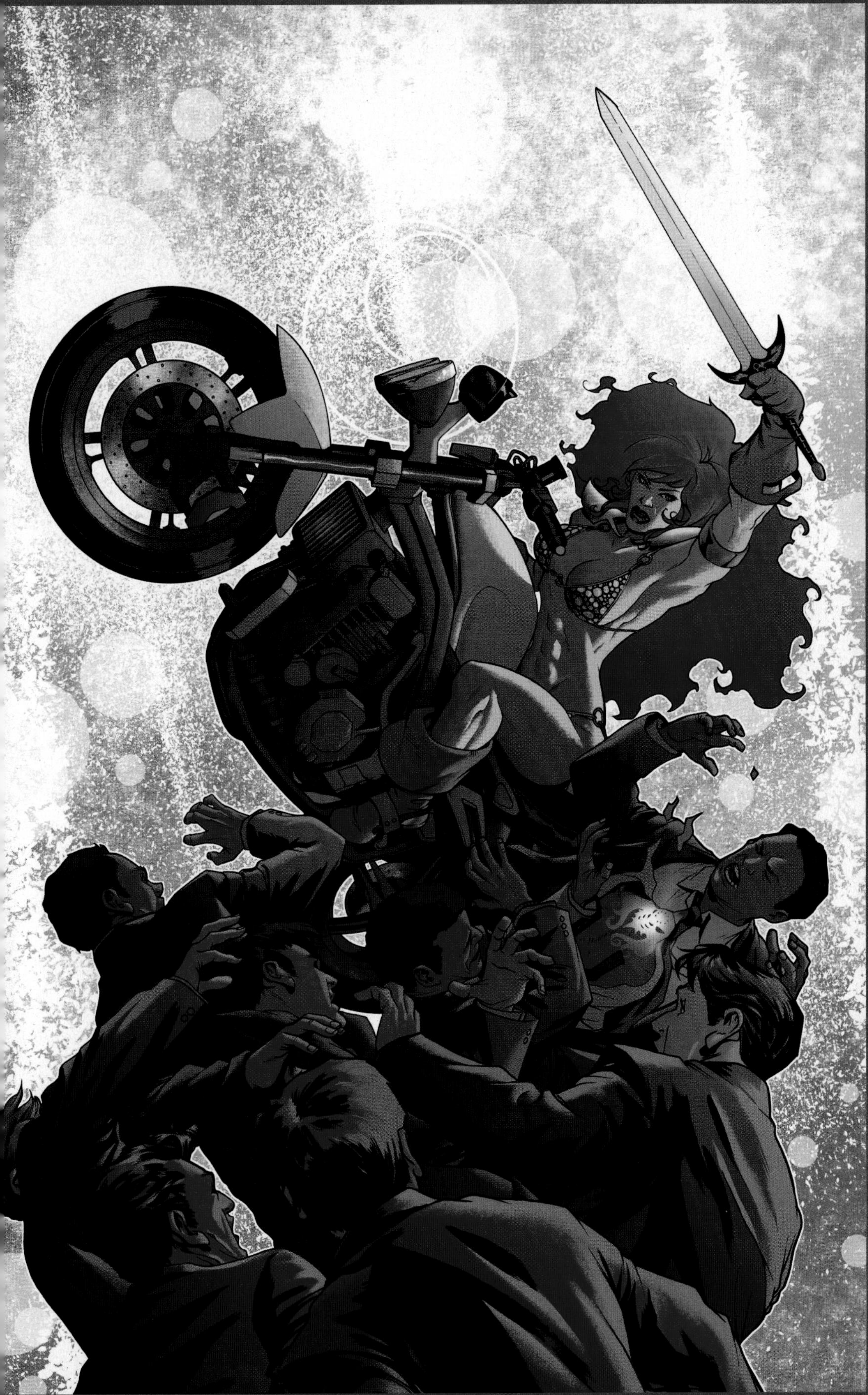

SSUE #3: COVER ART BY MIKE MCKONE

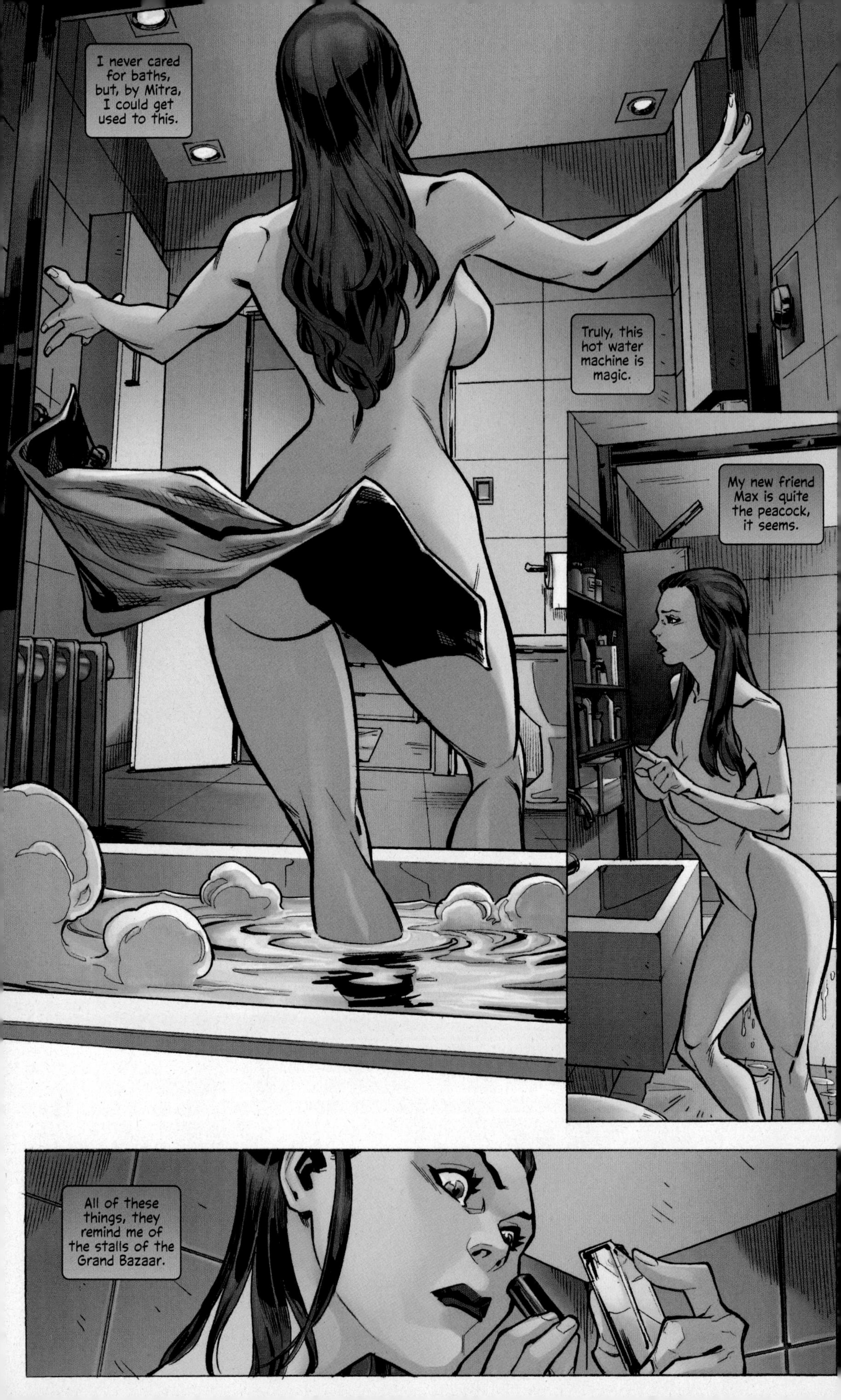
I never cared for baths, but, by Mitra, I could get used to this.
Truly, this hot water machine is magic.
My new friend Max is quite the peacock, it seems.
All of these things, they remind me of the stalls of the Grand Bazaar.

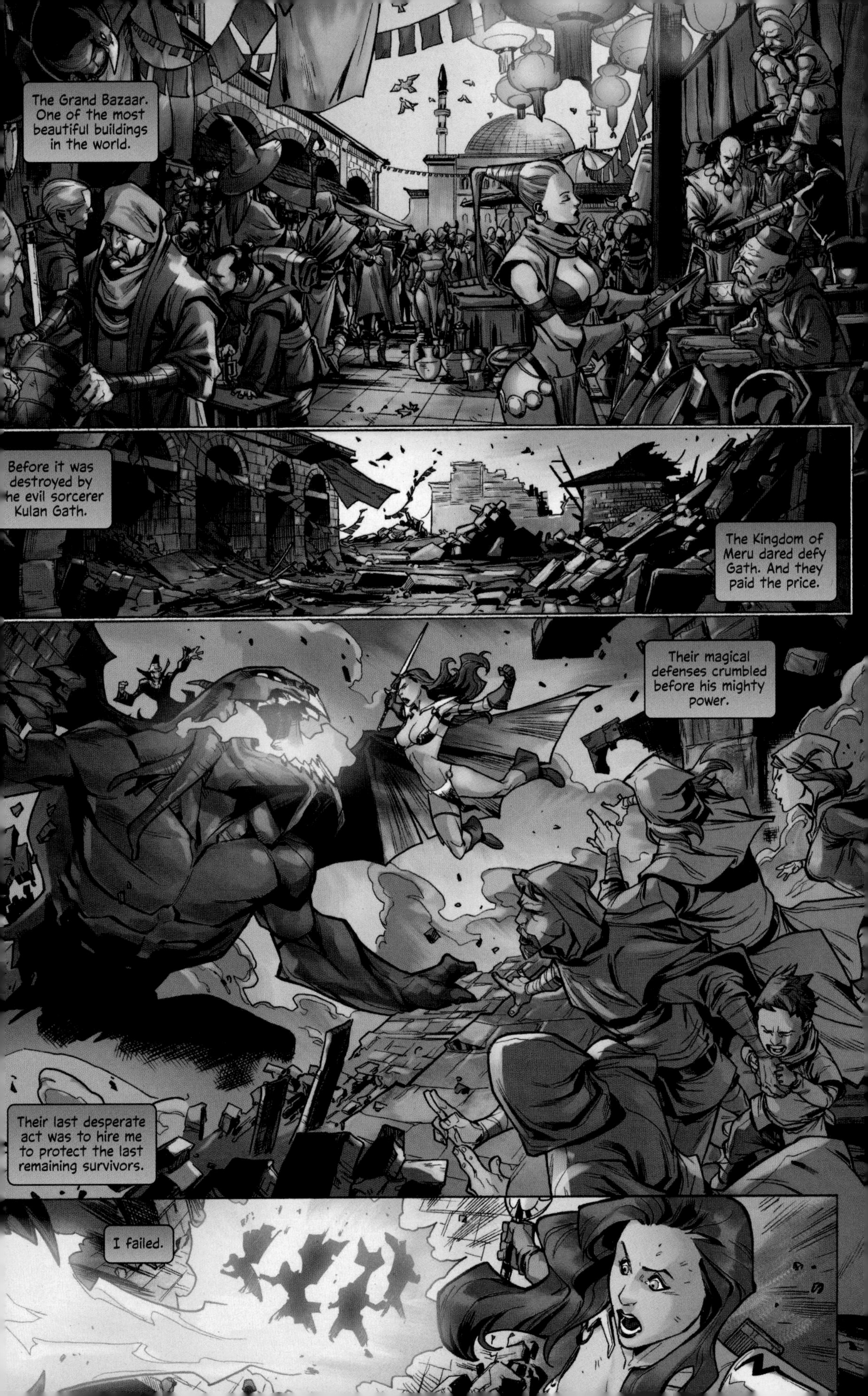
The Grand Bazaar. One of the most beautiful buildings in the world.
Before it was destroyed by he evil sorcerer Kulan Gath.
The Kingdom of Meru dared defy Gath. And they paid the price.
Their magical defenses crumbled before his mighty power.
Their last desperate act was to hire me to protect the last remaining survivors.
I failed.

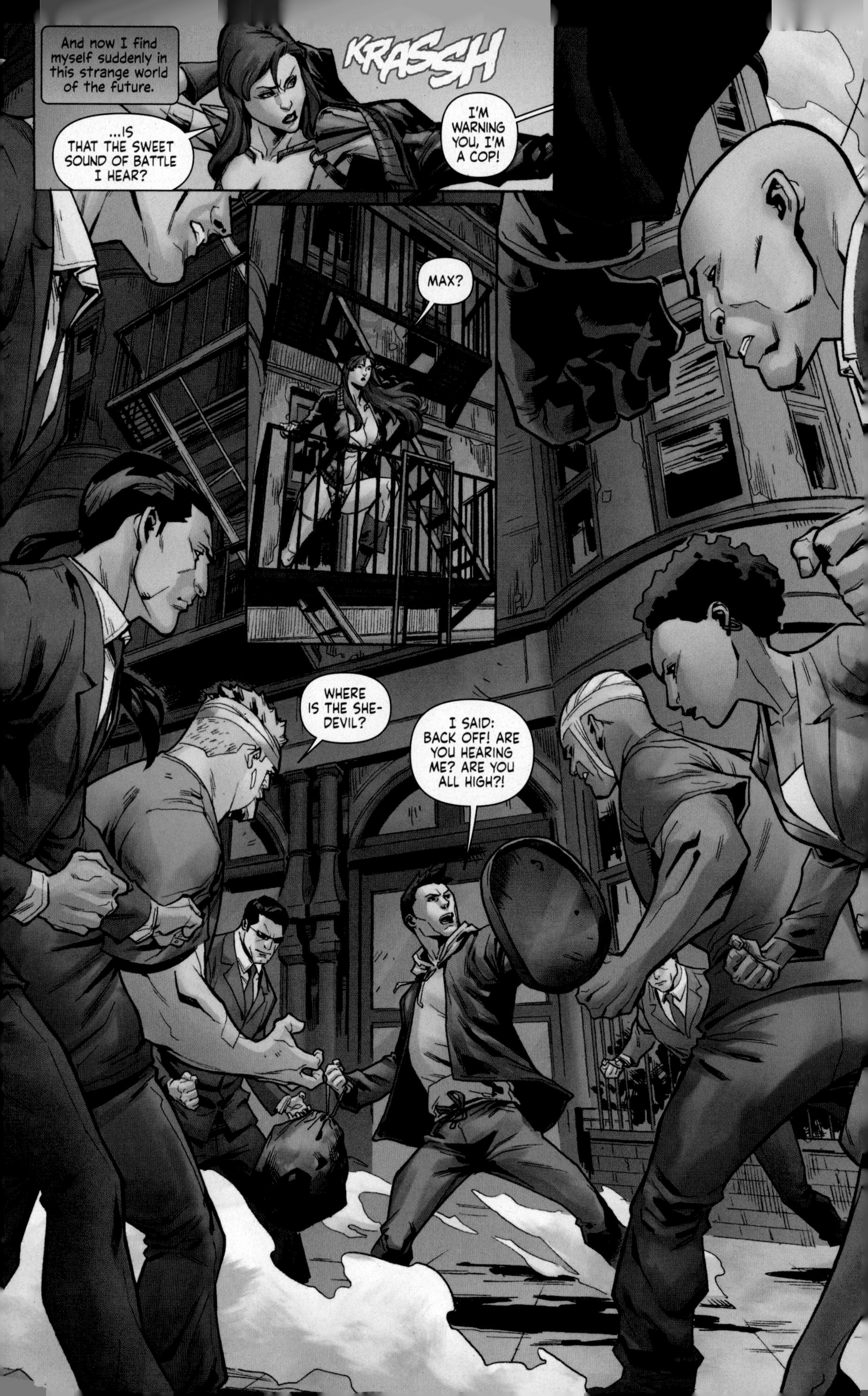
And now I find myself suddenly in this strange world of the future.
KRASSH
...IS THAT THE SWEET SOUND OF BATTLE I HEAR?
I'M WARNING YOU, I'M A COP!
MAX?
WHERE IS THE SHE-DEVIL?
I SAID: BACK OFF! ARE YOU HEARING ME? ARE YOU ALL HIGH?!

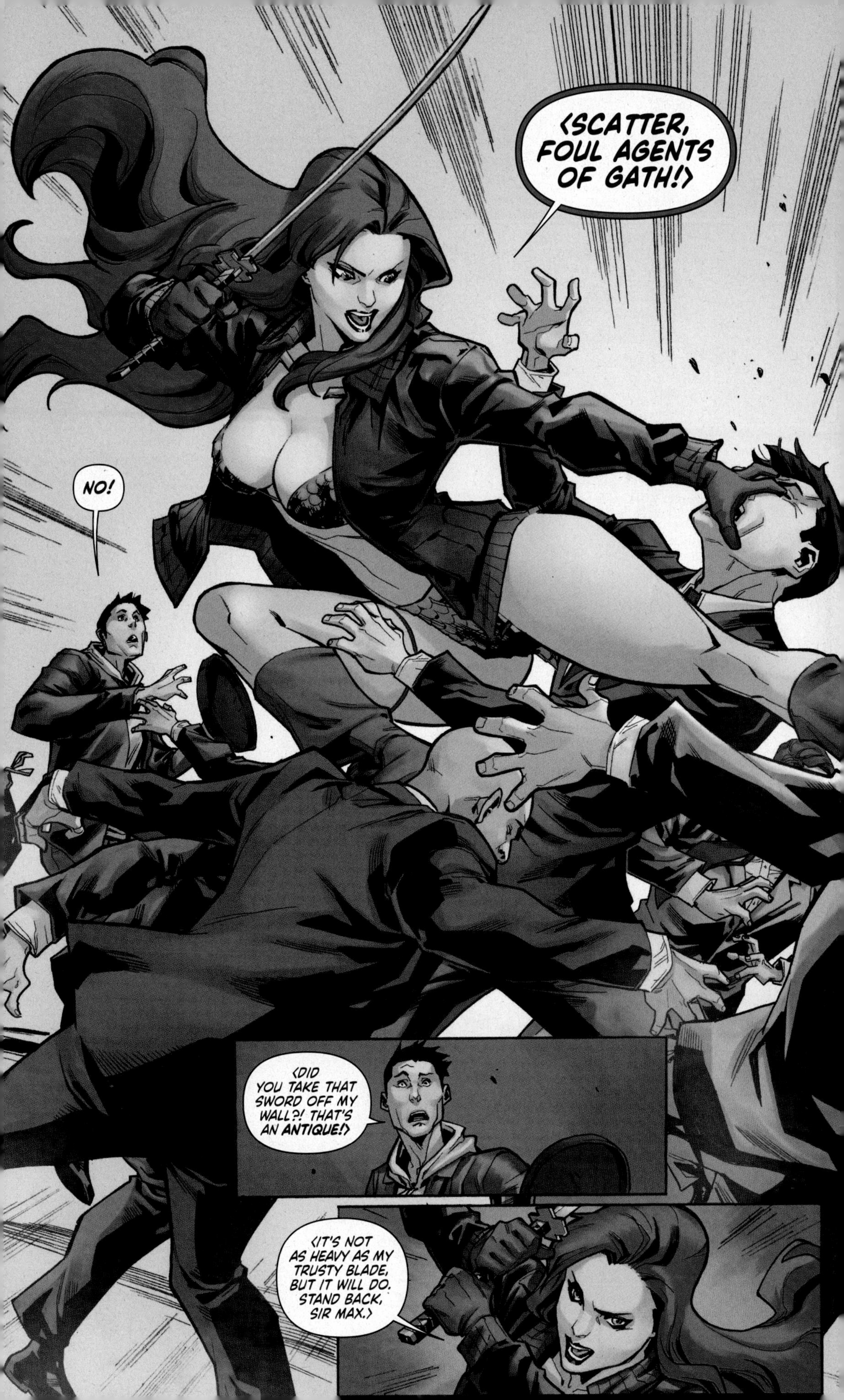
‹SCATTER, FOUL AGENTS OF GATH!›
NO!
‹DID YOU TAKE THAT SWORD OFF MY WALL?! THAT'S AN ANTIQUE!›
‹IT'S NOT AS HEAVY AS MY TRUSTY BLADE, BUT IT WILL DO. STAND BACK, SIR MAX.›

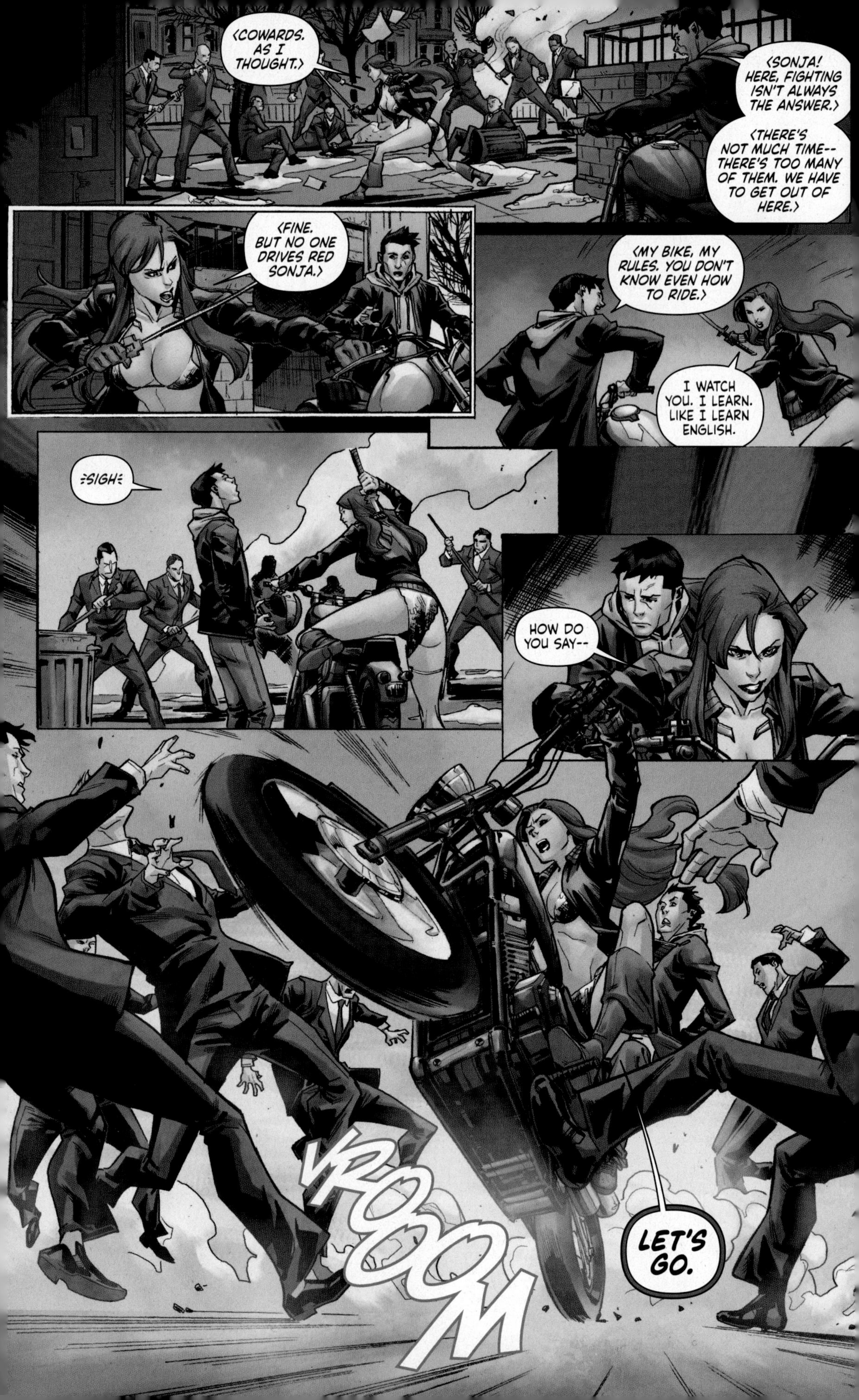

‹COWARDS. AS I THOUGHT.›
‹SONJA! HERE, FIGHTING ISN'T ALWAYS THE ANSWER.›
‹THERE'S NOT MUCH TIME-- THERE'S TOO MANY OF THEM. WE HAVE TO GET OUT OF HERE.›
‹FINE. BUT NO ONE DRIVES RED SONJA.›
‹MY BIKE, MY RULES. YOU DON'T KNOW EVEN HOW TO RIDE.›
I WATCH YOU. I LEARN. LIKE I LEARN ENGLISH.
SIGH
HOW DO YOU SAY--
VROOOM
LET'S GO.

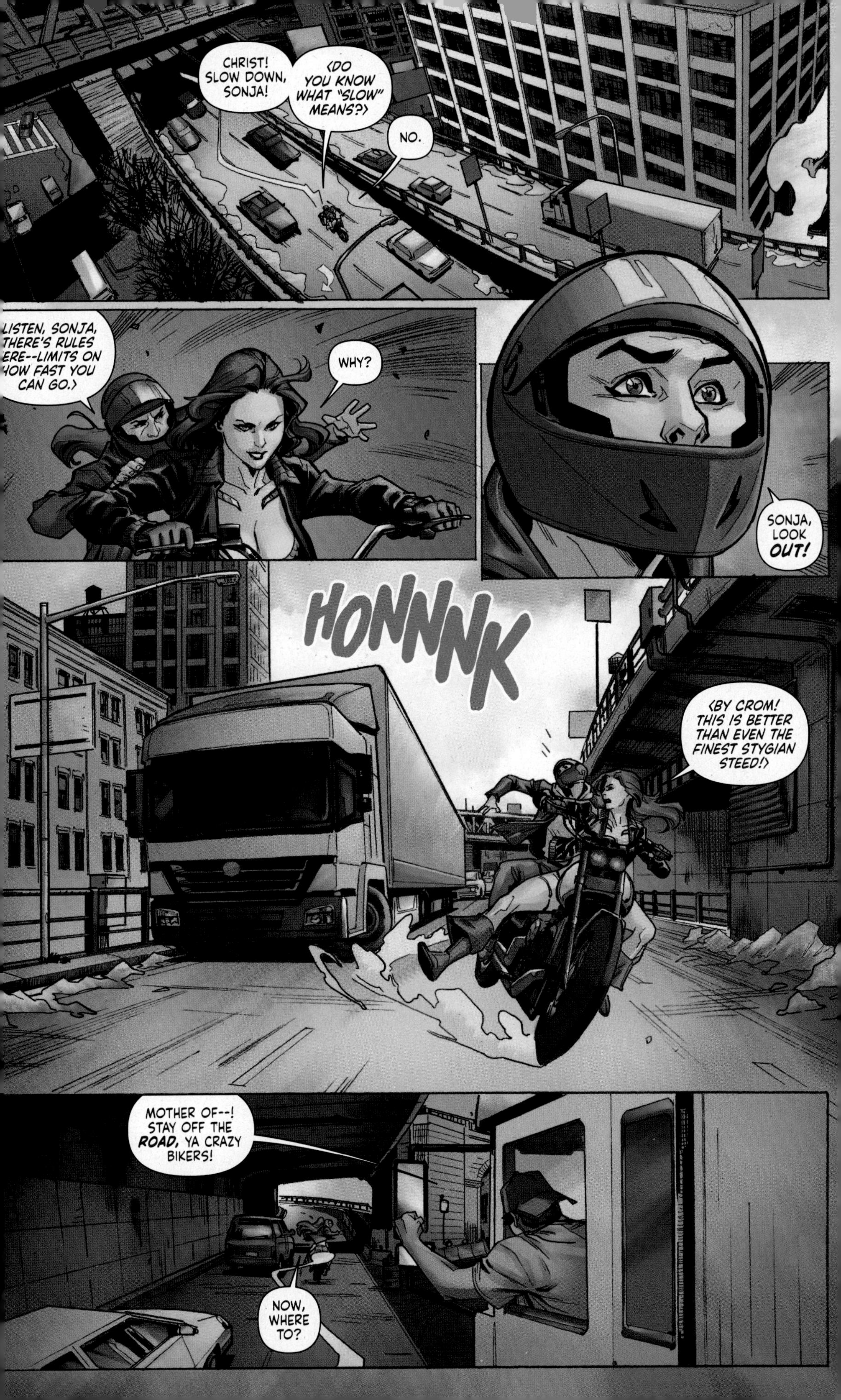
CHRIST! SLOW DOWN, SONJA!
‹DO YOU KNOW WHAT "SLOW" MEANS?›
NO.
‹LISTEN, SONJA, THERE'S RULES HERE--LIMITS ON HOW FAST YOU CAN GO.›
WHY?
SONJA, LOOK OUT!
HONNNK
‹BY CROM! THIS IS BETTER THAN EVEN THE FINEST STYGIAN STEED!›
MOTHER OF--! STAY OFF THE ROAD, YA CRAZY BIKERS!
NOW, WHERE TO?

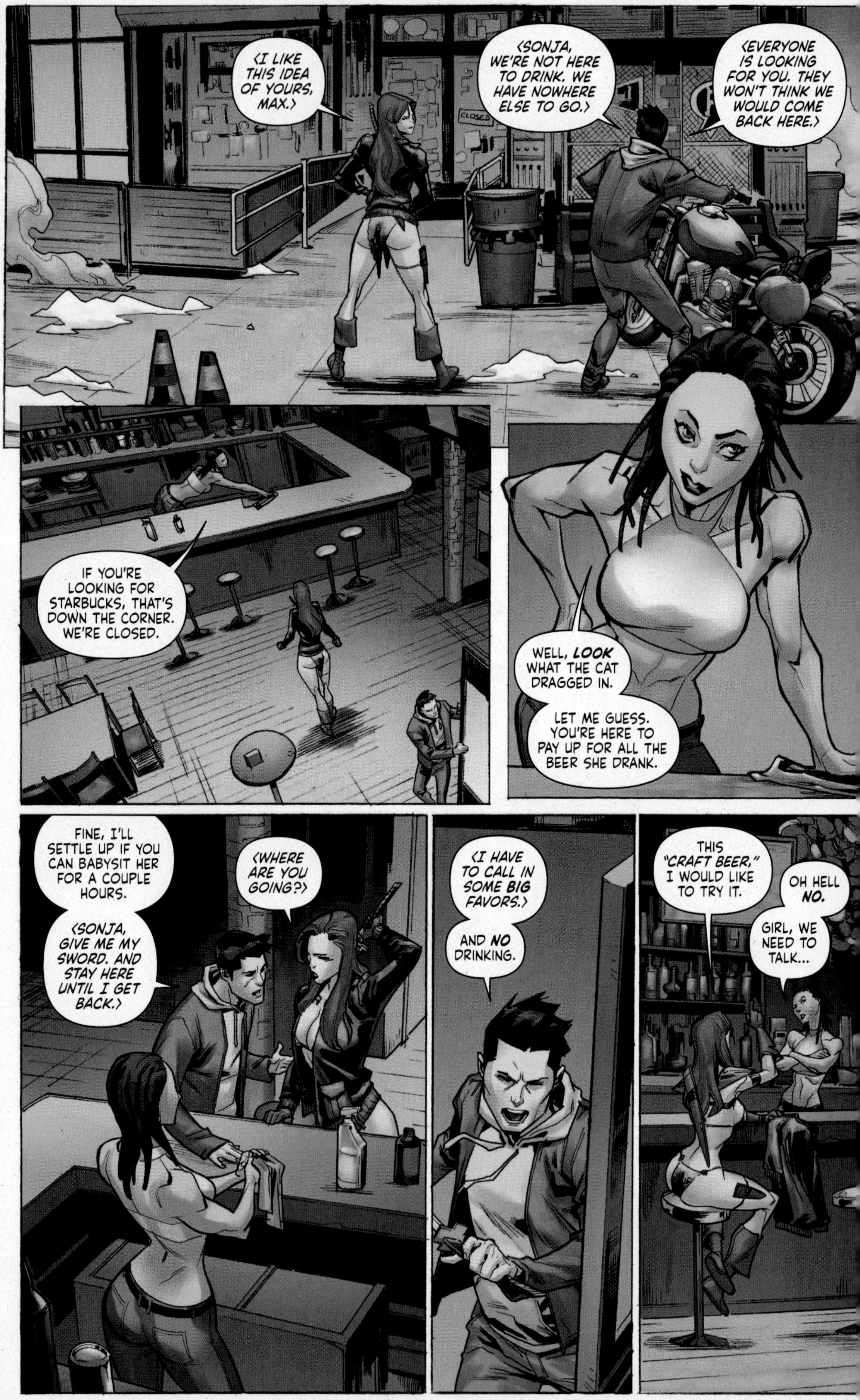

‹I LIKE THIS IDEA OF YOURS, MAX.›
‹SONJA, WE'RE NOT HERE TO DRINK. WE HAVE NOWHERE ELSE TO GO.›
‹EVERYONE IS LOOKING FOR YOU. THEY WON'T THINK WE WOULD COME BACK HERE.›
CLOSED
IF YOU'RE LOOKING FOR STARBUCKS, THAT'S DOWN THE CORNER. WE'RE CLOSED.
WELL, LOOK WHAT THE CAT DRAGGED IN.
LET ME GUESS. YOU'RE HERE TO PAY UP FOR ALL THE BEER SHE DRANK.
FINE, I'LL SETTLE UP IF YOU CAN BABYSIT HER FOR A COUPLE HOURS.
‹SONJA, GIVE ME MY SWORD. AND STAY HERE UNTIL I GET BACK.›
‹WHERE ARE YOU GOING?›
‹I HAVE TO CALL IN SOME BIG FAVORS.›
AND NO DRINKING.
THIS "CRAFT BEER," I WOULD LIKE TO TRY IT.
OH HELL NO.
GIRL, WE NEED TO TALK...

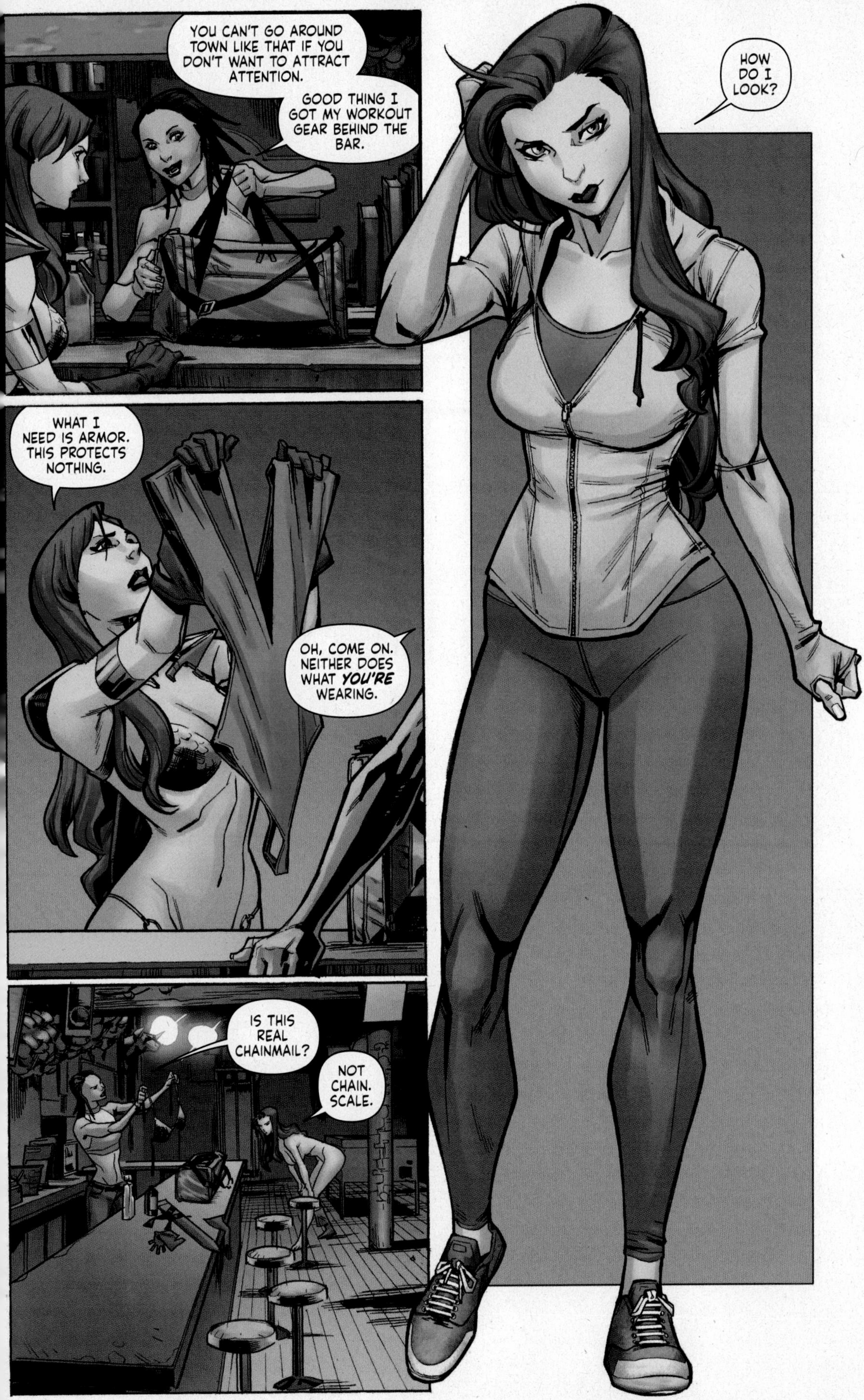
YOU CAN'T GO AROUND TOWN LIKE THAT IF YOU DON'T WANT TO ATTRACT ATTENTION.
GOOD THING I GOT MY WORKOUT GEAR BEHIND THE BAR.
WHAT I NEED IS ARMOR. THIS PROTECTS NOTHING.
OH, COME ON. NEITHER DOES WHAT *YOU'RE* WEARING.
IS THIS REAL CHAINMAIL?
NOT CHAIN. SCALE.
HOW DO I LOOK?

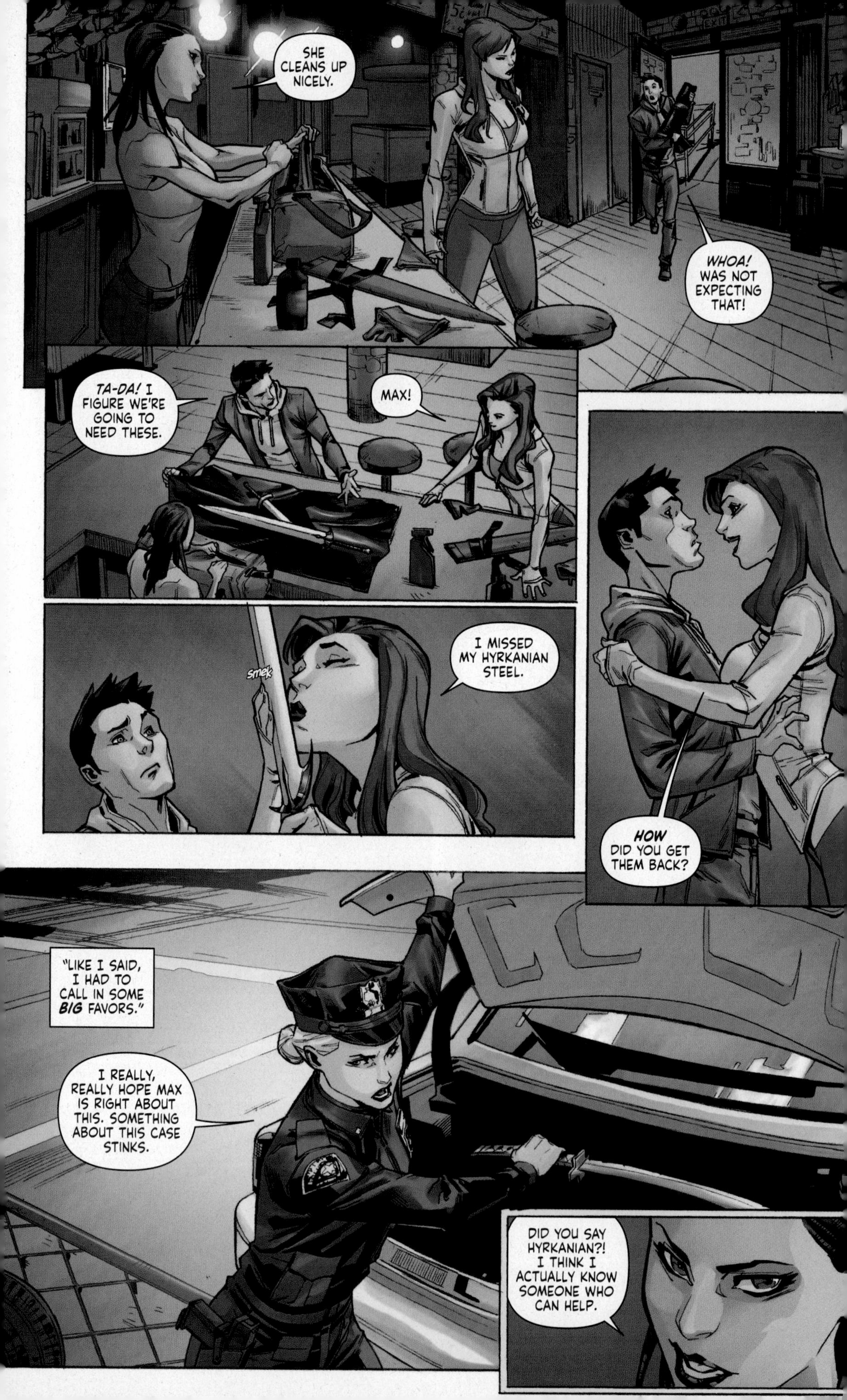

SHE CLEANS UP NICELY.
WHOA! WAS NOT EXPECTING THAT!
TA-DA! I FIGURE WE'RE GOING TO NEED THESE.
MAX!
SMEK
I MISSED MY HYRKANIAN STEEL.
HOW DID YOU GET THEM BACK?
"LIKE I SAID, I HAD TO CALL IN SOME BIG FAVORS."
I REALLY, REALLY HOPE MAX IS RIGHT ABOUT THIS. SOMETHING ABOUT THIS CASE STINKS.
DID YOU SAY HYRKANIAN?! I THINK I ACTUALLY KNOW SOMEONE WHO CAN HELP.

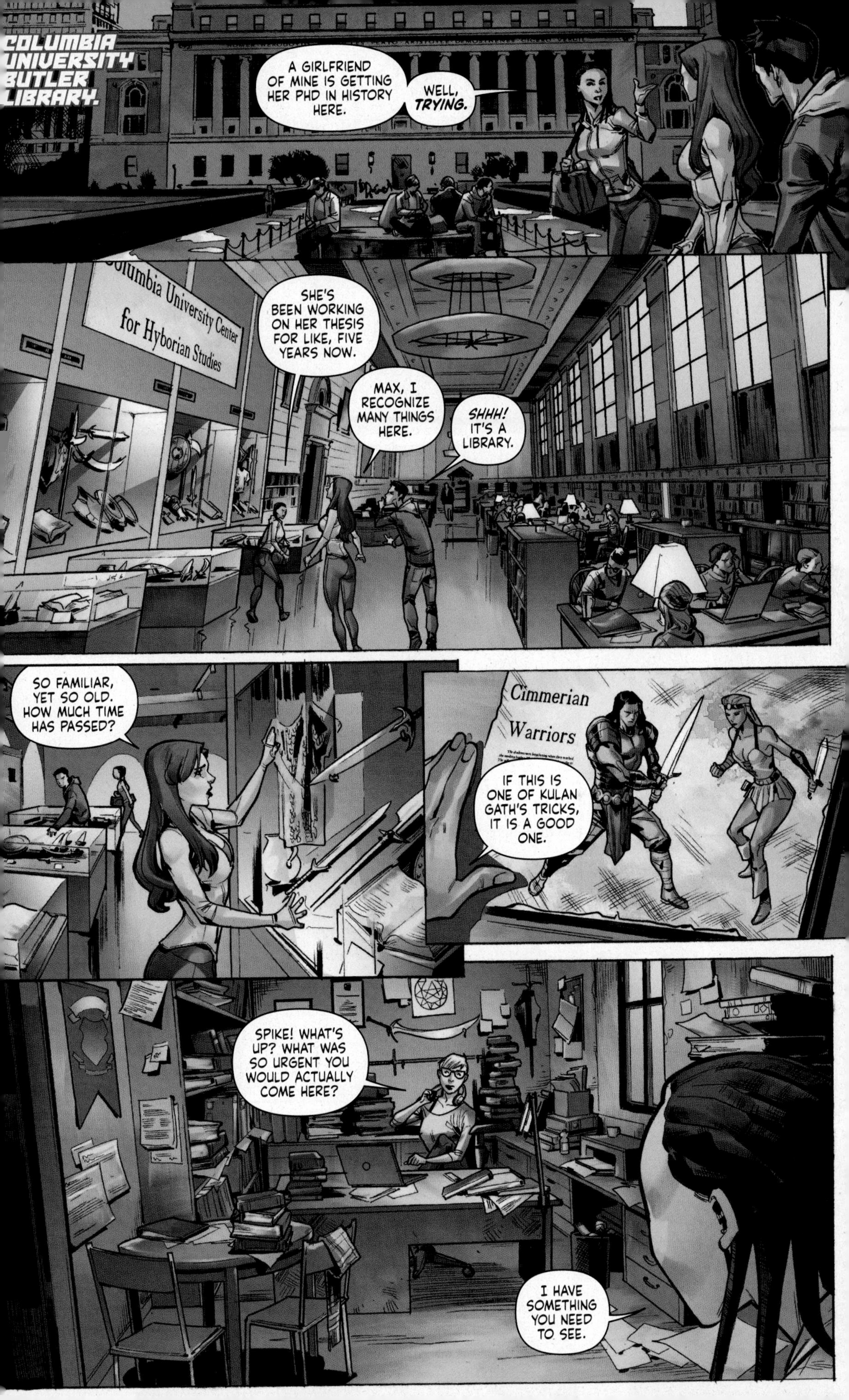
COLUMBIA UNIVERSITY BUTLER LIBRARY.
A GIRLFRIEND OF MINE IS GETTING HER PHD IN HISTORY HERE.
WELL, *TRYING.*
Columbia University Center for Hyborian Studies
SHE'S BEEN WORKING ON HER THESIS FOR LIKE, FIVE YEARS NOW.
MAX, I RECOGNIZE MANY THINGS HERE.
SHHH! IT'S A LIBRARY.
SO FAMILIAR, YET SO OLD. HOW MUCH TIME HAS PASSED?
Cimmerian Warriors
IF THIS IS ONE OF KULAN GATH'S TRICKS, IT IS A GOOD ONE.
SPIKE! WHAT'S UP? WHAT WAS SO URGENT YOU WOULD ACTUALLY COME HERE?
I HAVE SOMETHING YOU NEED TO SEE.

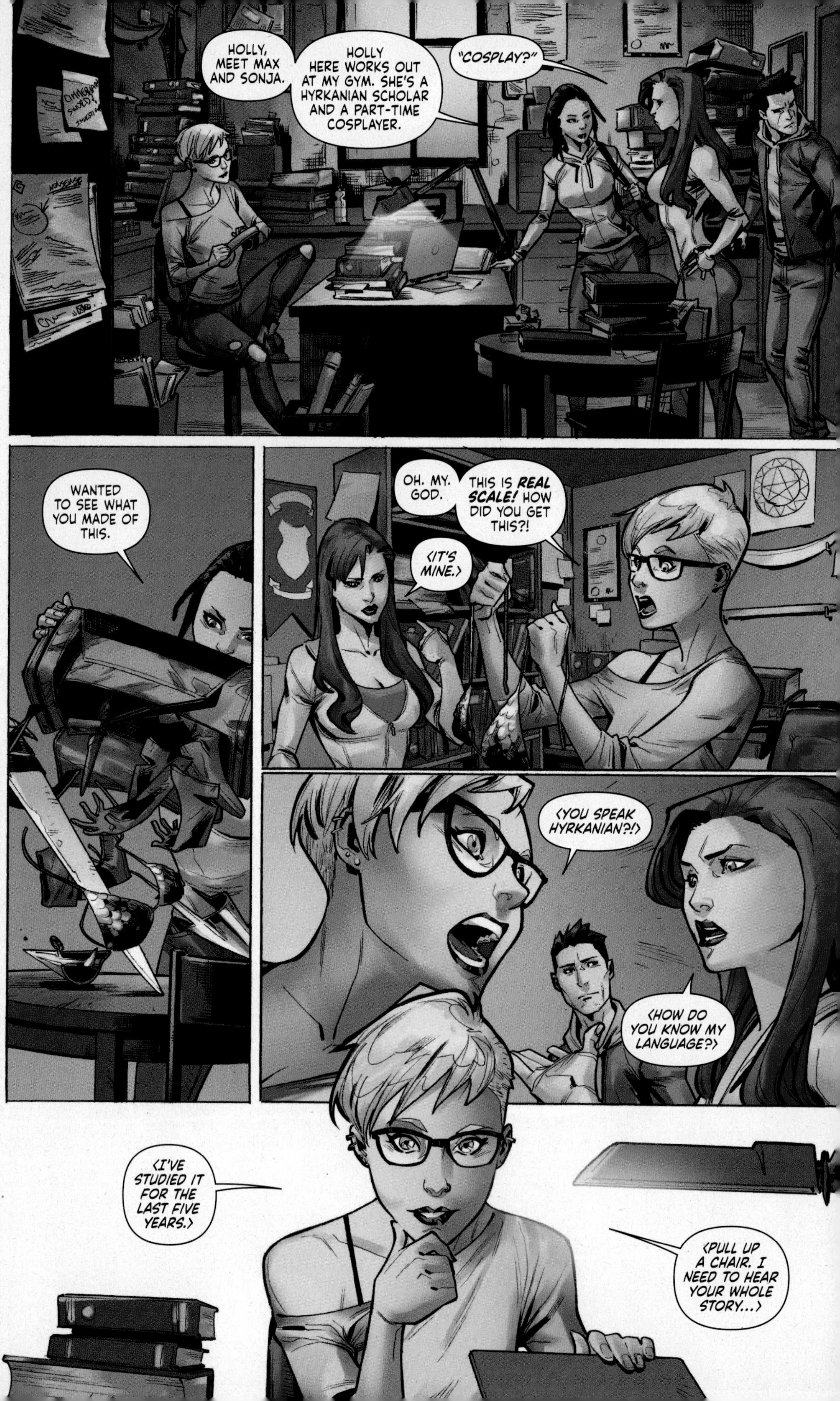

HOLLY, MEET MAX AND SONJA.
HOLLY HERE WORKS OUT AT MY GYM. SHE'S A HYRKANIAN SCHOLAR AND A PART-TIME COSPLAYER.
"COSPLAY?"
WANTED TO SEE WHAT YOU MADE OF THIS.
OH. MY. GOD.
THIS IS REAL SCALE! HOW DID YOU GET THIS?!
<IT'S MINE.>
<YOU SPEAK HYRKANIAN?!>
<HOW DO YOU KNOW MY LANGUAGE?>
<I'VE STUDIED IT FOR THE LAST FIVE YEARS.>
<PULL UP A CHAIR. I NEED TO HEAR YOUR WHOLE STORY...>

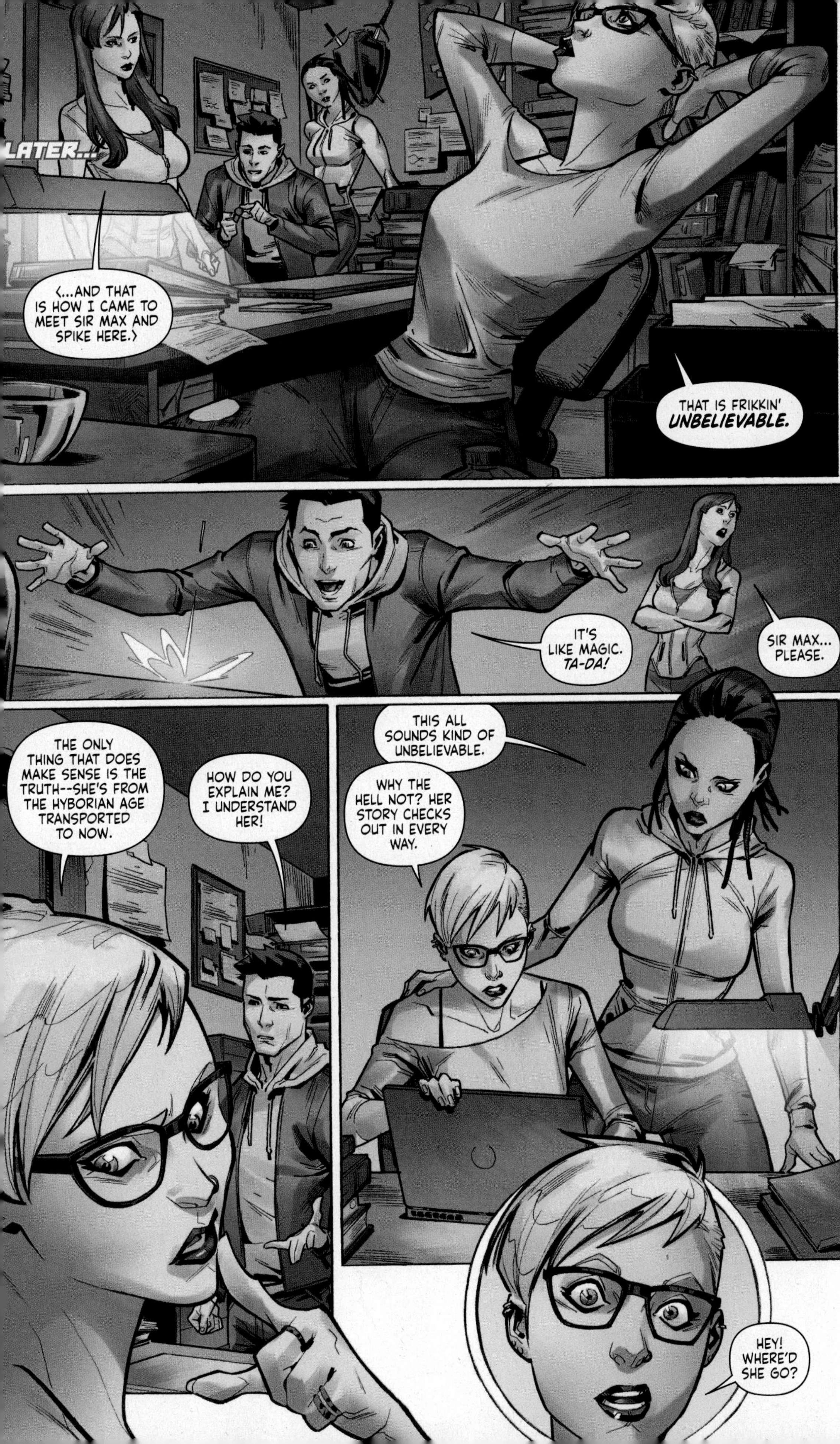
LATER...
<...AND THAT IS HOW I CAME TO MEET SIR MAX AND SPIKE HERE.>
THAT IS FRIKKIN' UNBELIEVABLE.
IT'S LIKE MAGIC. TA-DA!
SIR MAX... PLEASE.
THE ONLY THING THAT DOES MAKE SENSE IS THE TRUTH--SHE'S FROM THE HYBORIAN AGE TRANSPORTED TO NOW.
HOW DO YOU EXPLAIN ME? I UNDERSTAND HER!
THIS ALL SOUNDS KIND OF UNBELIEVABLE.
WHY THE HELL NOT? HER STORY CHECKS OUT IN EVERY WAY.
HEY! WHERE'D SHE GO?

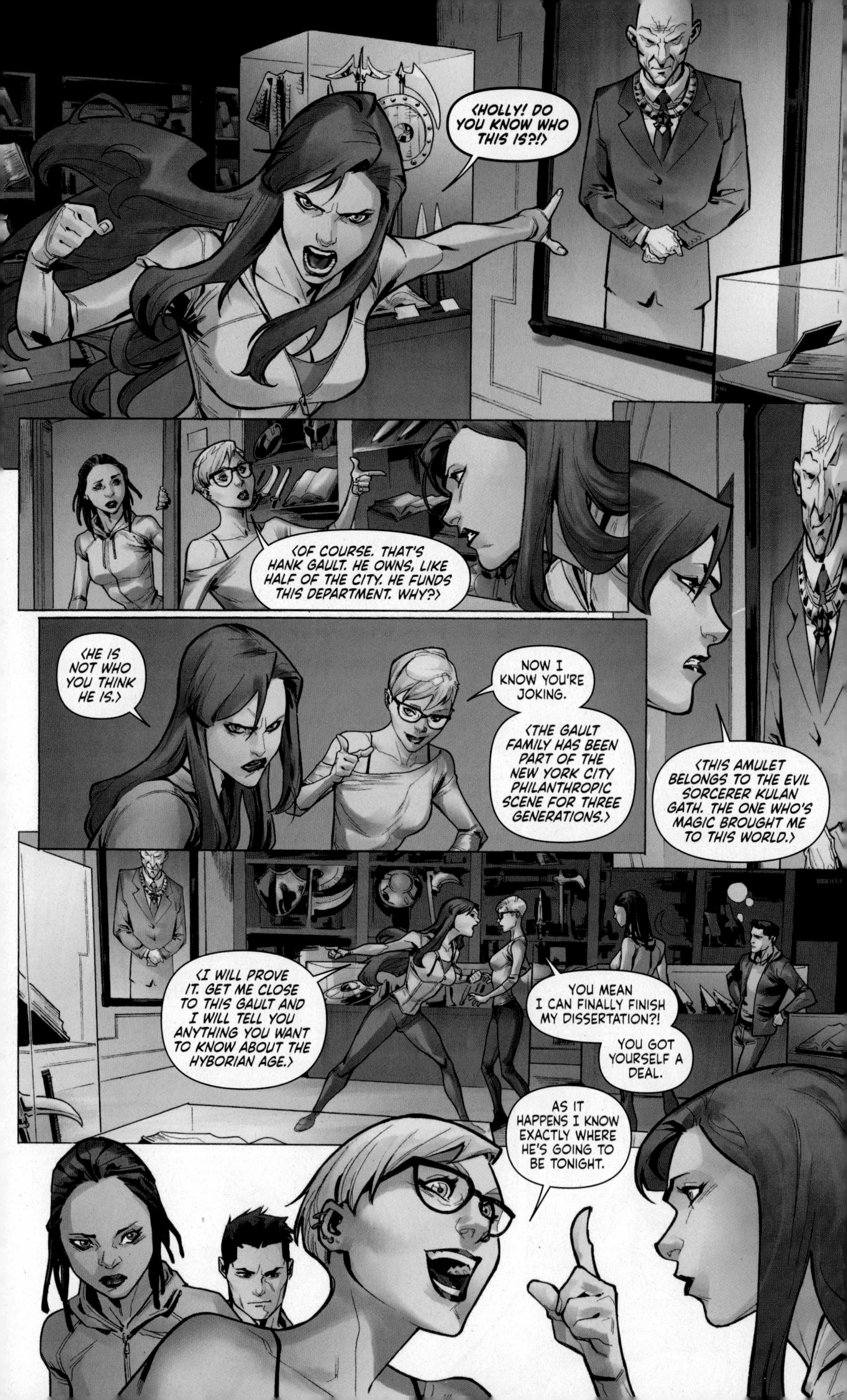

‹HOLLY! DO YOU KNOW WHO THIS IS?!›
‹OF COURSE. THAT'S HANK GAULT. HE OWNS, LIKE HALF OF THE CITY. HE FUNDS THIS DEPARTMENT. WHY?›
‹HE IS NOT WHO YOU THINK HE IS.›
NOW I KNOW YOU'RE JOKING.
‹THE GAULT FAMILY HAS BEEN PART OF THE NEW YORK CITY PHILANTHROPIC SCENE FOR THREE GENERATIONS.›
‹THIS AMULET BELONGS TO THE EVIL SORCERER KULAN GATH. THE ONE WHO'S MAGIC BROUGHT ME TO THIS WORLD.›
‹I WILL PROVE IT. GET ME CLOSE TO THIS GAULT AND I WILL TELL YOU ANYTHING YOU WANT TO KNOW ABOUT THE HYBORIAN AGE.›
YOU MEAN I CAN FINALLY FINISH MY DISSERTATION?!
YOU GOT YOURSELF A DEAL.
AS IT HAPPENS I KNOW EXACTLY WHERE HE'S GOING TO BE TONIGHT.

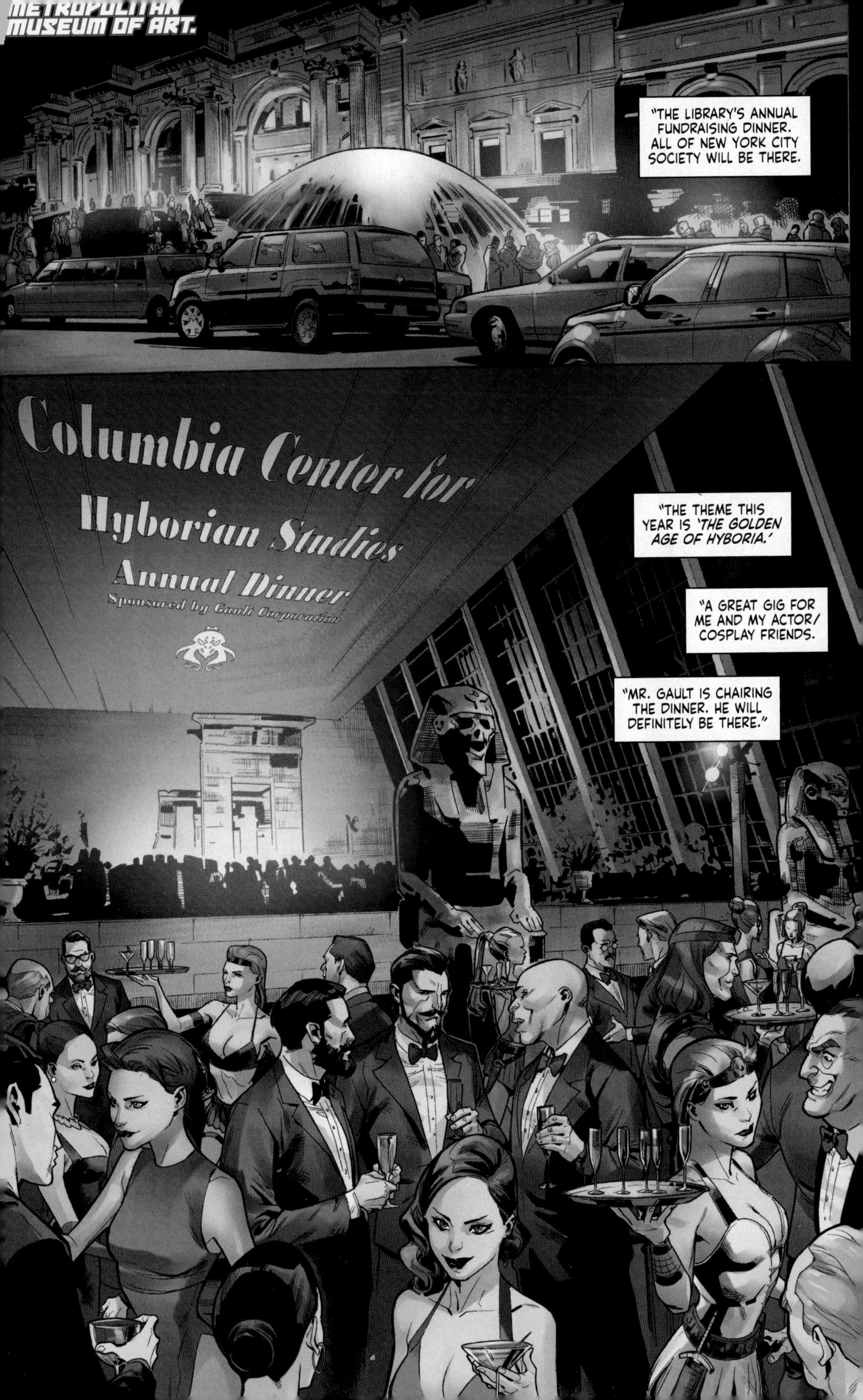
METROPOLITAN MUSEUM OF ART.
"THE LIBRARY'S ANNUAL FUNDRAISING DINNER. ALL OF NEW YORK CITY SOCIETY WILL BE THERE.
Columbia Center for Hyborian Studies
Annual Dinner
Sponsored by Gault Corporation
"THE THEME THIS YEAR IS 'THE GOLDEN AGE OF HYBORIA.'
"A GREAT GIG FOR ME AND MY ACTOR/ COSPLAY FRIENDS.
"MR. GAULT IS CHAIRING THE DINNER. HE WILL DEFINITELY BE THERE."

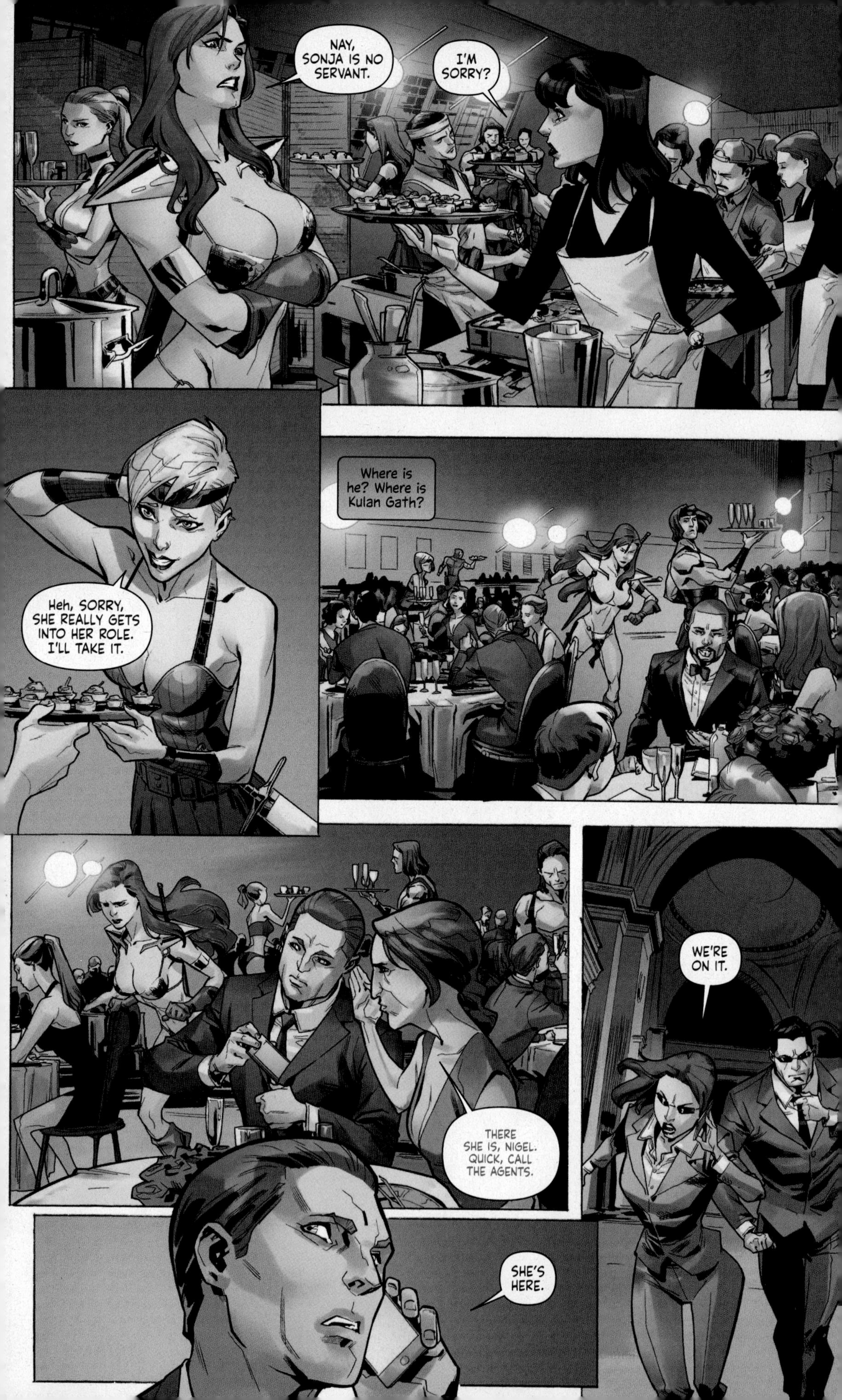

NAY, SONJA IS NO SERVANT.
I'M SORRY?
Heh, SORRY, SHE REALLY GETS INTO HER ROLE. I'LL TAKE IT.
Where is he? Where is Kulan Gath?
THERE SHE IS, NIGEL. QUICK, CALL THE AGENTS.
WE'RE ON IT.
SHE'S HERE.

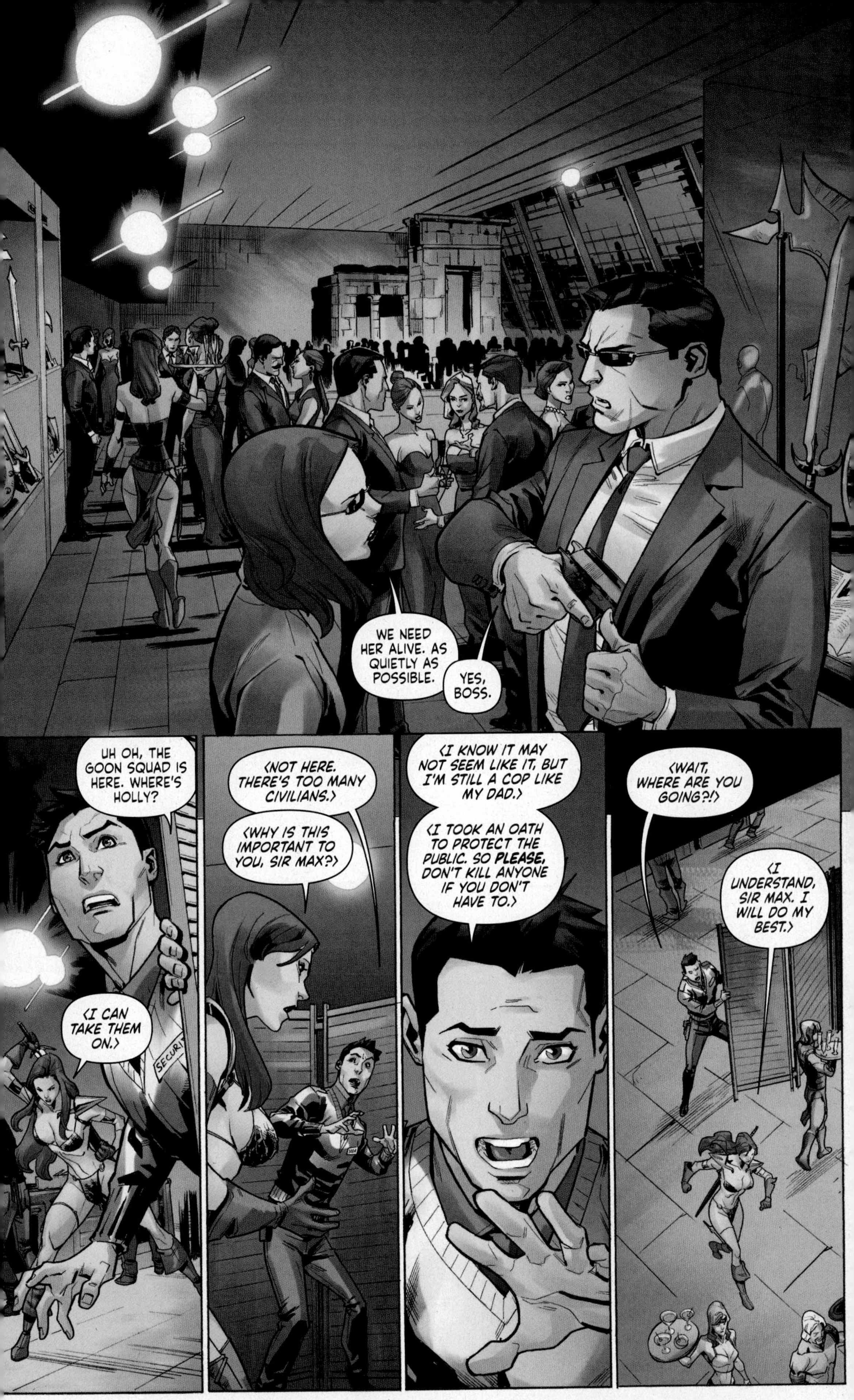
WE NEED HER ALIVE. AS QUIETLY AS POSSIBLE.
YES, BOSS.
UH OH, THE GOON SQUAD IS HERE. WHERE'S HOLLY?
<I CAN TAKE THEM ON.>
SECURI
<NOT HERE. THERE'S TOO MANY CIVILIANS.>
<WHY IS THIS IMPORTANT TO YOU, SIR MAX?>
<I KNOW IT MAY NOT SEEM LIKE IT, BUT I'M STILL A COP LIKE MY DAD.>
<I TOOK AN OATH TO PROTECT THE PUBLIC. SO PLEASE, DON'T KILL ANYONE IF YOU DON'T HAVE TO.>
<WAIT, WHERE ARE YOU GOING?!>
<I UNDERSTAND, SIR MAX. I WILL DO MY BEST.>

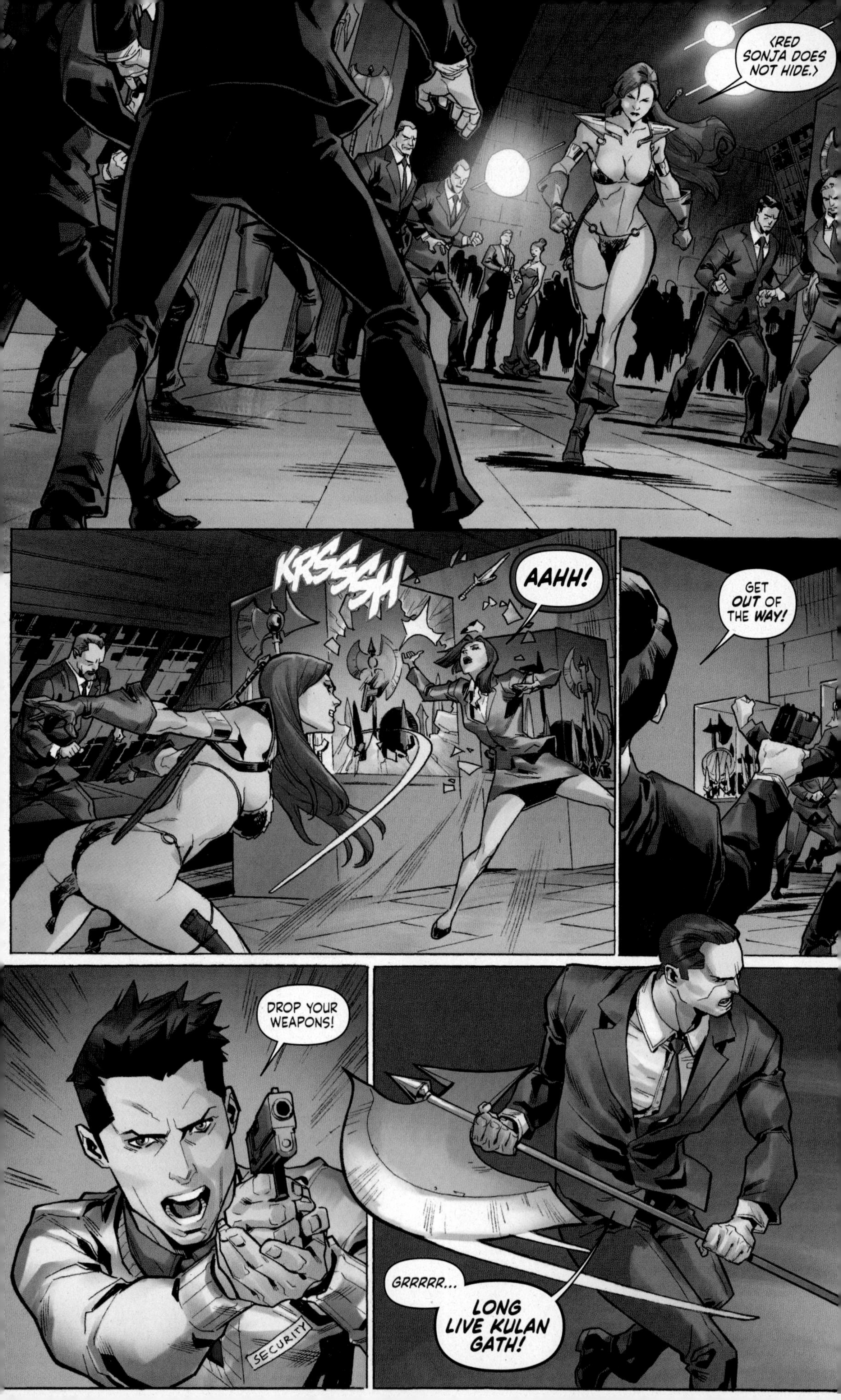
‹RED SONJA DOES NOT HIDE.›
KRSSSH
AAHH!
GET OUT OF THE WAY!
DROP YOUR WEAPONS!
SECURITY
GRRRRR...
LONG LIVE KULAN GATH!

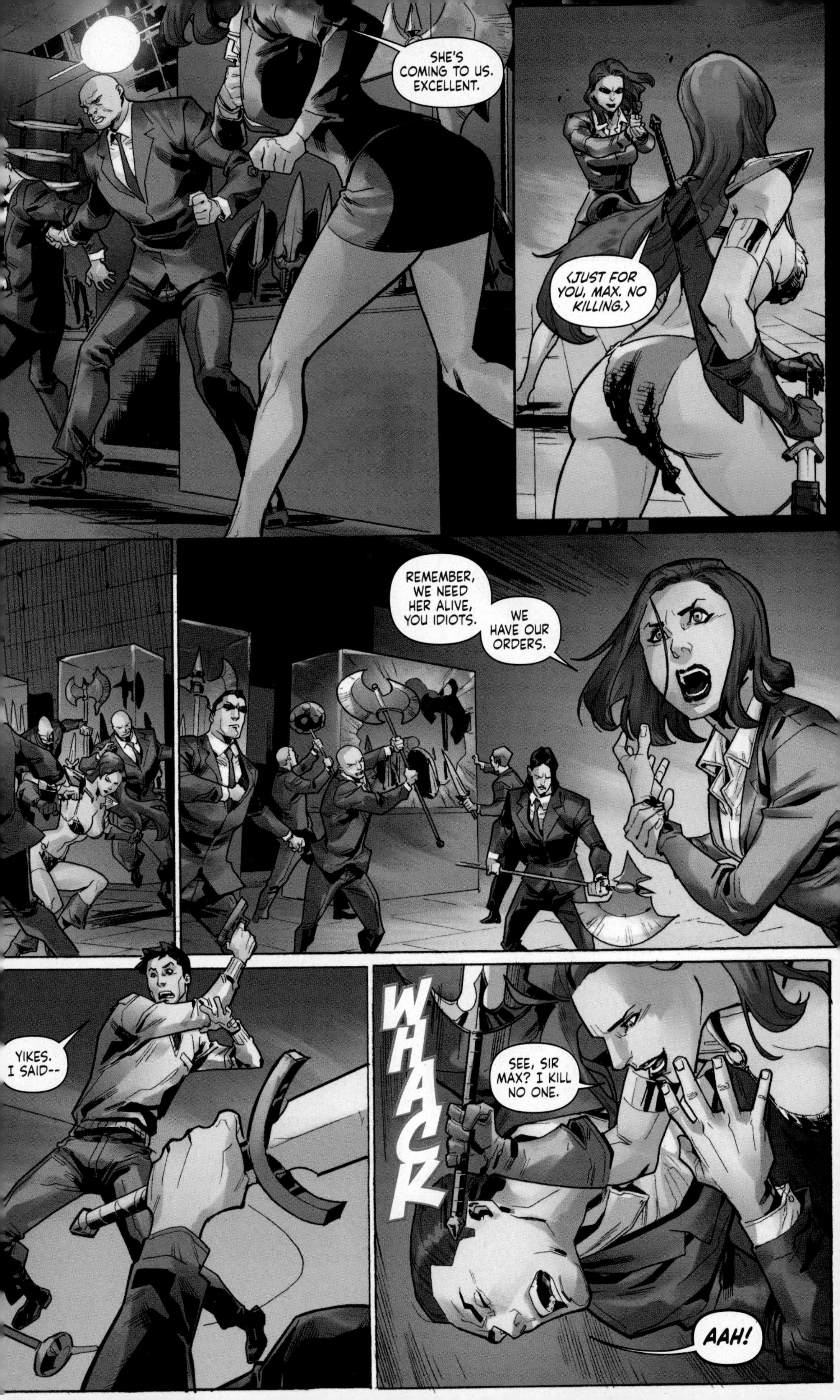
SHE'S COMING TO US. EXCELLENT.
<JUST FOR YOU, MAX. NO KILLING.>
REMEMBER, WE NEED HER ALIVE, YOU IDIOTS.
WE HAVE OUR ORDERS.
YIKES. I SAID--
WHACK
SEE, SIR MAX? I KILL NO ONE.
AAH!

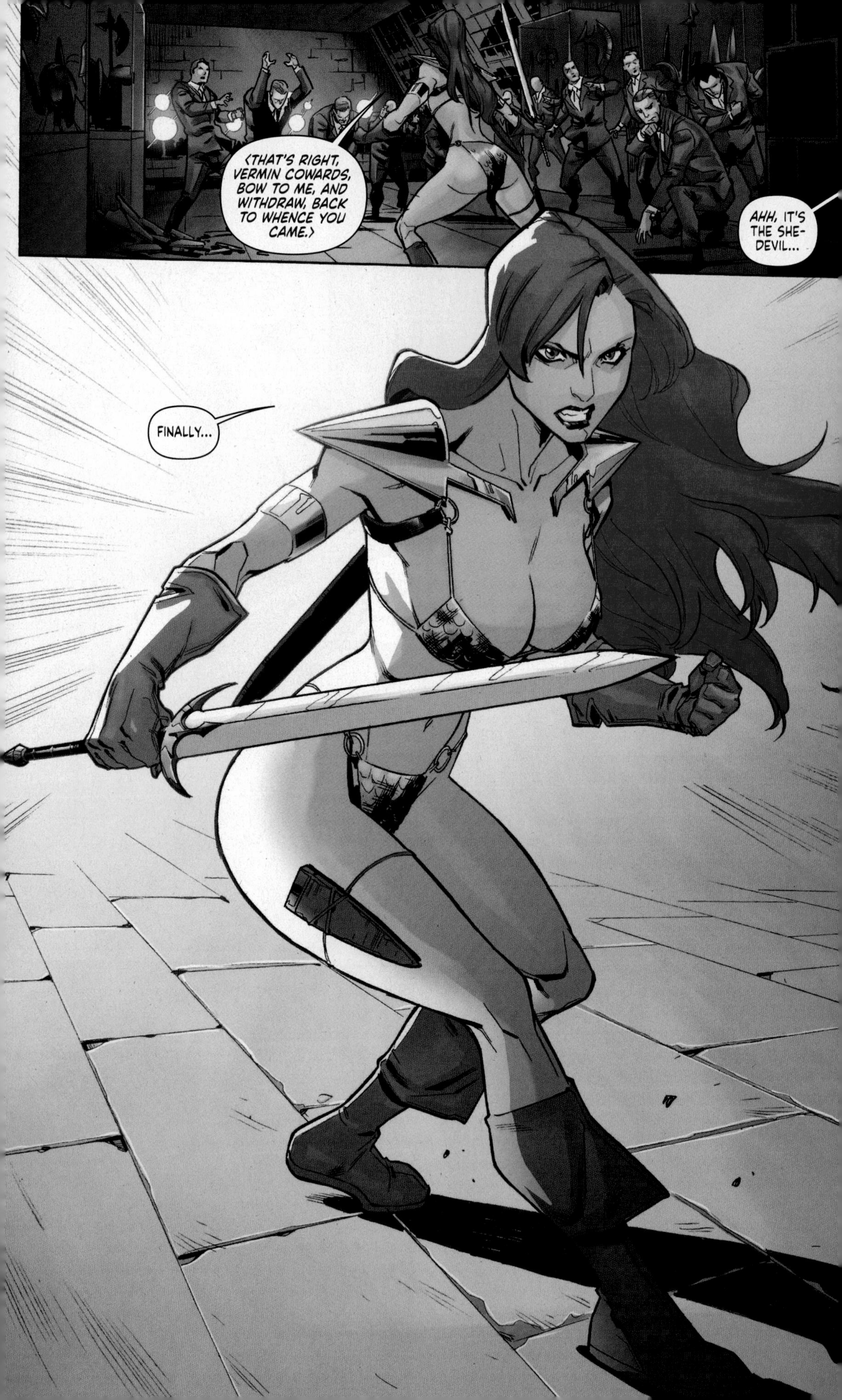

<THAT'S RIGHT, VERMIN COWARDS, BOW TO ME, AND WITHDRAW, BACK TO WHENCE YOU CAME.>
AHH, IT'S THE SHE-DEVIL...
FINALLY...

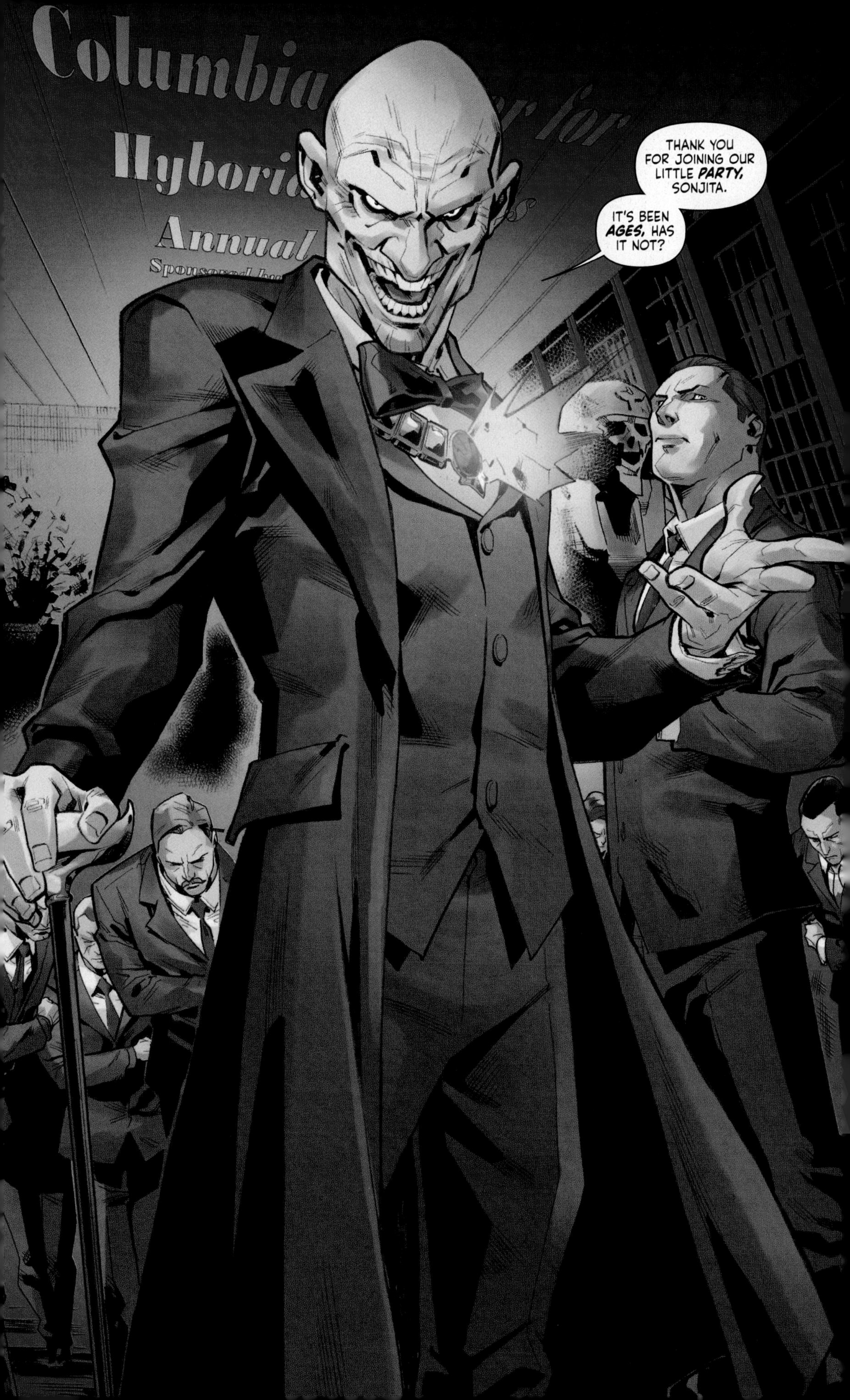
Columbia
Annual
THANK YOU FOR JOINING OUR LITTLE **PARTY,** SONJITA.
IT'S BEEN **AGES,** HAS IT NOT?

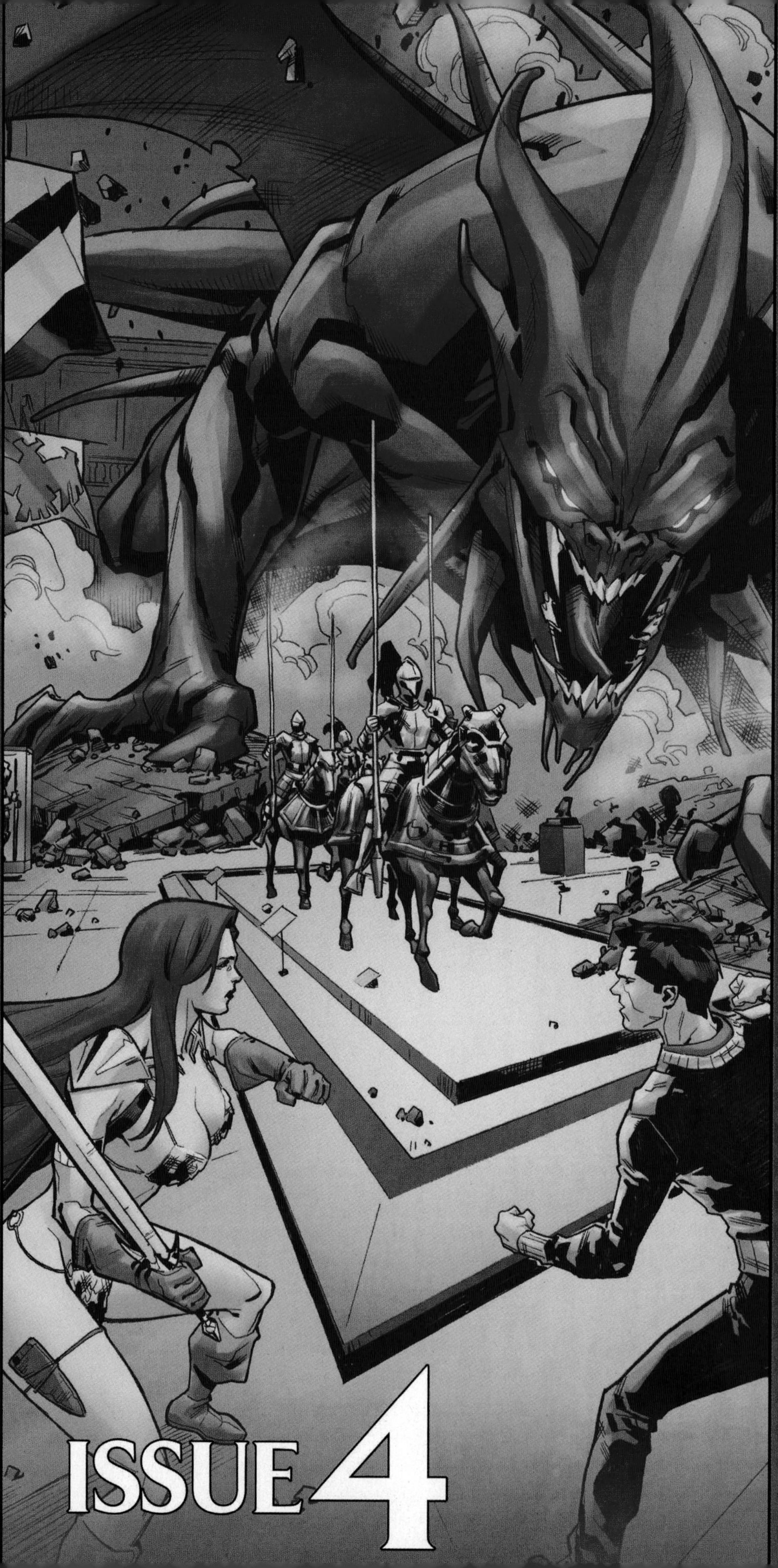
ISSUE 4

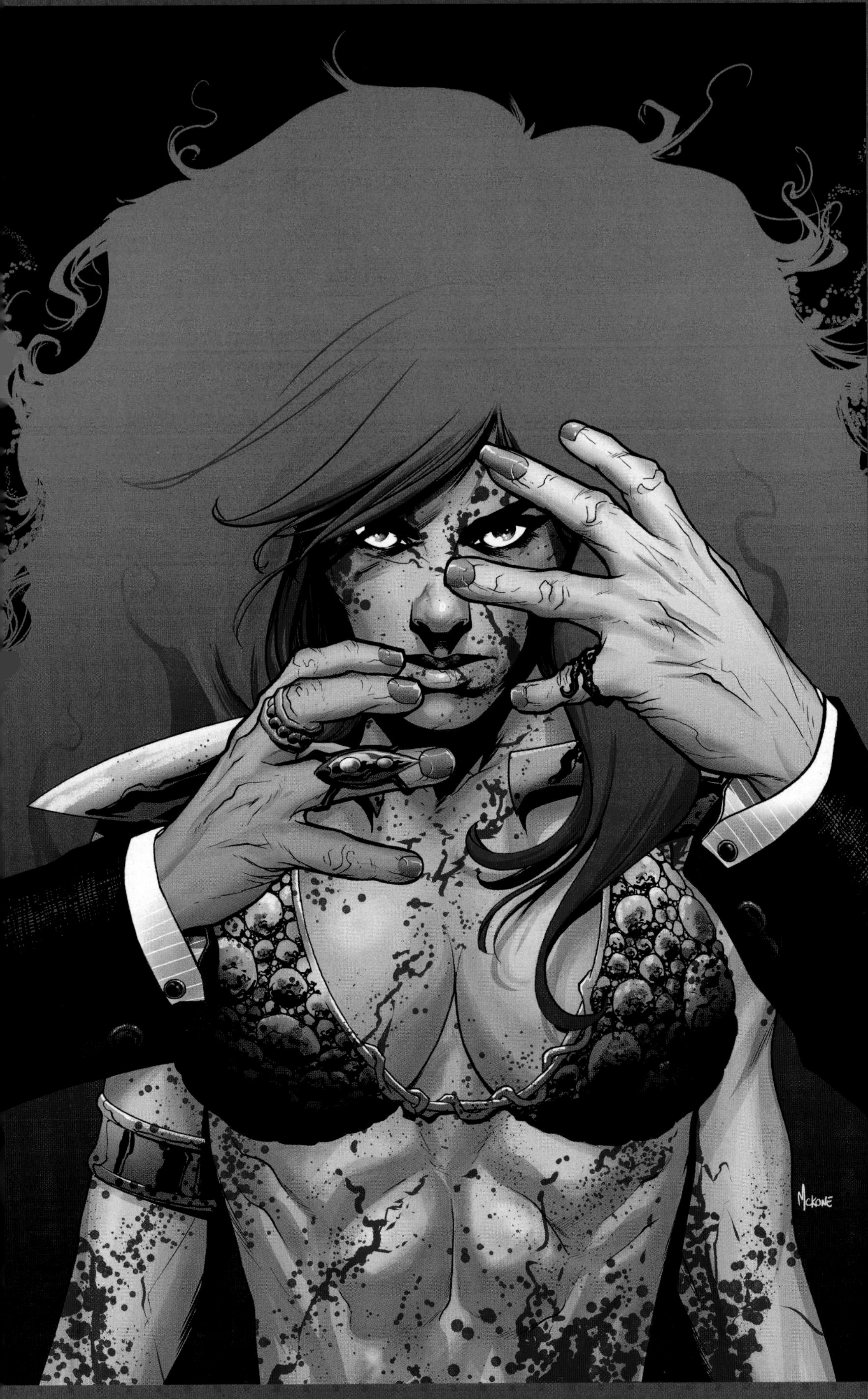
MCKONE

ISSUE #4: COVER ART BY MIKE MCKONE

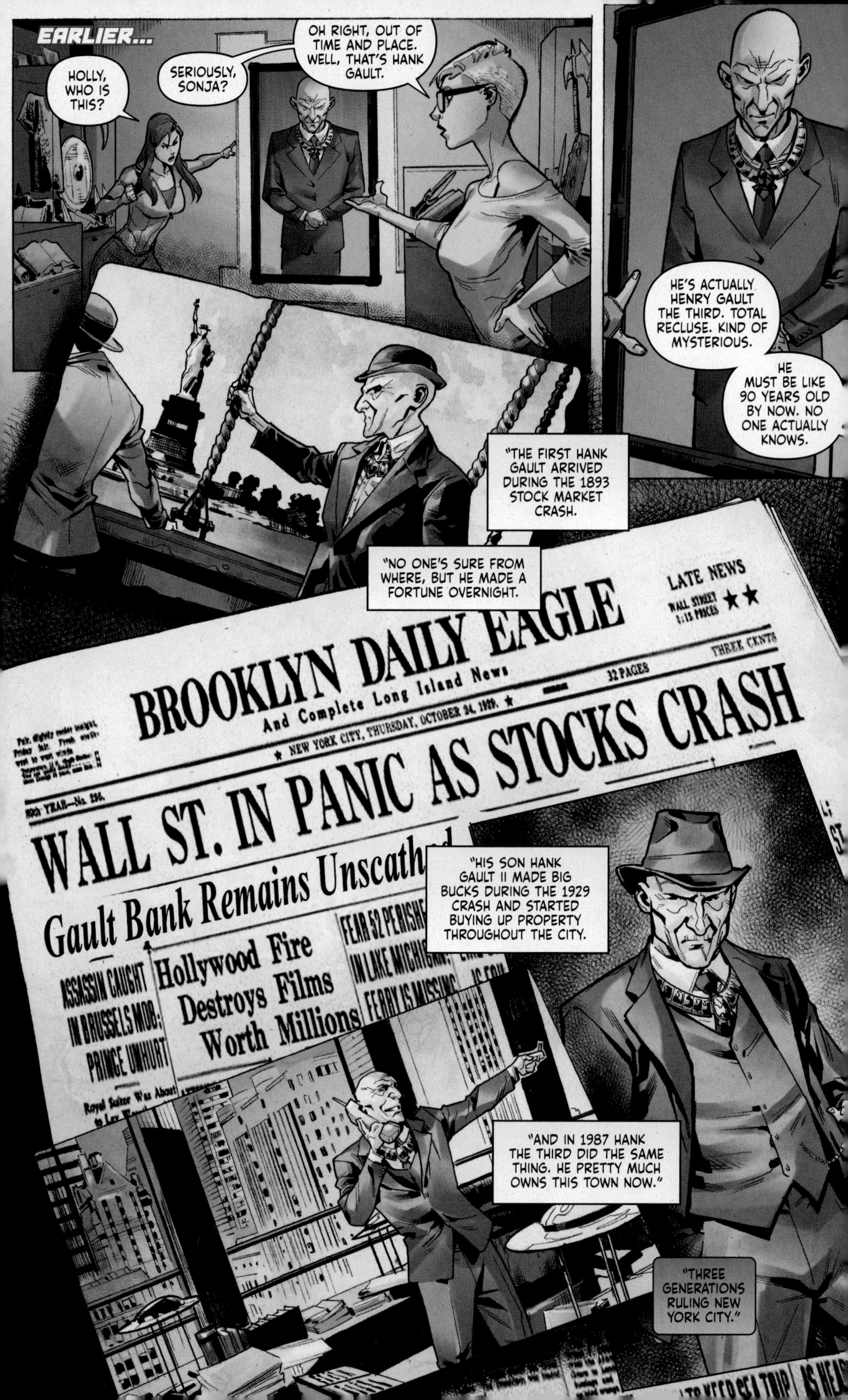
EARLIER...
HOLLY, WHO IS THIS?
SERIOUSLY, SONJA?
OH RIGHT, OUT OF TIME AND PLACE. WELL, THAT'S HANK GAULT.
HE'S ACTUALLY HENRY GAULT THE THIRD. TOTAL RECLUSE. KIND OF MYSTERIOUS.
HE MUST BE LIKE 90 YEARS OLD BY NOW. NO ONE ACTUALLY KNOWS.
"THE FIRST HANK GAULT ARRIVED DURING THE 1893 STOCK MARKET CRASH.
"NO ONE'S SURE FROM WHERE, BUT HE MADE A FORTUNE OVERNIGHT.
LATE NEWS
BROOKLYN DAILY EAGLE
And Complete Long Island News
THREE CENTS
32 PAGES
NEW YORK CITY, THURSDAY, OCTOBER 24, 1929.
WALL ST. IN PANIC AS STOCKS CRASH
Gault Bank Remains Unscath
ASSASSIN CAUGHT IN BRUSSELS MOB; PRINCE UNHURT
Hollywood Fire Destroys Films Worth Millions
FEAR 52 PERISH IN LAKE MICHIGAN; FERRY IS MISSING
"HIS SON HANK GAULT II MADE BIG BUCKS DURING THE 1929 CRASH AND STARTED BUYING UP PROPERTY THROUGHOUT THE CITY.
"AND IN 1987 HANK THE THIRD DID THE SAME THING. HE PRETTY MUCH OWNS THIS TOWN NOW."
"THREE GENERATIONS RULING NEW YORK CITY."

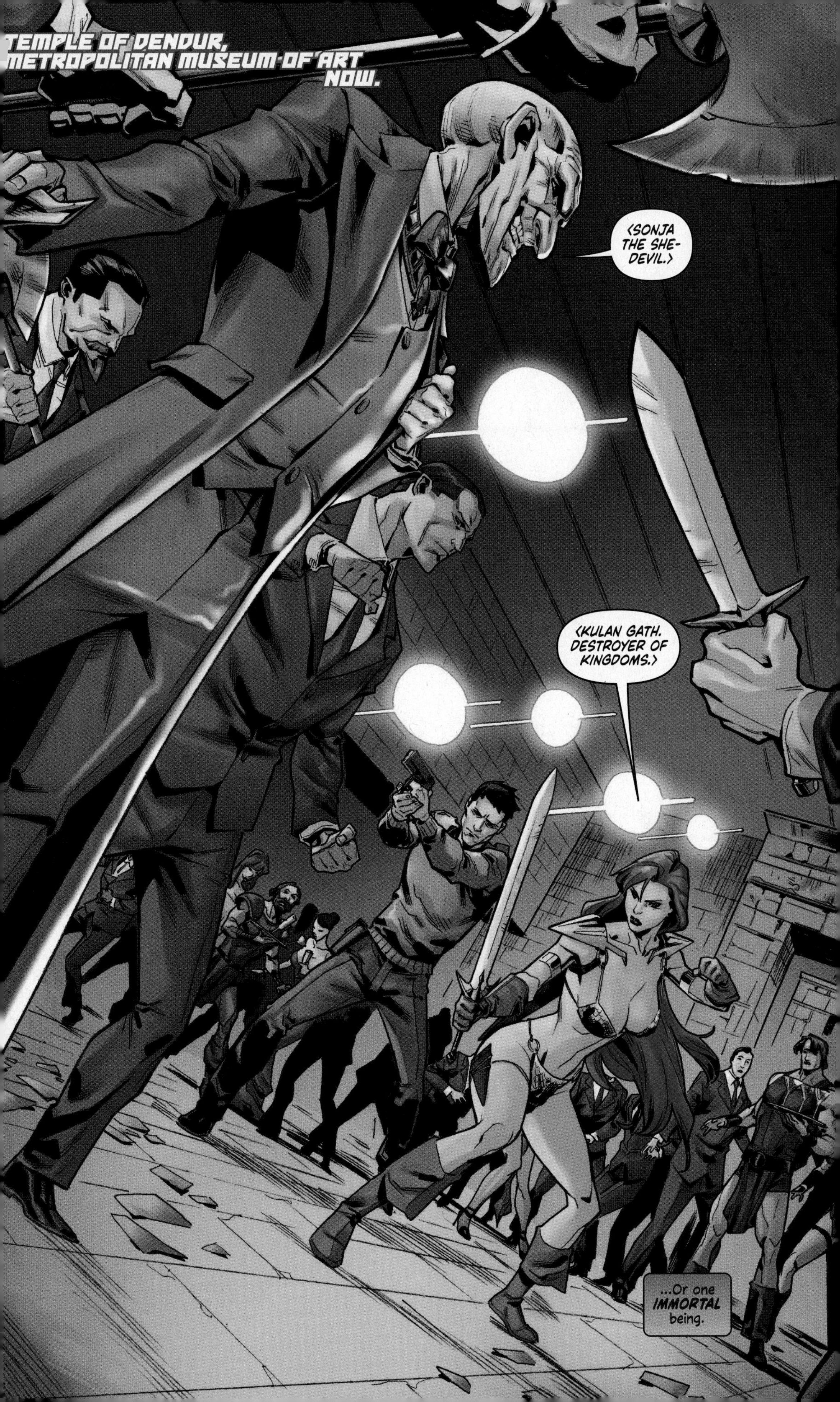
TEMPLE OF DENDUR, METROPOLITAN MUSEUM OF ART NOW.
‹SONJA THE SHE-DEVIL.›
‹KULAN GATH. DESTROYER OF KINGDOMS.›
...Or one IMMORTAL being.

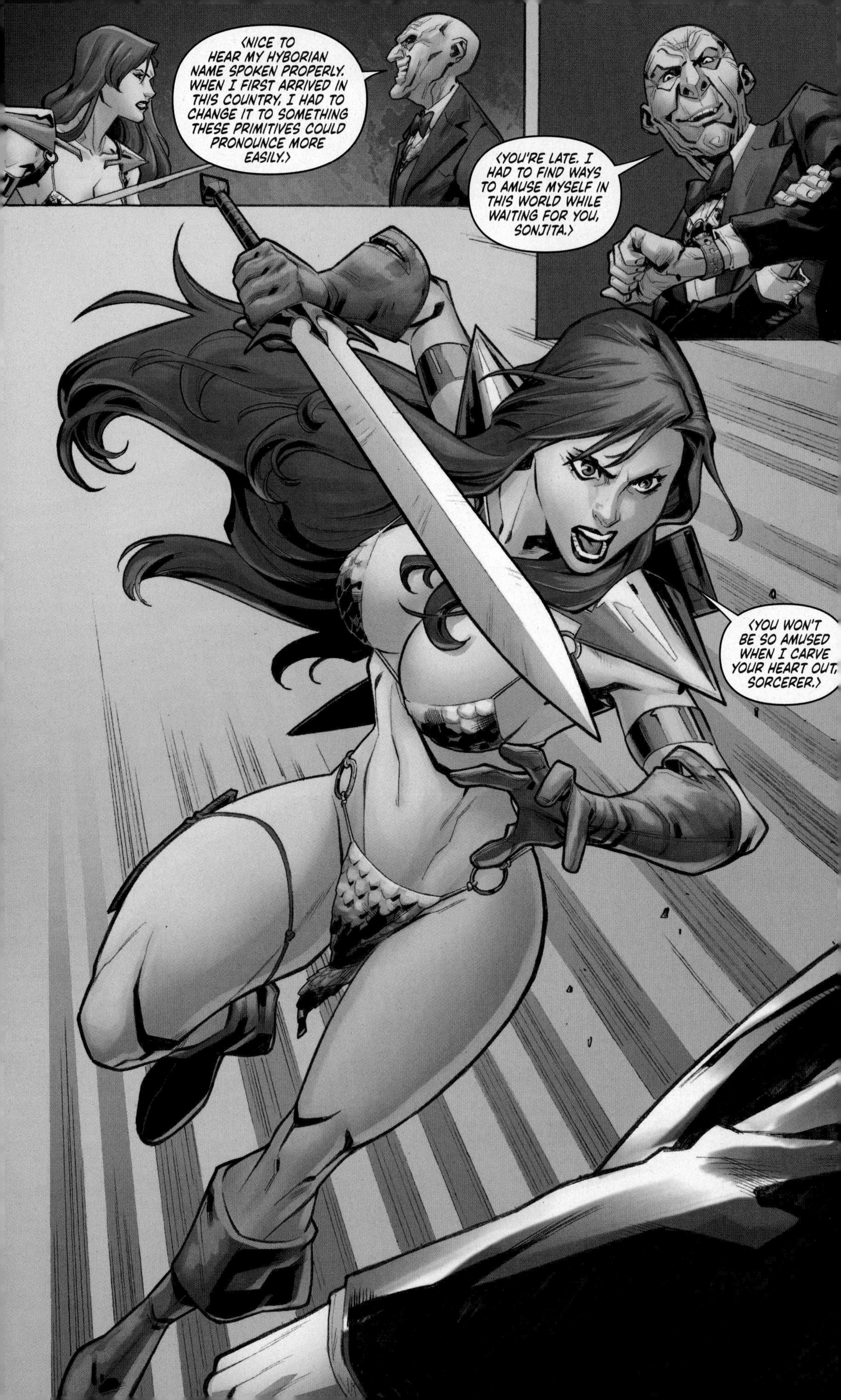

<NICE TO HEAR MY HYBORIAN NAME SPOKEN PROPERLY. WHEN I FIRST ARRIVED IN THIS COUNTRY, I HAD TO CHANGE IT TO SOMETHING THESE PRIMITIVES COULD PRONOUNCE MORE EASILY.>
<YOU'RE LATE. I HAD TO FIND WAYS TO AMUSE MYSELF IN THIS WORLD WHILE WAITING FOR YOU, SONJITA.>
<YOU WON'T BE SO AMUSED WHEN I CARVE YOUR HEART OUT, SORCERER.>

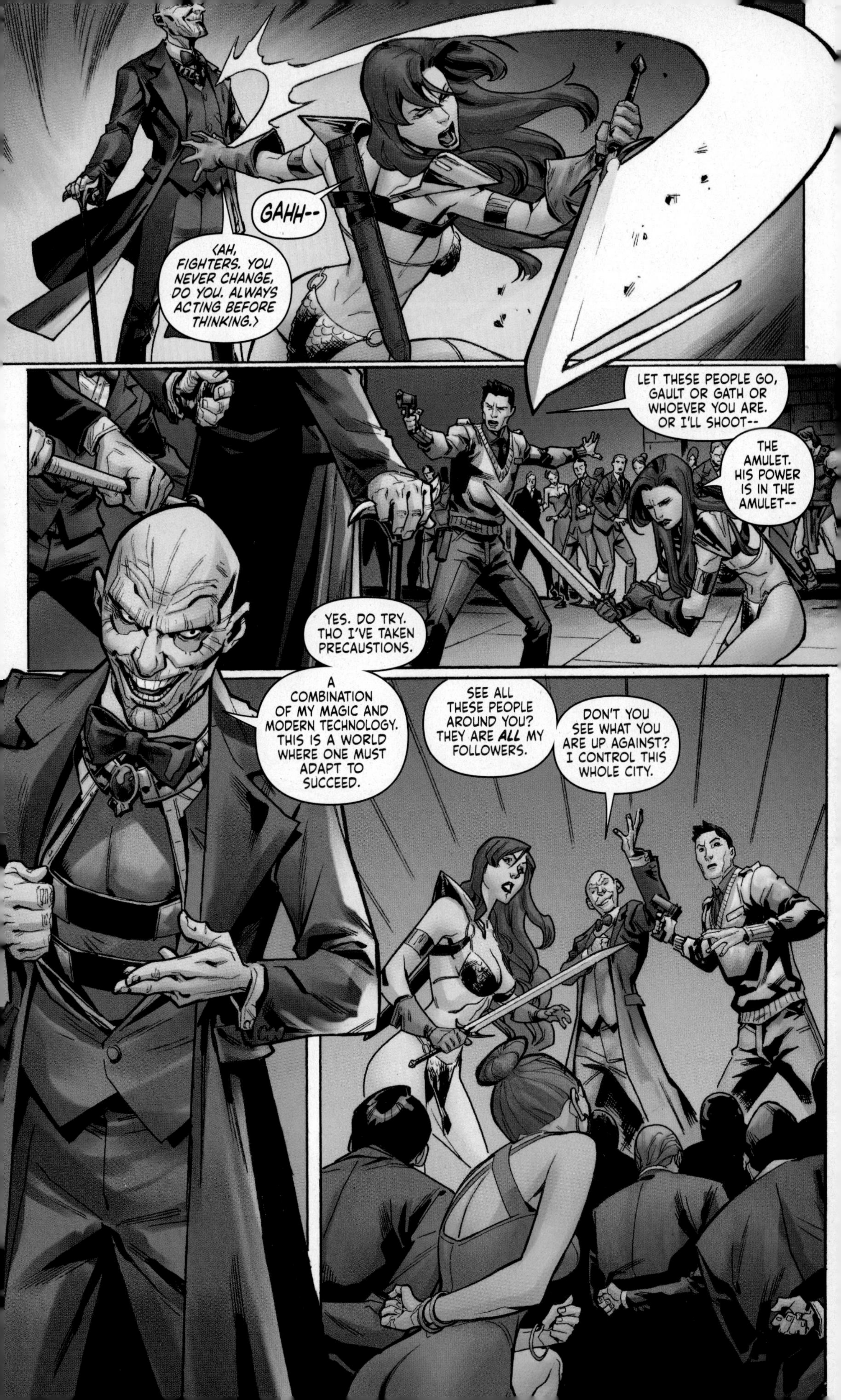

GAHH--
‹AH, FIGHTERS. YOU NEVER CHANGE, DO YOU. ALWAYS ACTING BEFORE THINKING.›
LET THESE PEOPLE GO, GAULT OR GATH OR WHOEVER YOU ARE. OR I'LL SHOOT--
THE AMULET. HIS POWER IS IN THE AMULET--
YES. DO TRY. THO I'VE TAKEN PRECAUSTIONS.
A COMBINATION OF MY MAGIC AND MODERN TECHNOLOGY. THIS IS A WORLD WHERE ONE MUST ADAPT TO SUCCEED.
SEE ALL THESE PEOPLE AROUND YOU? THEY ARE ALL MY FOLLOWERS.
DON'T YOU SEE WHAT YOU ARE UP AGAINST? I CONTROL THIS WHOLE CITY.

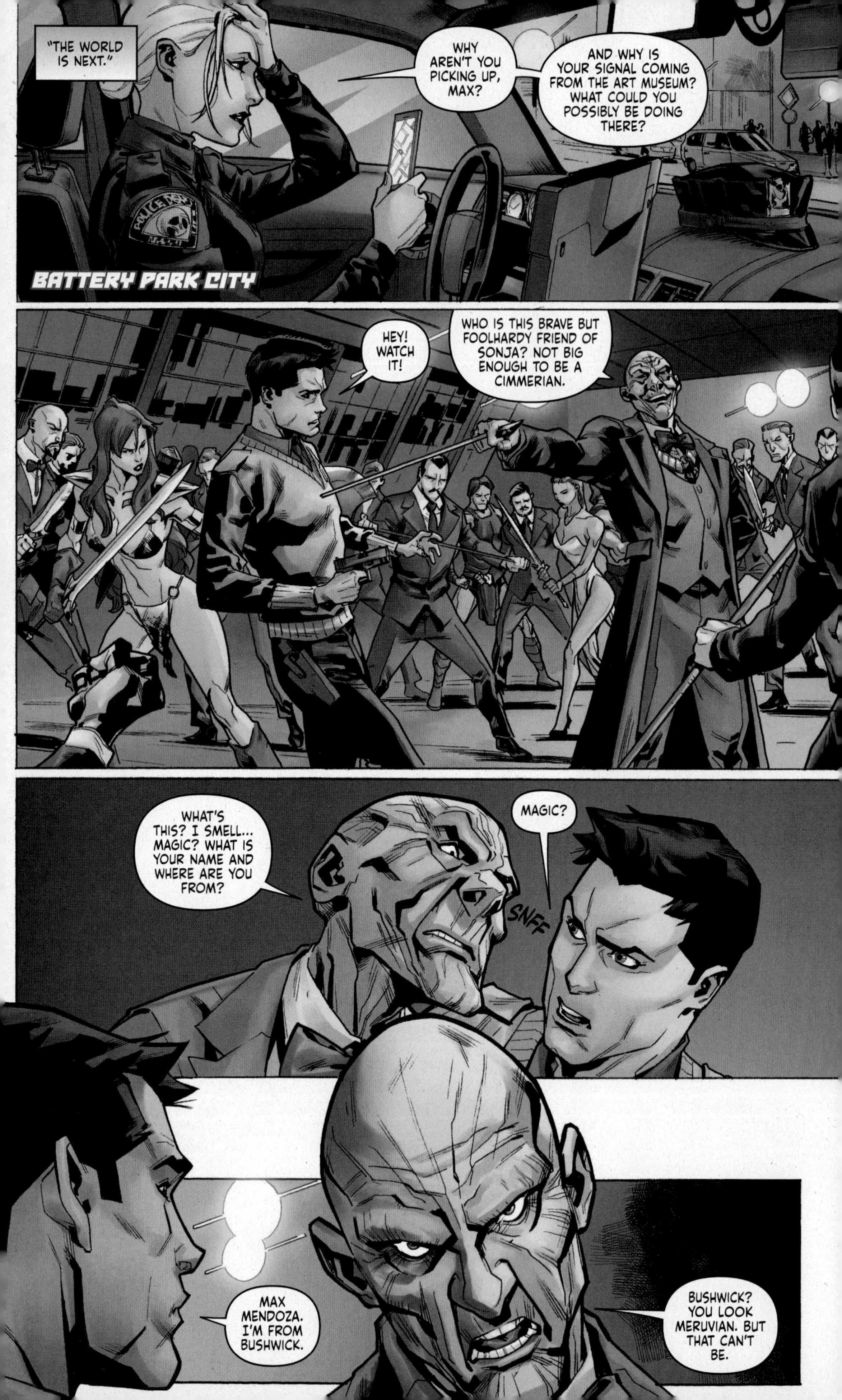

"THE WORLD IS NEXT."
WHY AREN'T YOU PICKING UP, MAX?
AND WHY IS YOUR SIGNAL COMING FROM THE ART MUSEUM? WHAT COULD YOU POSSIBLY BE DOING THERE?
BATTERY PARK CITY
HEY! WATCH IT!
WHO IS THIS BRAVE BUT FOOLHARDY FRIEND OF SONJA? NOT BIG ENOUGH TO BE A CIMMERIAN.
WHAT'S THIS? I SMELL... MAGIC? WHAT IS YOUR NAME AND WHERE ARE YOU FROM?
SNFF
MAGIC?
MAX MENDOZA. I'M FROM BUSHWICK.
BUSHWICK? YOU LOOK MERUVIAN. BUT THAT CAN'T BE.

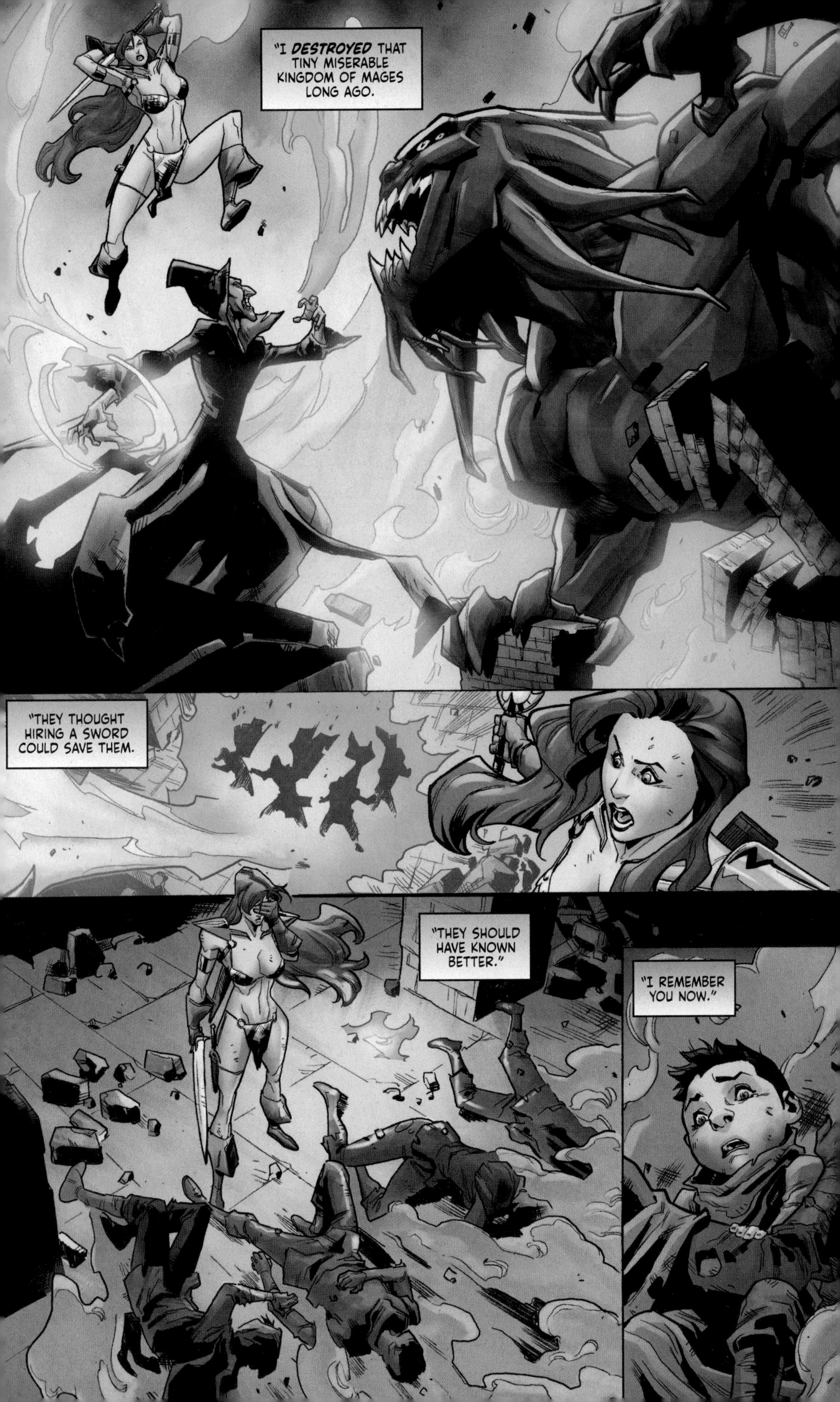
"I DESTROYED THAT TINY MISERABLE KINGDOM OF MAGES LONG AGO.
"THEY THOUGHT HIRING A SWORD COULD SAVE THEM.
"THEY SHOULD HAVE KNOWN BETTER."
"I REMEMBER YOU NOW."

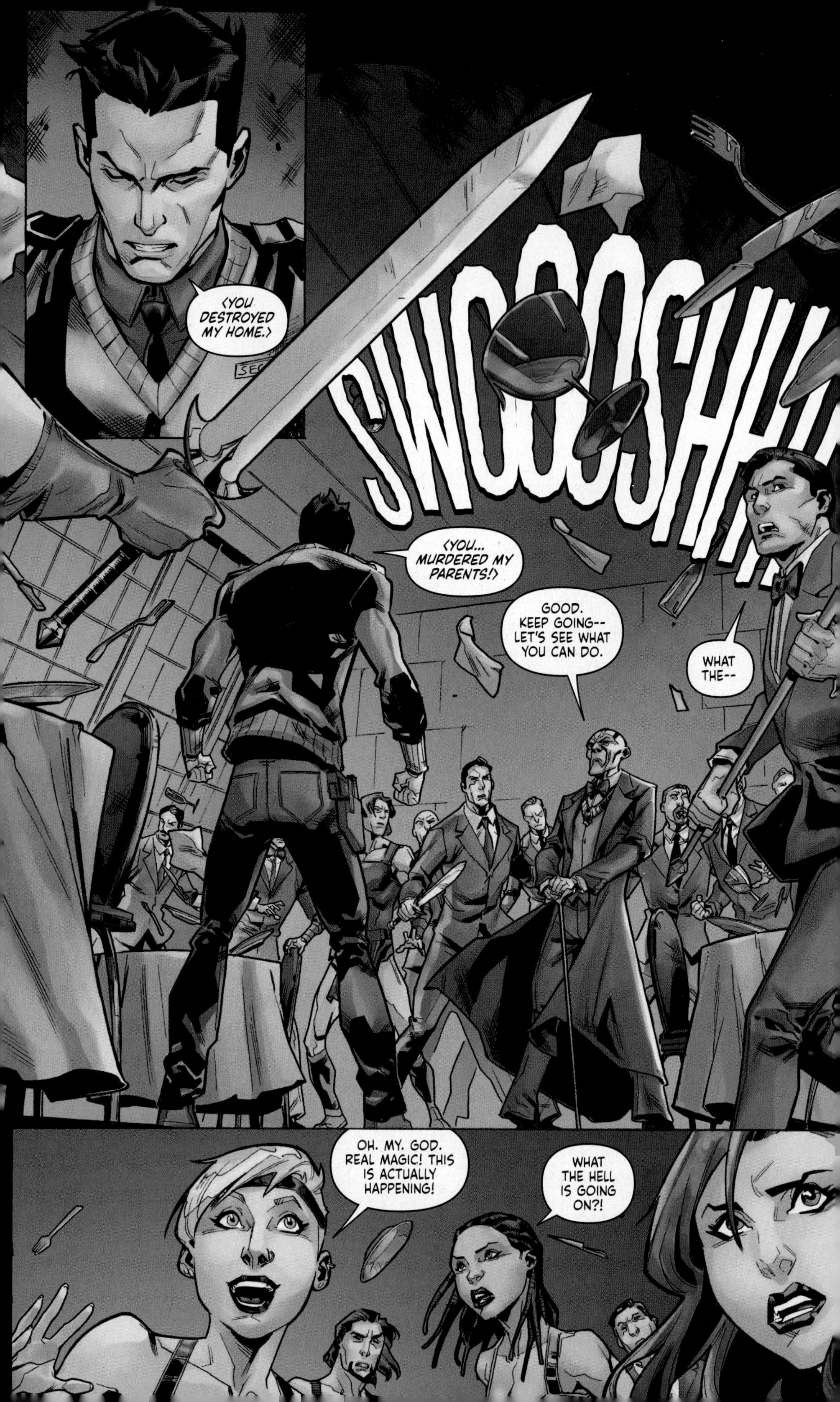
‹YOU DESTROYED MY HOME.›
SWOOOSHHH
‹YOU... MURDERED MY PARENTS!›
GOOD. KEEP GOING-- LET'S SEE WHAT YOU CAN DO.
WHAT THE--
OH. MY. GOD. REAL MAGIC! THIS IS ACTUALLY HAPPENING!
WHAT THE HELL IS GOING ON?!

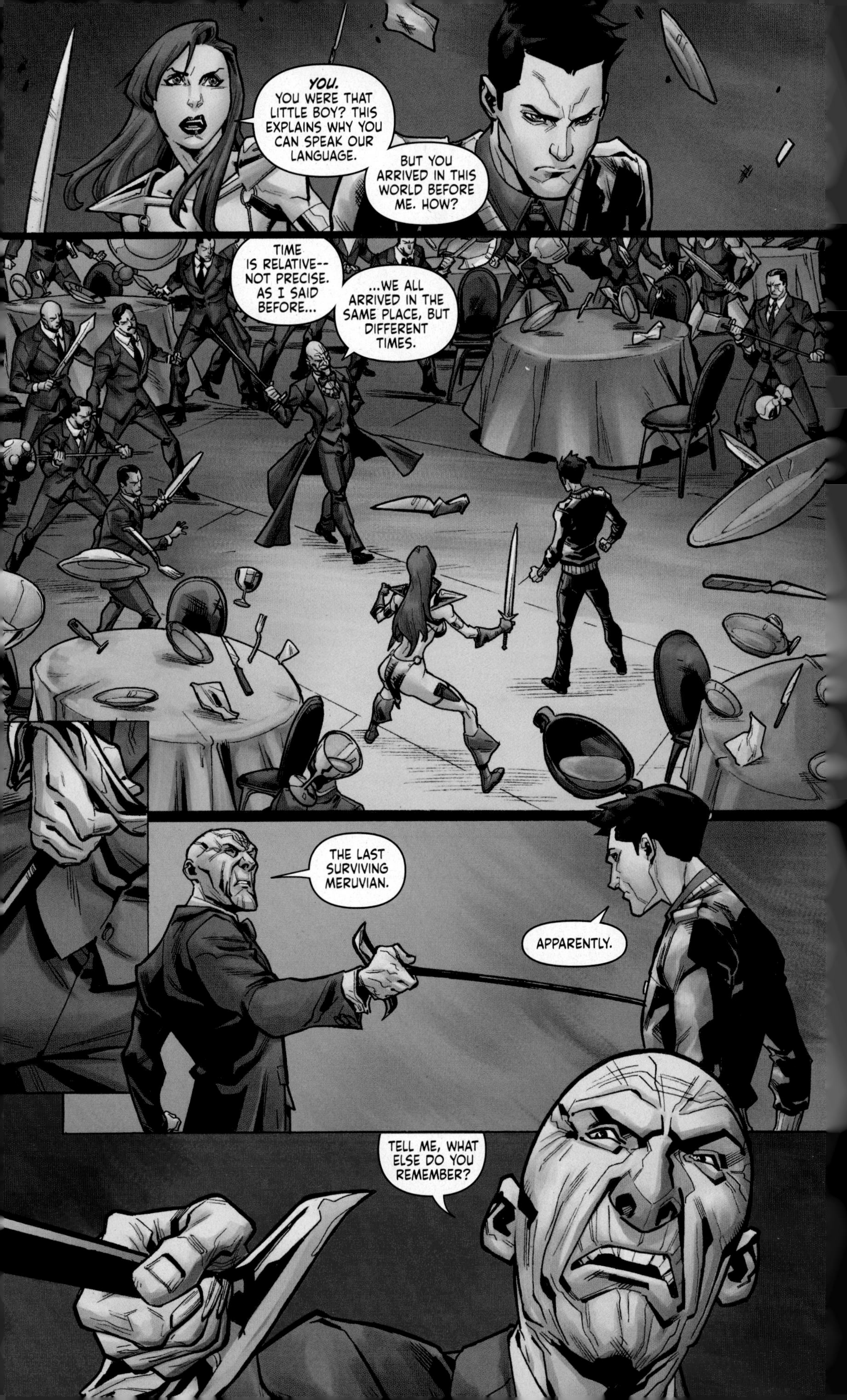
YOU. YOU WERE THAT LITTLE BOY? THIS EXPLAINS WHY YOU CAN SPEAK OUR LANGUAGE.
BUT YOU ARRIVED IN THIS WORLD BEFORE ME. HOW?
TIME IS RELATIVE-- NOT PRECISE. AS I SAID BEFORE...
...WE ALL ARRIVED IN THE SAME PLACE, BUT DIFFERENT TIMES.
THE LAST SURVIVING MERUVIAN.
APPARENTLY.
TELL ME, WHAT ELSE DO YOU REMEMBER?

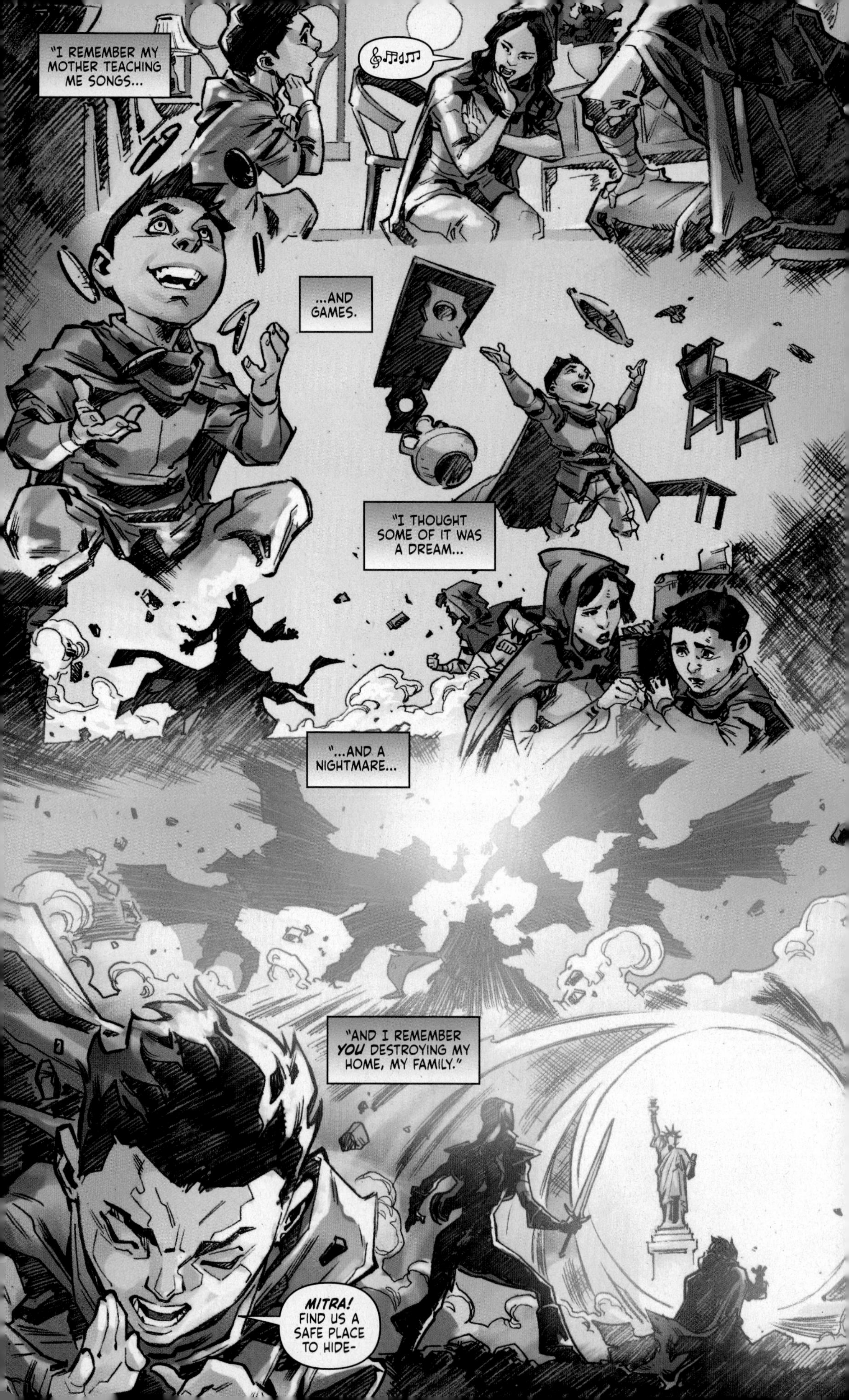
"I REMEMBER MY MOTHER TEACHING ME SONGS...
...AND GAMES.
"I THOUGHT SOME OF IT WAS A DREAM...
"...AND A NIGHTMARE...
"AND I REMEMBER *YOU* DESTROYING MY HOME, MY FAMILY."
MITRA! FIND US A SAFE PLACE TO HIDE-

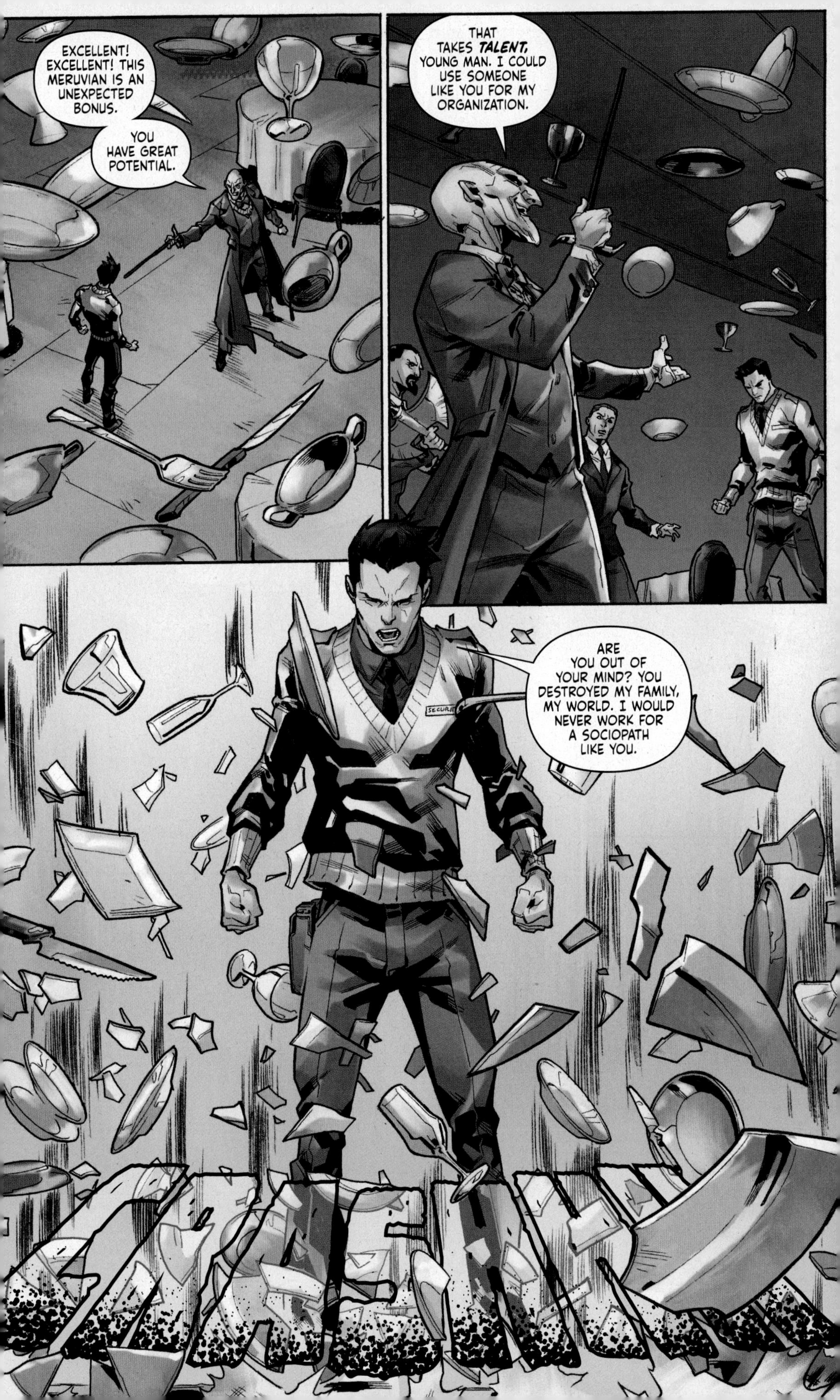
EXCELLENT! EXCELLENT! THIS MERUVIAN IS AN UNEXPECTED BONUS.
YOU HAVE GREAT POTENTIAL.
THAT TAKES TALENT, YOUNG MAN. I COULD USE SOMEONE LIKE YOU FOR MY ORGANIZATION.
ARE YOU OUT OF YOUR MIND? YOU DESTROYED MY FAMILY, MY WORLD. I WOULD NEVER WORK FOR A SOCIOPATH LIKE YOU.

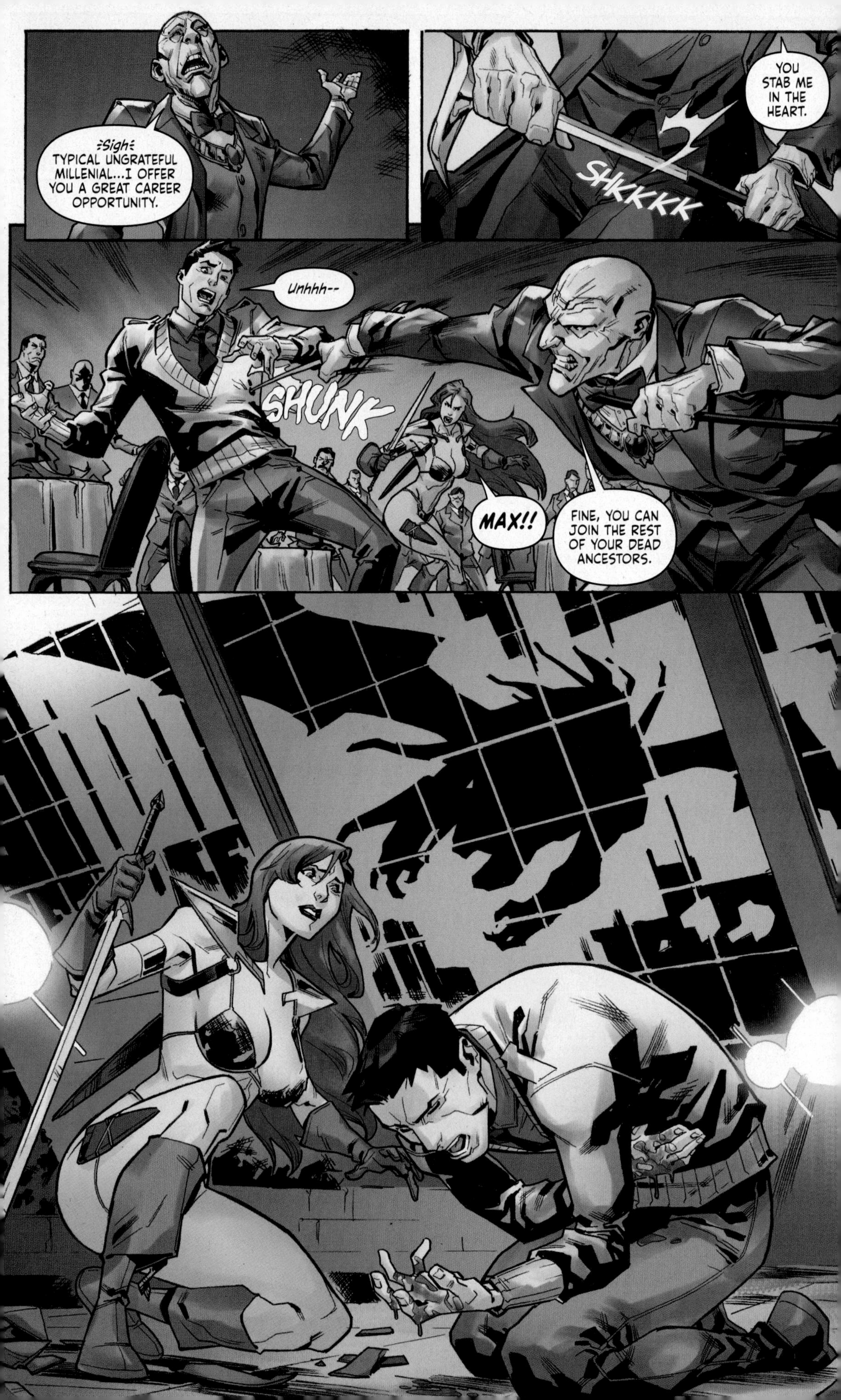

Sigh
TYPICAL UNGRATEFUL MILLENIAL...I OFFER YOU A GREAT CAREER OPPORTUNITY.
YOU STAB ME IN THE HEART.
SHKKKK
Unhhh--
SHUNK
MAX!!
FINE, YOU CAN JOIN THE REST OF YOUR DEAD ANCESTORS.

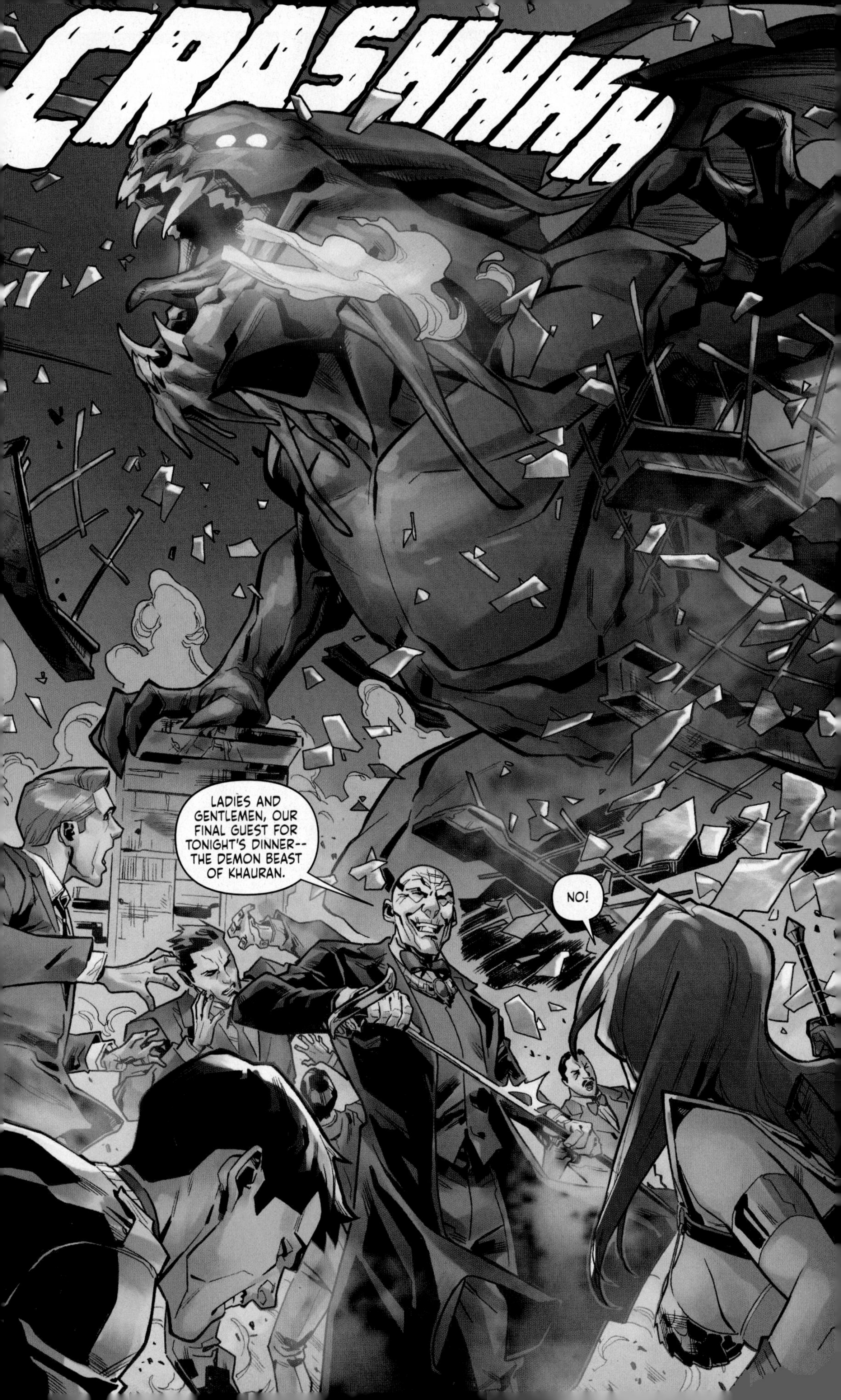
CRASHHHH
LADIES AND GENTLEMEN, OUR FINAL GUEST FOR TONIGHT'S DINNER-- THE DEMON BEAST OF KHAURAN.
NO!

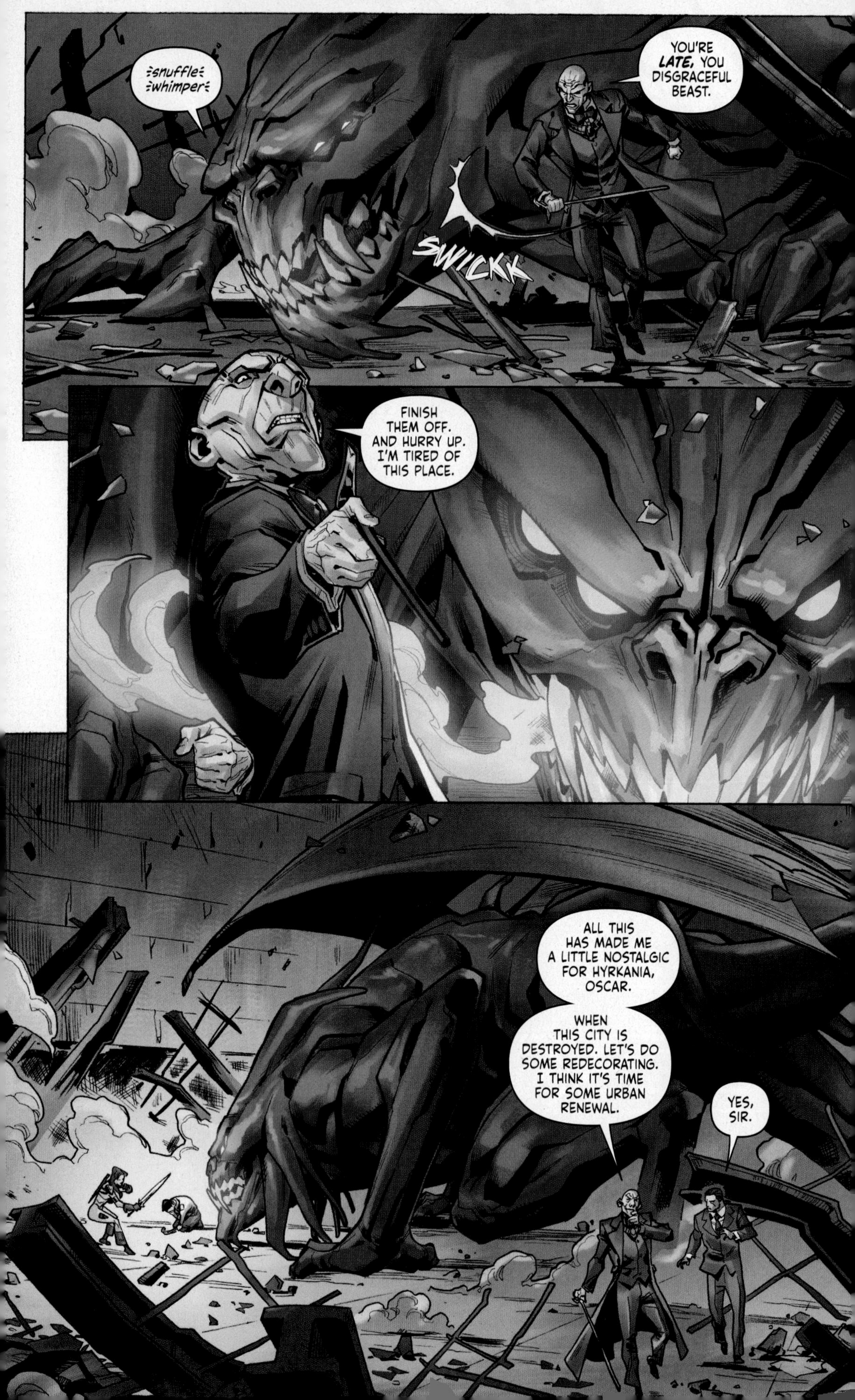

snuffle whimper
YOU'RE LATE, YOU DISGRACEFUL BEAST.
SWICKK
FINISH THEM OFF. AND HURRY UP. I'M TIRED OF THIS PLACE.
ALL THIS HAS MADE ME A LITTLE NOSTALGIC FOR HYRKANIA, OSCAR.
WHEN THIS CITY IS DESTROYED. LET'S DO SOME REDECORATING. I THINK IT'S TIME FOR SOME URBAN RENEWAL.
YES, SIR.

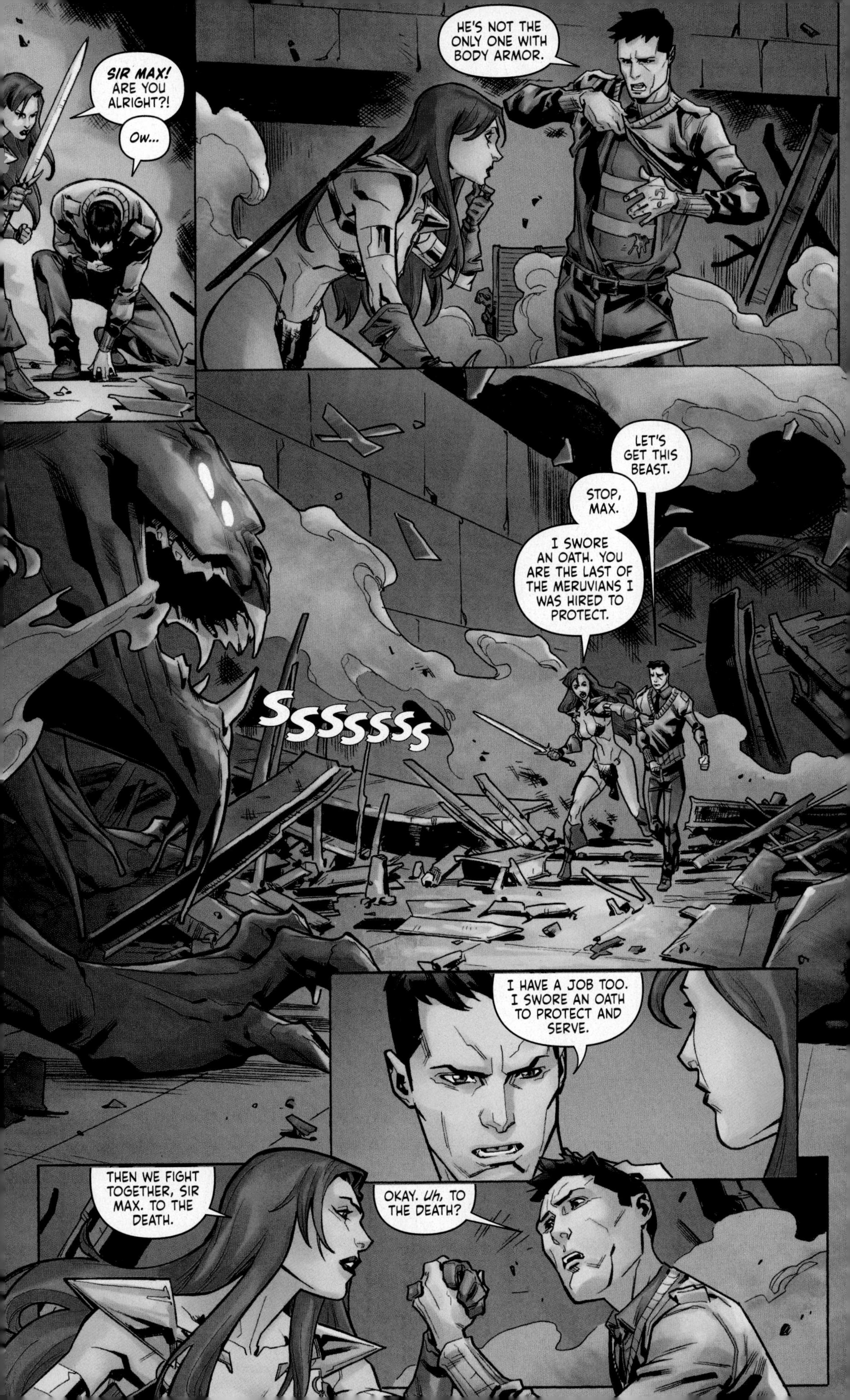
SIR MAX! ARE YOU ALRIGHT?!
OW...
HE'S NOT THE ONLY ONE WITH BODY ARMOR.
LET'S GET THIS BEAST.
STOP, MAX.
I SWORE AN OATH. YOU ARE THE LAST OF THE MERUVIANS I WAS HIRED TO PROTECT.
SSSSSSS
I HAVE A JOB TOO. I SWORE AN OATH TO PROTECT AND SERVE.
THEN WE FIGHT TOGETHER, SIR MAX. TO THE DEATH.
OKAY. *Uh,* TO THE DEATH?

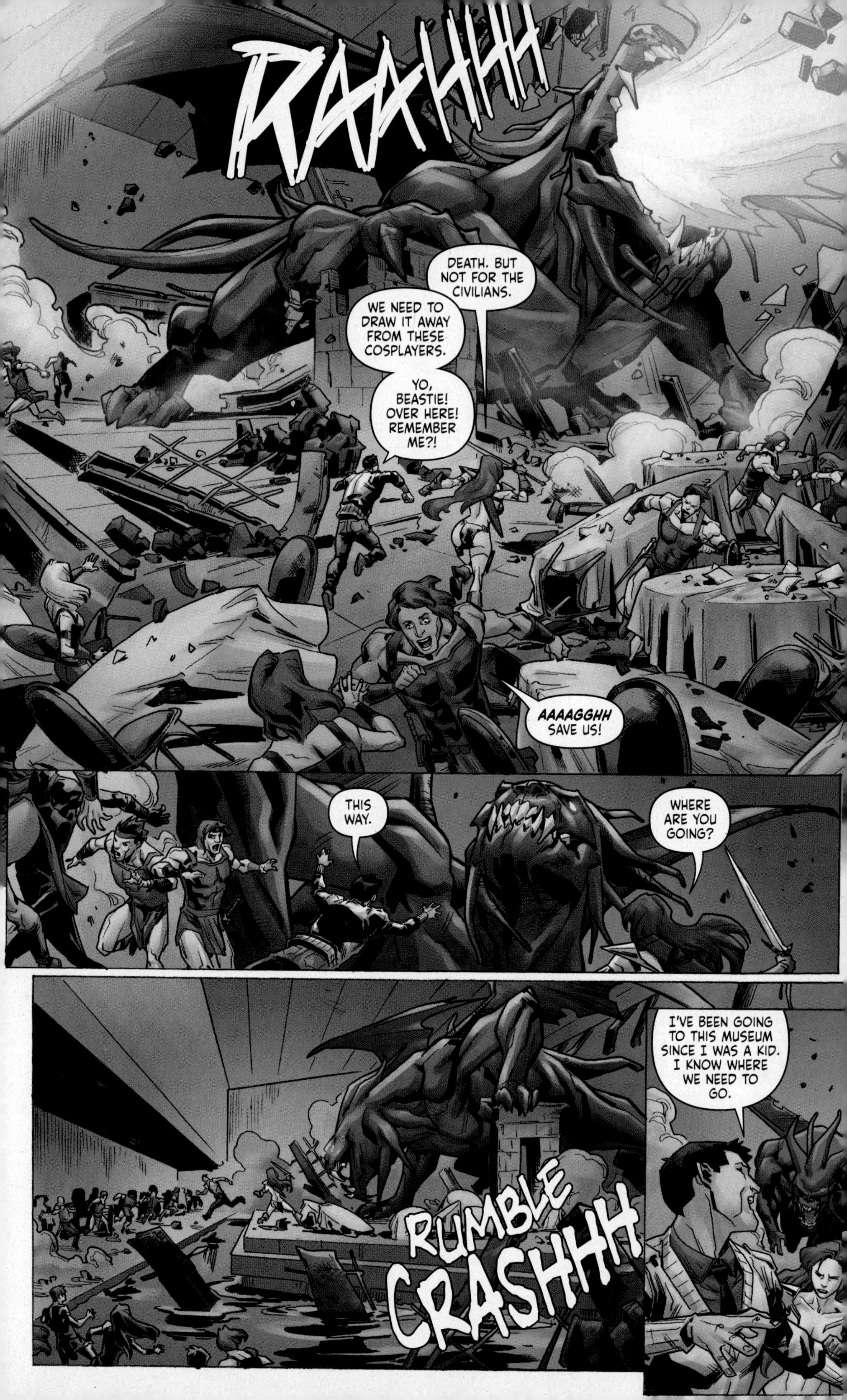
RAAHHH
WE NEED TO DRAW IT AWAY FROM THESE COSPLAYERS.
DEATH. BUT NOT FOR THE CIVILIANS.
YO, BEASTIE! OVER HERE! REMEMBER ME?!
AAAAGGHH SAVE US!
THIS WAY.
WHERE ARE YOU GOING?
I'VE BEEN GOING TO THIS MUSEUM SINCE I WAS A KID. I KNOW WHERE WE NEED TO GO.
RUMBLE
CRASHHH

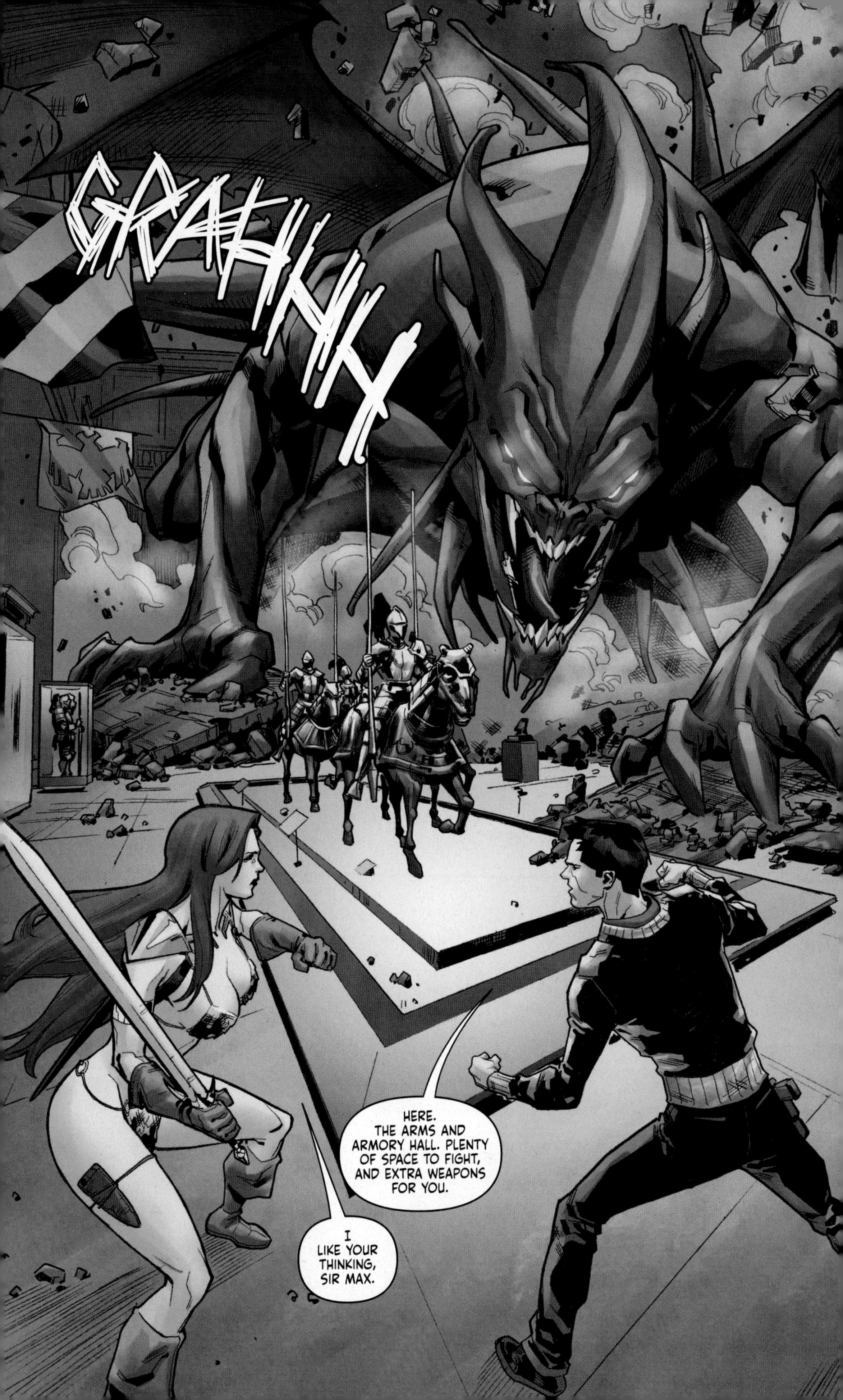
GRAAHHH
HERE. THE ARMS AND ARMORY HALL. PLENTY OF SPACE TO FIGHT, AND EXTRA WEAPONS FOR YOU.
I LIKE YOUR THINKING, SIR MAX.

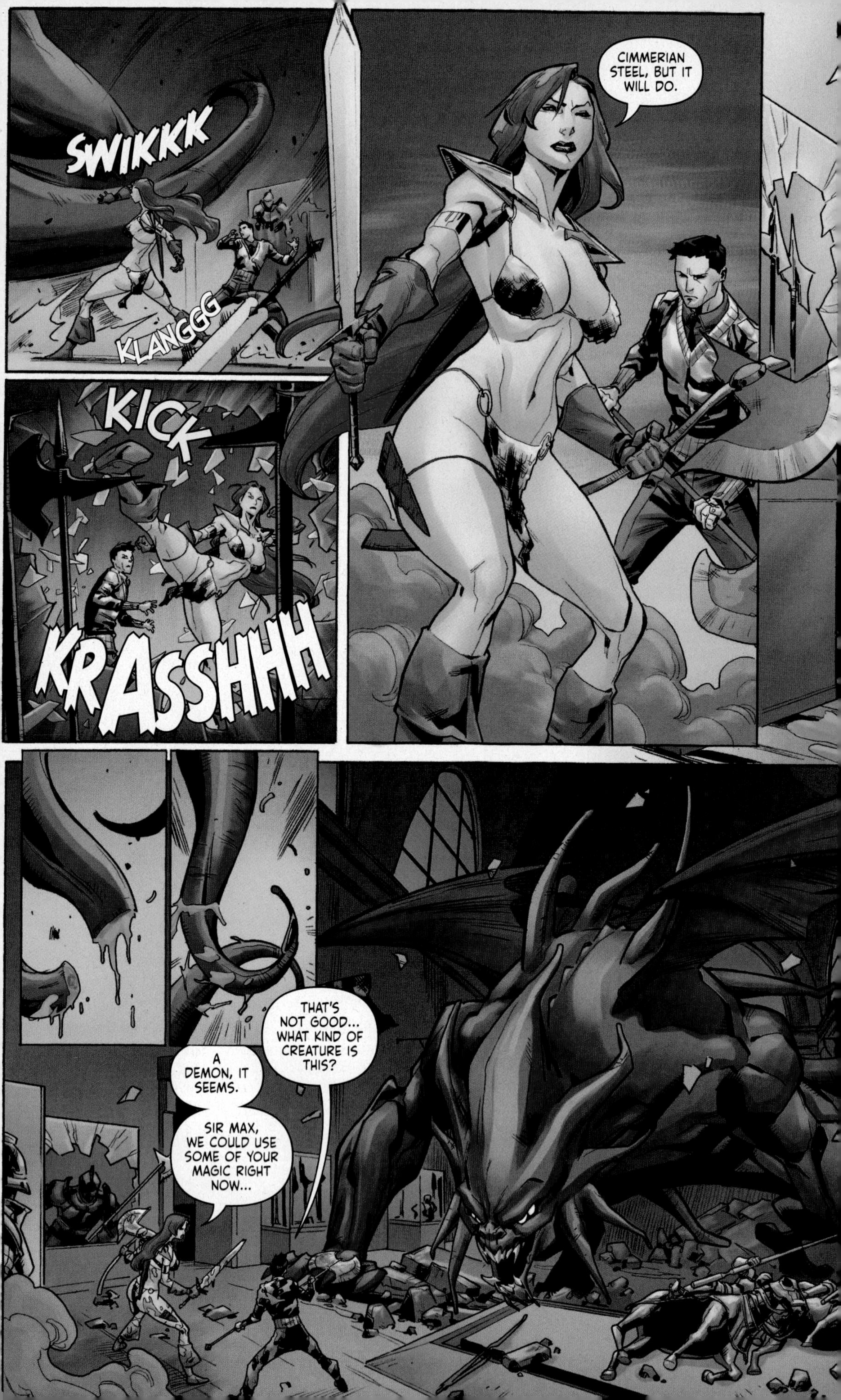
SWIKKK
KLANGGG
CIMMERIAN STEEL, BUT IT WILL DO.
KICK
KRASSHHH
THAT'S NOT GOOD... WHAT KIND OF CREATURE IS THIS?
A DEMON, IT SEEMS.
SIR MAX, WE COULD USE SOME OF YOUR MAGIC RIGHT NOW...

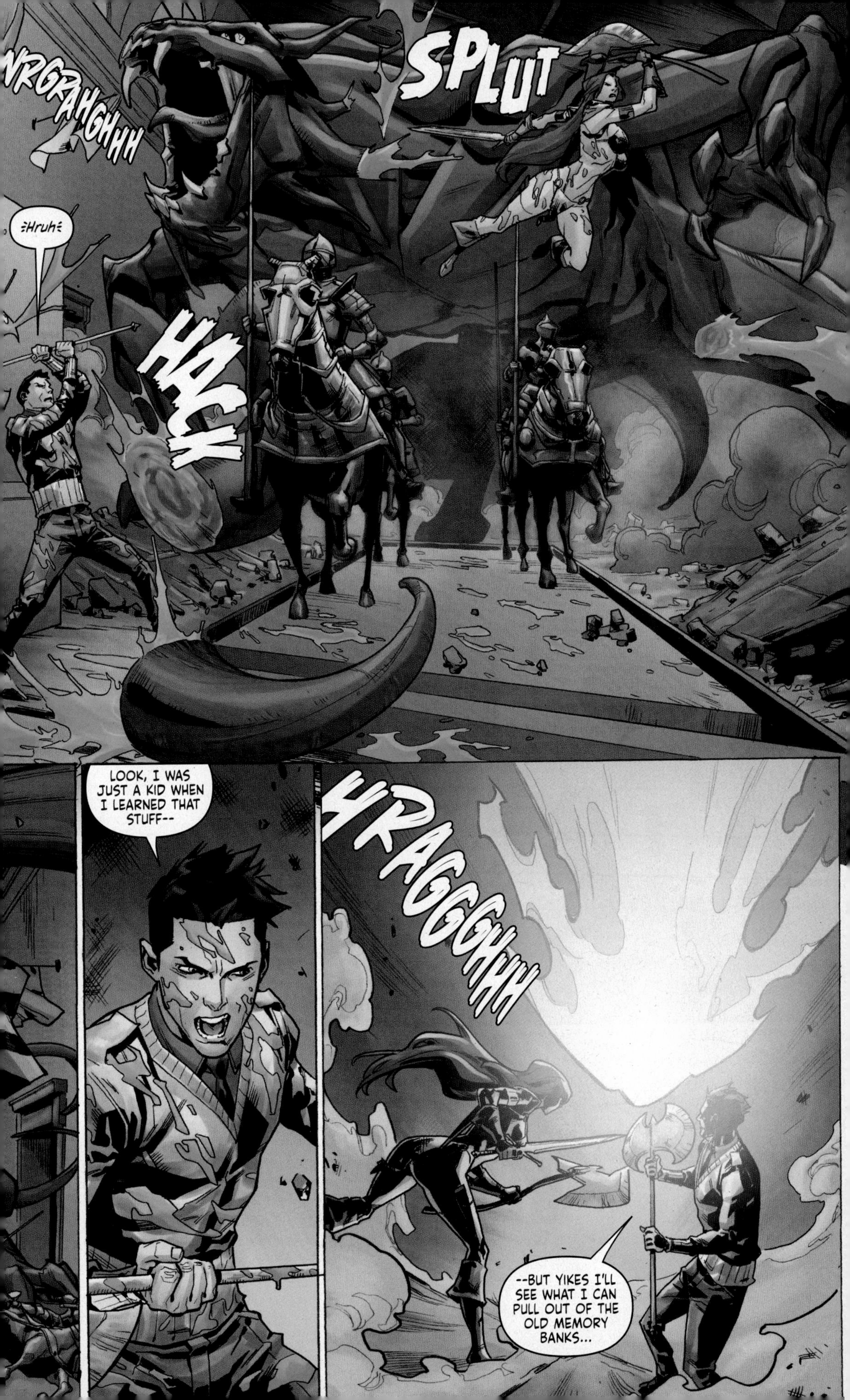
NRGRAHGHHH
SPLUT
Hruh
HACK
LOOK, I WAS JUST A KID WHEN I LEARNED THAT STUFF--
YRAGGGHHH
--BUT YIKES I'LL SEE WHAT I CAN PULL OUT OF THE OLD MEMORY BANKS...

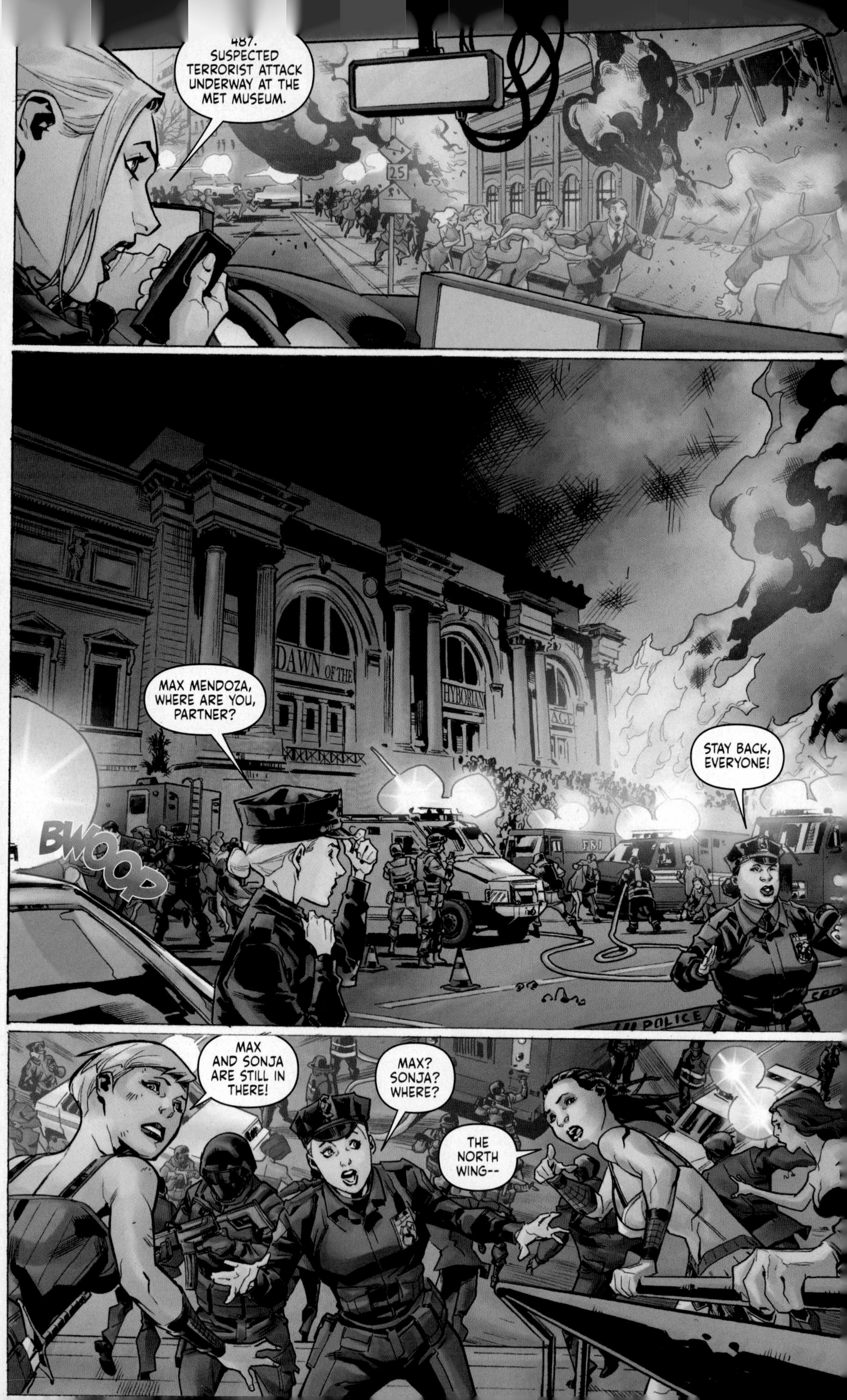
487. SUSPECTED TERRORIST ATTACK UNDERWAY AT THE MET MUSEUM.
25
DAWN OF THE HYBORIAN AGE
MAX MENDOZA, WHERE ARE YOU, PARTNER?
STAY BACK, EVERYONE!
BWOOP
FBI
POLICE
MAX AND SONJA ARE STILL IN THERE!
MAX? SONJA? WHERE?
THE NORTH WING--

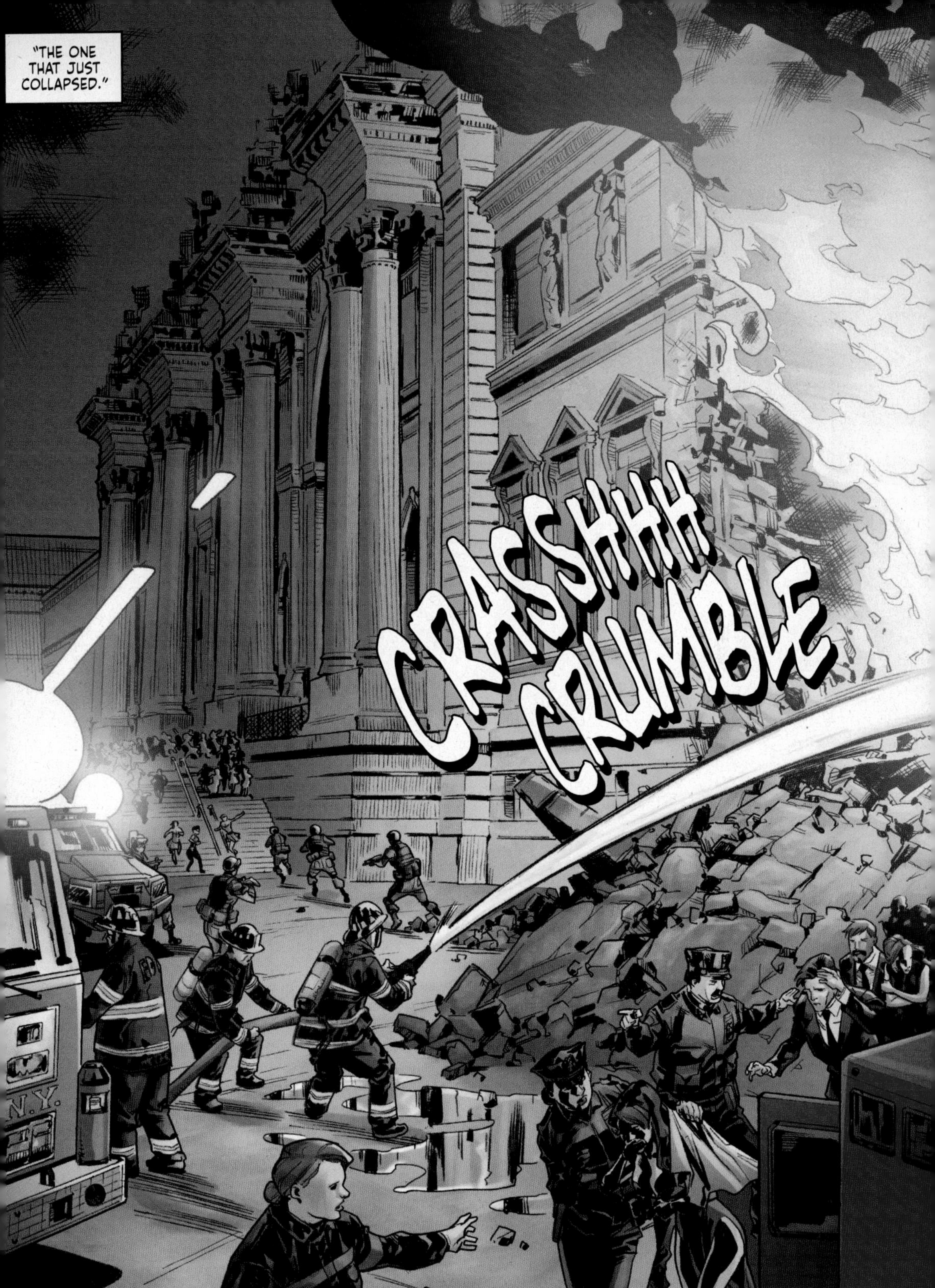
"THE ONE THAT JUST COLLAPSED."
CRASHHH
CRUMBLE

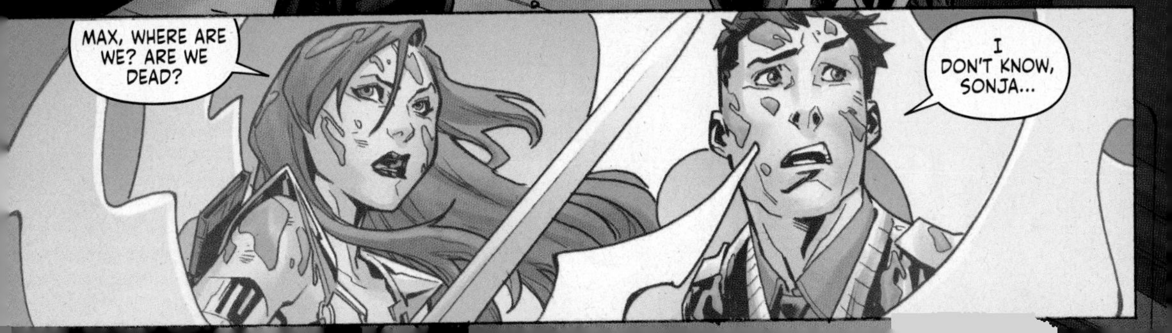
MAX, WHERE ARE WE? ARE WE DEAD?
I DON'T KNOW, SONJA...

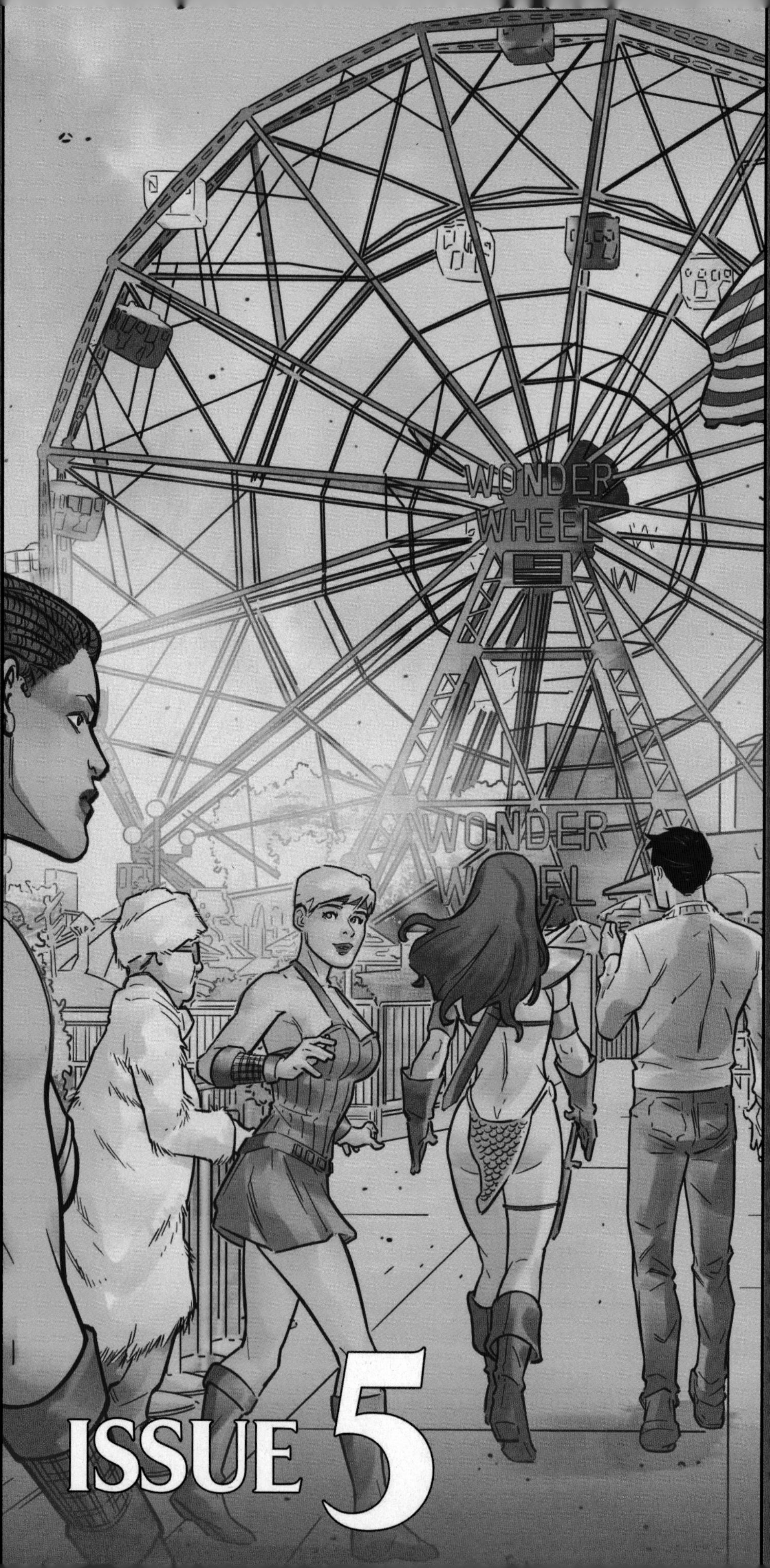
WONDER WHEEL
WONDER WHEEL

ISSUE 5

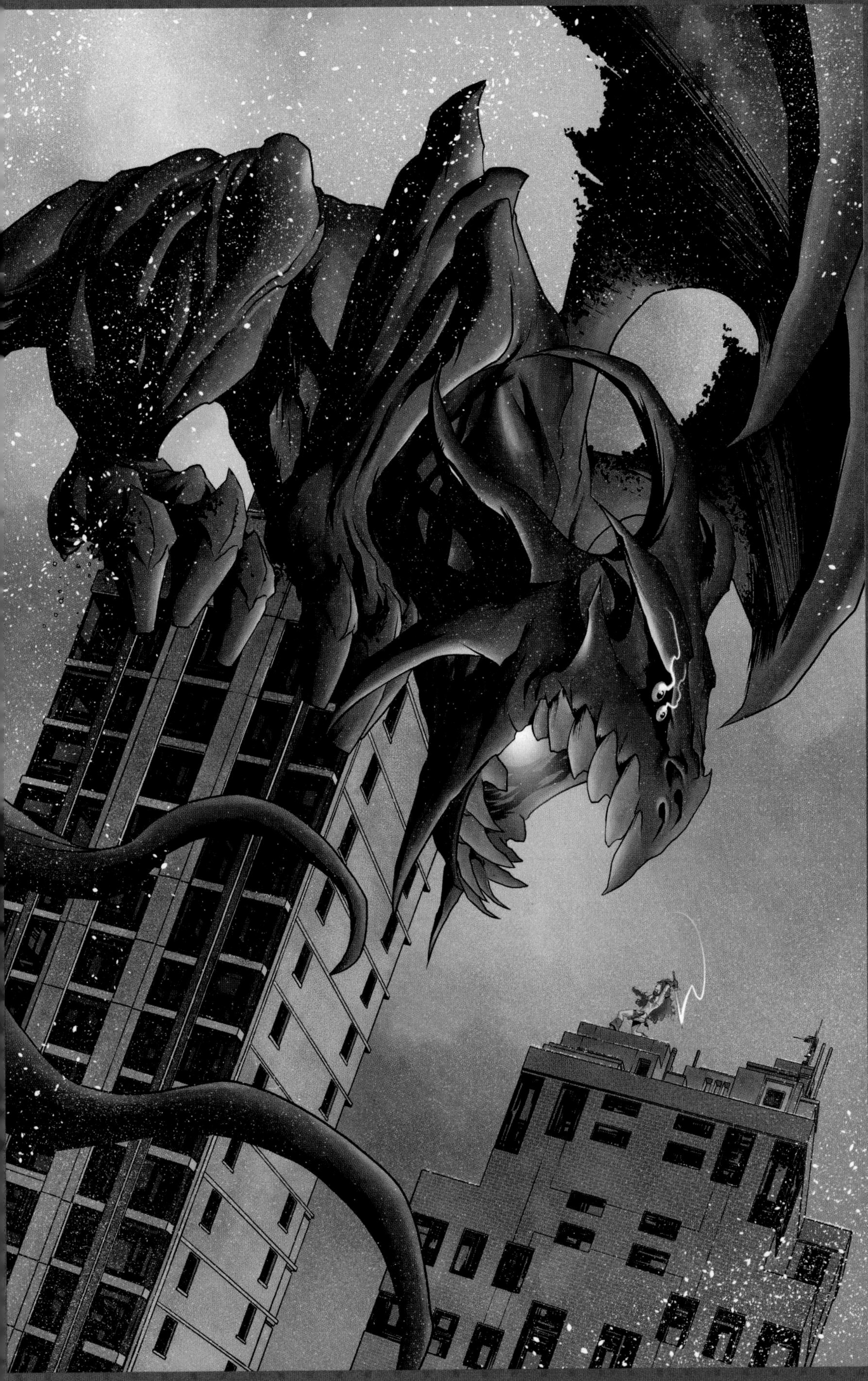

ISSUE #5: COVER ART BY **MIKE MCKONE**

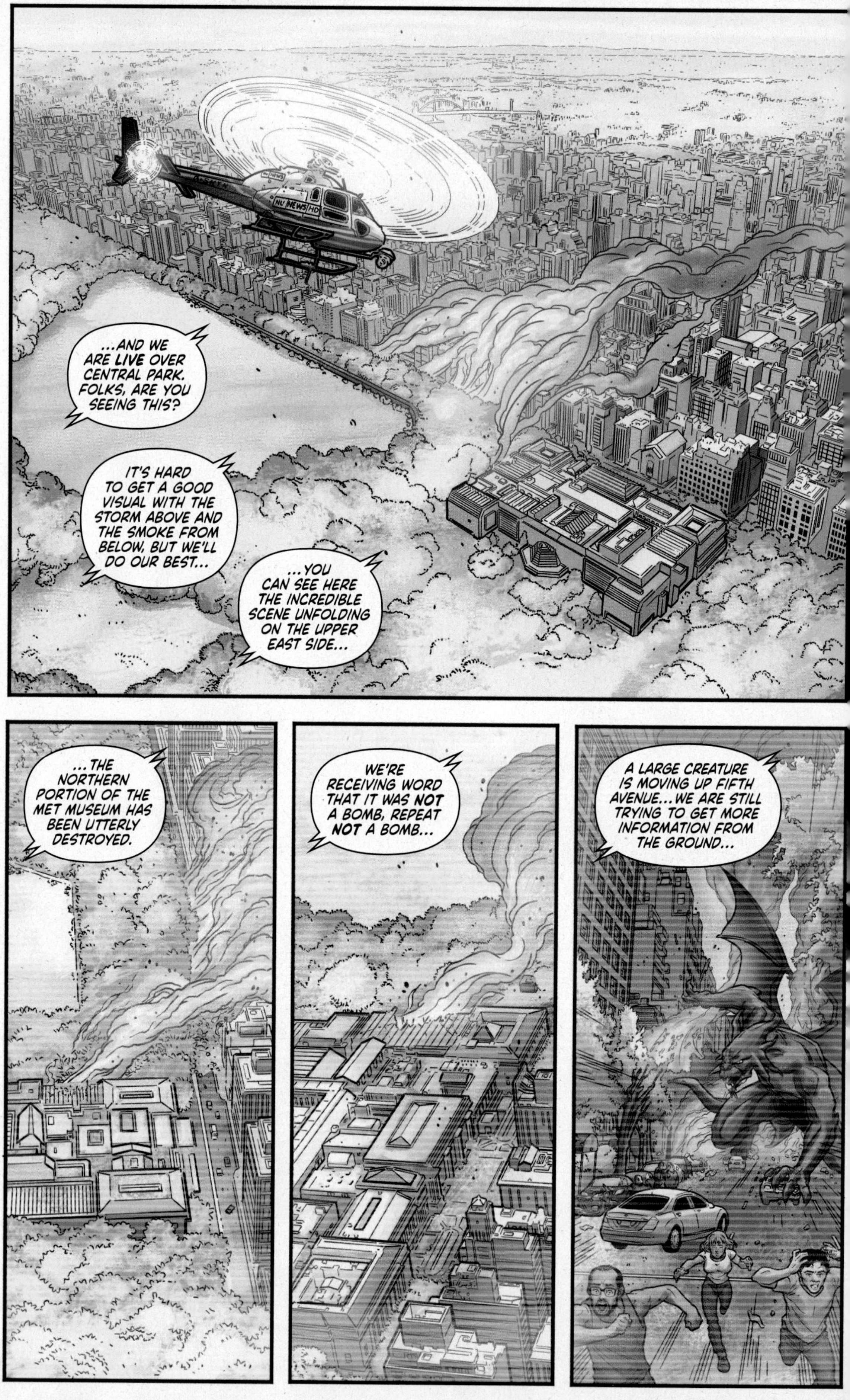
...AND WE ARE LIVE OVER CENTRAL PARK. FOLKS, ARE YOU SEEING THIS?
IT'S HARD TO GET A GOOD VISUAL WITH THE STORM ABOVE AND THE SMOKE FROM BELOW, BUT WE'LL DO OUR BEST...
...YOU CAN SEE HERE THE INCREDIBLE SCENE UNFOLDING ON THE UPPER EAST SIDE...
...THE NORTHERN PORTION OF THE MET MUSEUM HAS BEEN UTTERLY DESTROYED.
WE'RE RECEIVING WORD THAT IT WAS **NOT** A BOMB, REPEAT **NOT** A BOMB...
A LARGE CREATURE IS MOVING UP FIFTH AVENUE...WE ARE STILL TRYING TO GET MORE INFORMATION FROM THE GROUND...

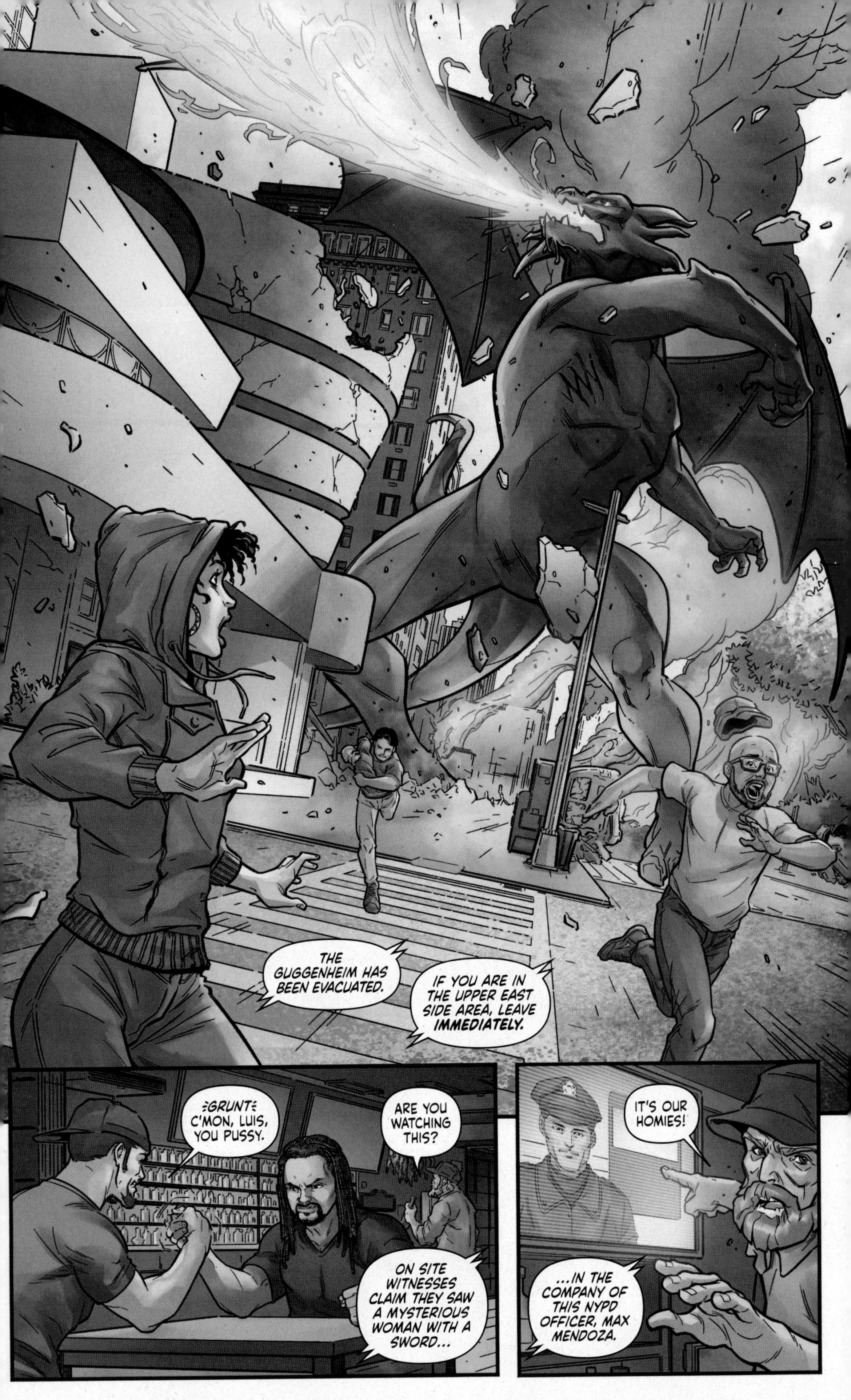
THE GUGGENHEIM HAS BEEN EVACUATED.
IF YOU ARE IN THE UPPER EAST SIDE AREA, LEAVE IMMEDIATELY.
GRUNT C'MON, LUIS, YOU PUSSY.
ARE YOU WATCHING THIS?
ON SITE WITNESSES CLAIM THEY SAW A MYSTERIOUS WOMAN WITH A SWORD...
IT'S OUR HOMIES!
...IN THE COMPANY OF THIS NYPD OFFICER, MAX MENDOZA.

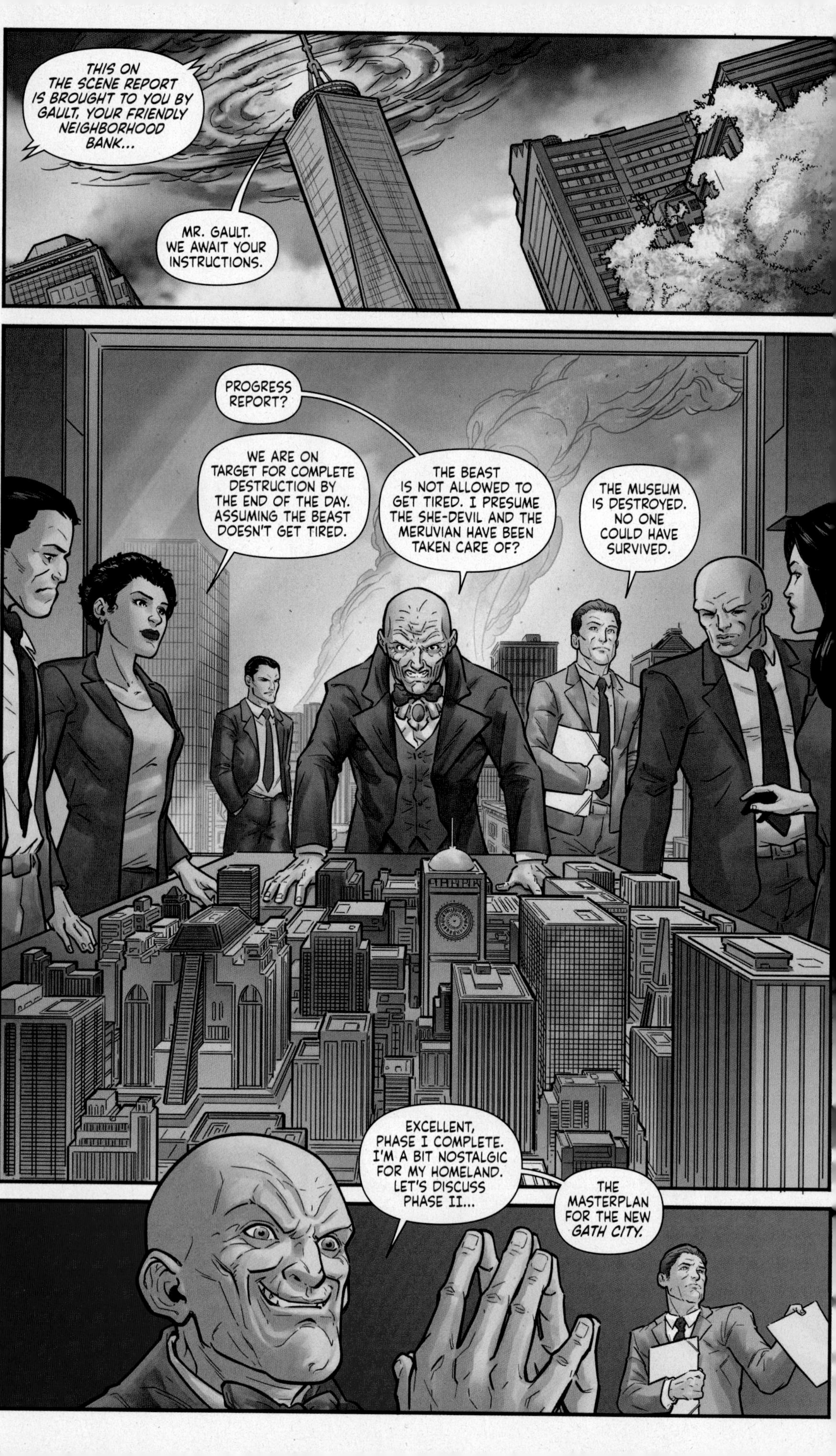
THIS ON THE SCENE REPORT IS BROUGHT TO YOU BY GAULT, YOUR FRIENDLY NEIGHBORHOOD BANK...
MR. GAULT. WE AWAIT YOUR INSTRUCTIONS.
PROGRESS REPORT?
WE ARE ON TARGET FOR COMPLETE DESTRUCTION BY THE END OF THE DAY. ASSUMING THE BEAST DOESN'T GET TIRED.
THE BEAST IS NOT ALLOWED TO GET TIRED. I PRESUME THE SHE-DEVIL AND THE MERUVIAN HAVE BEEN TAKEN CARE OF?
THE MUSEUM IS DESTROYED. NO ONE COULD HAVE SURVIVED.
EXCELLENT, PHASE I COMPLETE. I'M A BIT NOSTALGIC FOR MY HOMELAND. LET'S DISCUSS PHASE II...
THE MASTERPLAN FOR THE NEW GATH CITY.

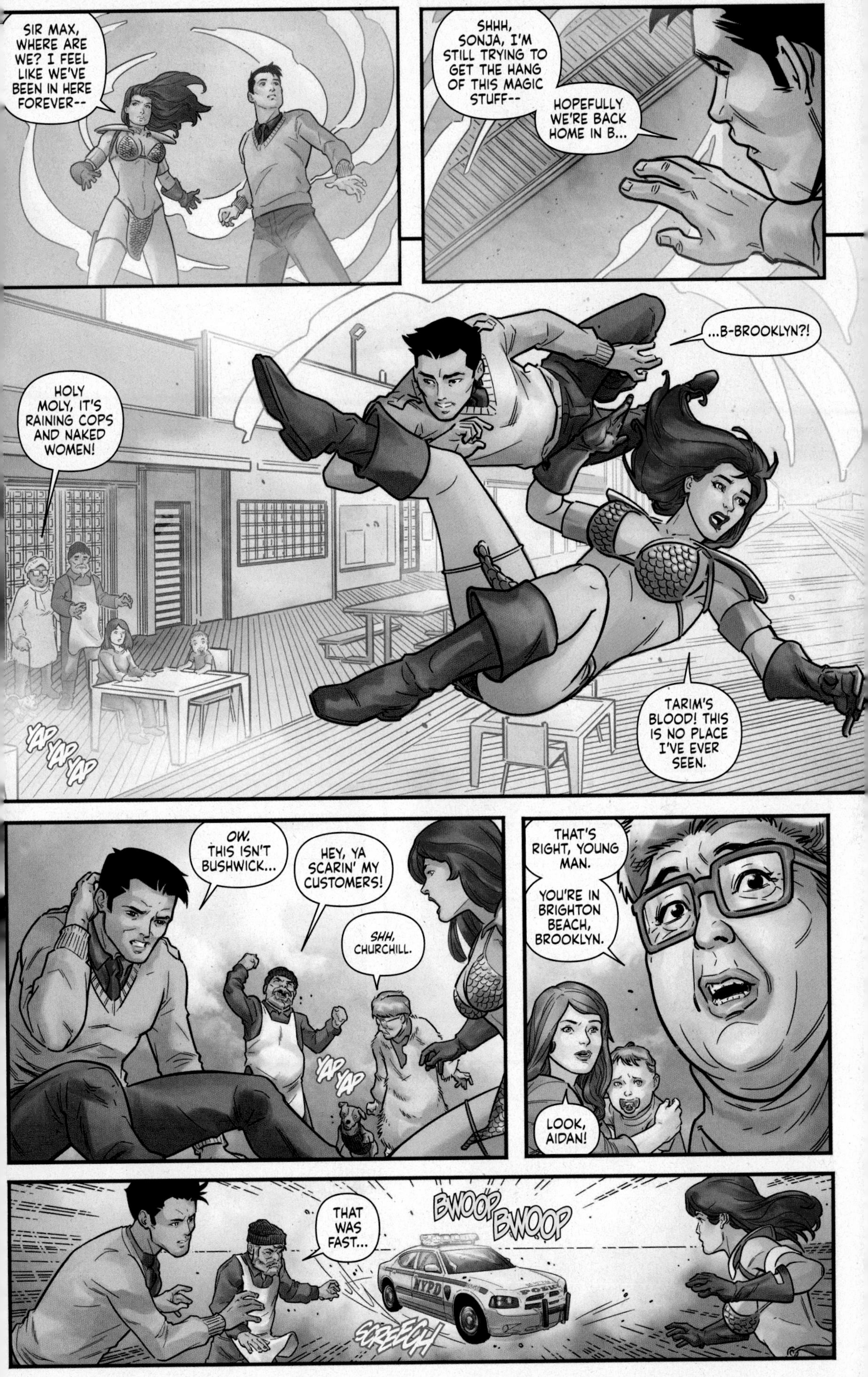
SIR MAX, WHERE ARE WE? I FEEL LIKE WE'VE BEEN IN HERE FOREVER--
SHHH, SONJA, I'M STILL TRYING TO GET THE HANG OF THIS MAGIC STUFF--
HOPEFULLY WE'RE BACK HOME IN B...
...B-BROOKLYN?!
HOLY MOLY, IT'S RAINING COPS AND NAKED WOMEN!
TARIM'S BLOOD! THIS IS NO PLACE I'VE EVER SEEN.
YAP YAP YAP
OW. THIS ISN'T BUSHWICK...
HEY, YA SCARIN' MY CUSTOMERS!
SHH, CHURCHILL.
YAP YAP
THAT'S RIGHT, YOUNG MAN.
YOU'RE IN BRIGHTON BEACH, BROOKLYN.
LOOK, AIDAN!
THAT WAS FAST...
BWOOP BWOOP
NYPD
POLICE
SCREEECH

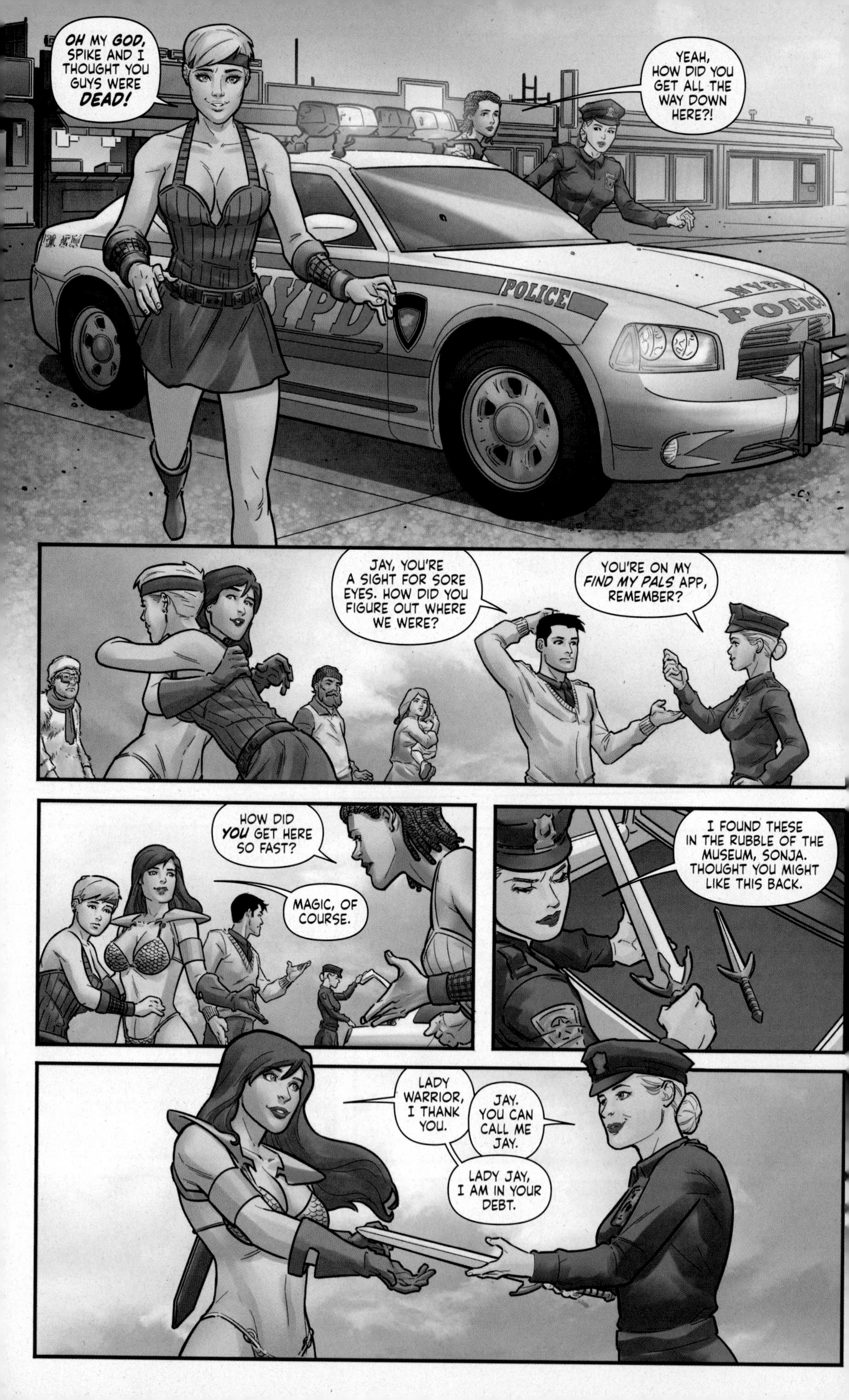
OH MY GOD, SPIKE AND I THOUGHT YOU GUYS WERE DEAD!
YEAH, HOW DID YOU GET ALL THE WAY DOWN HERE?!
POLICE
NYPD
JAY, YOU'RE A SIGHT FOR SORE EYES. HOW DID YOU FIGURE OUT WHERE WE WERE?
YOU'RE ON MY FIND MY PALS APP, REMEMBER?
HOW DID YOU GET HERE SO FAST?
MAGIC, OF COURSE.
I FOUND THESE IN THE RUBBLE OF THE MUSEUM, SONJA. THOUGHT YOU MIGHT LIKE THIS BACK.
LADY WARRIOR, I THANK YOU.
JAY. YOU CAN CALL ME JAY.
LADY JAY, I AM IN YOUR DEBT.

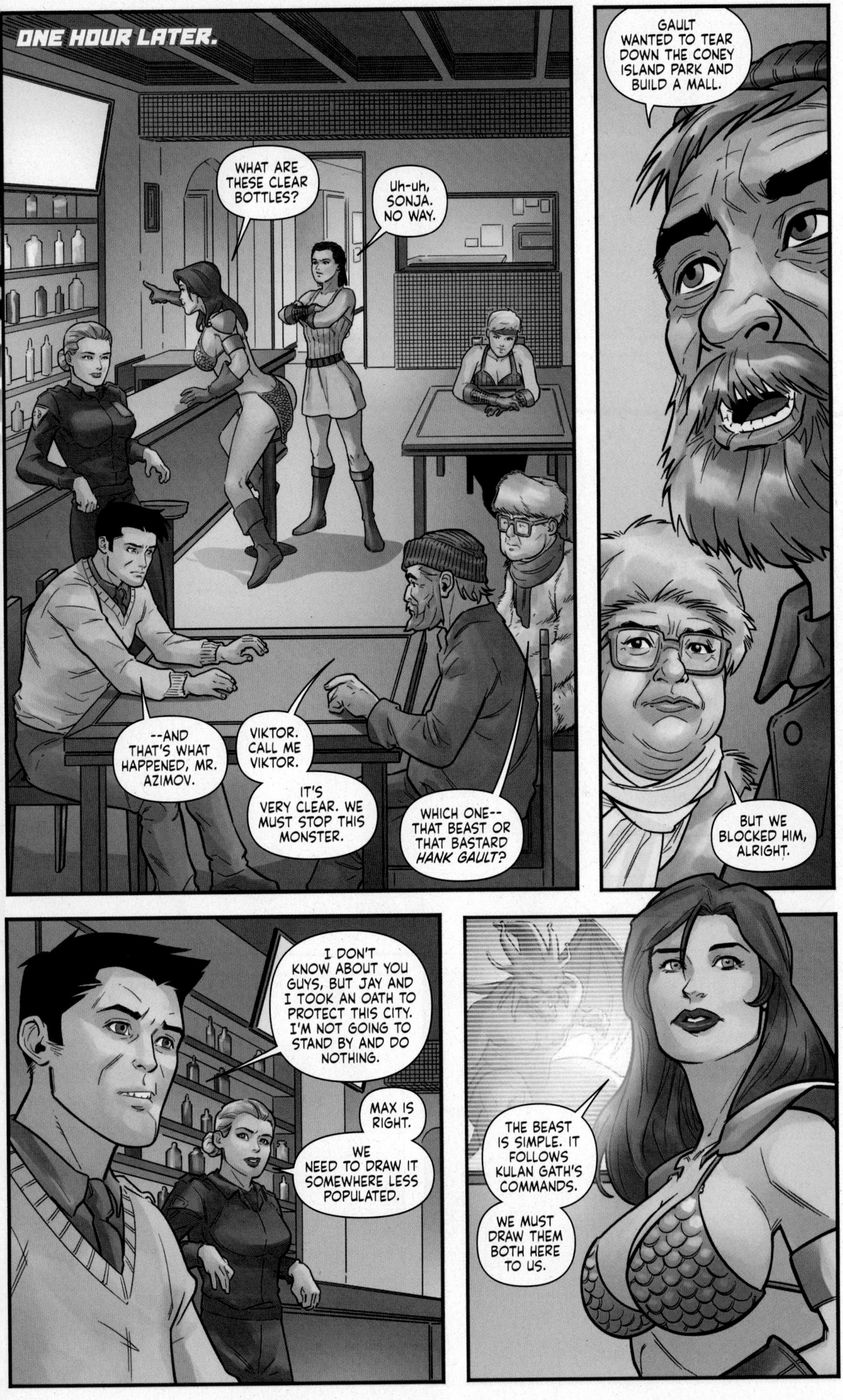
ONE HOUR LATER.
WHAT ARE THESE CLEAR BOTTLES?
Uh-uh, SONJA. NO WAY.
--AND THAT'S WHAT HAPPENED, MR. AZIMOV.
VIKTOR. CALL ME VIKTOR.
IT'S VERY CLEAR. WE MUST STOP THIS MONSTER.
WHICH ONE-- THAT BEAST OR THAT BASTARD *HANK GAULT?*
GAULT WANTED TO TEAR DOWN THE CONEY ISLAND PARK AND BUILD A MALL.
BUT WE BLOCKED HIM, ALRIGHT.
I DON'T KNOW ABOUT YOU GUYS, BUT JAY AND I TOOK AN OATH TO PROTECT THIS CITY. I'M NOT GOING TO STAND BY AND DO NOTHING.
MAX IS RIGHT.
WE NEED TO DRAW IT SOMEWHERE LESS POPULATED.
THE BEAST IS SIMPLE. IT FOLLOWS KULAN GATH'S COMMANDS.
WE MUST DRAW THEM BOTH HERE TO US.

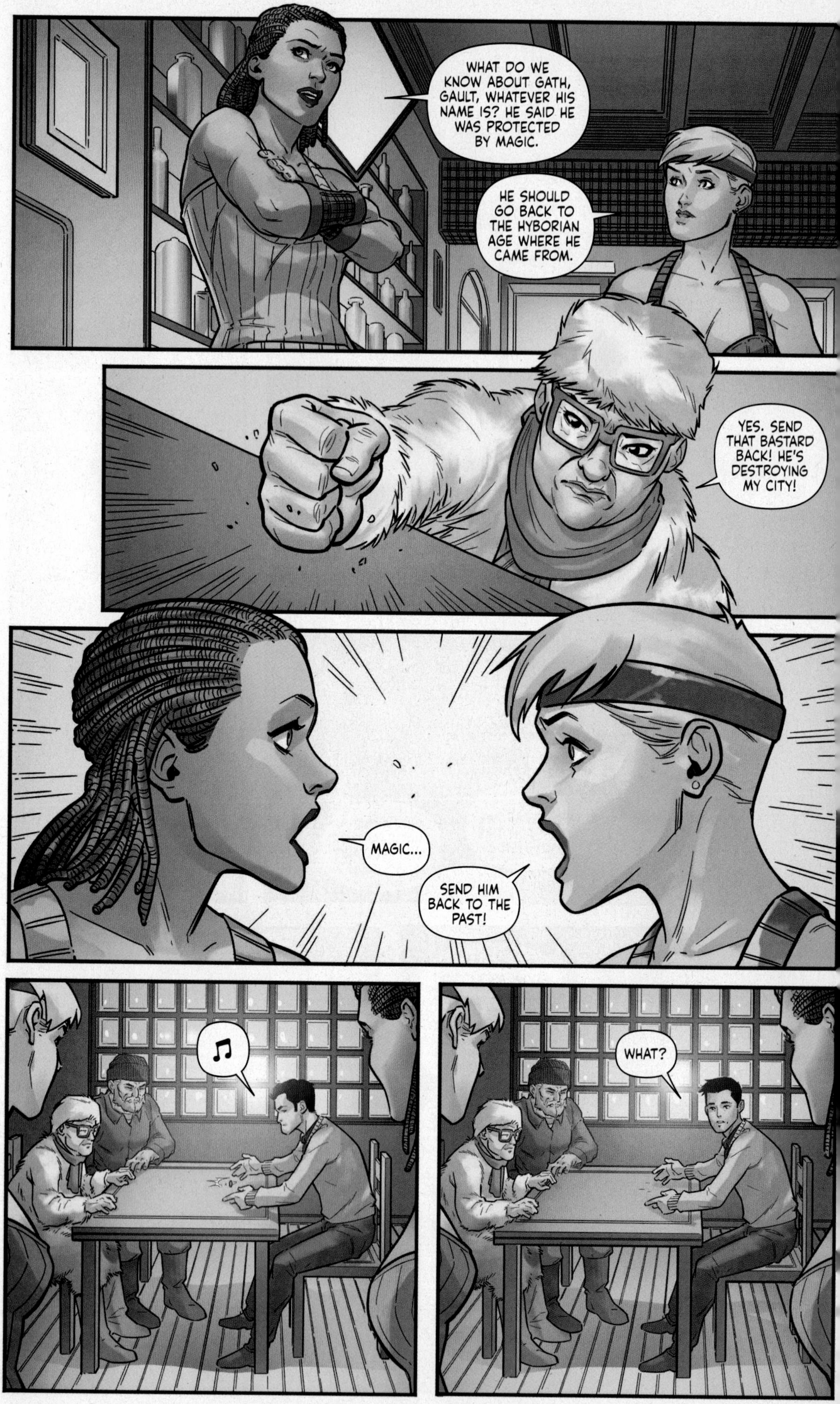
WHAT DO WE KNOW ABOUT GATH, GAULT, WHATEVER HIS NAME IS? HE SAID HE WAS PROTECTED BY MAGIC.
HE SHOULD GO BACK TO THE HYBORIAN AGE WHERE HE CAME FROM.
YES. SEND THAT BASTARD BACK! HE'S DESTROYING MY CITY!
MAGIC...
SEND HIM BACK TO THE PAST!
♫
WHAT?

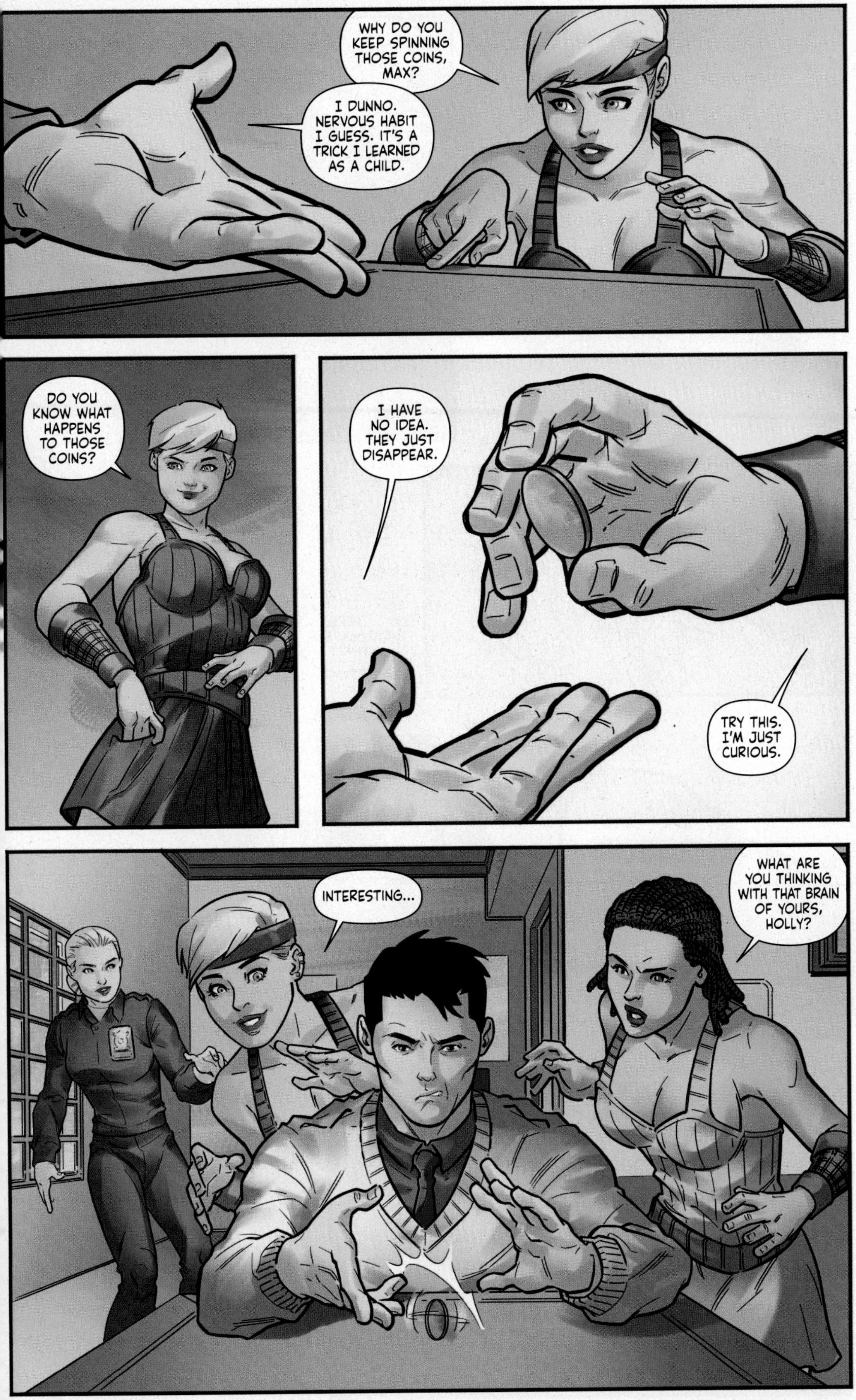
WHY DO YOU KEEP SPINNING THOSE COINS, MAX?
I DUNNO. NERVOUS HABIT I GUESS. IT'S A TRICK I LEARNED AS A CHILD.
DO YOU KNOW WHAT HAPPENS TO THOSE COINS?
I HAVE NO IDEA. THEY JUST DISAPPEAR.
TRY THIS. I'M JUST CURIOUS.
INTERESTING...
WHAT ARE YOU THINKING WITH THAT BRAIN OF YOURS, HOLLY?

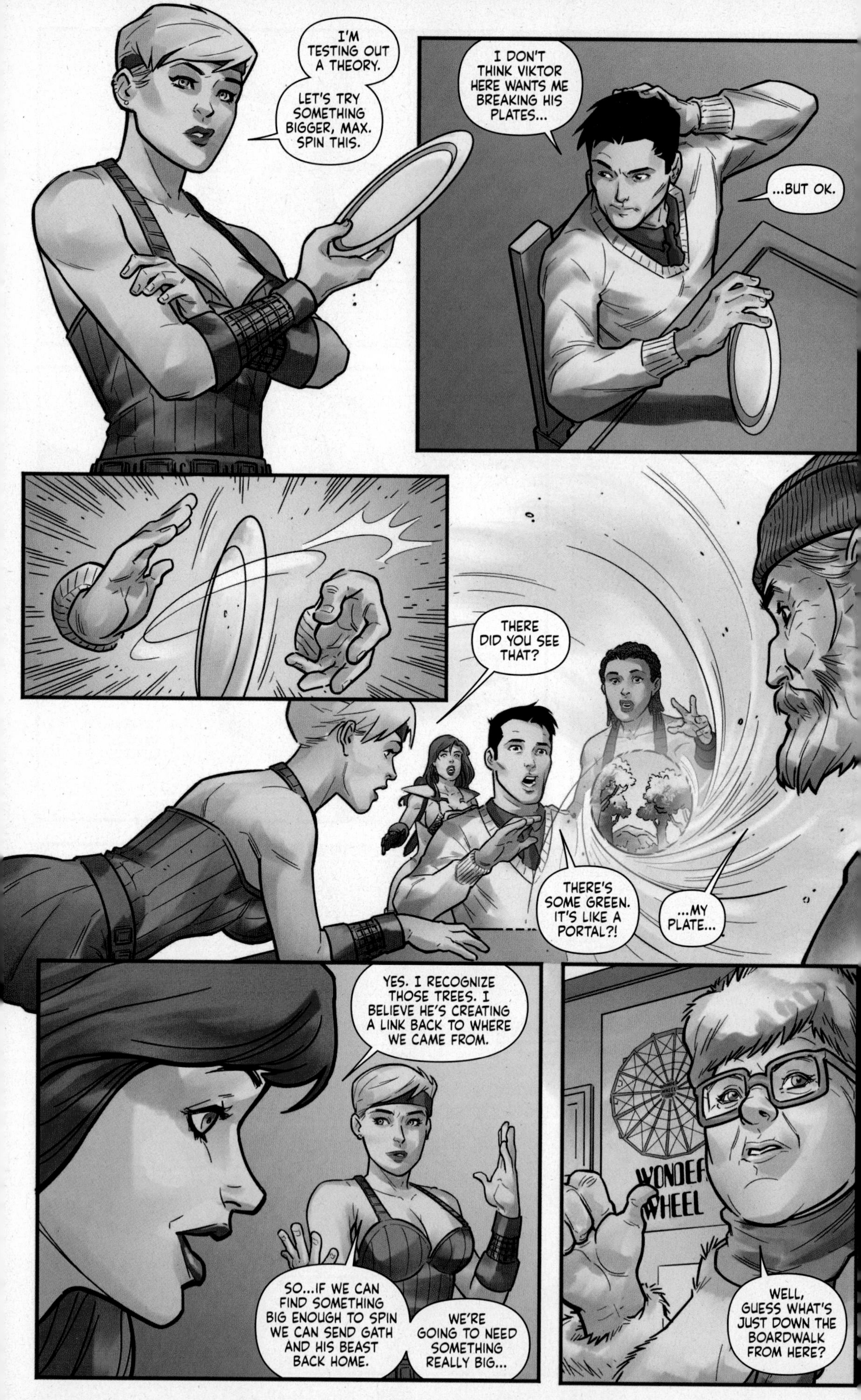
I'M TESTING OUT A THEORY.
LET'S TRY SOMETHING BIGGER, MAX. SPIN THIS.
I DON'T THINK VIKTOR HERE WANTS ME BREAKING HIS PLATES...
...BUT OK.
THERE DID YOU SEE THAT?
THERE'S SOME GREEN. IT'S LIKE A PORTAL?!
...MY PLATE...
YES. I RECOGNIZE THOSE TREES. I BELIEVE HE'S CREATING A LINK BACK TO WHERE WE CAME FROM.
SO...IF WE CAN FIND SOMETHING BIG ENOUGH TO SPIN WE CAN SEND GATH AND HIS BEAST BACK HOME.
WE'RE GOING TO NEED SOMETHING REALLY BIG...
WELL, GUESS WHAT'S JUST DOWN THE BOARDWALK FROM HERE?

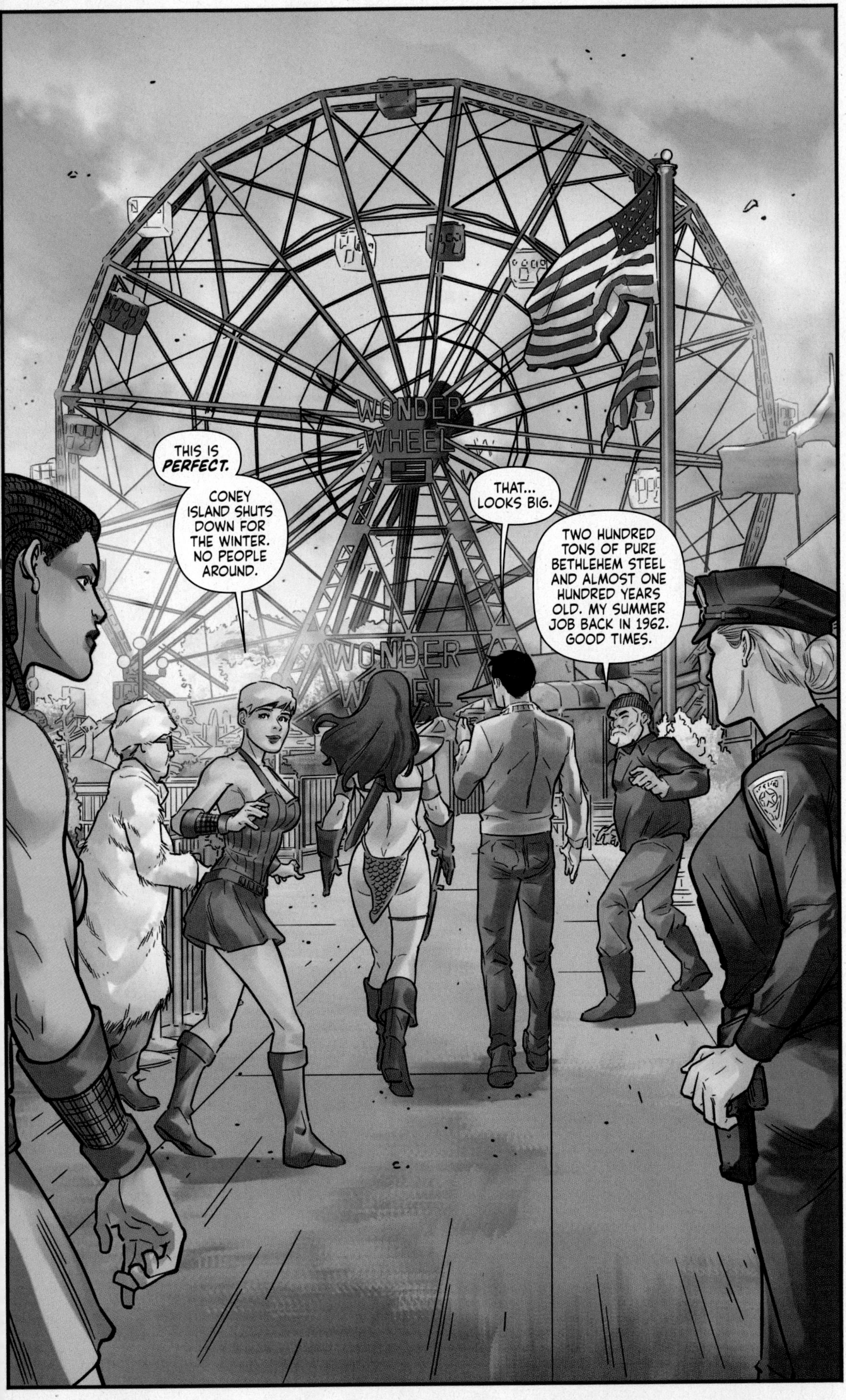

WONDER WHEEL
THIS IS *PERFECT.*
CONEY ISLAND SHUTS DOWN FOR THE WINTER. NO PEOPLE AROUND.
THAT... LOOKS BIG.
TWO HUNDRED TONS OF PURE BETHLEHEM STEEL AND ALMOST ONE HUNDRED YEARS OLD. MY SUMMER JOB BACK IN 1962. GOOD TIMES.

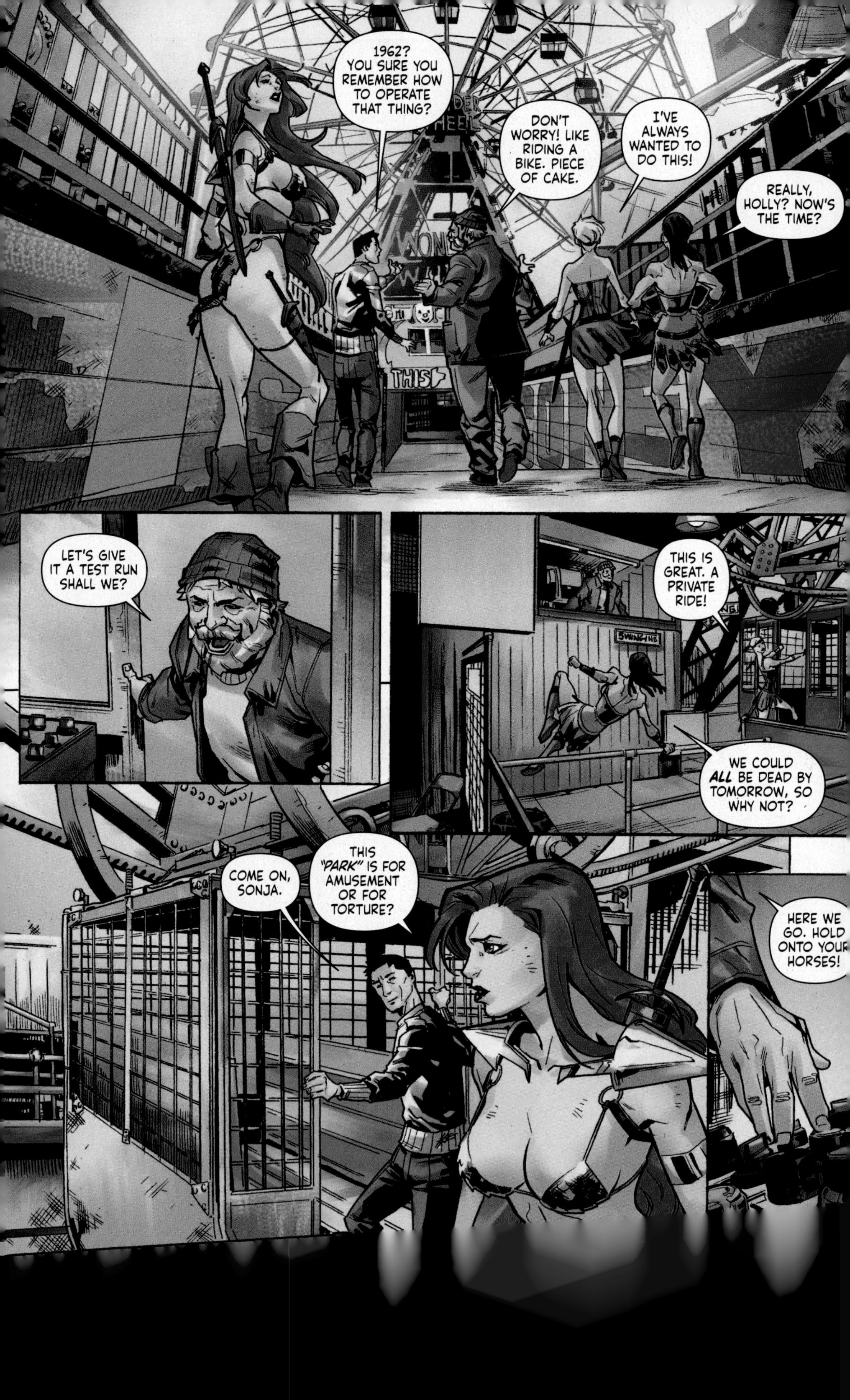
1962? YOU SURE YOU REMEMBER HOW TO OPERATE THAT THING?
DON'T WORRY! LIKE RIDING A BIKE. PIECE OF CAKE.
I'VE ALWAYS WANTED TO DO THIS!
REALLY, HOLLY? NOW'S THE TIME?
THIS
LET'S GIVE IT A TEST RUN SHALL WE?
THIS IS GREAT. A PRIVATE RIDE!
WE COULD ALL BE DEAD BY TOMORROW, SO WHY NOT?
COME ON, SONJA.
THIS "PARK" IS FOR AMUSEMENT OR FOR TORTURE?
HERE WE GO. HOLD ONTO YOUR HORSES!

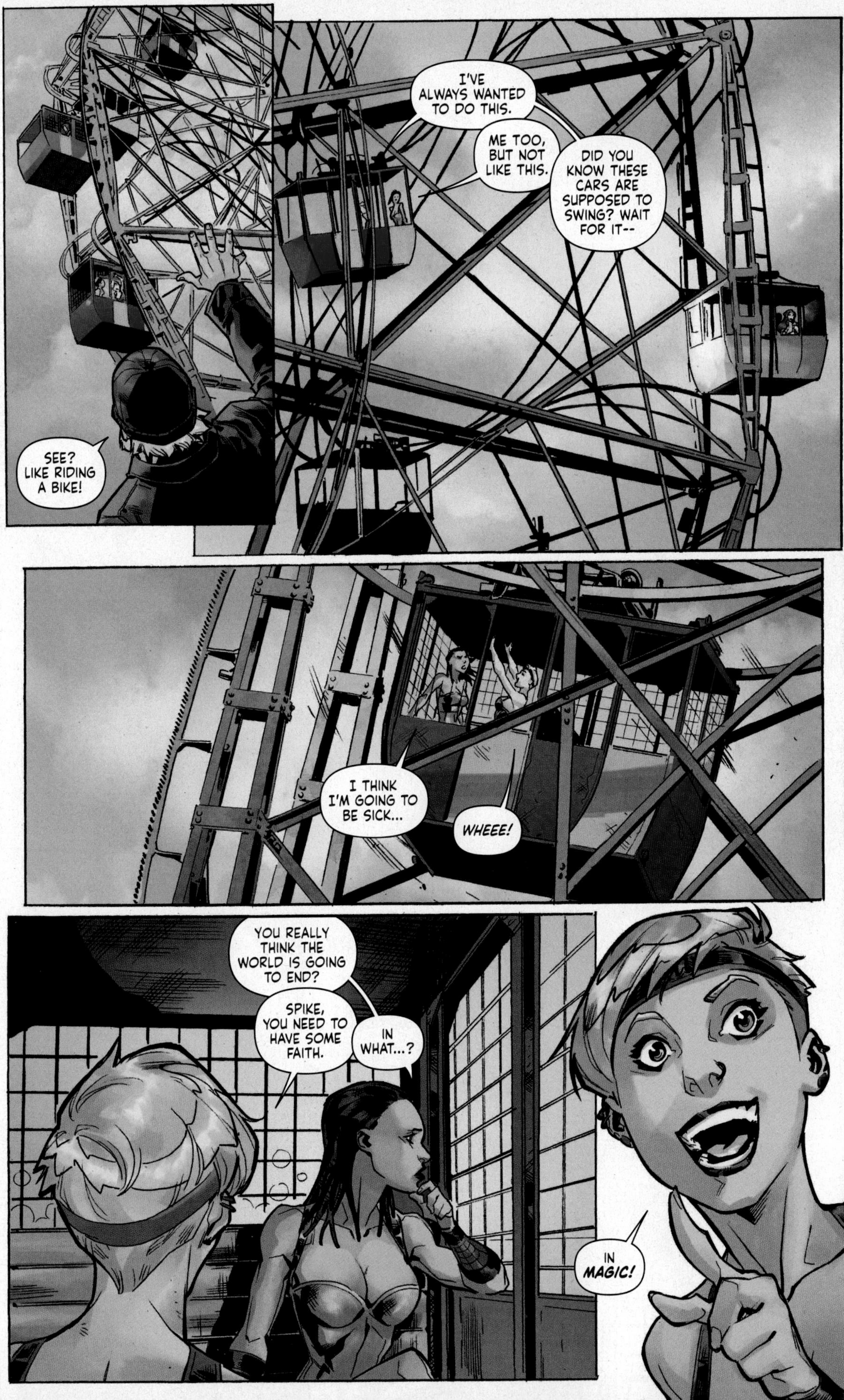
I'VE ALWAYS WANTED TO DO THIS.
ME TOO, BUT NOT LIKE THIS.
DID YOU KNOW THESE CARS ARE SUPPOSED TO SWING? WAIT FOR IT--
SEE? LIKE RIDING A BIKE!
I THINK I'M GOING TO BE SICK...
WHEEE!
YOU REALLY THINK THE WORLD IS GOING TO END?
SPIKE, YOU NEED TO HAVE SOME FAITH.
IN WHAT...?
IN MAGIC!

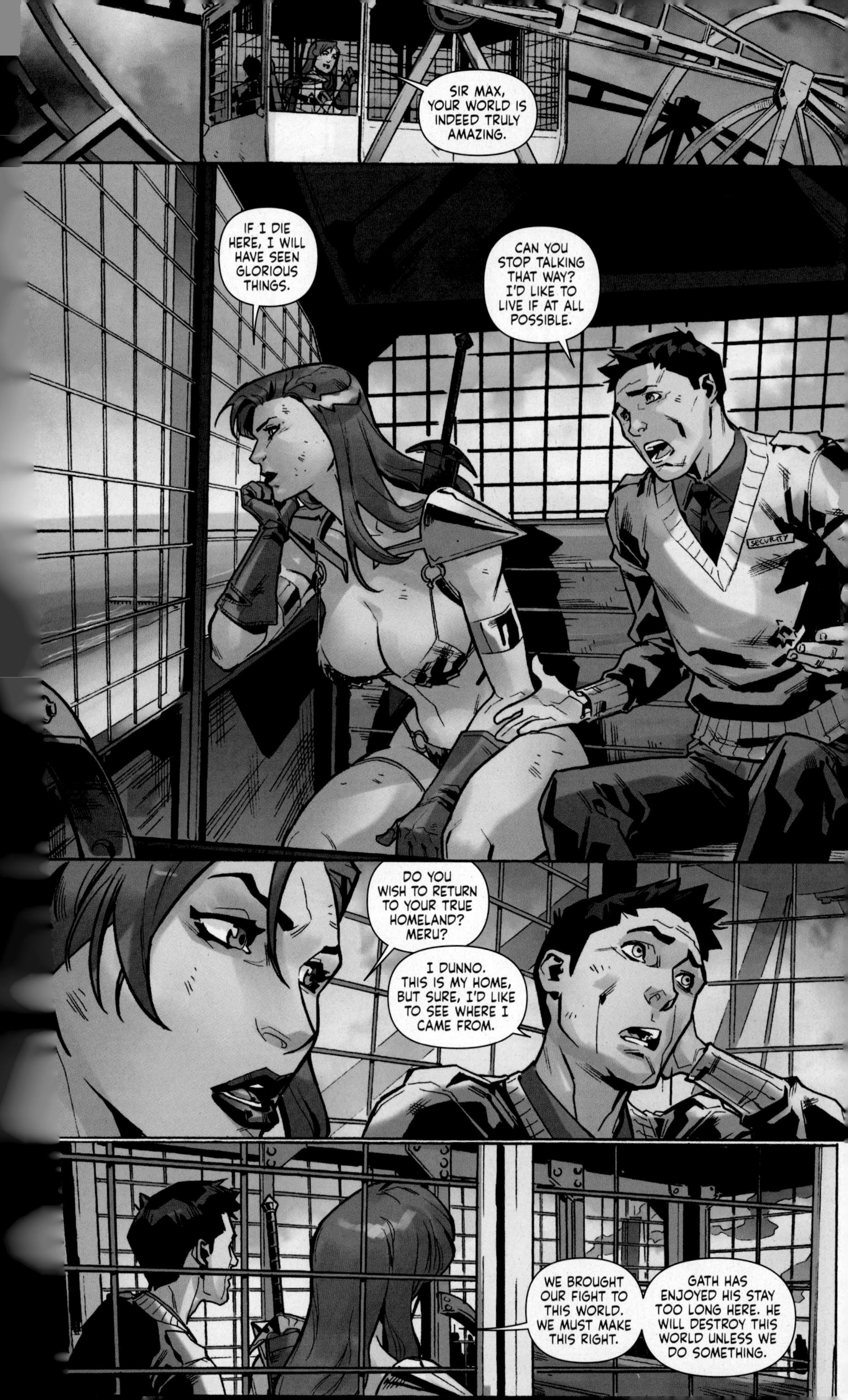
SIR MAX, YOUR WORLD IS INDEED TRULY AMAZING.
IF I DIE HERE, I WILL HAVE SEEN GLORIOUS THINGS.
CAN YOU STOP TALKING THAT WAY? I'D LIKE TO LIVE IF AT ALL POSSIBLE.
SECURITY
DO YOU WISH TO RETURN TO YOUR TRUE HOMELAND? MERU?
I DUNNO. THIS IS MY HOME, BUT SURE, I'D LIKE TO SEE WHERE I CAME FROM.
WE BROUGHT OUR FIGHT TO THIS WORLD. WE MUST MAKE THIS RIGHT.
GATH HAS ENJOYED HIS STAY TOO LONG HERE. HE WILL DESTROY THIS WORLD UNLESS WE DO SOMETHING.

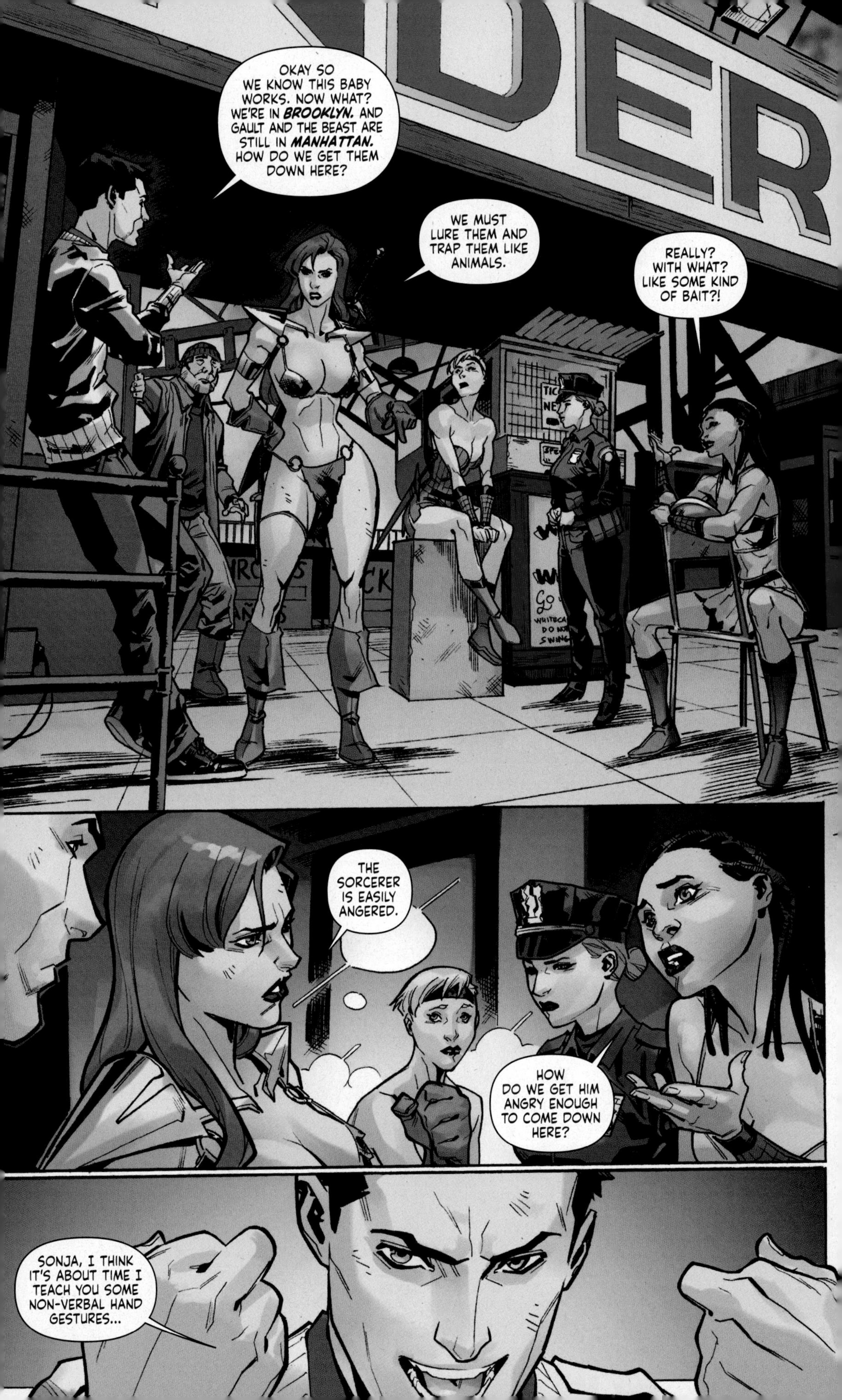
OKAY SO WE KNOW THIS BABY WORKS. NOW WHAT? WE'RE IN ***BROOKLYN.*** AND GAULT AND THE BEAST ARE STILL IN ***MANHATTAN.*** HOW DO WE GET THEM DOWN HERE?
WE MUST LURE THEM AND TRAP THEM LIKE ANIMALS.
REALLY? WITH WHAT? LIKE SOME KIND OF BAIT?!
THE SORCERER IS EASILY ANGERED.
HOW DO WE GET HIM ANGRY ENOUGH TO COME DOWN HERE?
SONJA, I THINK IT'S ABOUT TIME I TEACH YOU SOME NON-VERBAL HAND GESTURES...

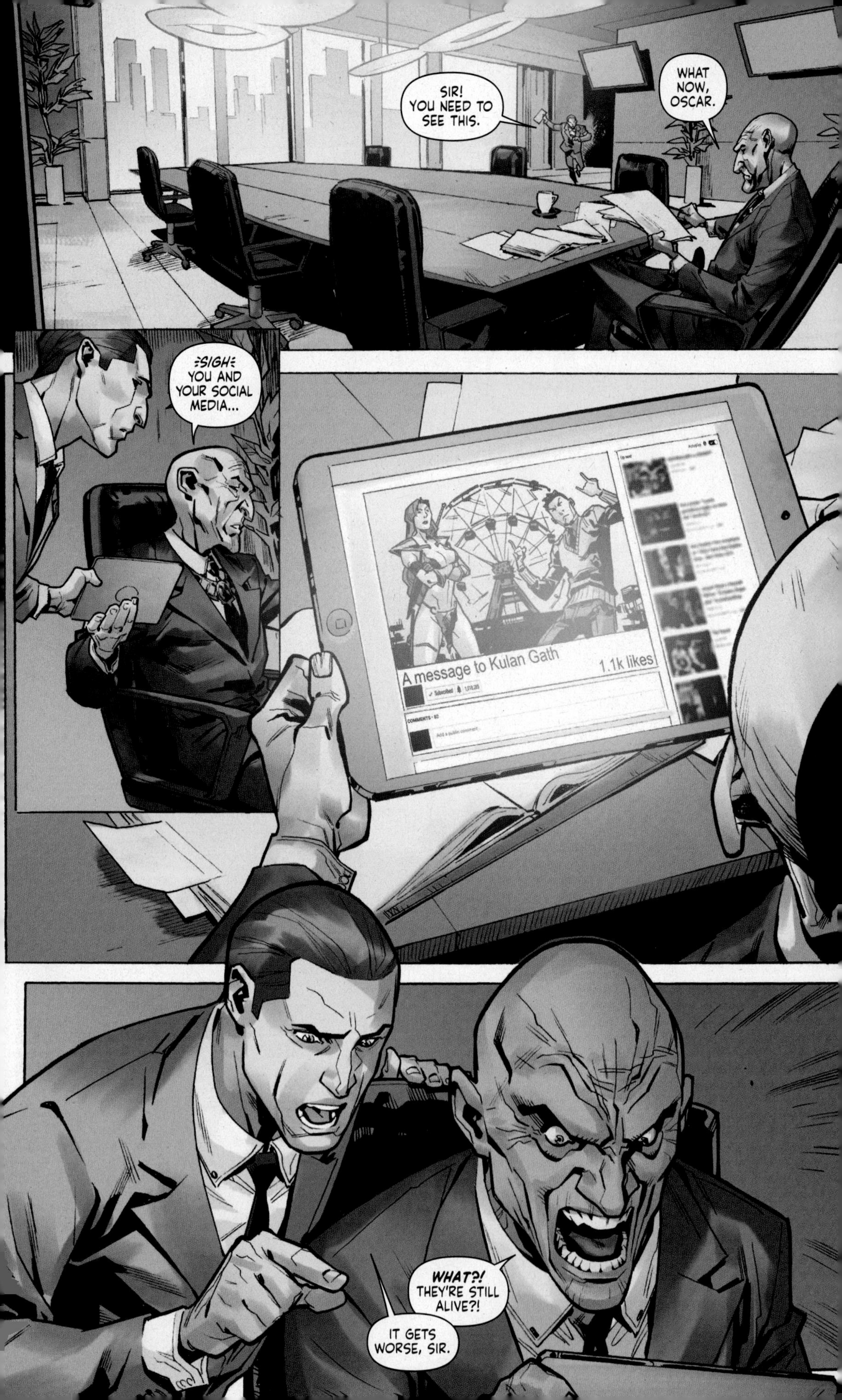

SIR! YOU NEED TO SEE THIS.
WHAT NOW, OSCAR.
SIGH
YOU AND YOUR SOCIAL MEDIA...
A message to Kulan Gath
1.1k likes
WHAT?! THEY'RE STILL ALIVE?!
IT GETS WORSE, SIR.

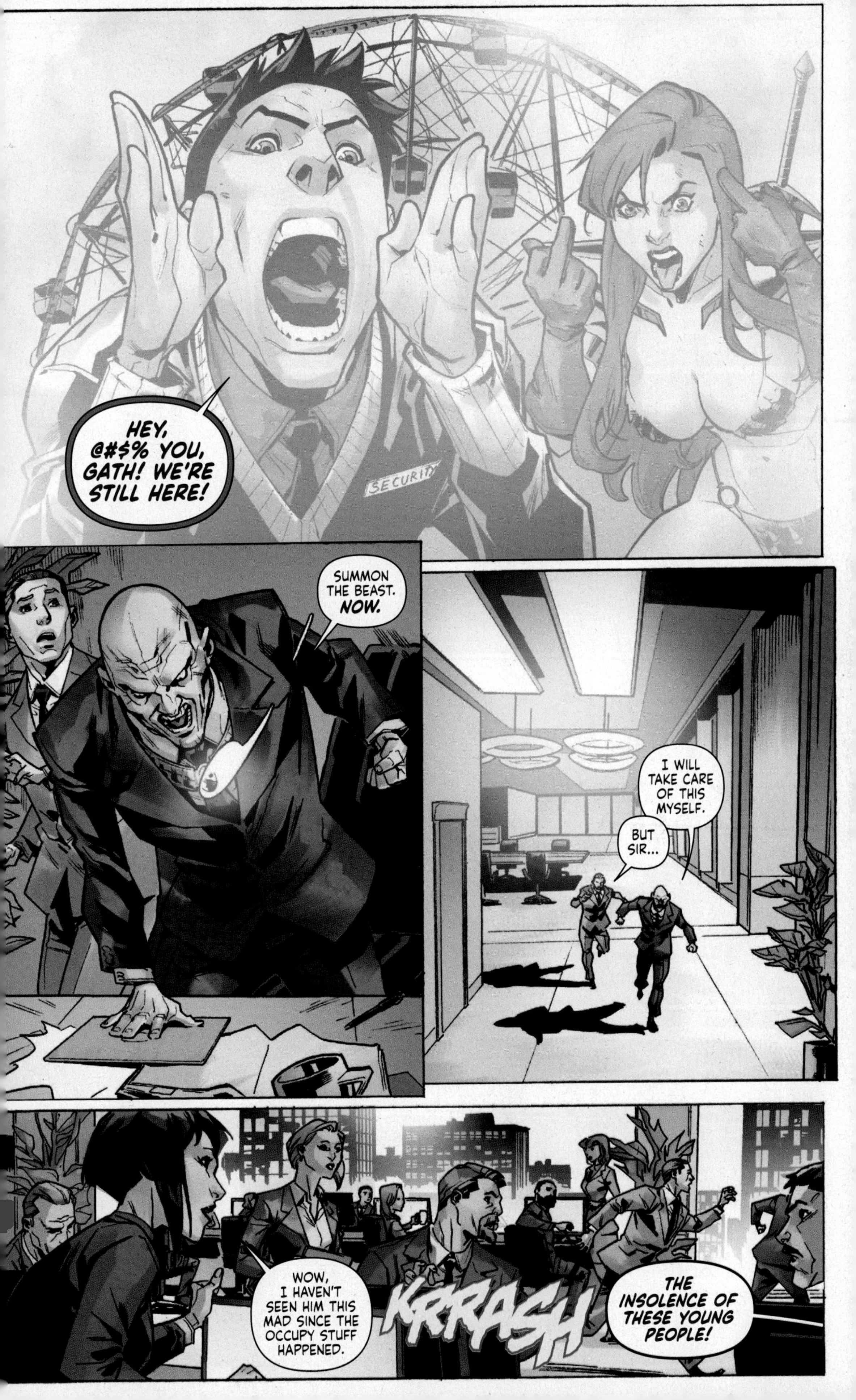
HEY, @#$% YOU, GATH! WE'RE STILL HERE!
SECURITY
SUMMON THE BEAST. NOW.
I WILL TAKE CARE OF THIS MYSELF.
BUT SIR...
WOW, I HAVEN'T SEEN HIM THIS MAD SINCE THE OCCUPY STUFF HAPPENED.
KRRASH
THE INSOLENCE OF THESE YOUNG PEOPLE!

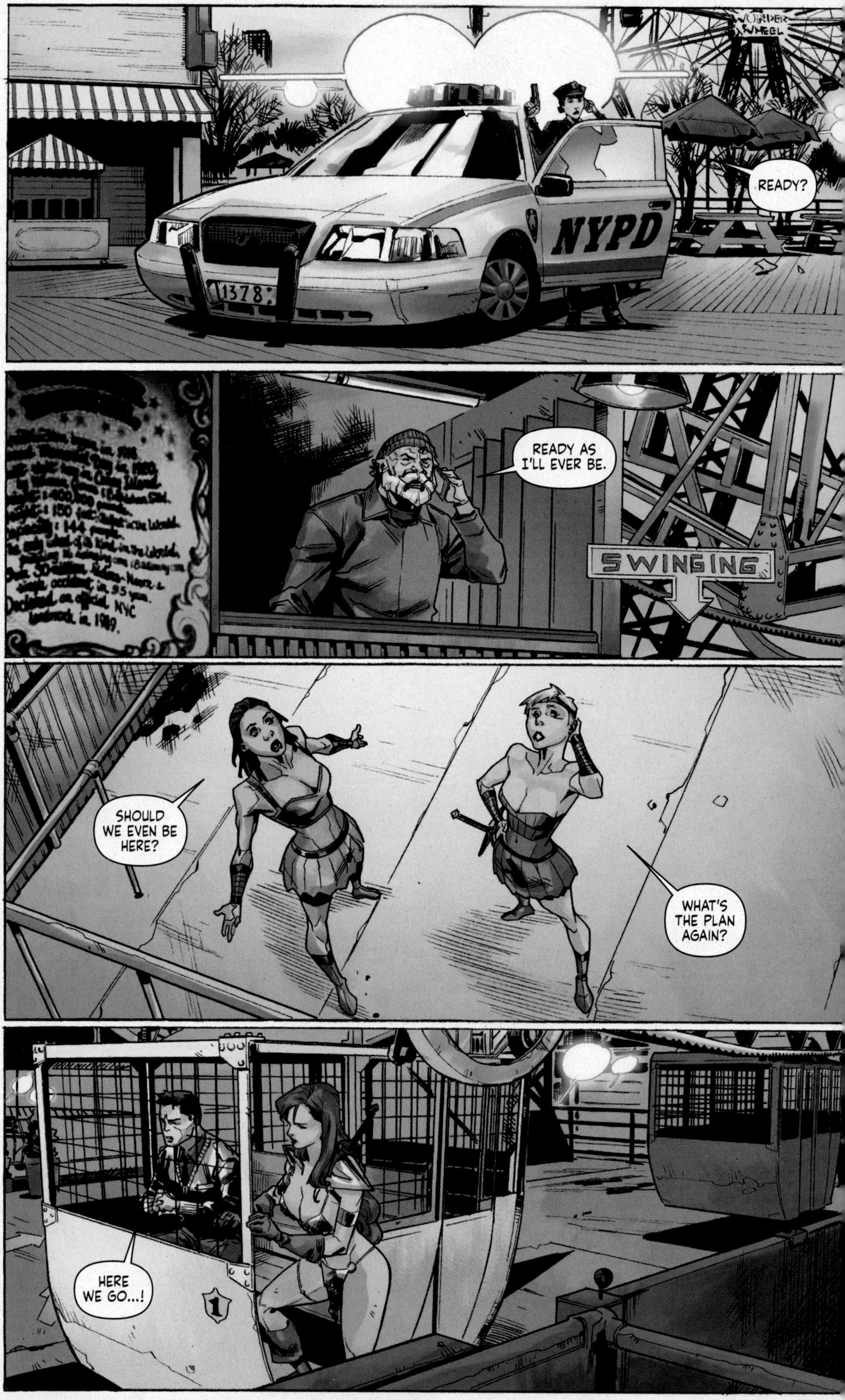
WONDER WHEEL
NYPD
1378
READY?
READY AS I'LL EVER BE.
SWINGING
SHOULD WE EVEN BE HERE?
WHAT'S THE PLAN AGAIN?
HERE WE GO...!
1

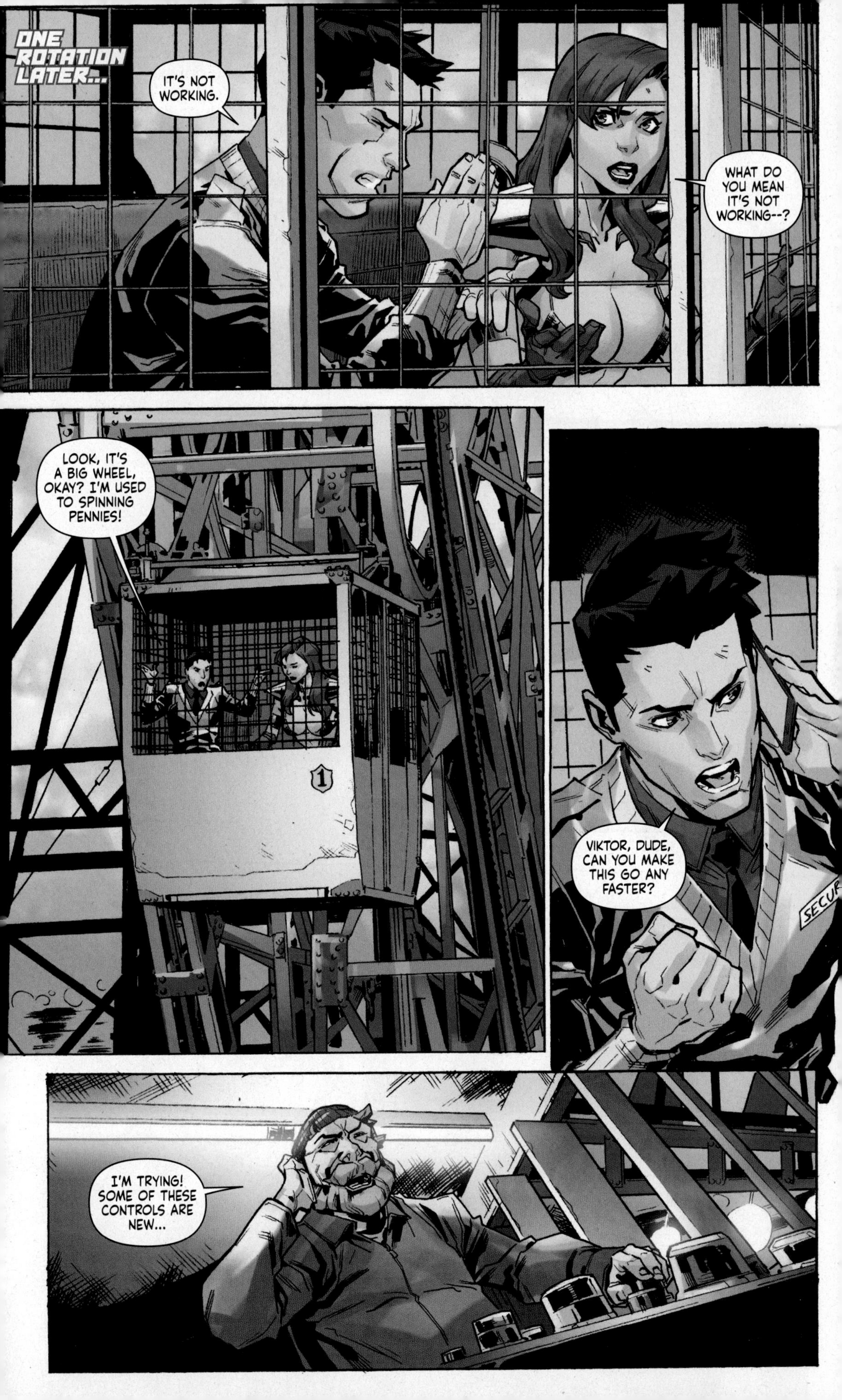
ONE ROTATION LATER...
IT'S NOT WORKING.
WHAT DO YOU MEAN IT'S NOT WORKING--?
LOOK, IT'S A BIG WHEEL, OKAY? I'M USED TO SPINNING PENNIES!
1
VIKTOR, DUDE, CAN YOU MAKE THIS GO ANY FASTER?
SECUR
I'M TRYING! SOME OF THESE CONTROLS ARE NEW...

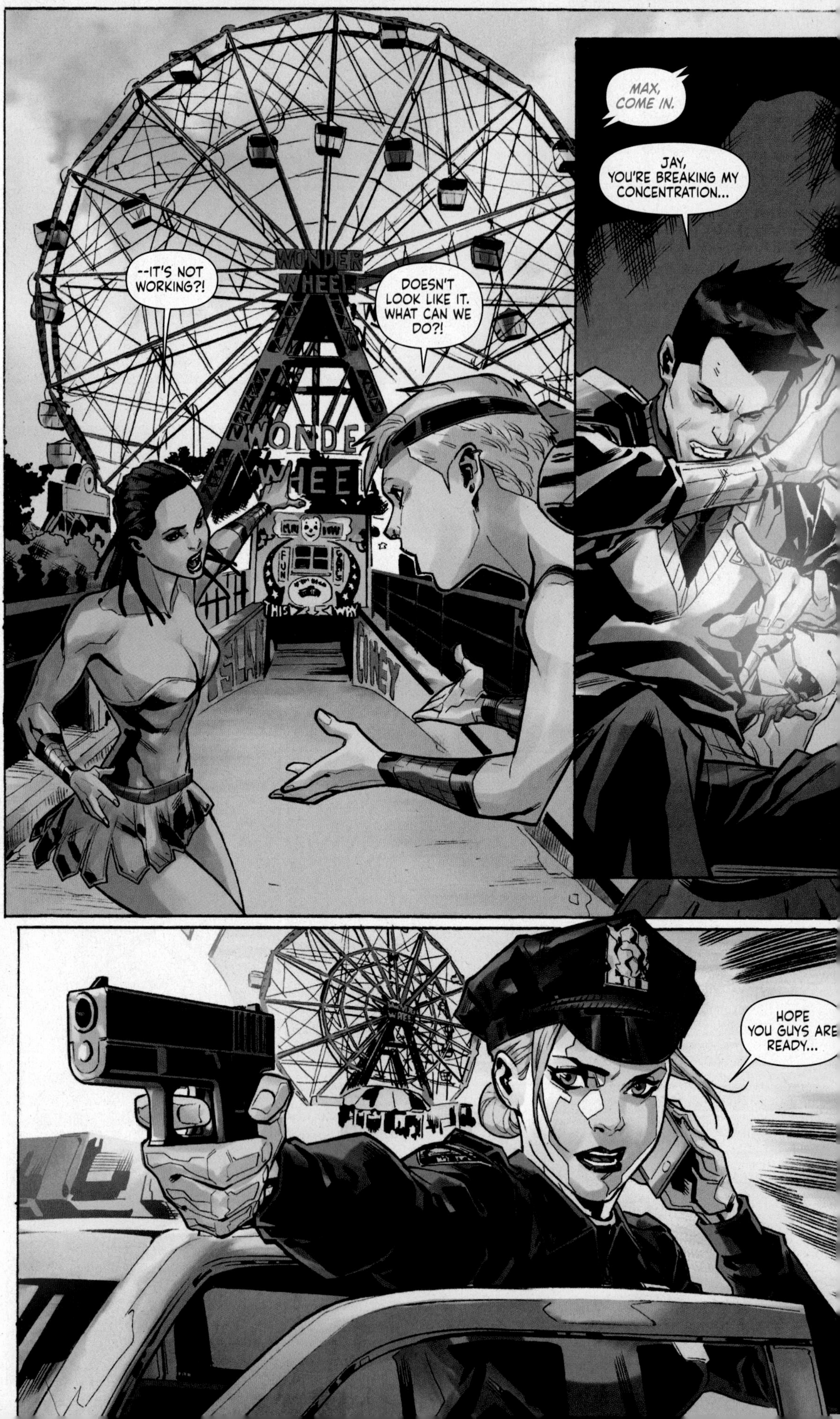
WONDER WHEEL
--IT'S NOT WORKING?!
DOESN'T LOOK LIKE IT. WHAT CAN WE DO?!
MAX, COME IN.
JAY, YOU'RE BREAKING MY CONCENTRATION...
HOPE YOU GUYS ARE READY...

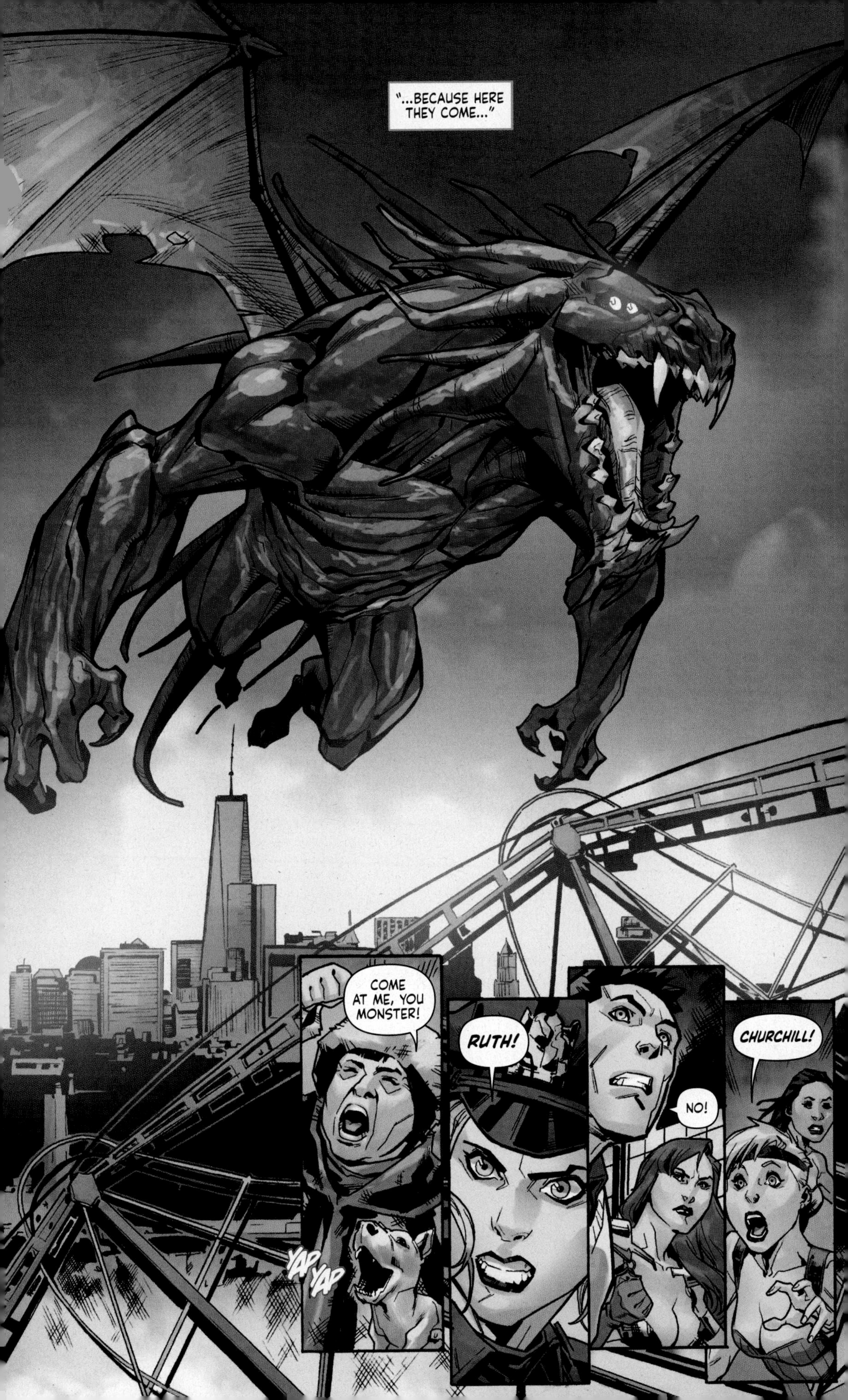
"...BECAUSE HERE THEY COME..."
COME AT ME, YOU MONSTER!
YAP YAP
RUTH!
NO!
CHURCHILL!

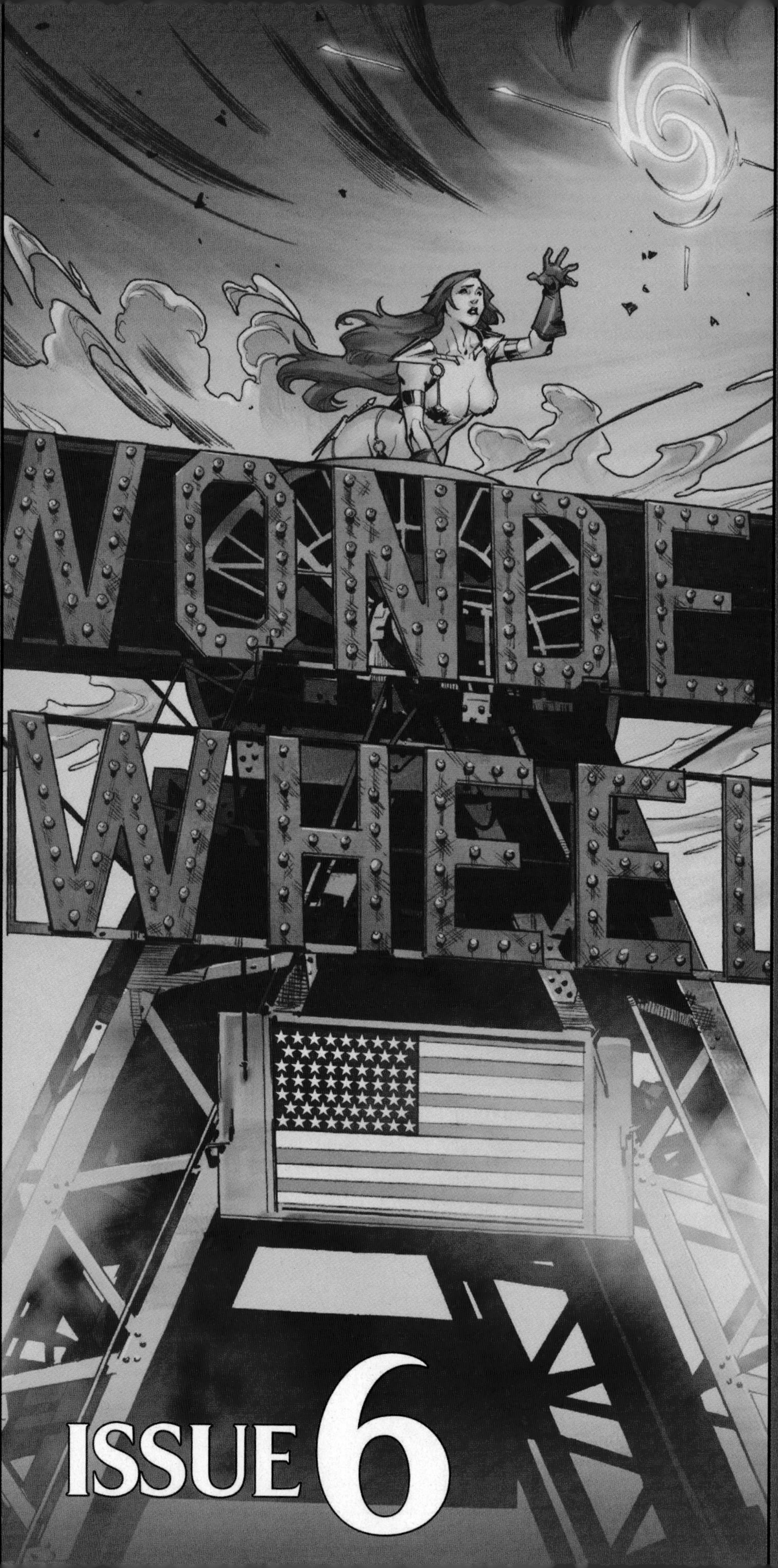
WONDE
WHEE

ISSUE 6

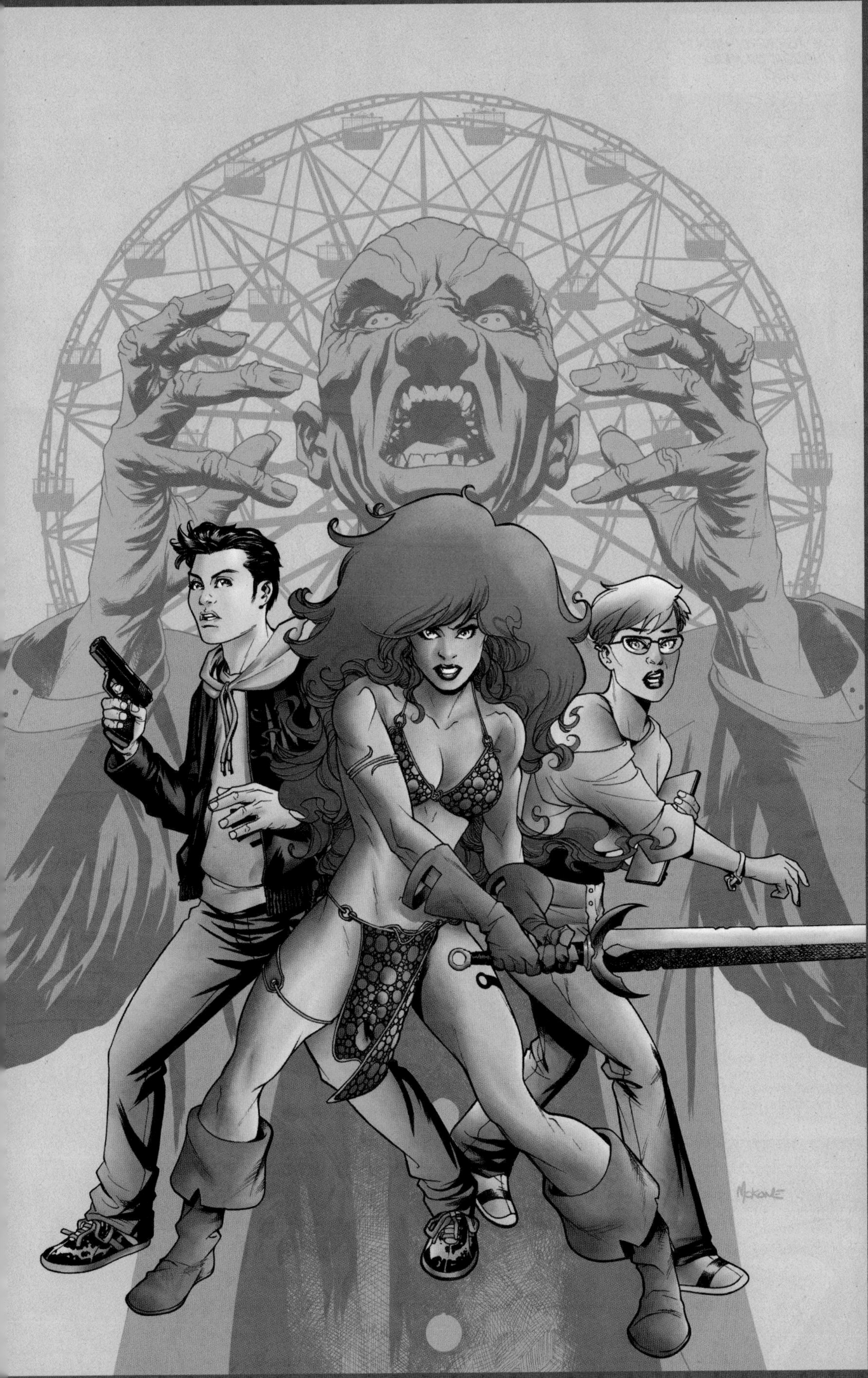
MCKONE

ISSUE #6: COVER ART BY **MIKE MCKONE**

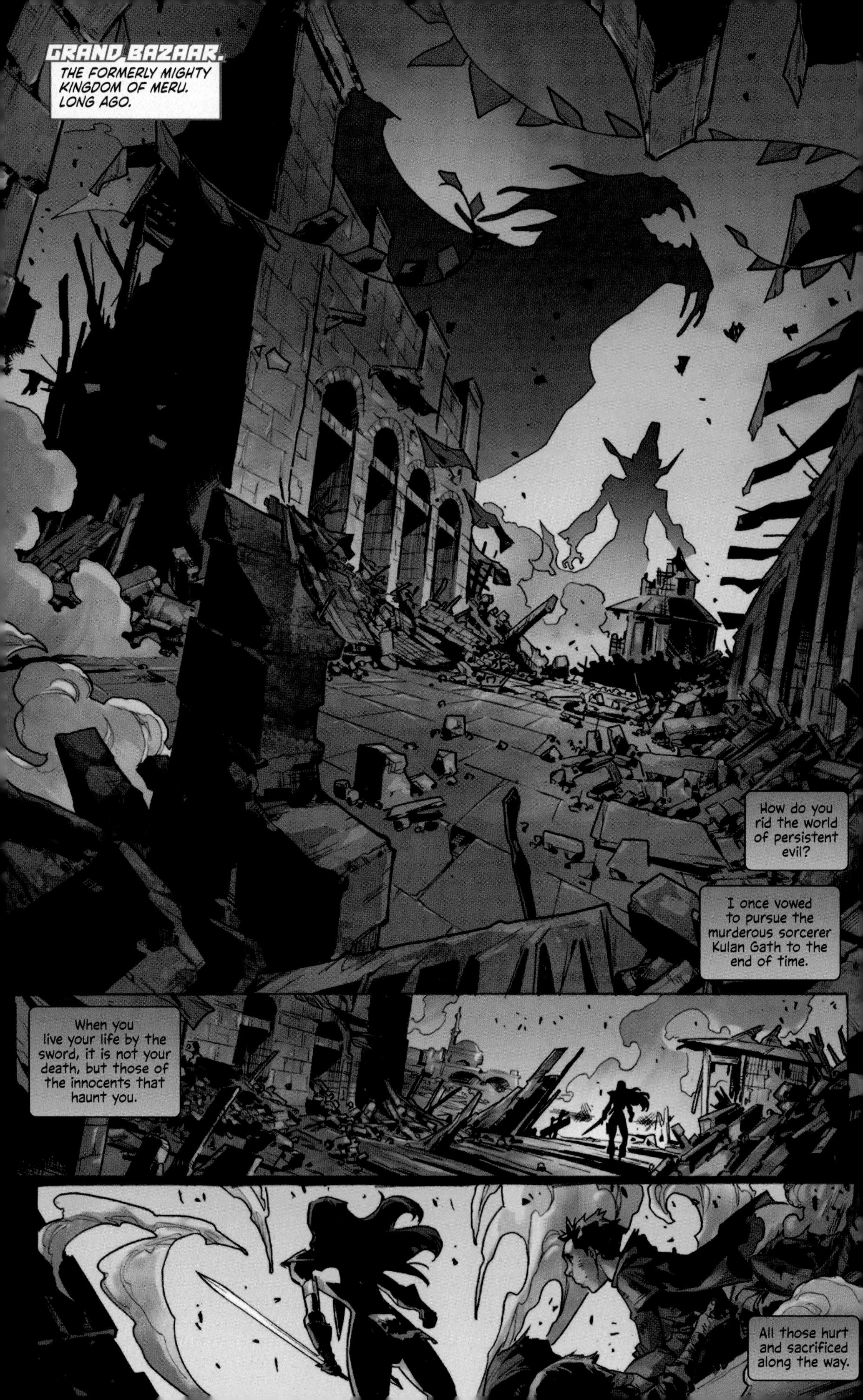
GRAND BAZAAR.
THE FORMERLY MIGHTY KINGDOM OF MERU. LONG AGO.
How do you rid the world of persistent evil?
I once vowed to pursue the murderous sorcerer Kulan Gath to the end of time.
When you live your life by the sword, it is not your death, but those of the innocents that haunt you.
All those hurt and sacrificed along the way.

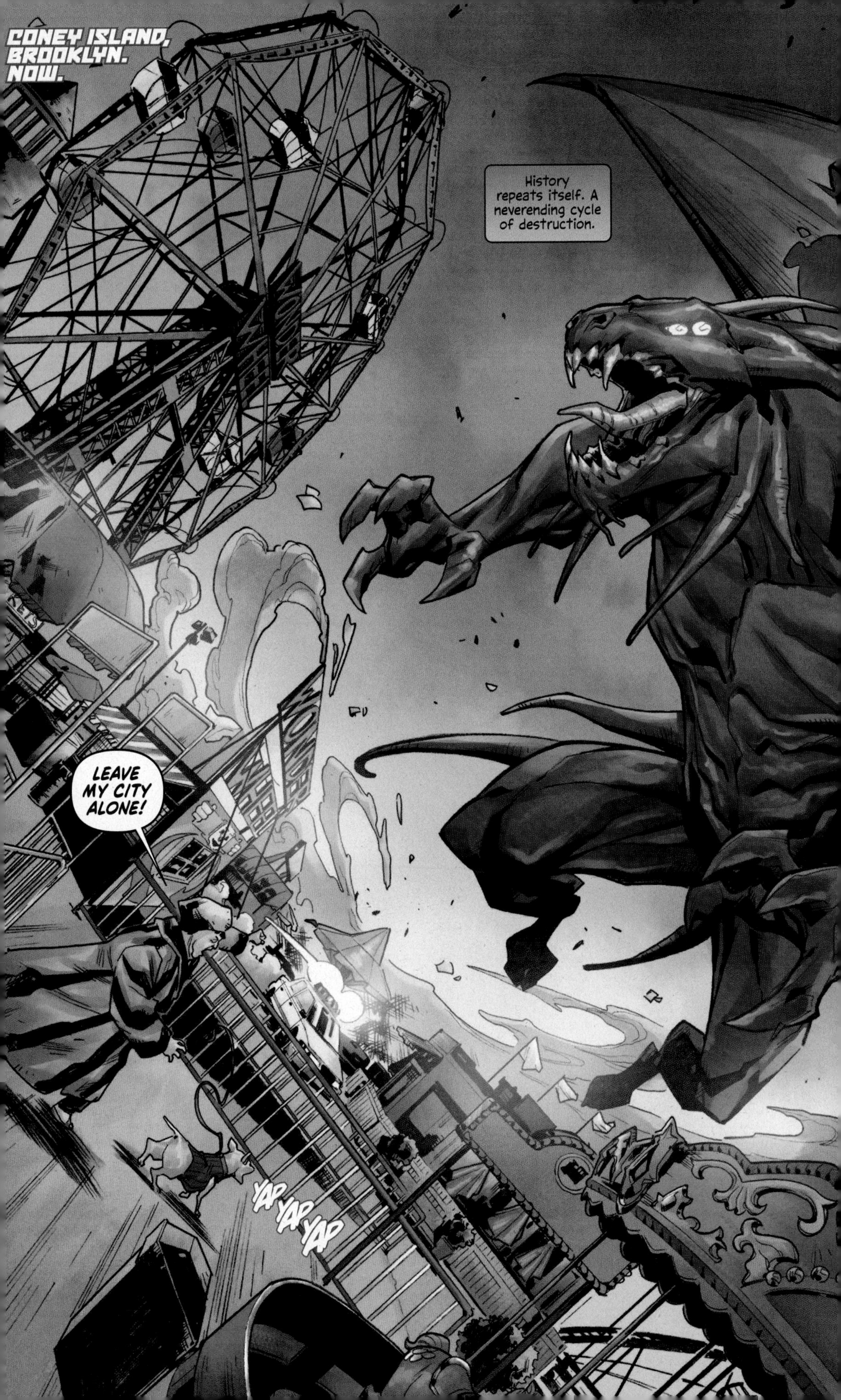
CONEY ISLAND, BROOKLYN. NOW.
History repeats itself. A neverending cycle of destruction.
LEAVE MY CITY ALONE!
YAP YAP YAP

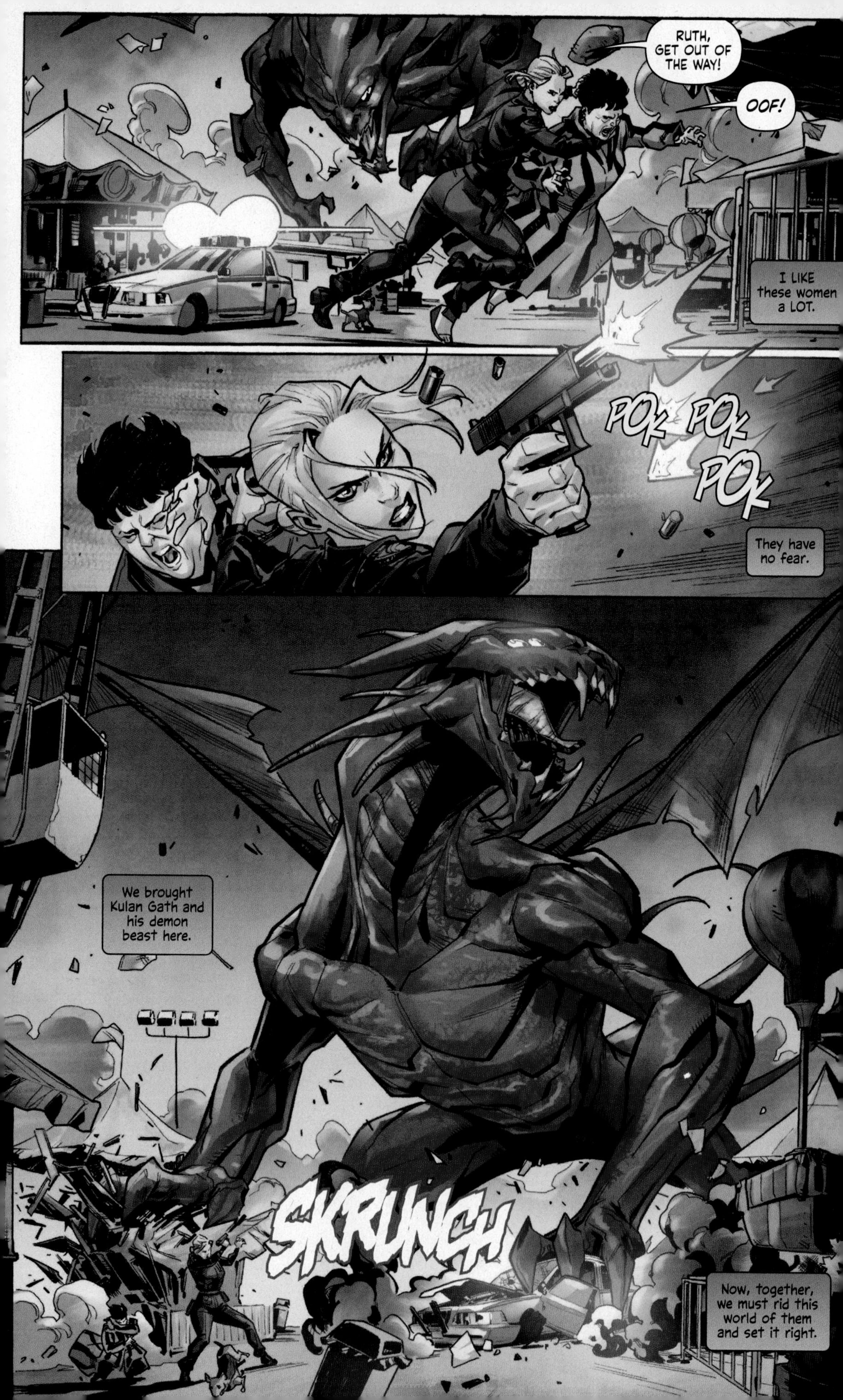

RUTH, GET OUT OF THE WAY!
OOF!
I LIKE these women a LOT.
POK POK POK
They have no fear.
We brought Kulan Gath and his demon beast here.
SKRUNCH
Now, together, we must rid this world of them and set it right.

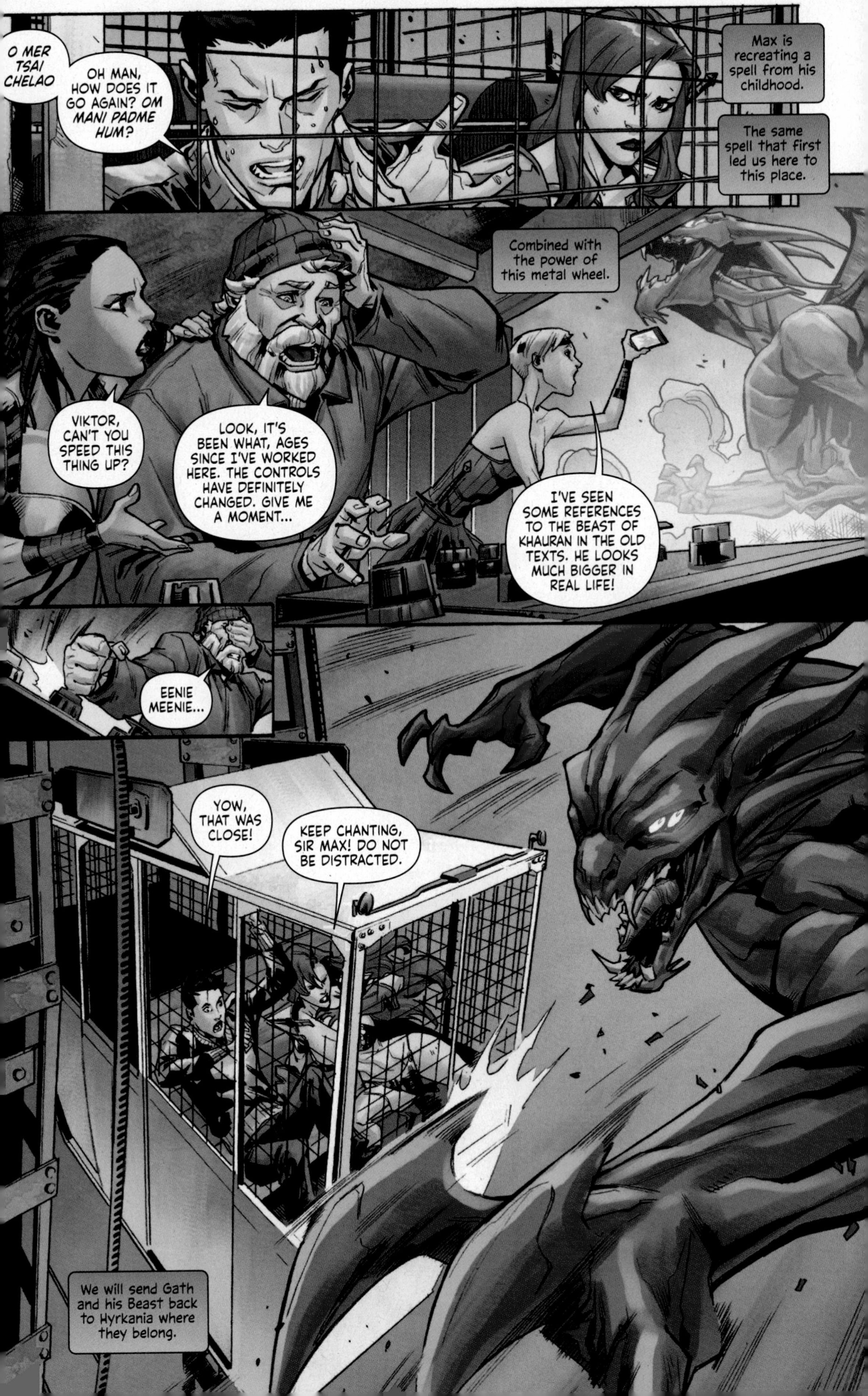
O MER TSAI CHELAO
OH MAN, HOW DOES IT GO AGAIN? OM MANI PADME HUM?
Max is recreating a spell from his childhood.
The same spell that first led us here to this place.
Combined with the power of this metal wheel.
VIKTOR, CAN'T YOU SPEED THIS THING UP?
LOOK, IT'S BEEN WHAT, AGES SINCE I'VE WORKED HERE. THE CONTROLS HAVE DEFINITELY CHANGED. GIVE ME A MOMENT...
I'VE SEEN SOME REFERENCES TO THE BEAST OF KHAURAN IN THE OLD TEXTS. HE LOOKS MUCH BIGGER IN REAL LIFE!
EENIE MEENIE...
YOW, THAT WAS CLOSE!
KEEP CHANTING, SIR MAX! DO NOT BE DISTRACTED.
We will send Gath and his Beast back to Hyrkania where they belong.

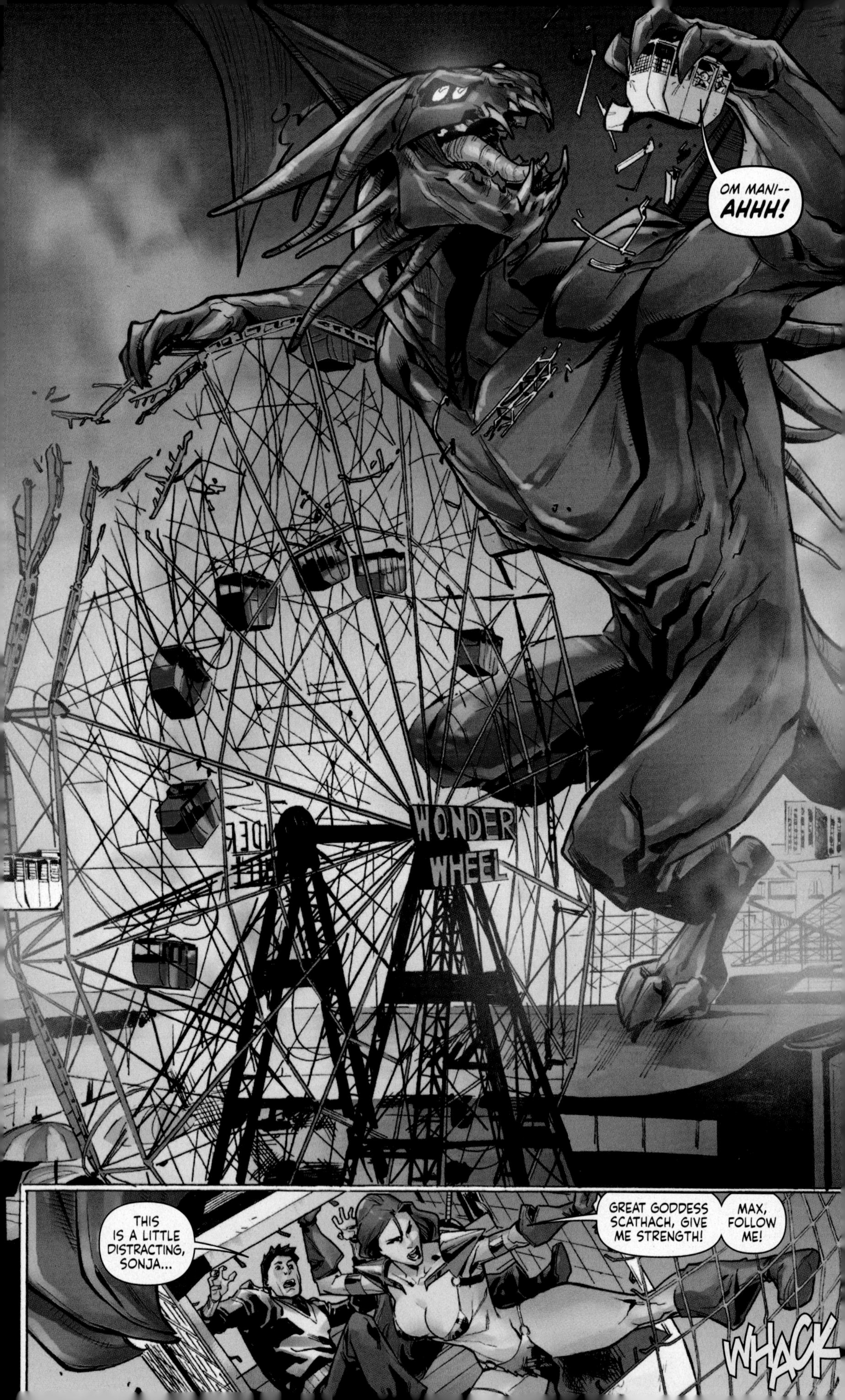
OM MANI--
AHHH!
WONDER
WHEEL
THIS IS A LITTLE DISTRACTING, SONJA...
GREAT GODDESS SCATHACH, GIVE ME STRENGTH!
MAX, FOLLOW ME!
WHACK

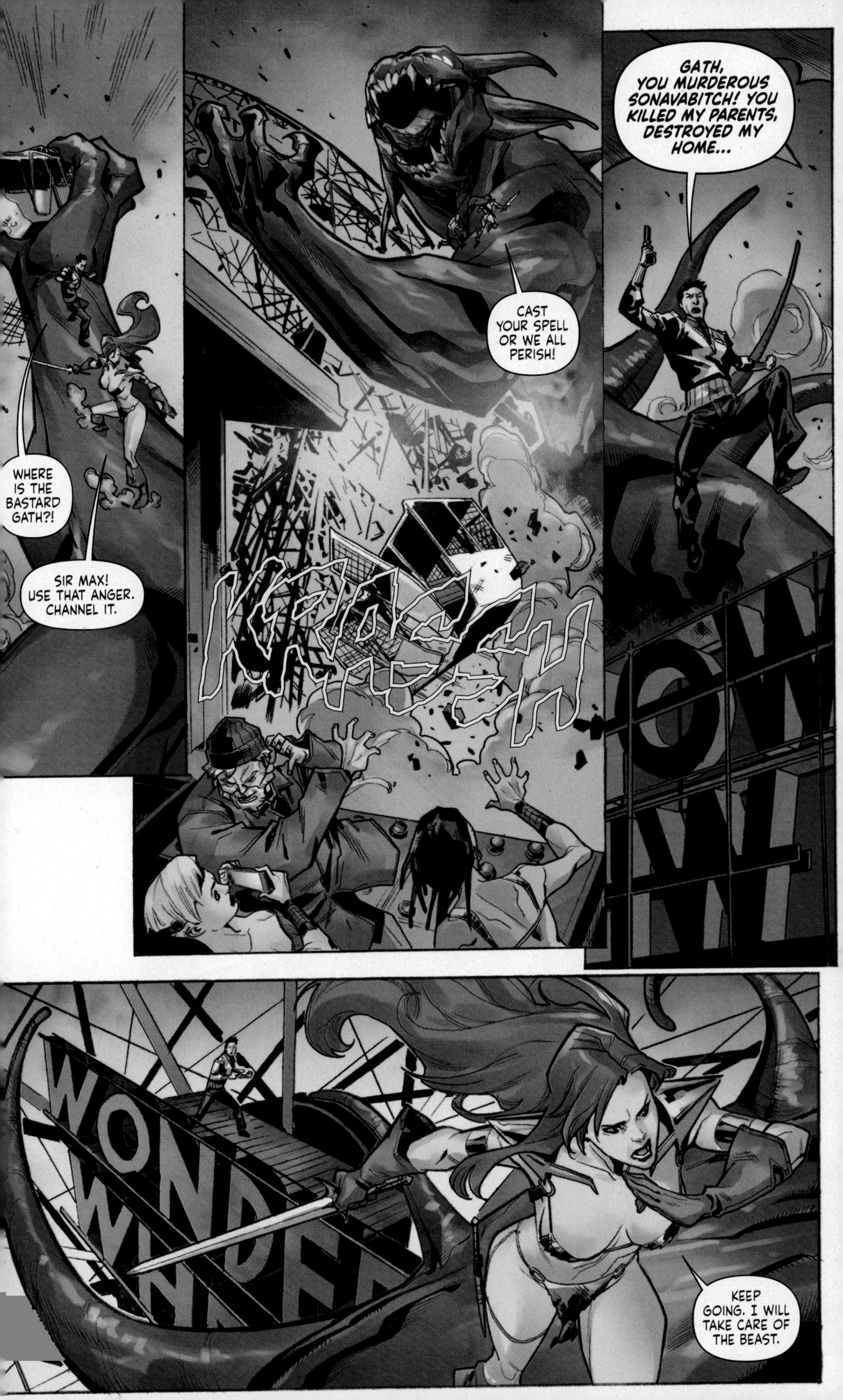
WHERE IS THE BASTARD GATH?!
SIR MAX! USE THAT ANGER. CHANNEL IT.
CAST YOUR SPELL OR WE ALL PERISH!
KRAAAKK
GATH, YOU MURDEROUS SONAVABITCH! YOU KILLED MY PARENTS, DESTROYED MY HOME...
KEEP GOING. I WILL TAKE CARE OF THE BEAST.

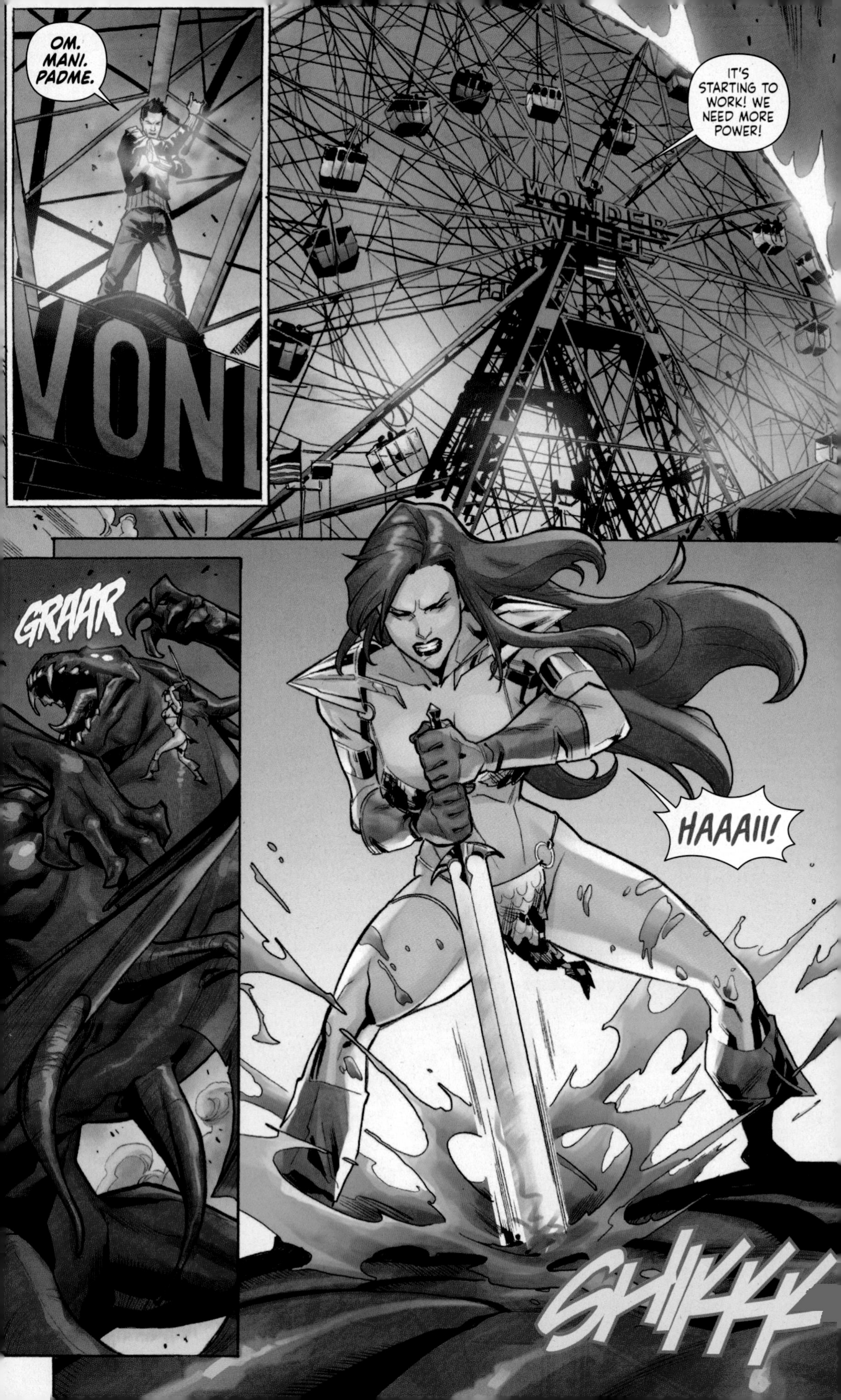
OM. MANI. PADME.
IT'S STARTING TO WORK! WE NEED MORE POWER!
WONDER WHEEL
GRAAR
HAAAII!
SHKKK

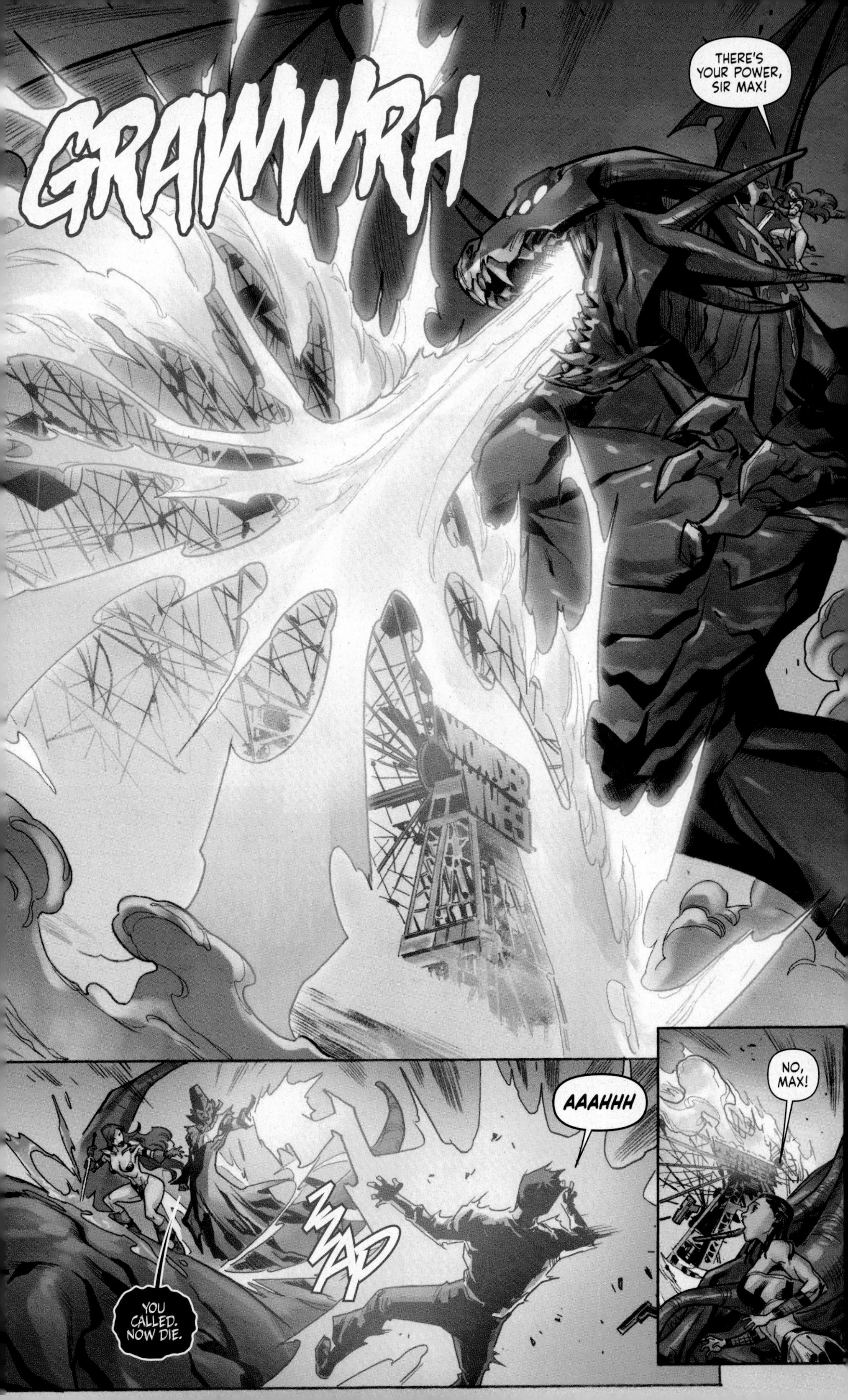
GRAWWRH
THERE'S YOUR POWER, SIR MAX!
YOU CALLED. NOW DIE.
ZZAP
AAAHHH
NO, MAX!

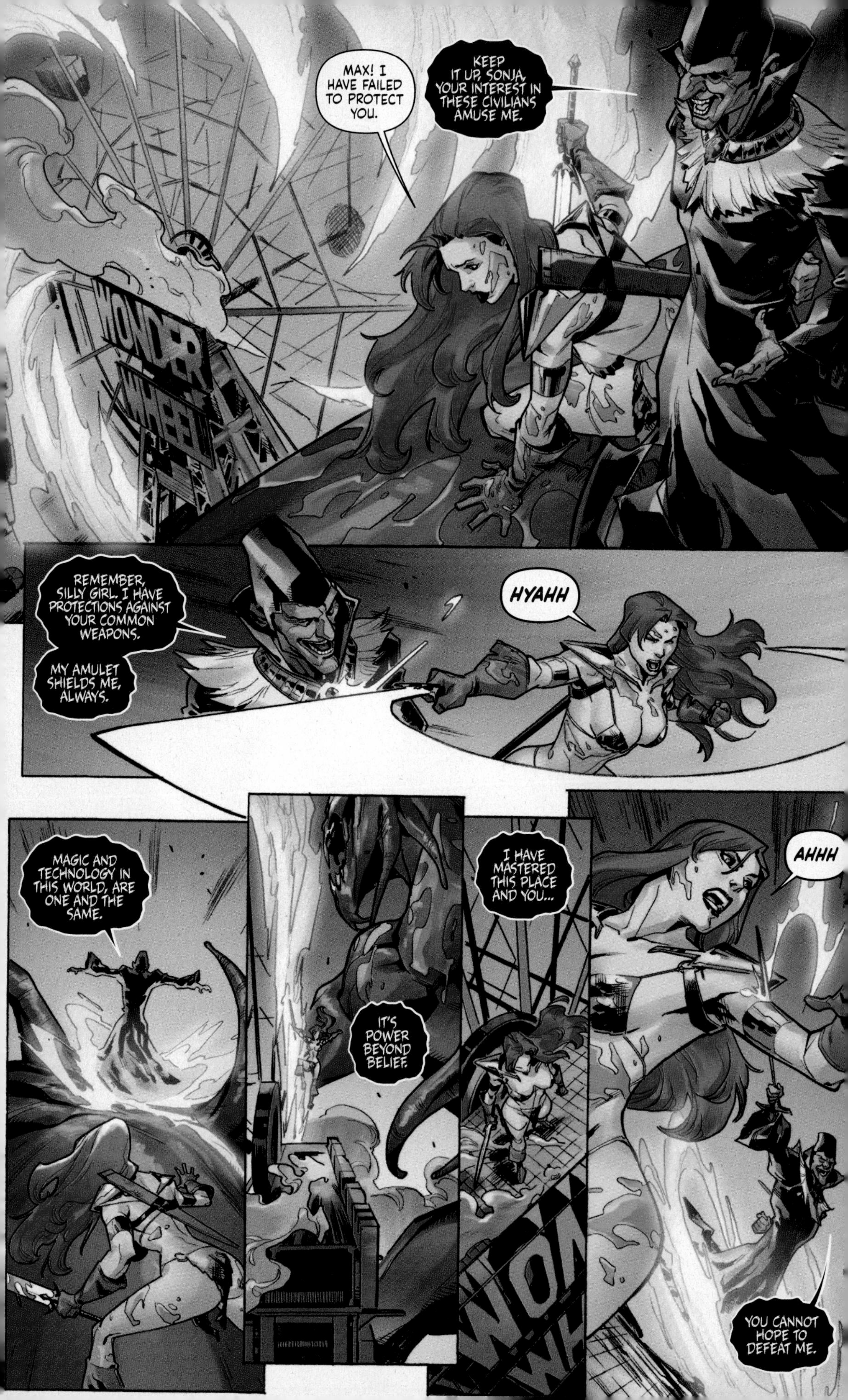
MAX! I HAVE FAILED TO PROTECT YOU.
KEEP IT UP, SONJA, YOUR INTEREST IN THESE CIVILIANS AMUSE ME.
WONDER WHEEL
REMEMBER, SILLY GIRL. I HAVE PROTECTIONS AGAINST YOUR COMMON WEAPONS.
MY AMULET SHIELDS ME, ALWAYS.
HYAHH
MAGIC AND TECHNOLOGY IN THIS WORLD, ARE ONE AND THE SAME.
IT'S POWER BEYOND BELIEF.
I HAVE MASTERED THIS PLACE AND YOU...
AHHH
YOU CANNOT HOPE TO DEFEAT ME.

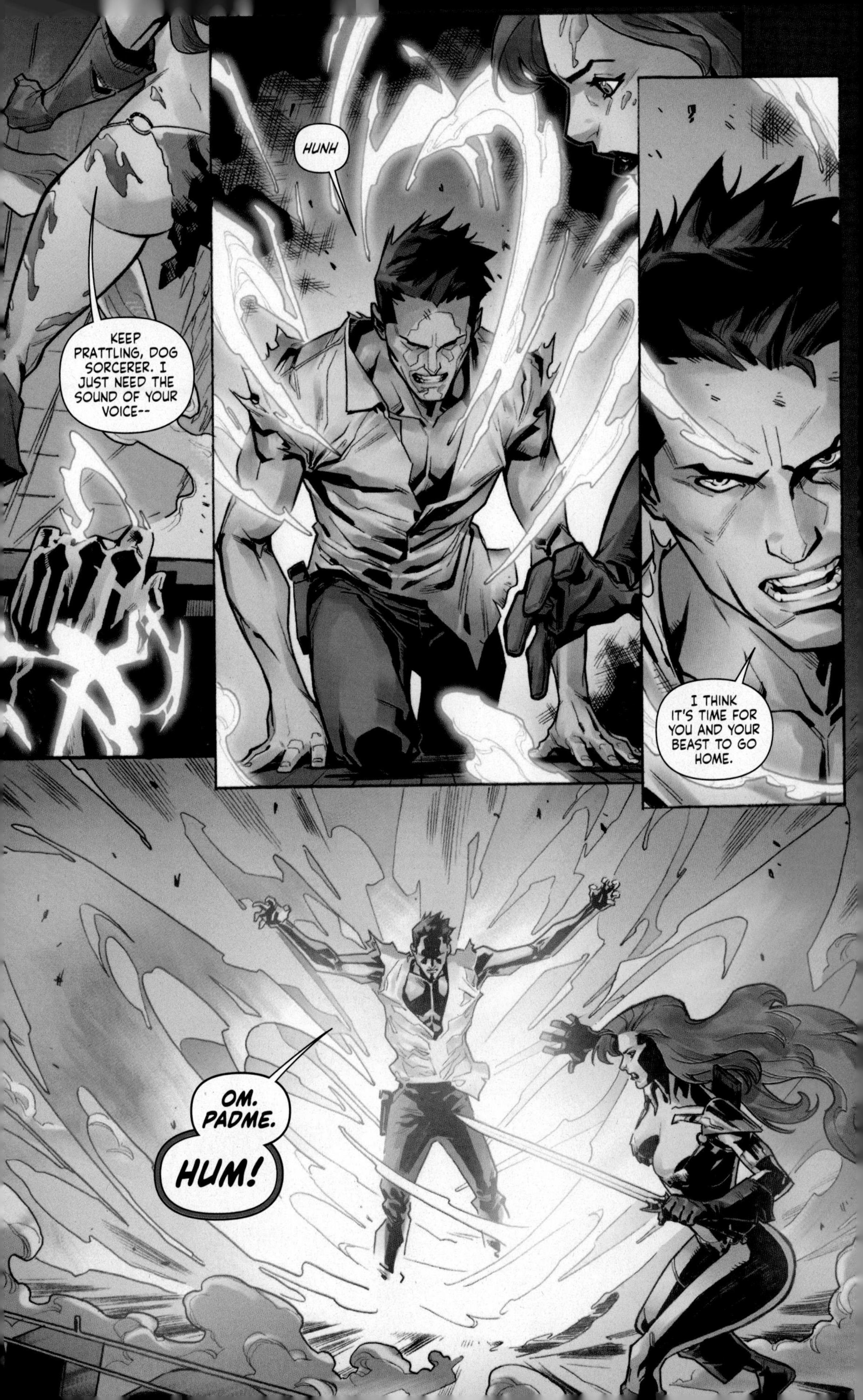
KEEP PRATTLING, DOG SORCERER. I JUST NEED THE SOUND OF YOUR VOICE--
HUNH
I THINK IT'S TIME FOR YOU AND YOUR BEAST TO GO HOME.
OM. PADME.
HUM!

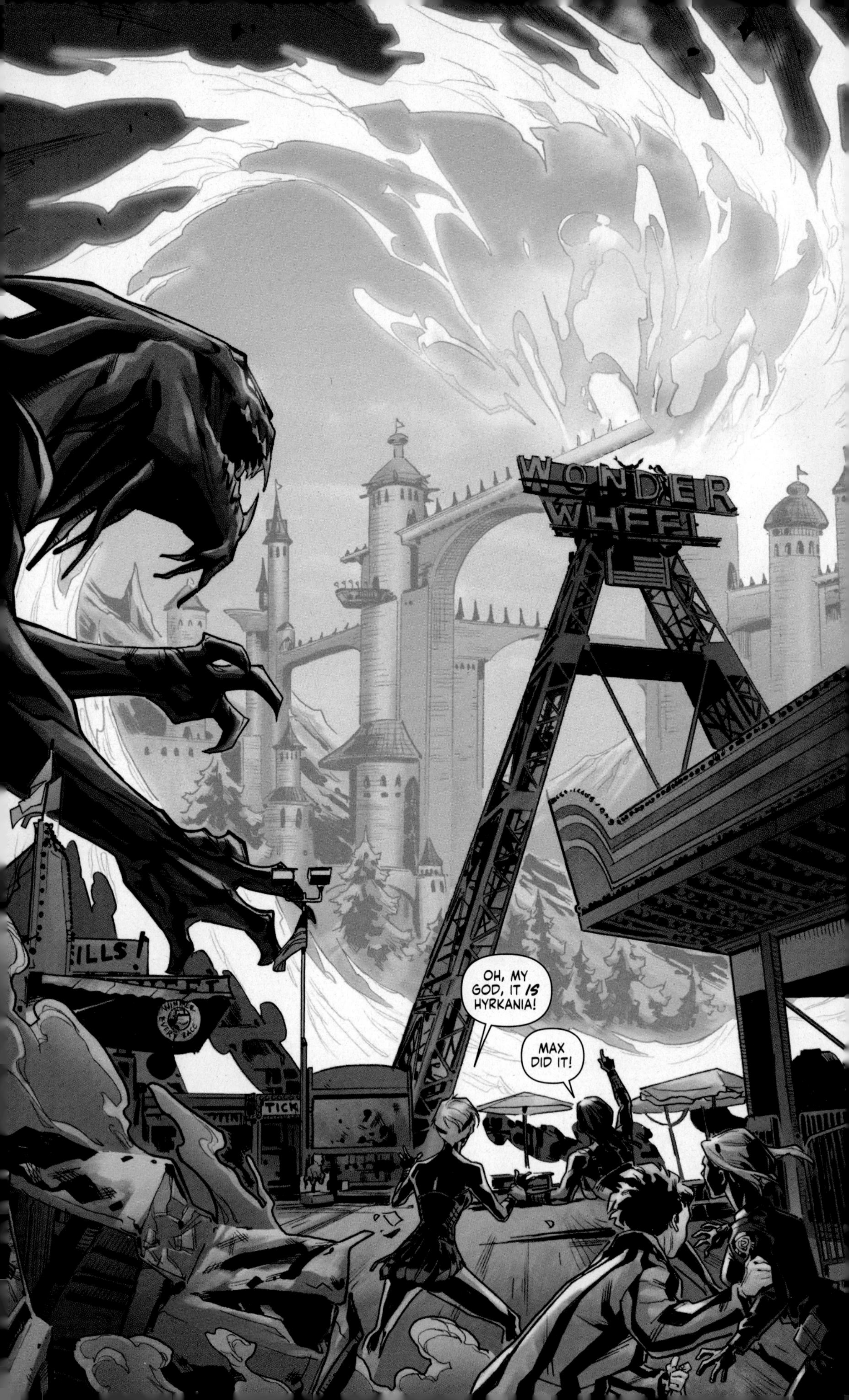
WONDER
OH, MY GOD, IT *IS* HYRKANIA!
MAX DID IT!

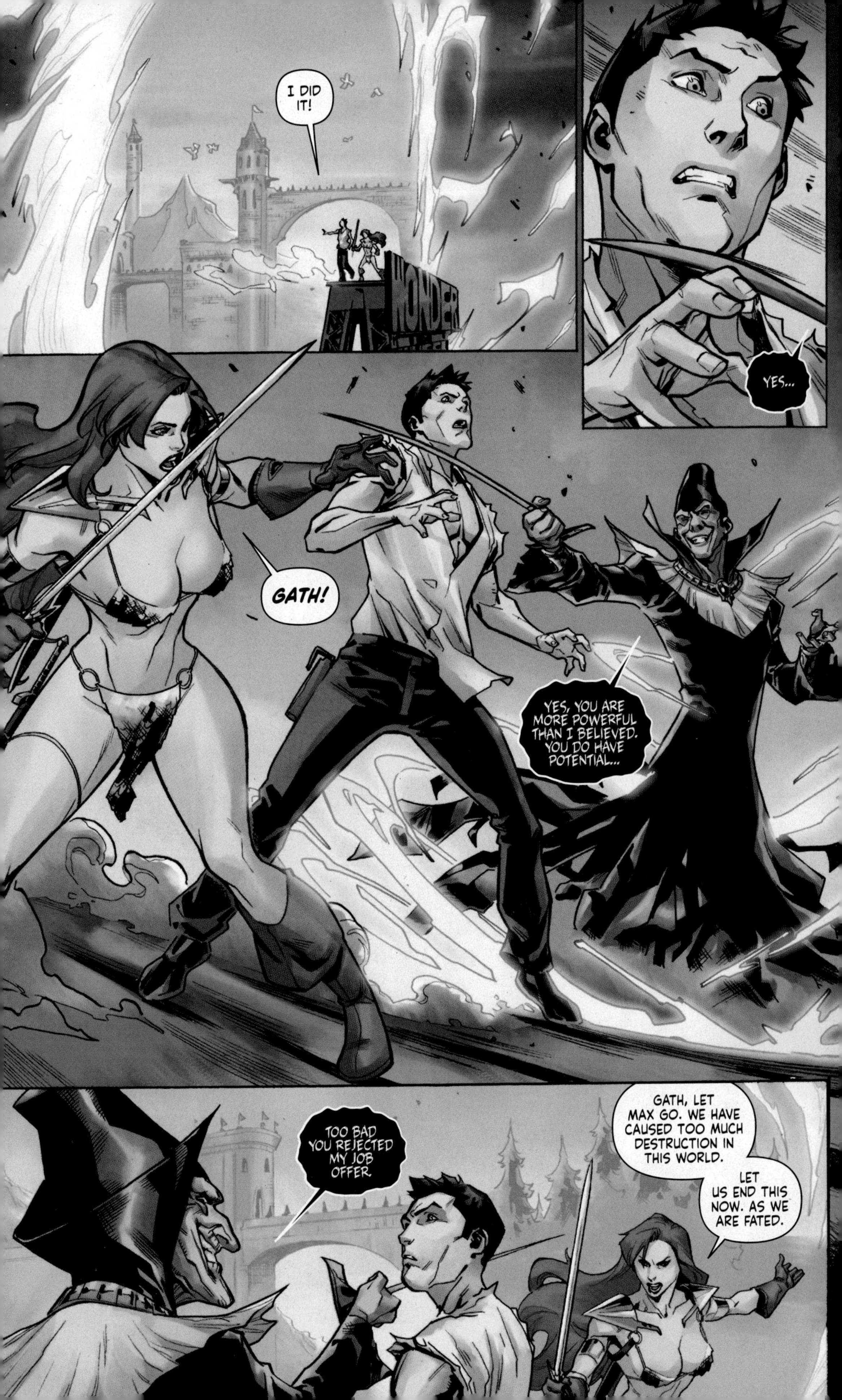
I DID IT!
WONDER
YES...
GATH!
YES, YOU ARE MORE POWERFUL THAN I BELIEVED. YOU DO HAVE POTENTIAL...
TOO BAD YOU REJECTED MY JOB OFFER.
GATH, LET MAX GO. WE HAVE CAUSED TOO MUCH DESTRUCTION IN THIS WORLD.
LET US END THIS NOW. AS WE ARE FATED.

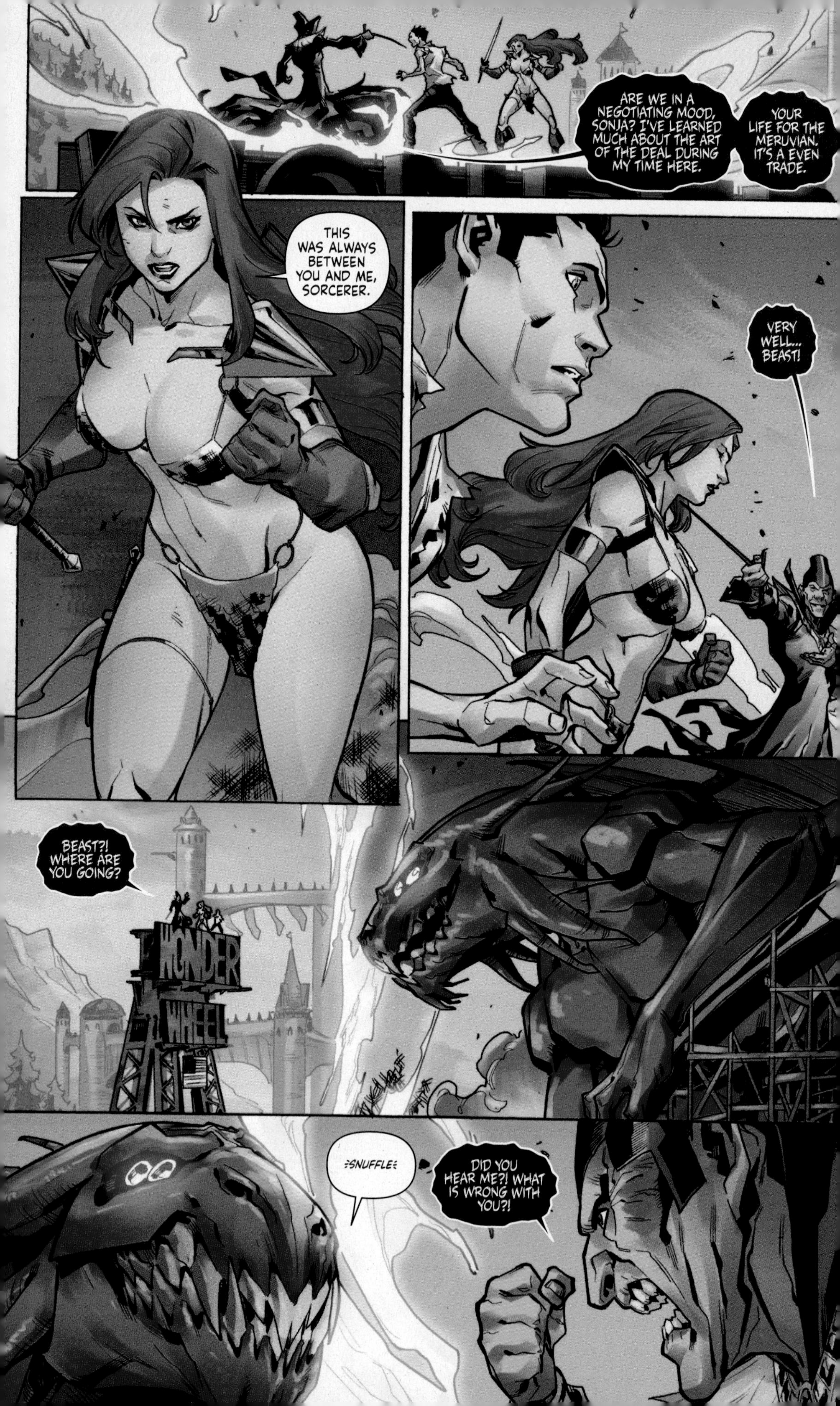

ARE WE IN A NEGOTIATING MOOD, SONJA? I'VE LEARNED MUCH ABOUT THE ART OF THE DEAL DURING MY TIME HERE.
YOUR LIFE FOR THE MERUVIAN. IT'S A EVEN TRADE.
THIS WAS ALWAYS BETWEEN YOU AND ME, SORCERER.
VERY WELL... BEAST!
BEAST?! WHERE ARE YOU GOING?
WONDER WHEEL
SNUFFLE
DID YOU HEAR ME?! WHAT IS WRONG WITH YOU?!

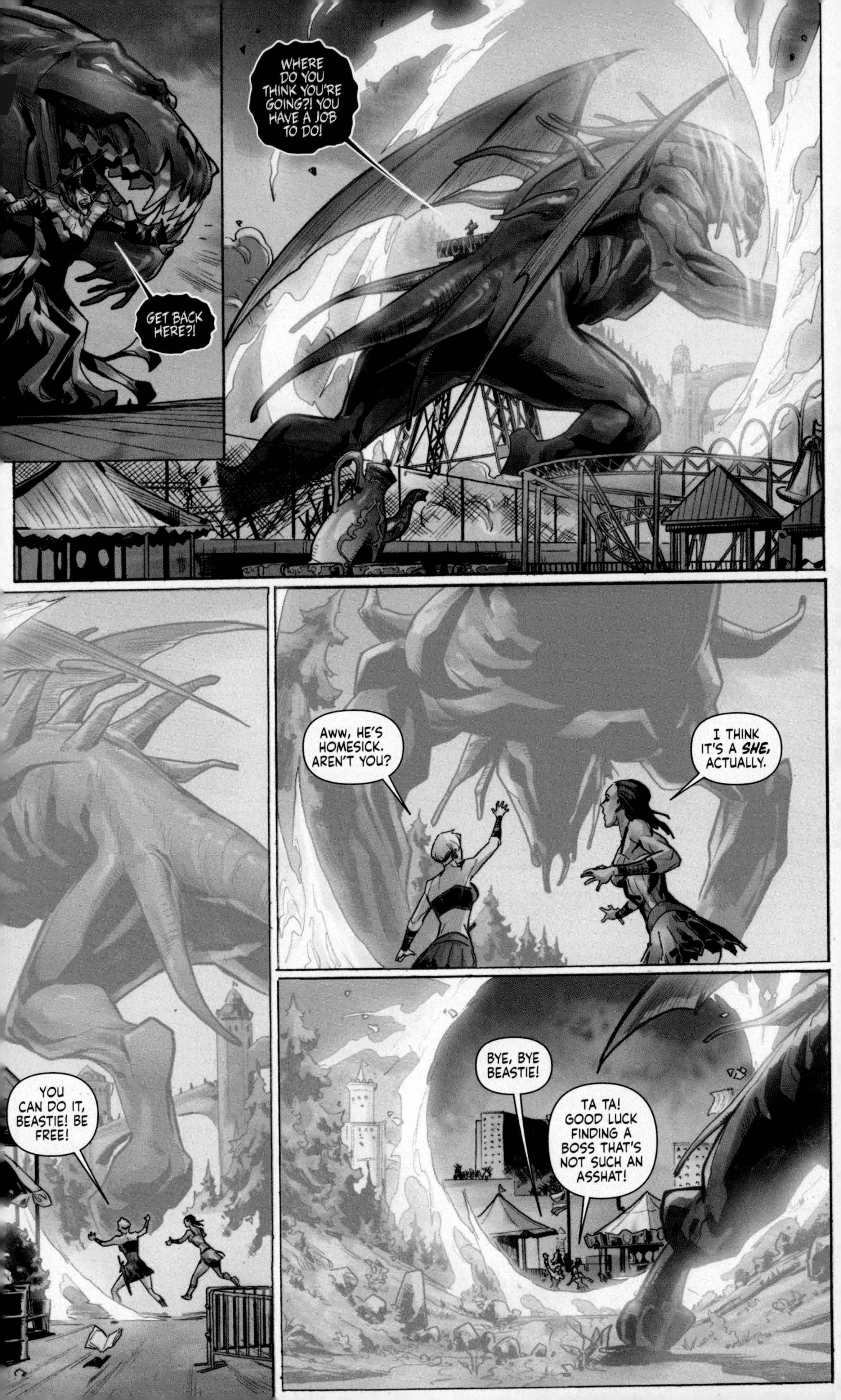
GET BACK HERE?!
WHERE DO YOU THINK YOU'RE GOING?! YOU HAVE A JOB TO DO!
YOU CAN DO IT, BEASTIE! BE FREE!
AWW, HE'S HOMESICK. AREN'T YOU?
I THINK IT'S A SHE, ACTUALLY.
BYE, BYE BEASTIE!
TA TA! GOOD LUCK FINDING A BOSS THAT'S NOT SUCH AN ASSHAT!

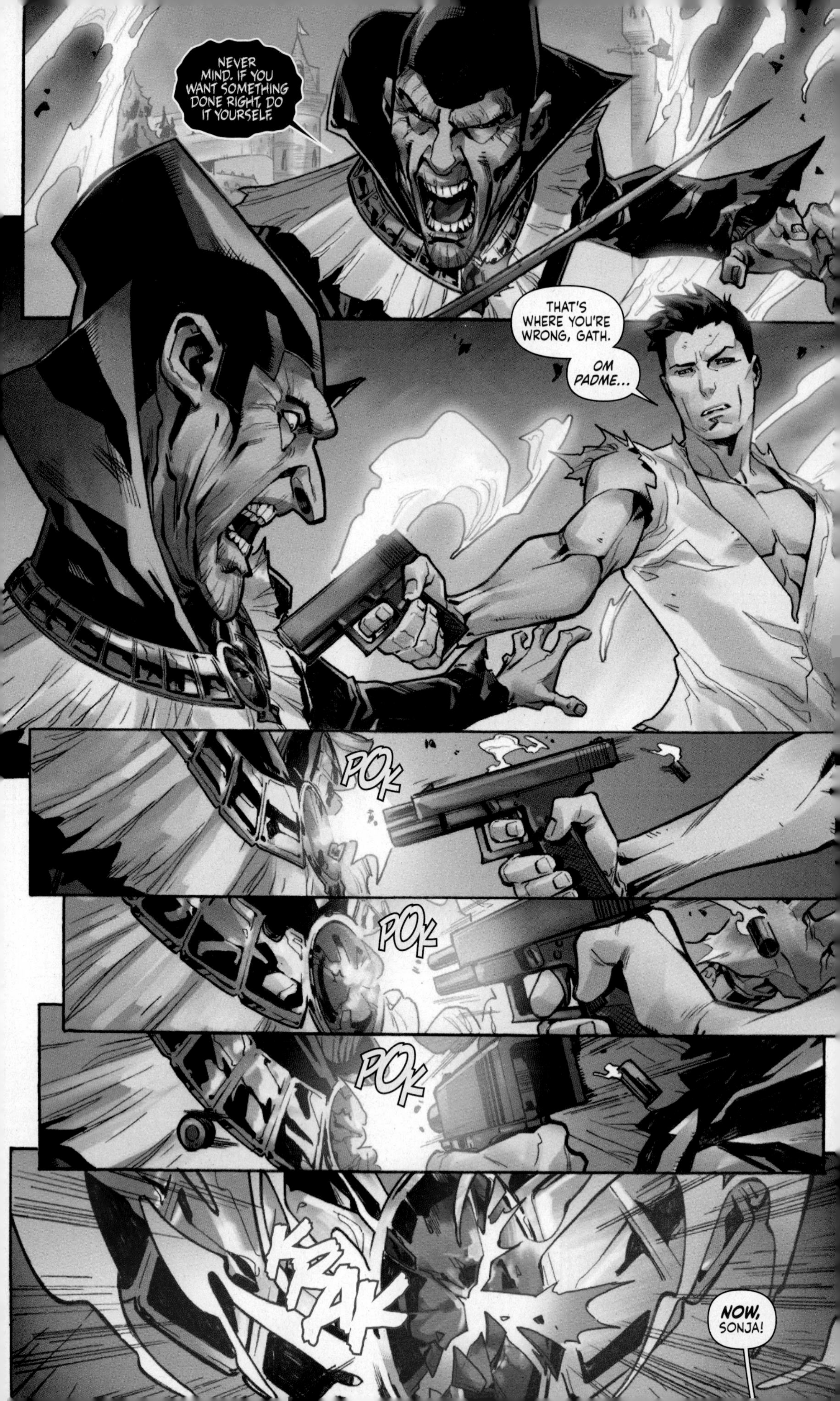
NEVER MIND. IF YOU WANT SOMETHING DONE RIGHT, DO IT YOURSELF.
THAT'S WHERE YOU'RE WRONG, GATH.
OM PADME...
POK
POK
POK
KRAK
NOW, SONJA!

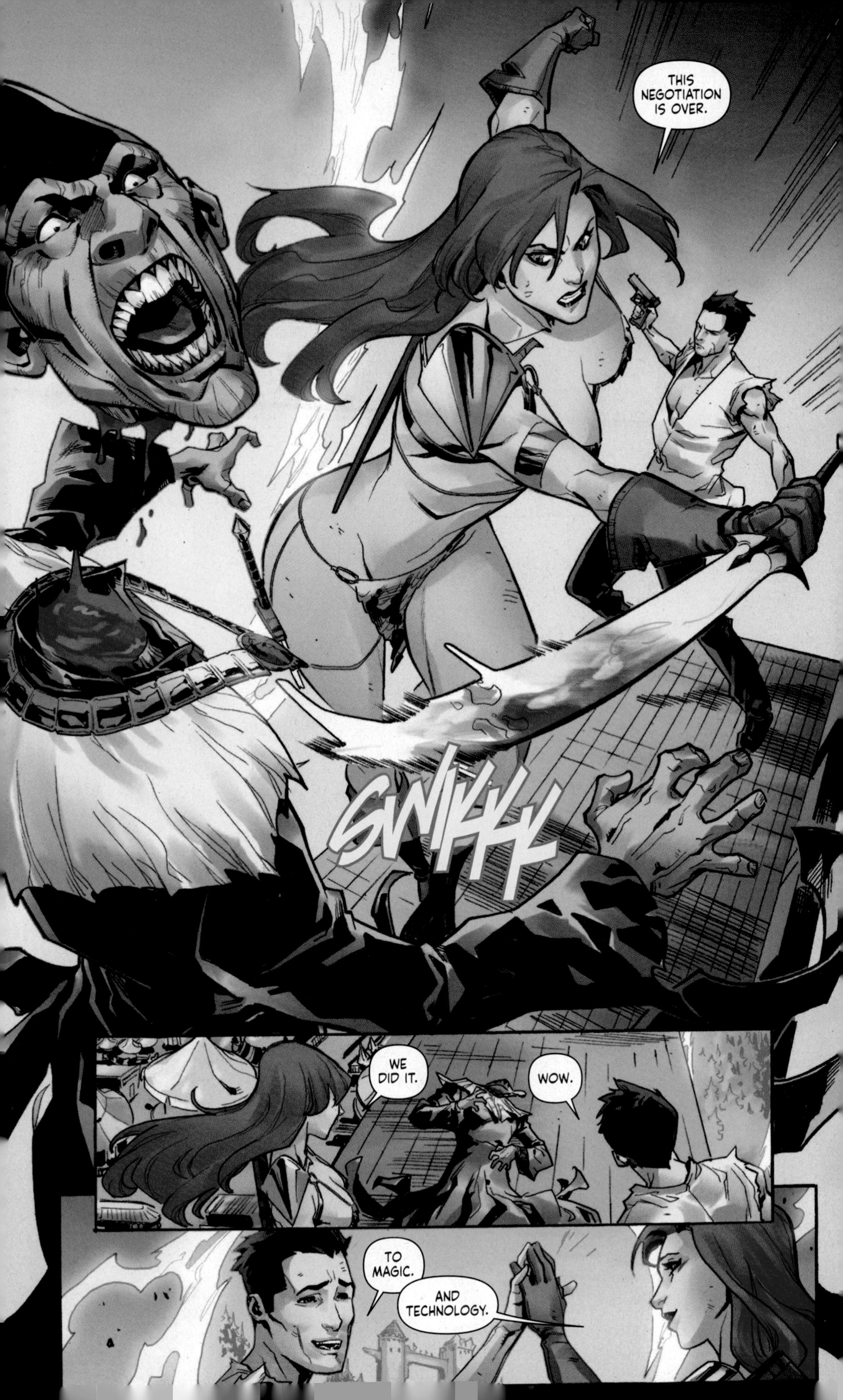

THIS NEGOTIATION IS OVER.
SWIKKK
WE DID IT.
WOW.
TO MAGIC.
AND TECHNOLOGY.

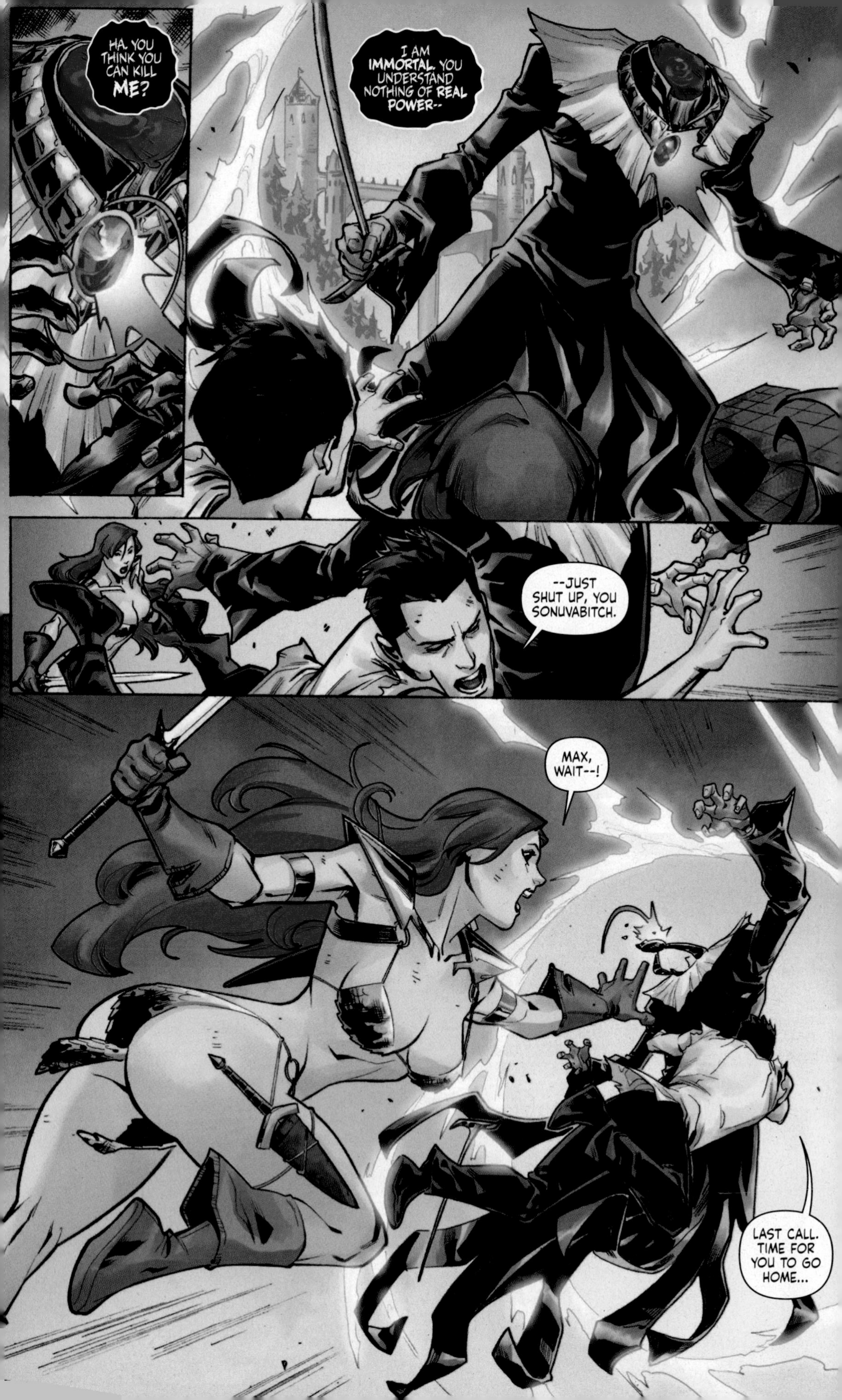
HA. YOU THINK YOU CAN KILL ME?
I AM IMMORTAL. YOU UNDERSTAND NOTHING OF REAL POWER--
--JUST SHUT UP, YOU SONUVABITCH.
MAX, WAIT--!
LAST CALL. TIME FOR YOU TO GO HOME...

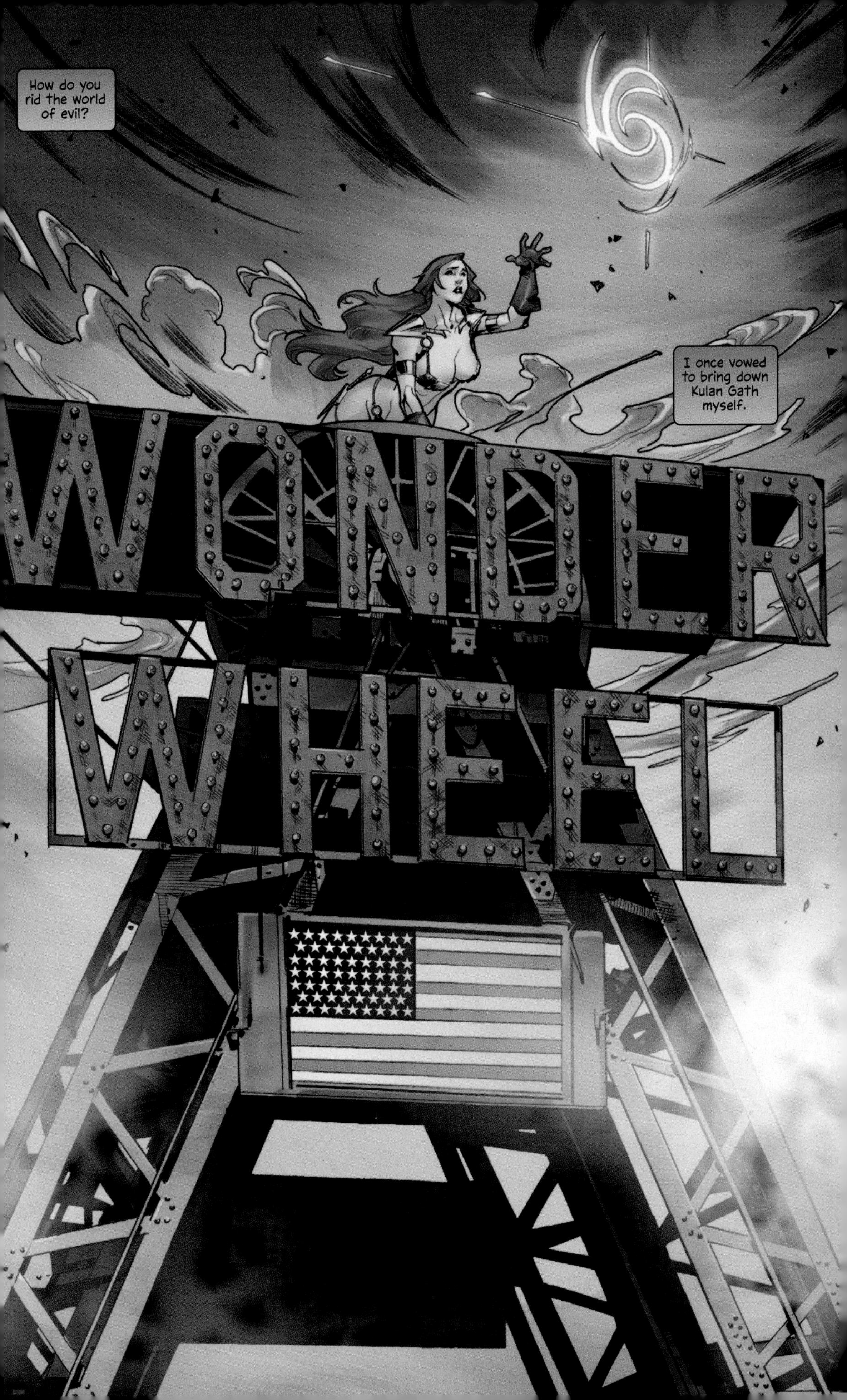
How do you rid the world of evil?
I once vowed to bring down Kulan Gath myself.
WONDER WHEEL

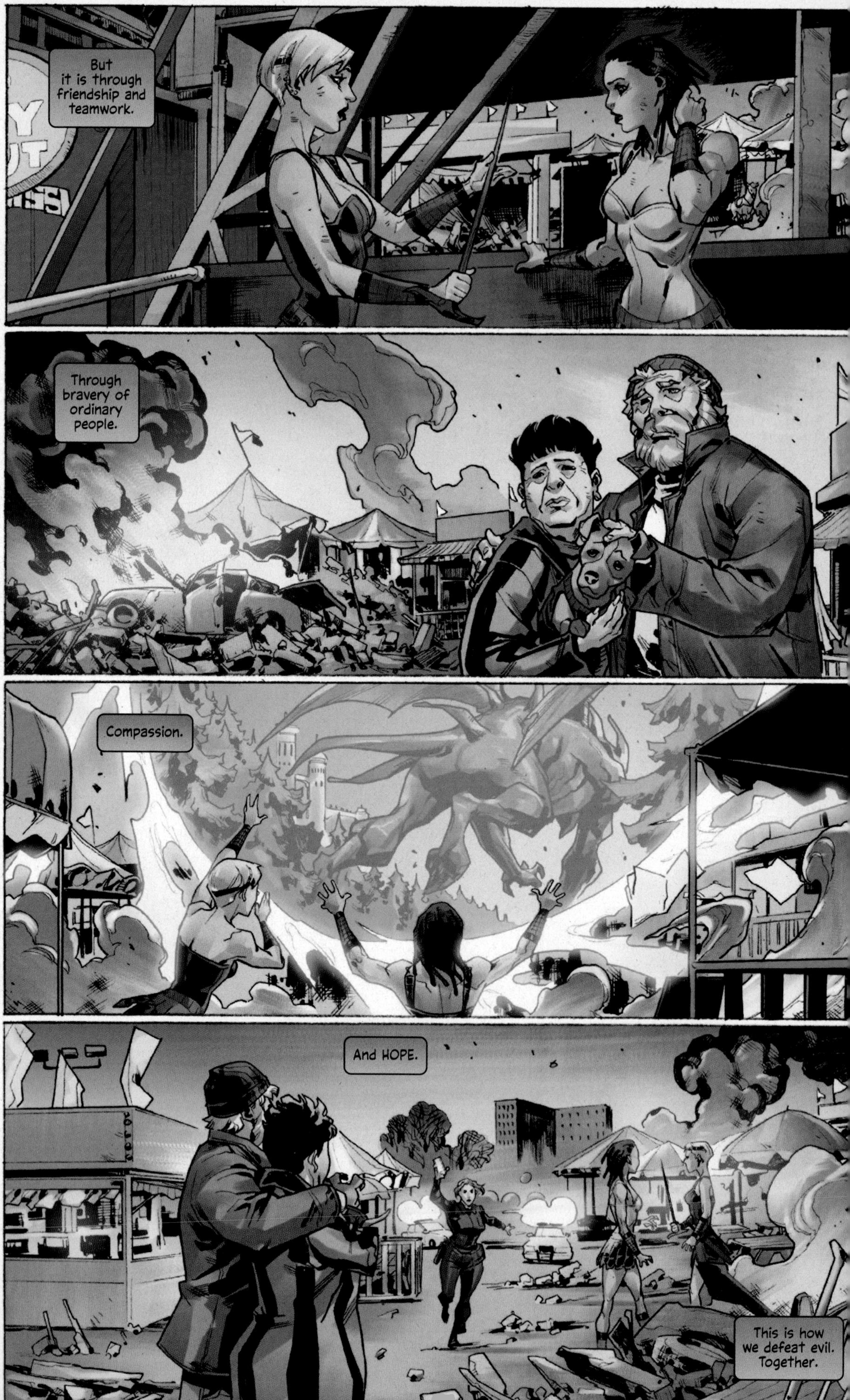
But it is through friendship and teamwork.
Through bravery of ordinary people.
Compassion.
And HOPE.
This is how we defeat evil. Together.

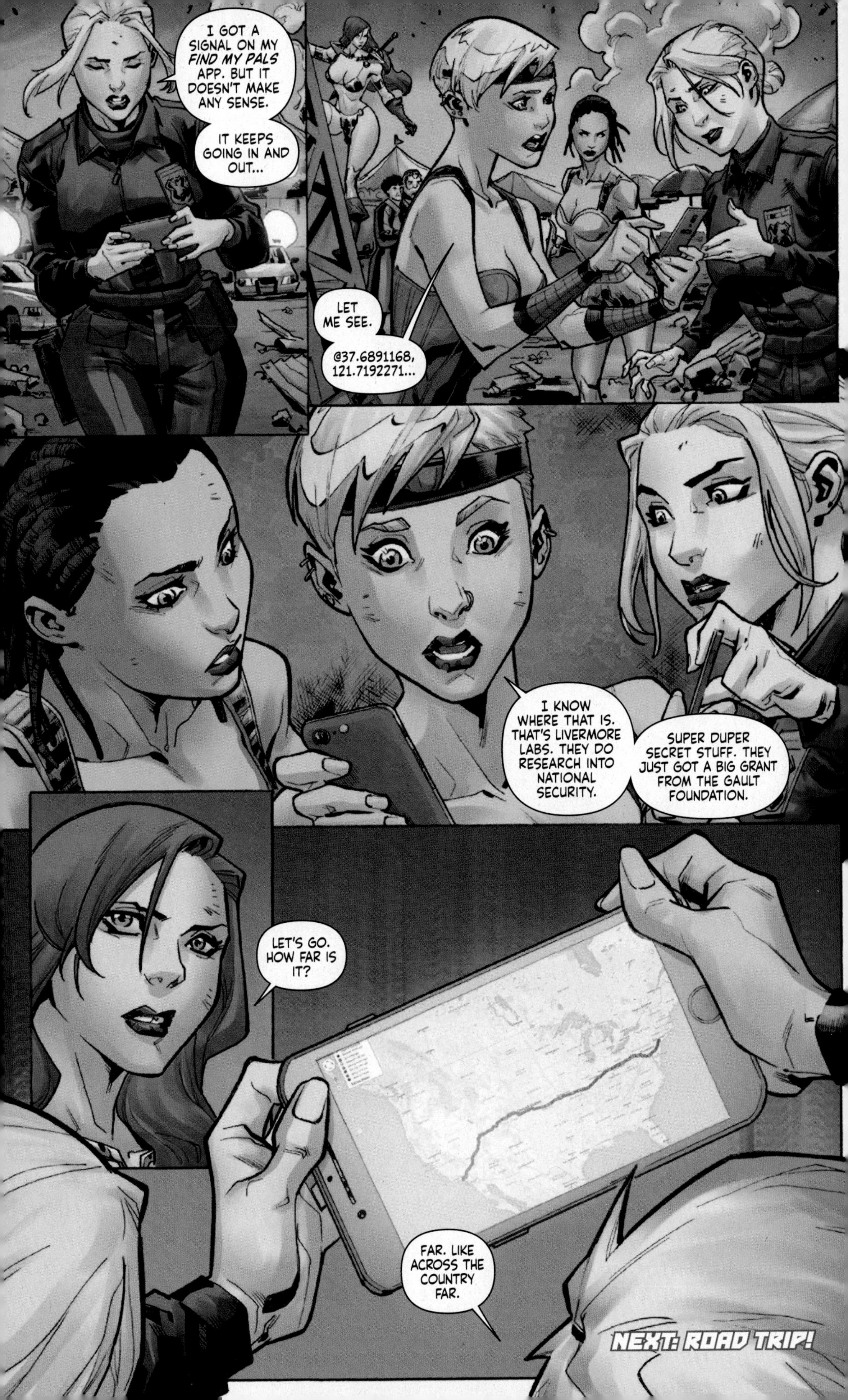
I GOT A SIGNAL ON MY *FIND MY PALS* APP. BUT IT DOESN'T MAKE ANY SENSE.
IT KEEPS GOING IN AND OUT...
LET ME SEE.
@37.6891168, 121.7192271...
I KNOW WHERE THAT IS. THAT'S LIVERMORE LABS. THEY DO RESEARCH INTO NATIONAL SECURITY.
SUPER DUPER SECRET STUFF. THEY JUST GOT A BIG GRANT FROM THE GAULT FOUNDATION.
LET'S GO. HOW FAR IS IT?
FAR. LIKE ACROSS THE COUNTRY FAR.
NEXT: ROAD TRIP!

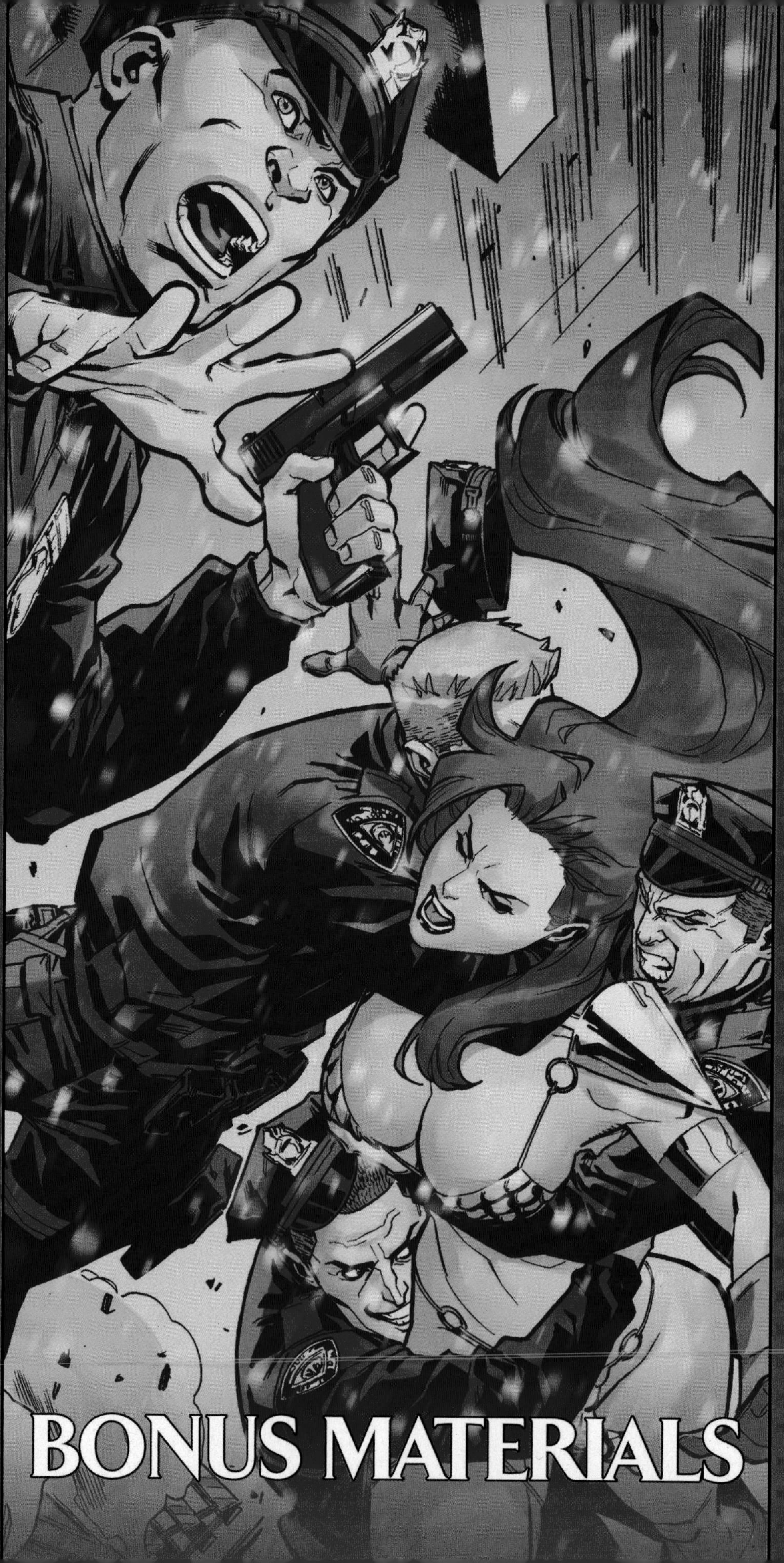

BONUS MATERIALS

COVER GALLERY

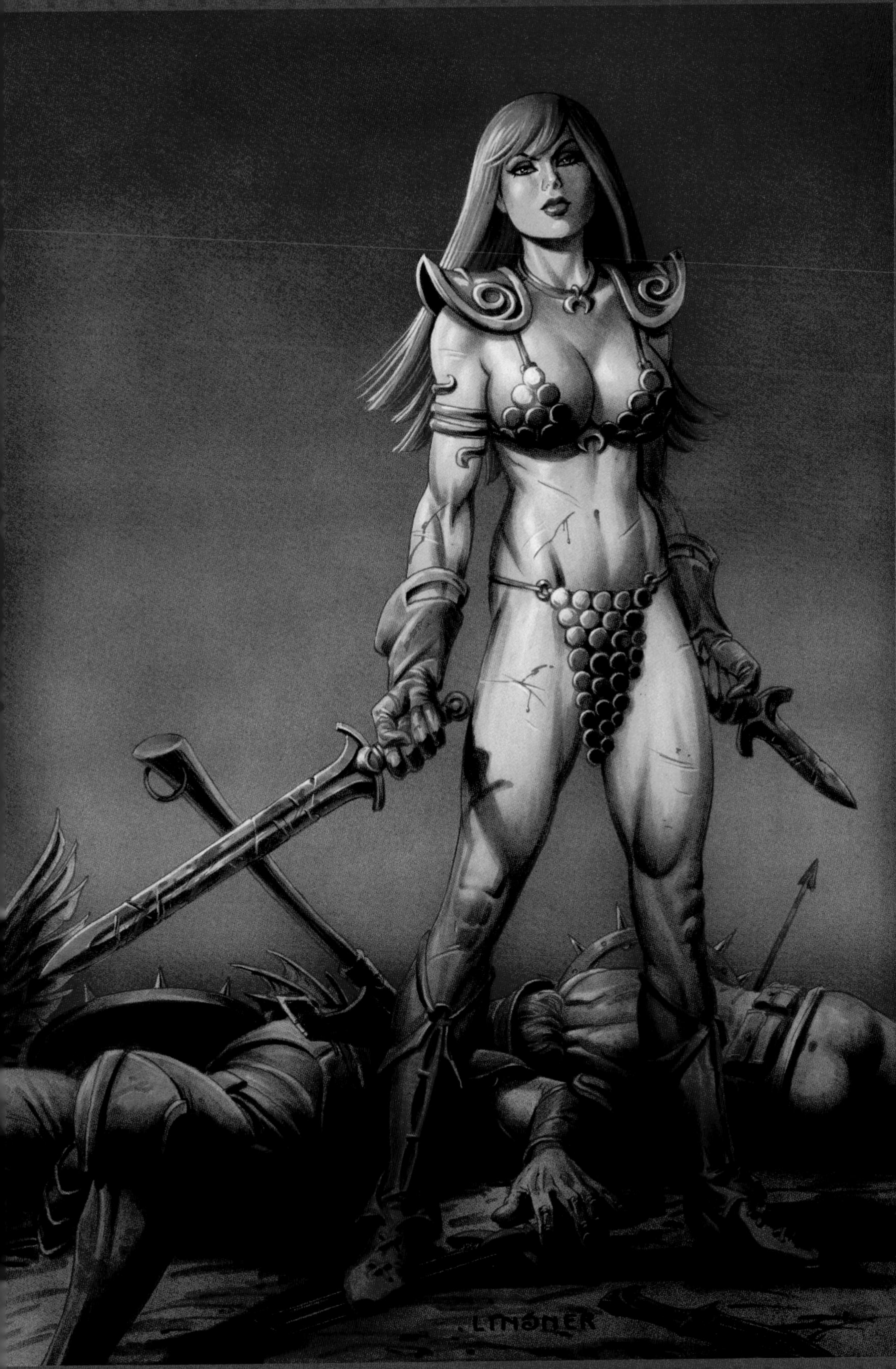

ISSUE#0: BAM!BOX EXCLUSIVE COVER ART BY **JOSEPH MICHAEL LINSNER**

COVER GALLERY

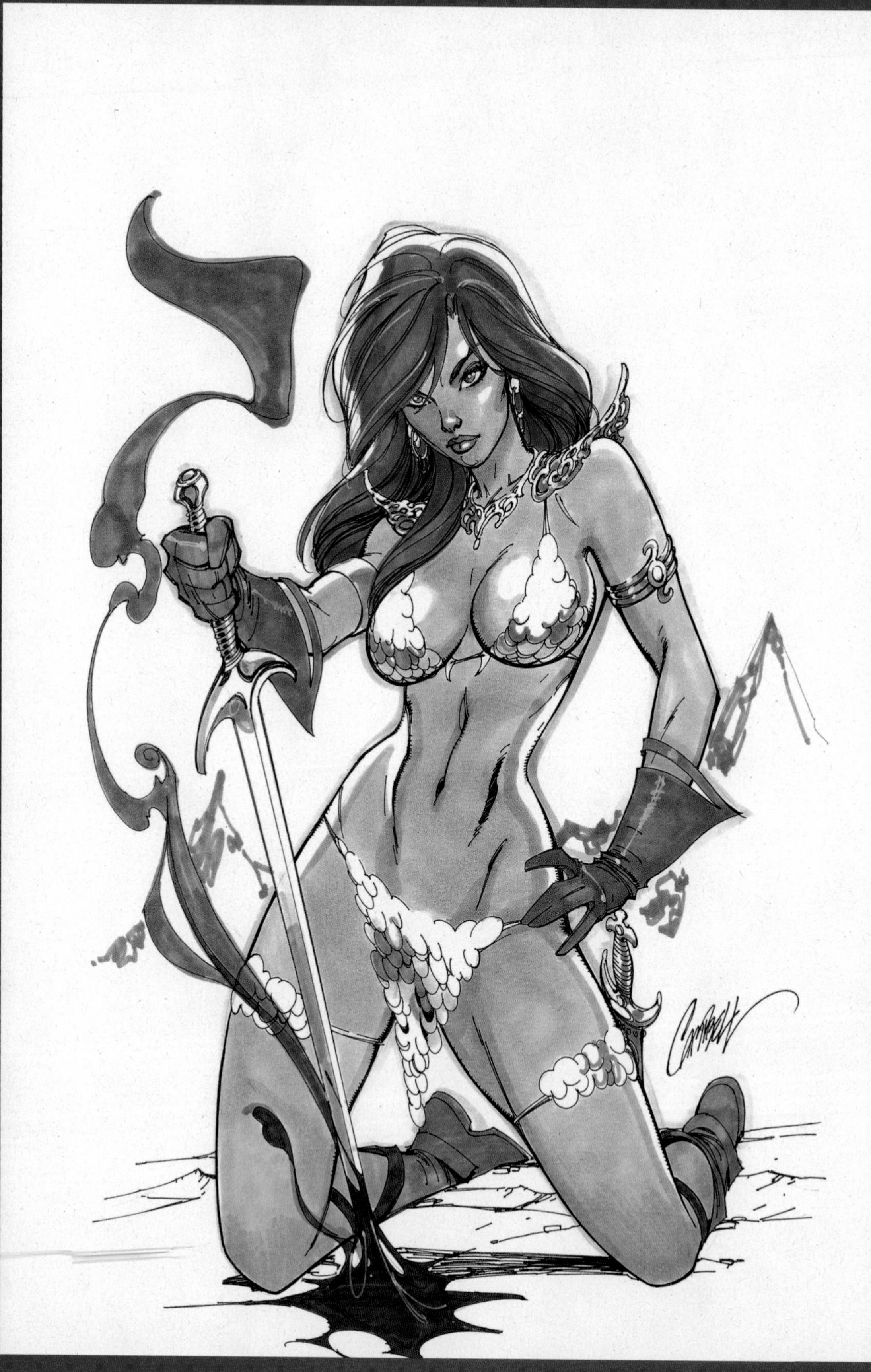

ISSUE #1: COVER ART BY **J. SCOTT CAMPBELL**

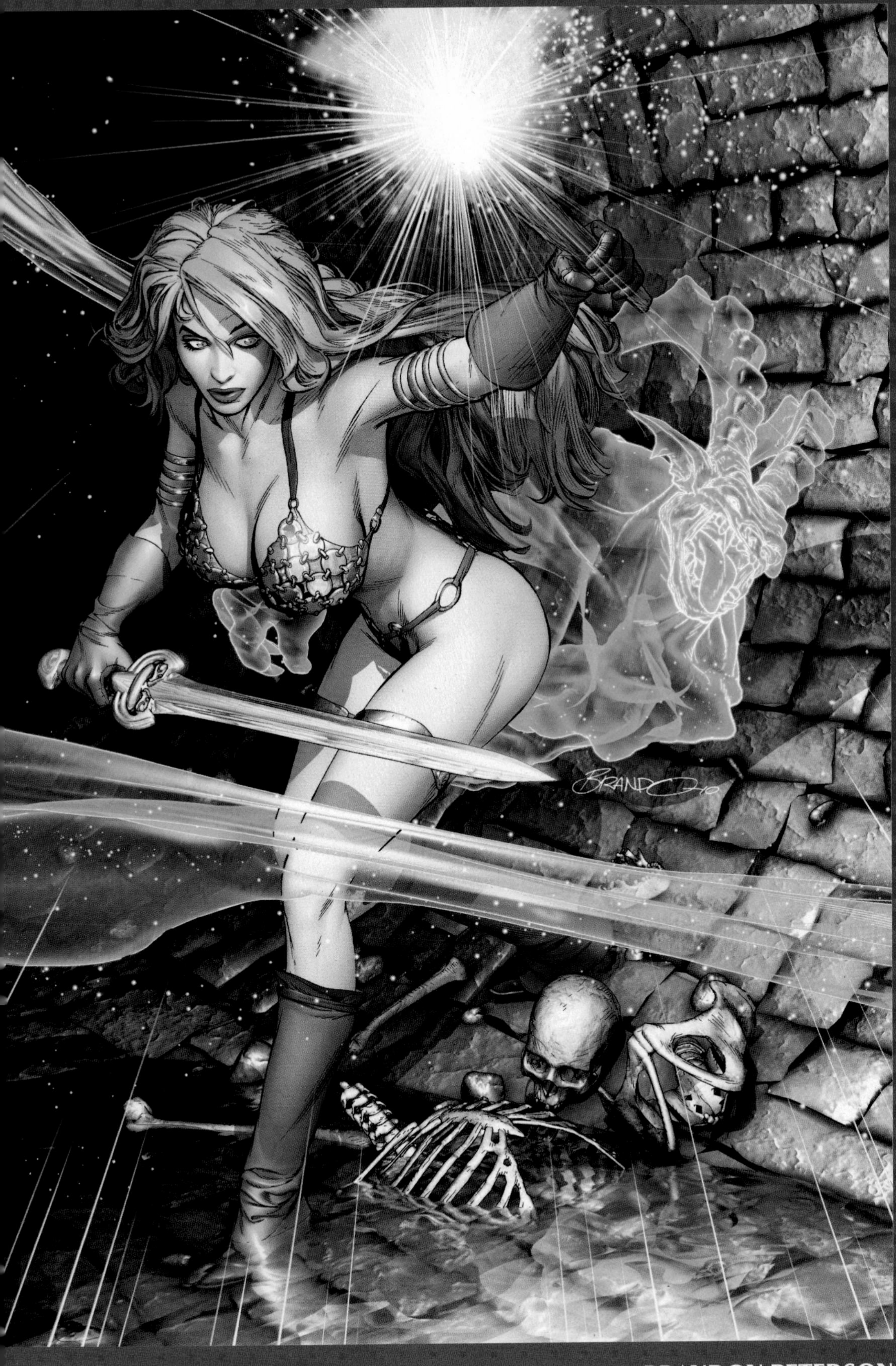

ISSUE #1: COVER ART BY **BRANDON PETERSON**

COVER GALLERY

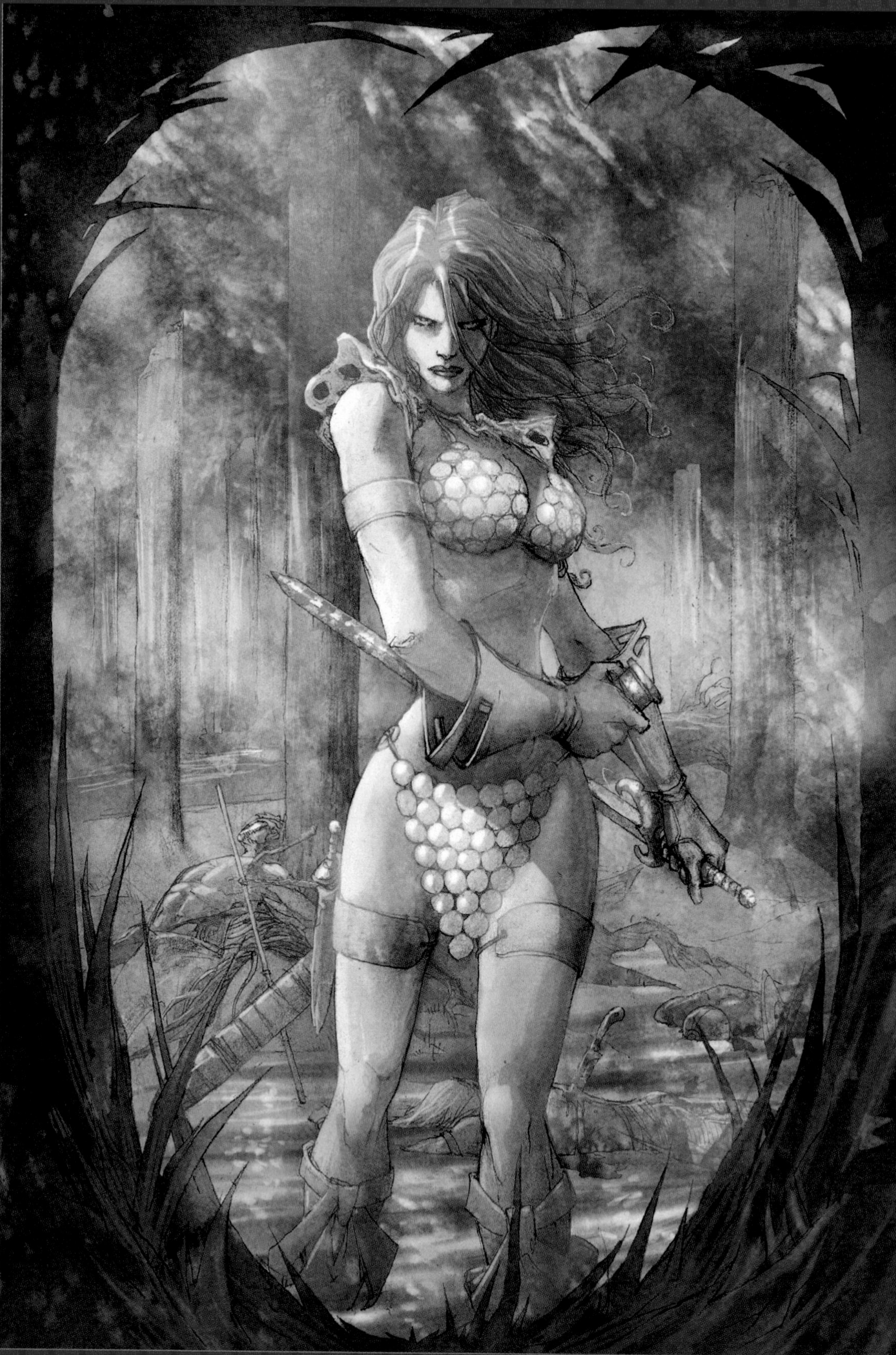

ISSUE #1: COVER ART BY **GIUSEPPE CAMUNCOLI**, COLORS BY **JOSE VILLARRUBIA**

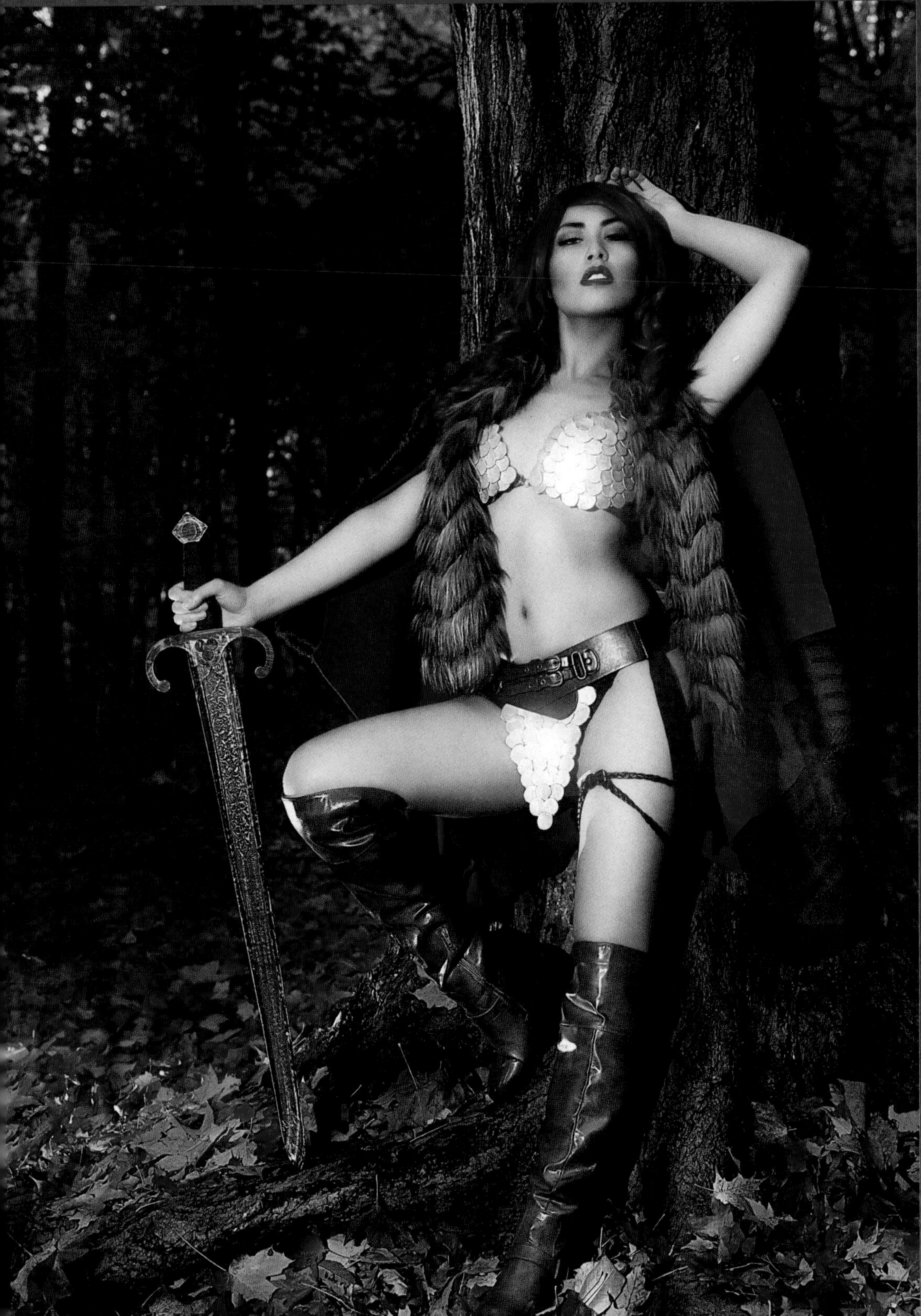

ISSUE #1: COSPLAY VARIANT
MODEL: ASHLEY DU (TWITTER: @UNDEADDU), PHOTOGRAPHER: ERIK PAREDES

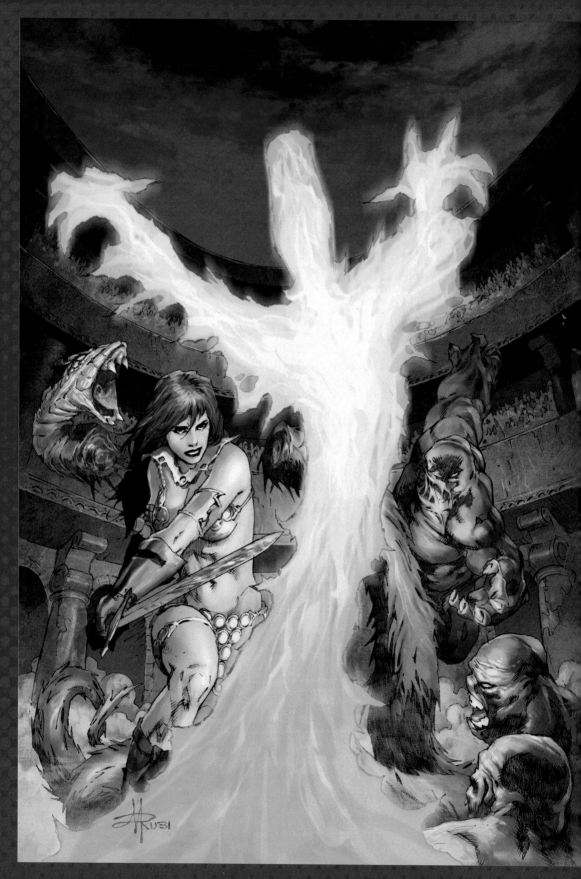

ISSUE #1: COVER ART BY **MEL RUBI**, COLORS BY **MOHAN**

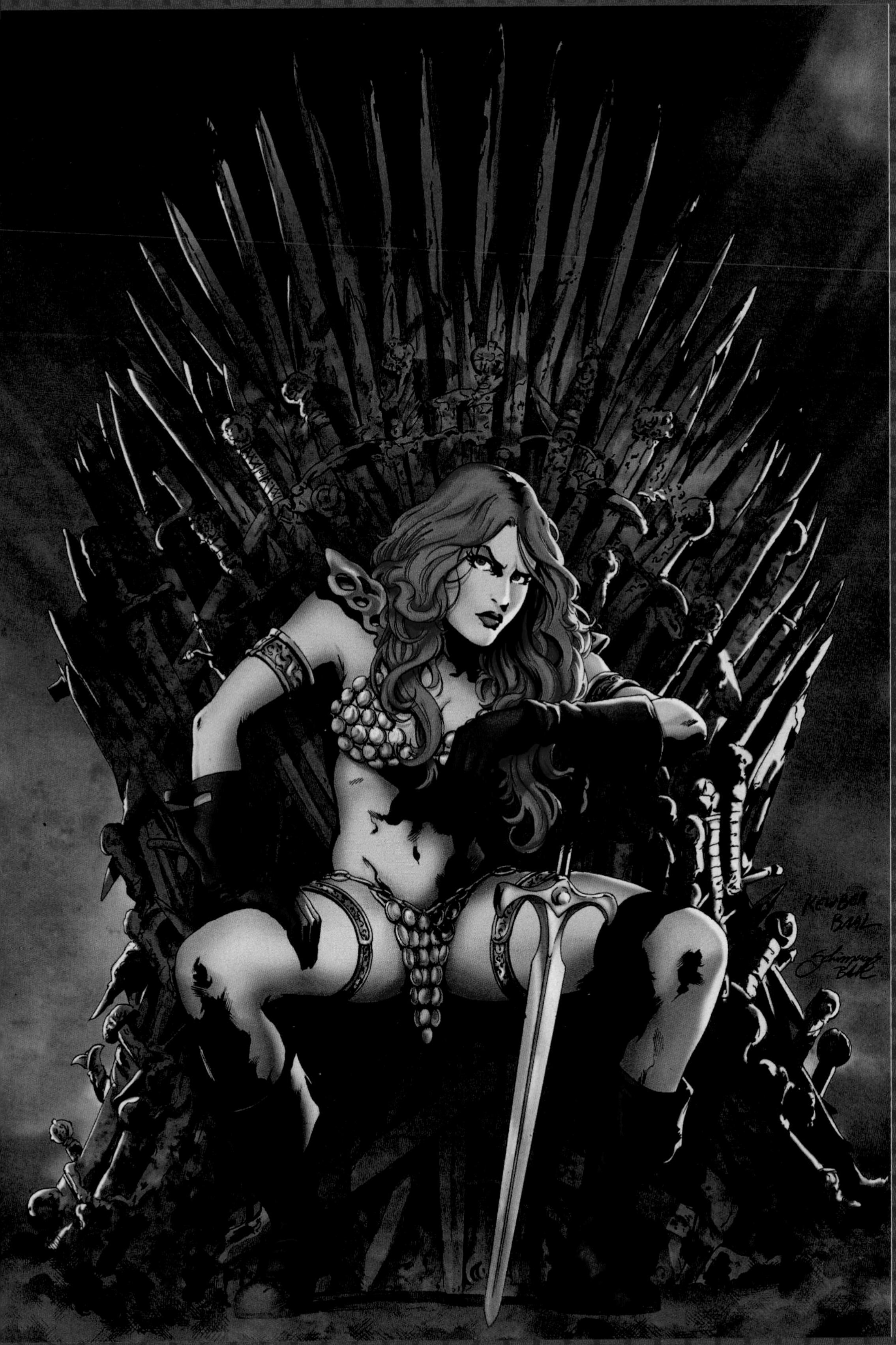
KEWBER BAAL

ISSUE #1: DYNAMIC FORCES EXCLUSIVE

COVER ART BY KEWBER BAAL, COLORS BY SCHIMERYS BAAL

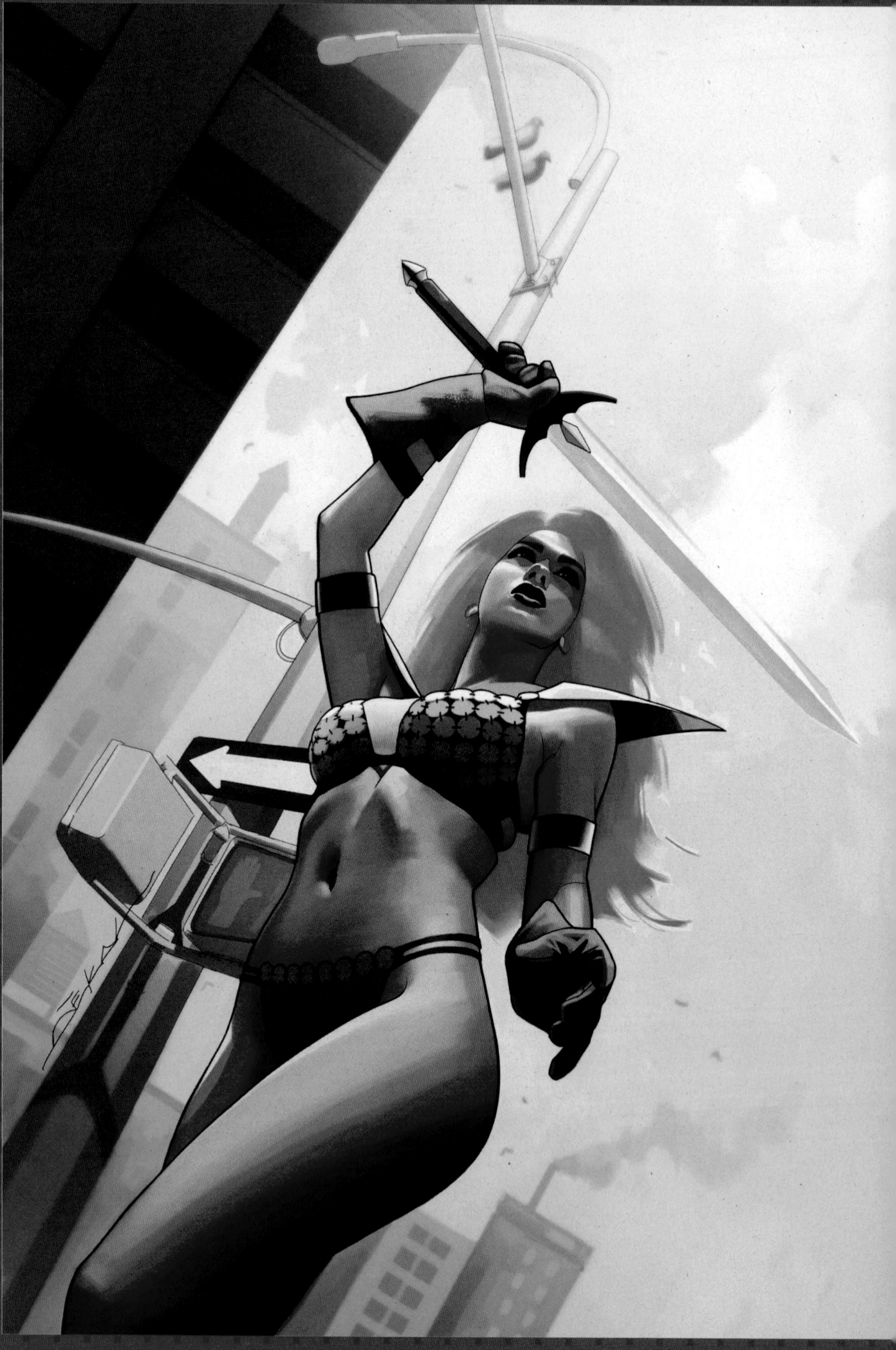

ISSUE #1: NERDBLOCK EXCLUSIVE COVER ART BY JEFF DEKAL

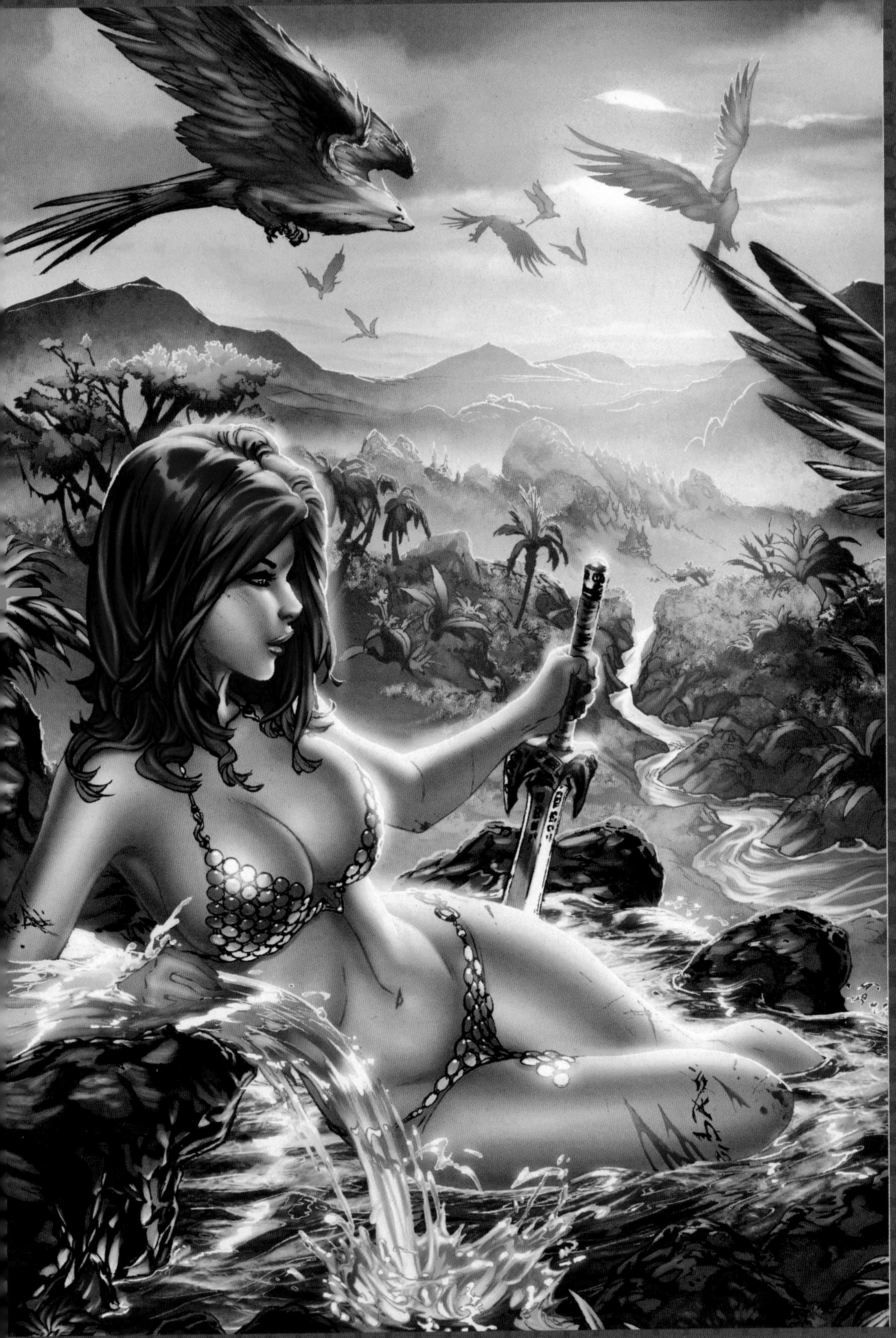

ISSUE #1: STEAMPUNK COMIC SHOP EXCLUSIVE
COVER ART BY ERIC BASALDUA, COLORS BY NEI RUFFINO

COVER GALLERY

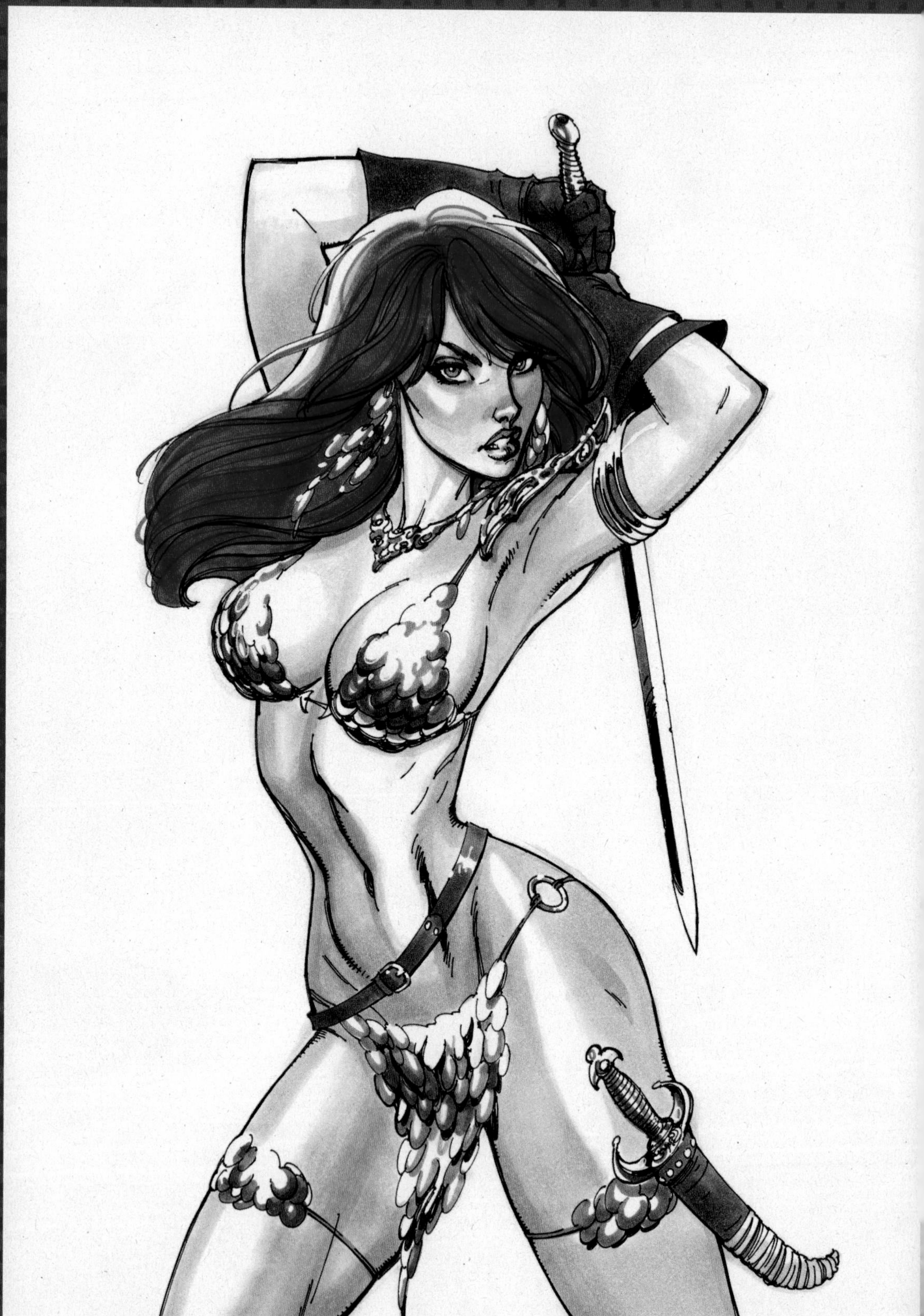

ISSUE #2: COVER ART BY J. SCOTT CAMPBELL

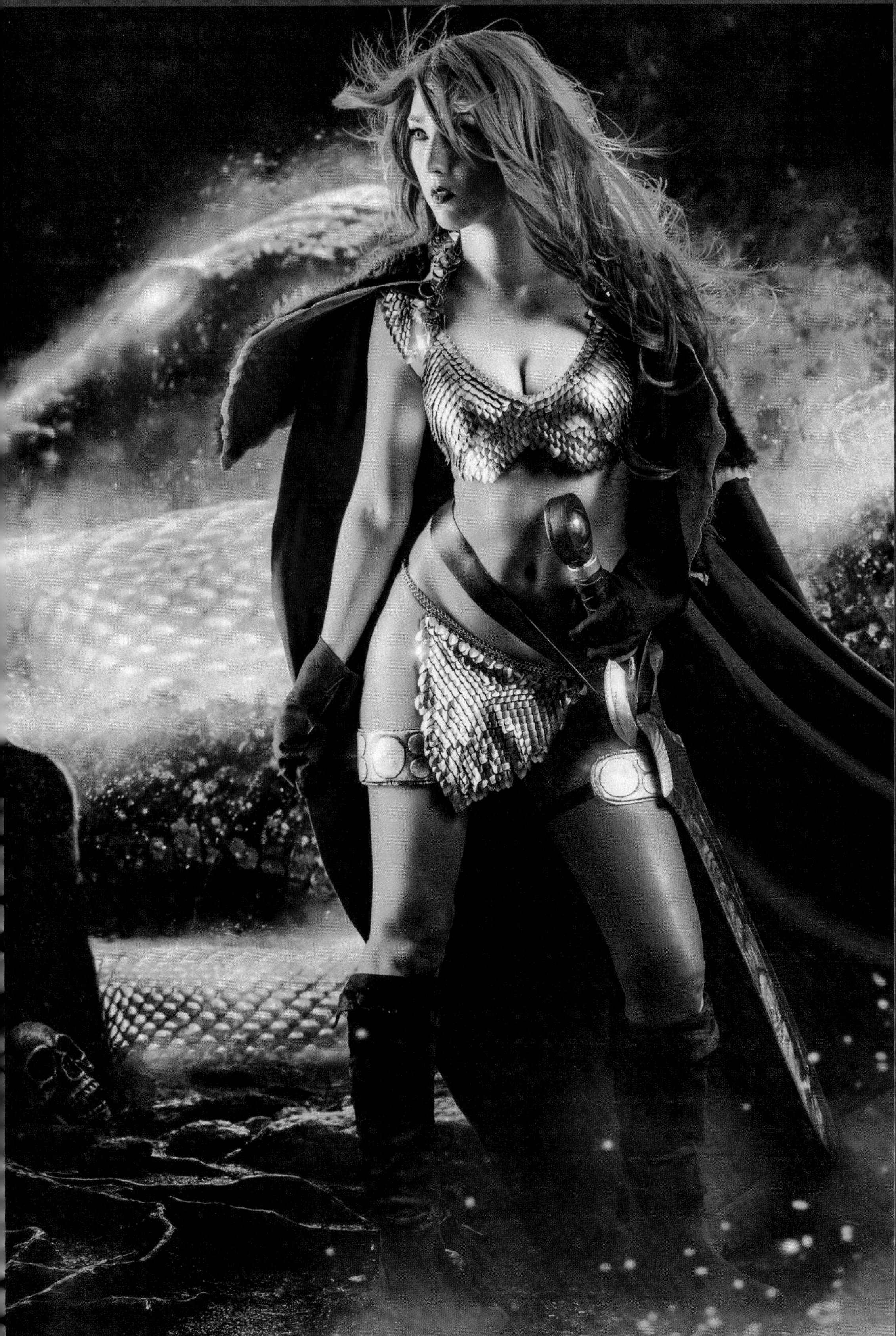

ISSUE #2: COSPLAY VARIANT
MODEL: JENIFER ANN (TWITTER: @OJENIFERANN), PHOTOGRAPHER: DAVID LOVE

COVER GALLERY

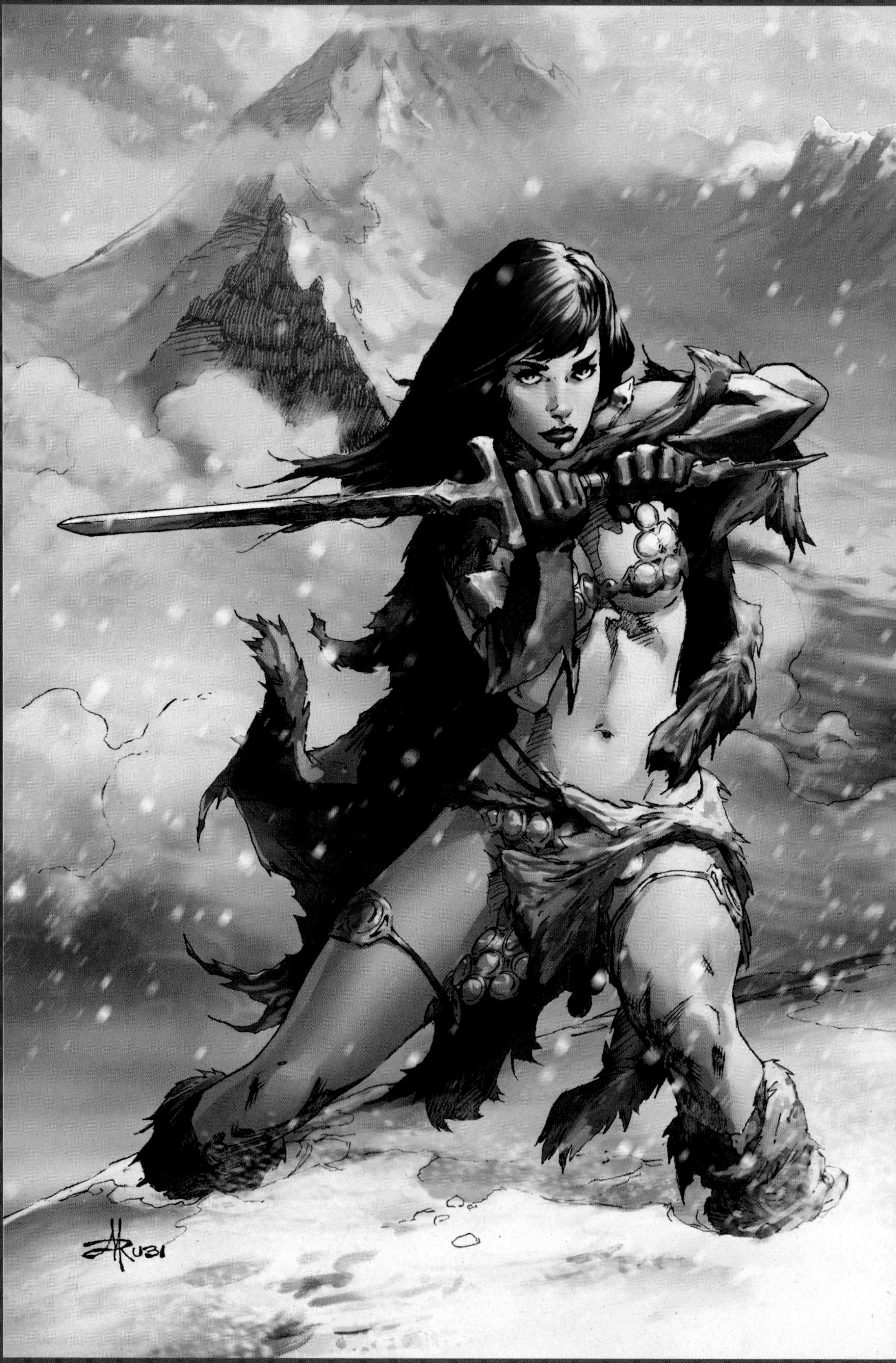
RUBI

ISSUE #2: COVER ART BY MEL RUBI, COLORS BY MOHAN

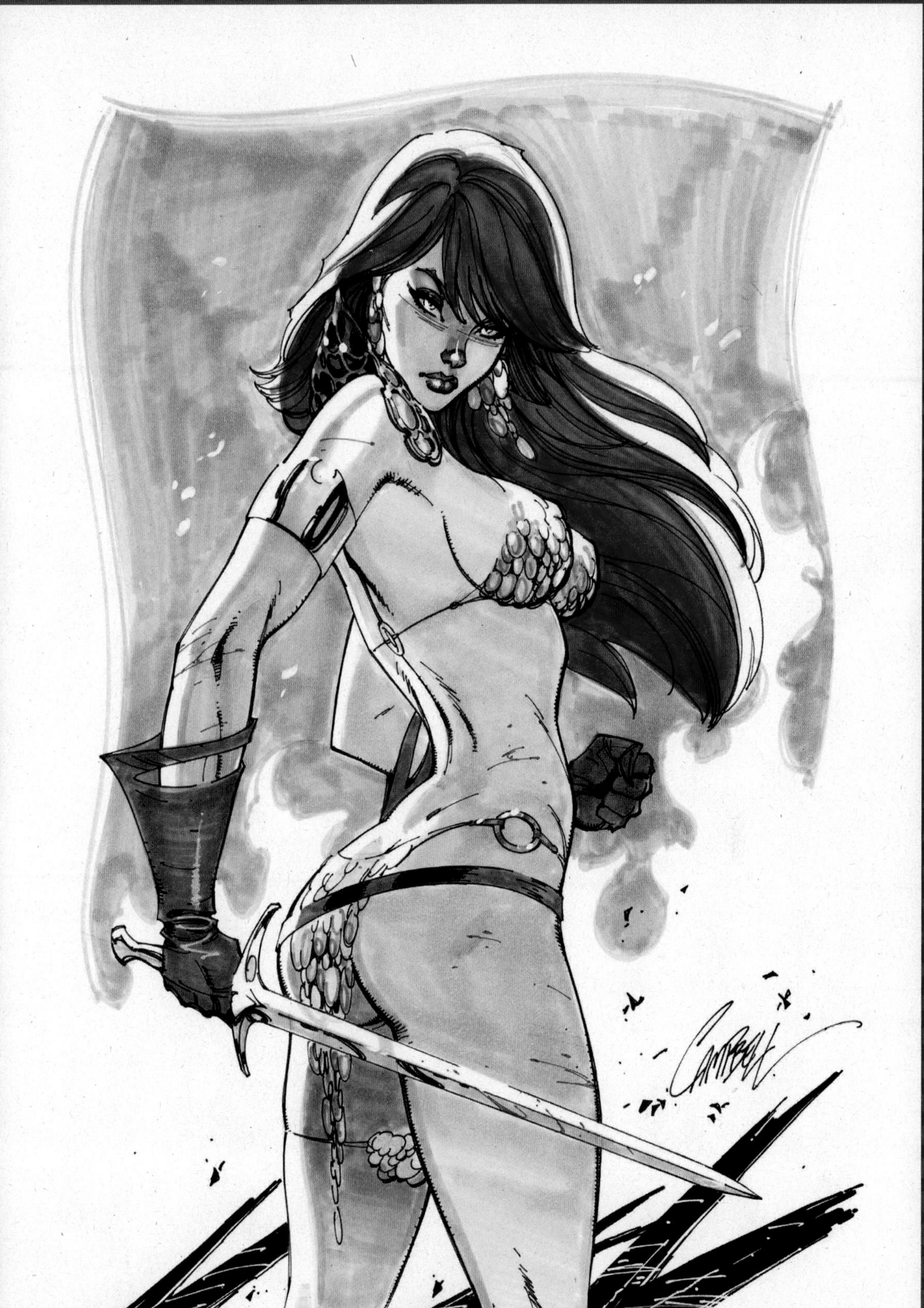

ISSUE #3: COVER ART BY J. SCOTT CAMPBELL

COVER GALLERY

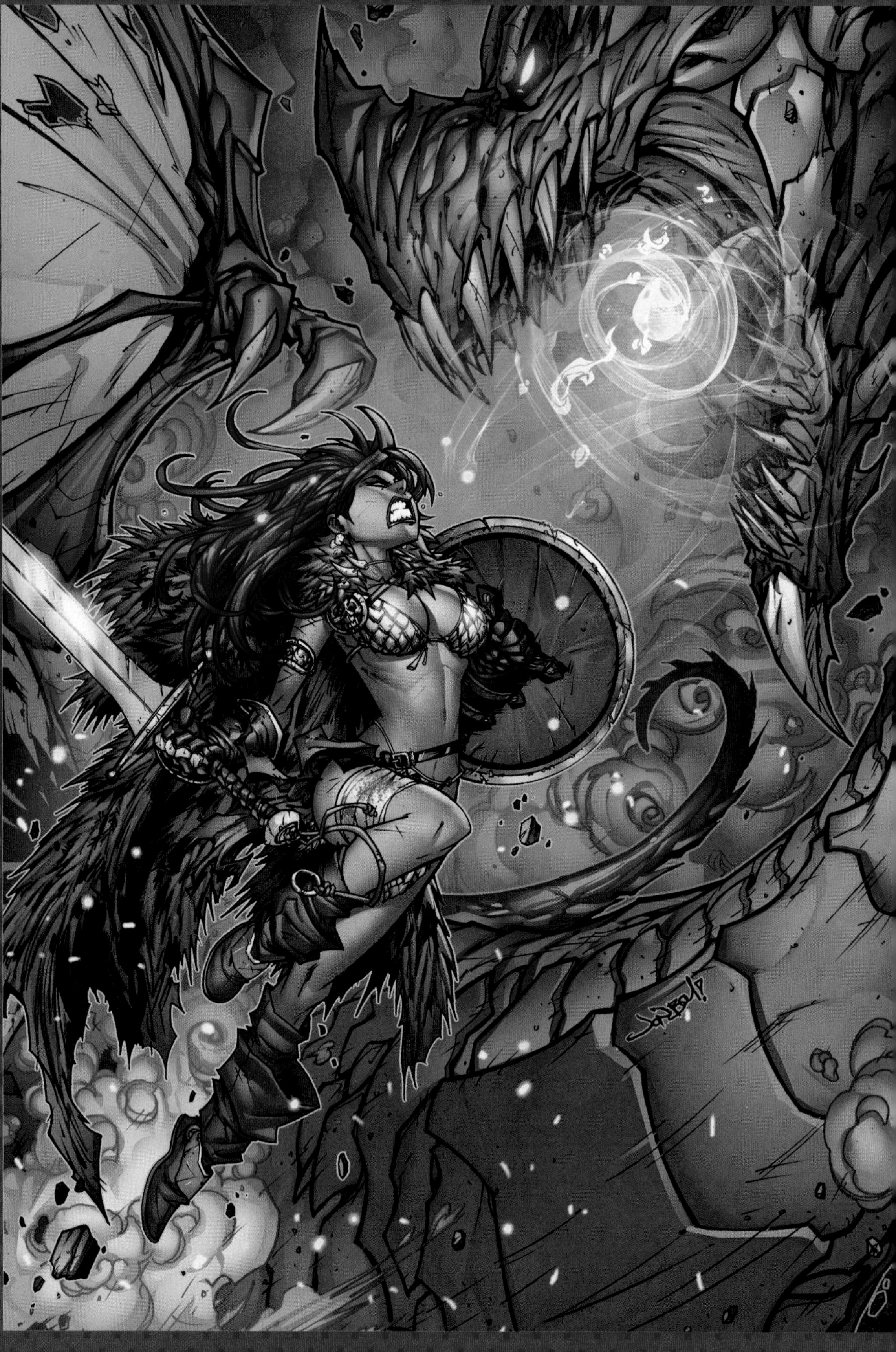

ISSUE #3: COVER ART BY **JONBOY MEYERS**

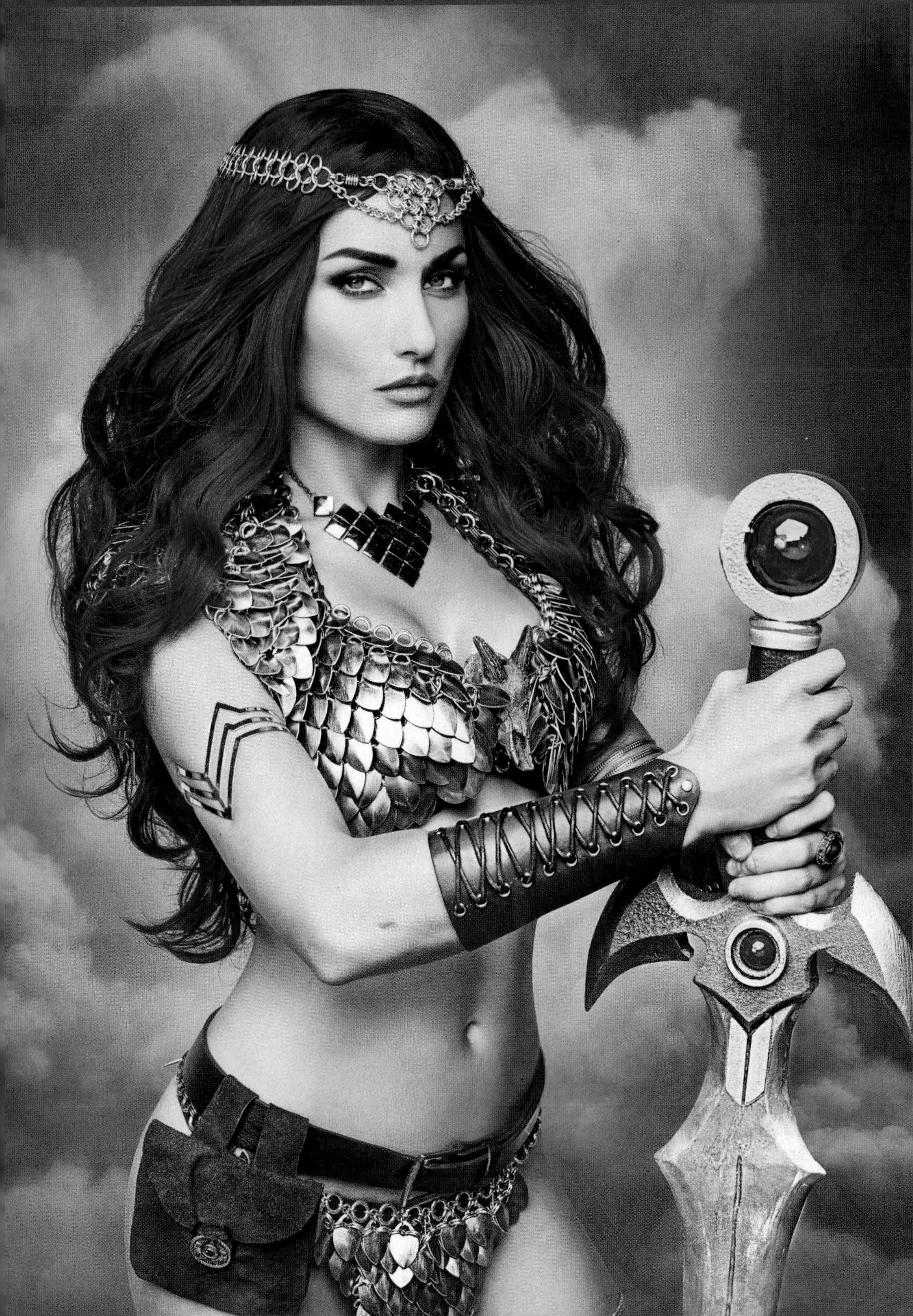

ISSUE #3: COSPLAY VARIANT
MODEL: TATIANA DEKHTYAR (TWITTER: @TATIANA DEKHTYAR), PHOTOGRAPHER: JOE RUBINSTEIN

COVER GALLERY

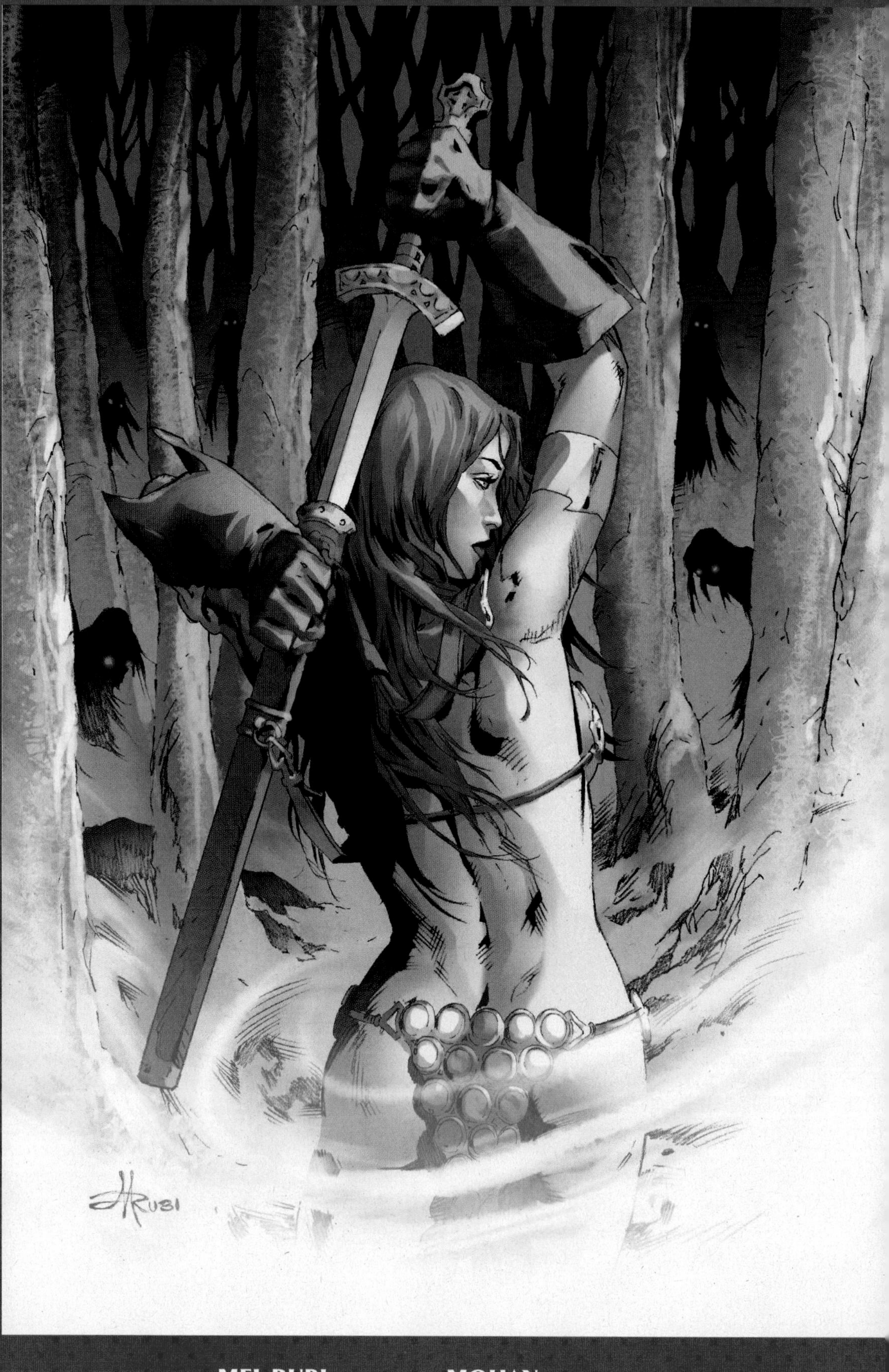
RUBI

ISSUE #3: COVER ART BY **MEL RUBI**, COLORS BY **MOHAN**

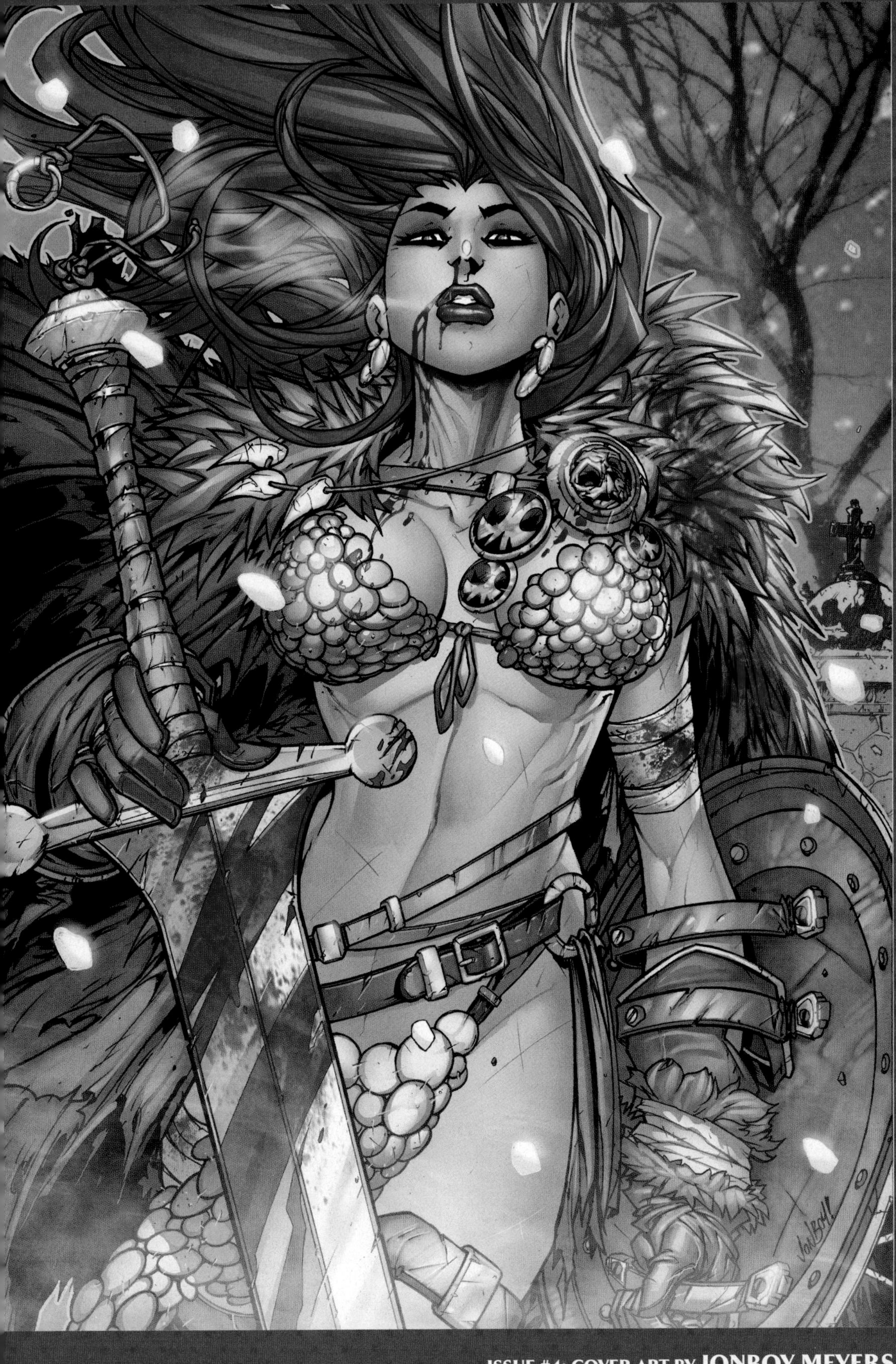

ISSUE #4: COVER ART BY **JONBOY MEYERS**

COVER GALLERY

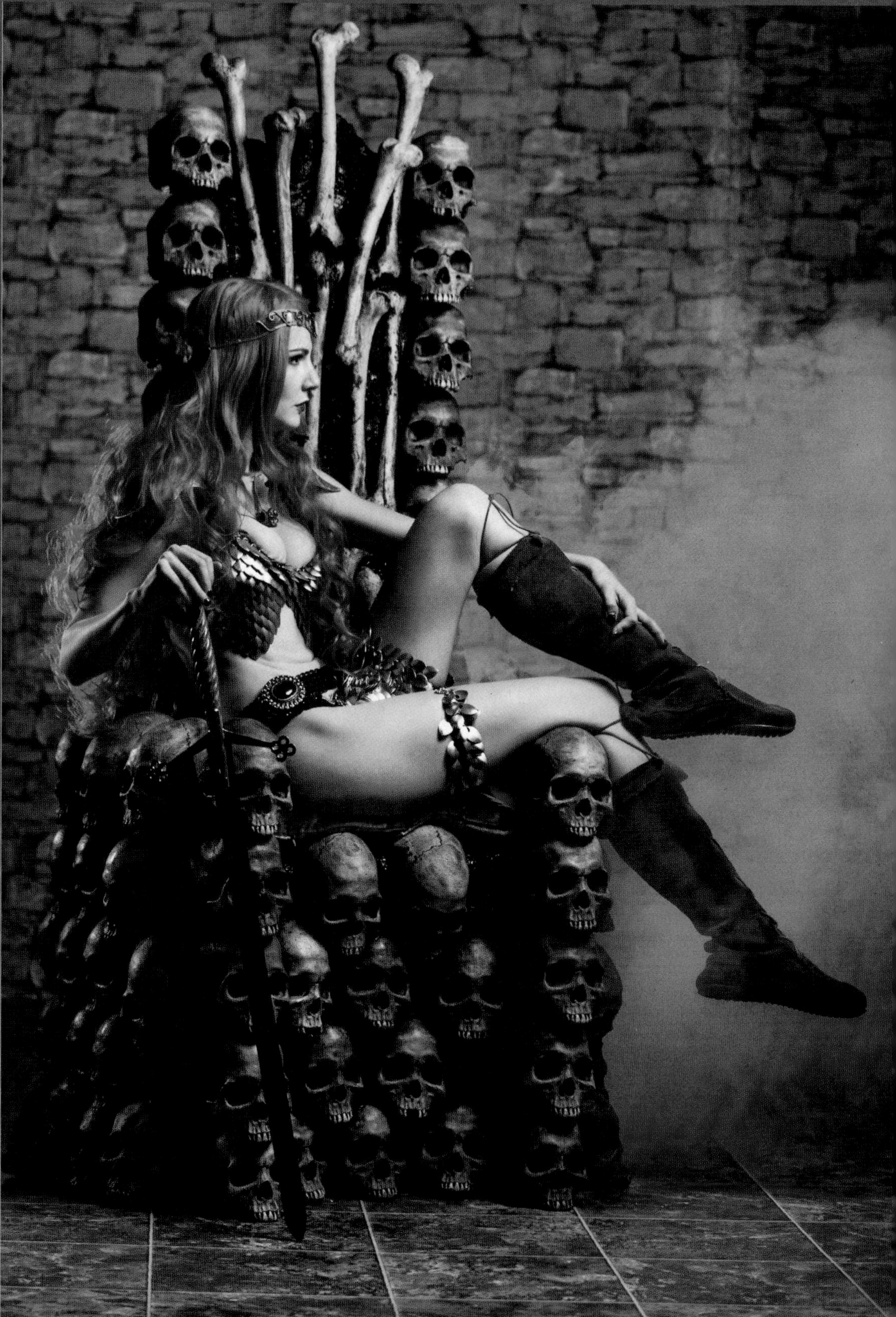

ISSUE #4: COSPLAY VARIANT
MODEL: KAT SHERIDAN (TWITTER: @KatKombat), PHOTOGRAPHER: SLEVIN MORS

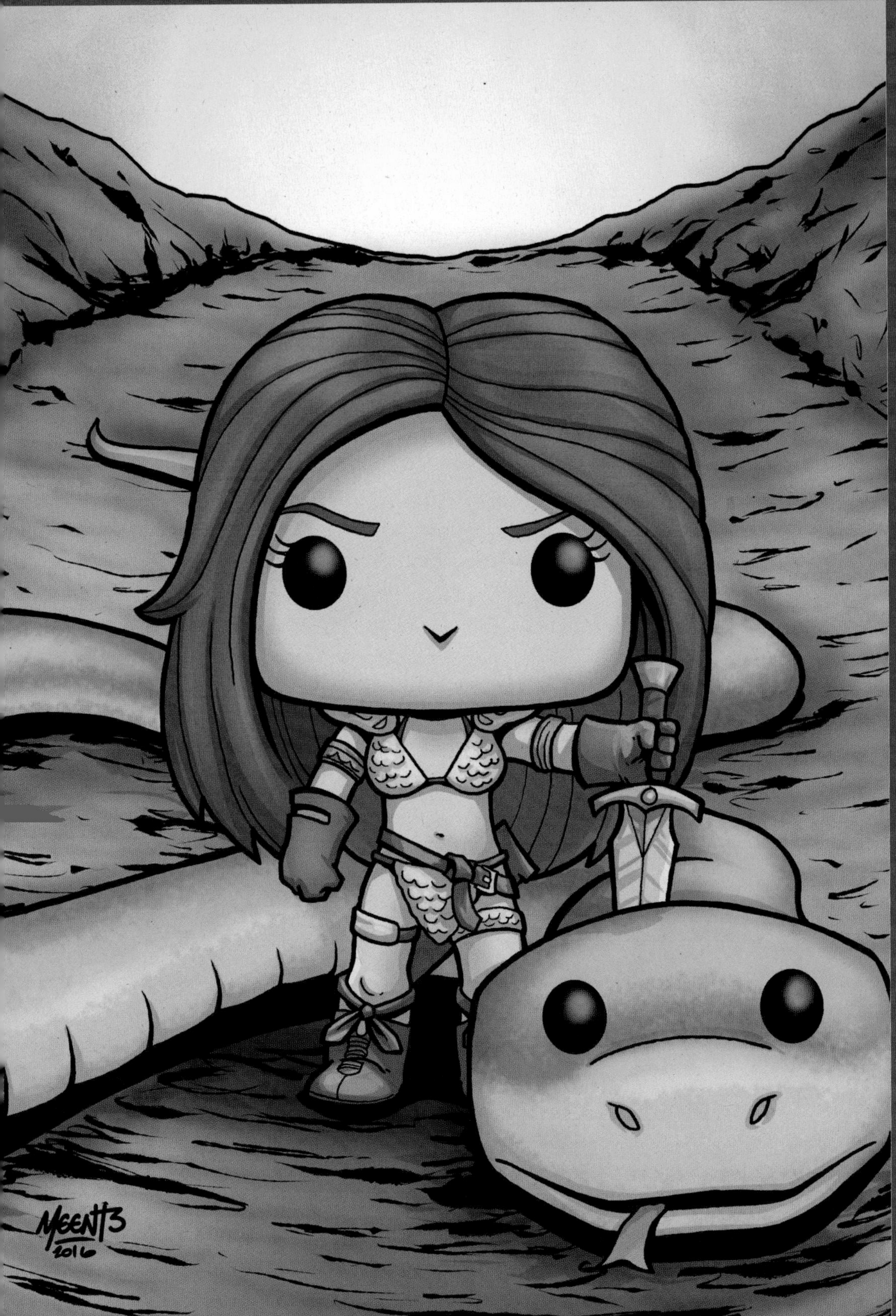
MEENTS
2016

ISSUE #4: FUNKO VARIANT, COVER ART BY **JASON MEENTS**

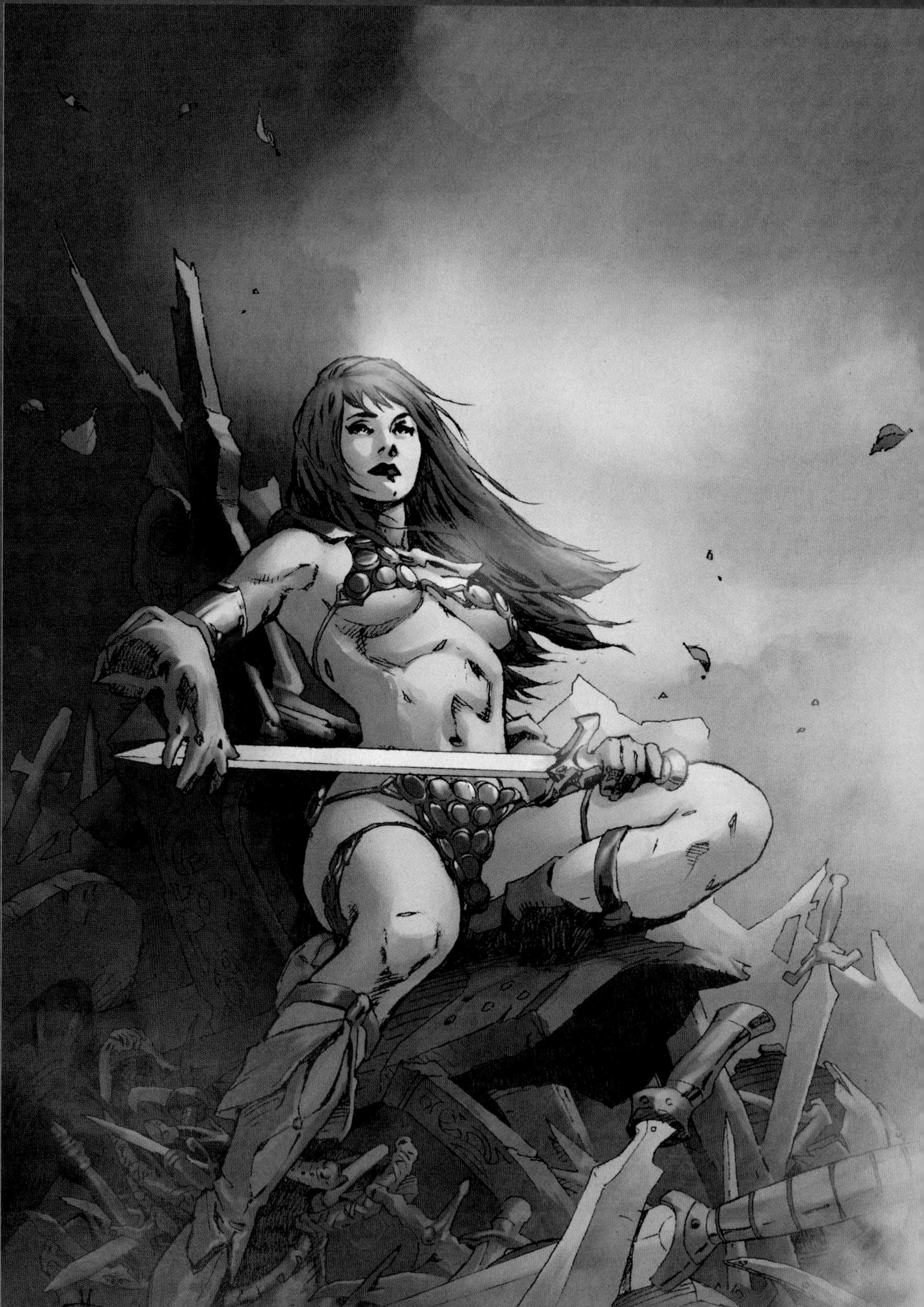

ISSUE #4: COVER ART BY MEL RUBI, COLORS BY MOHAN

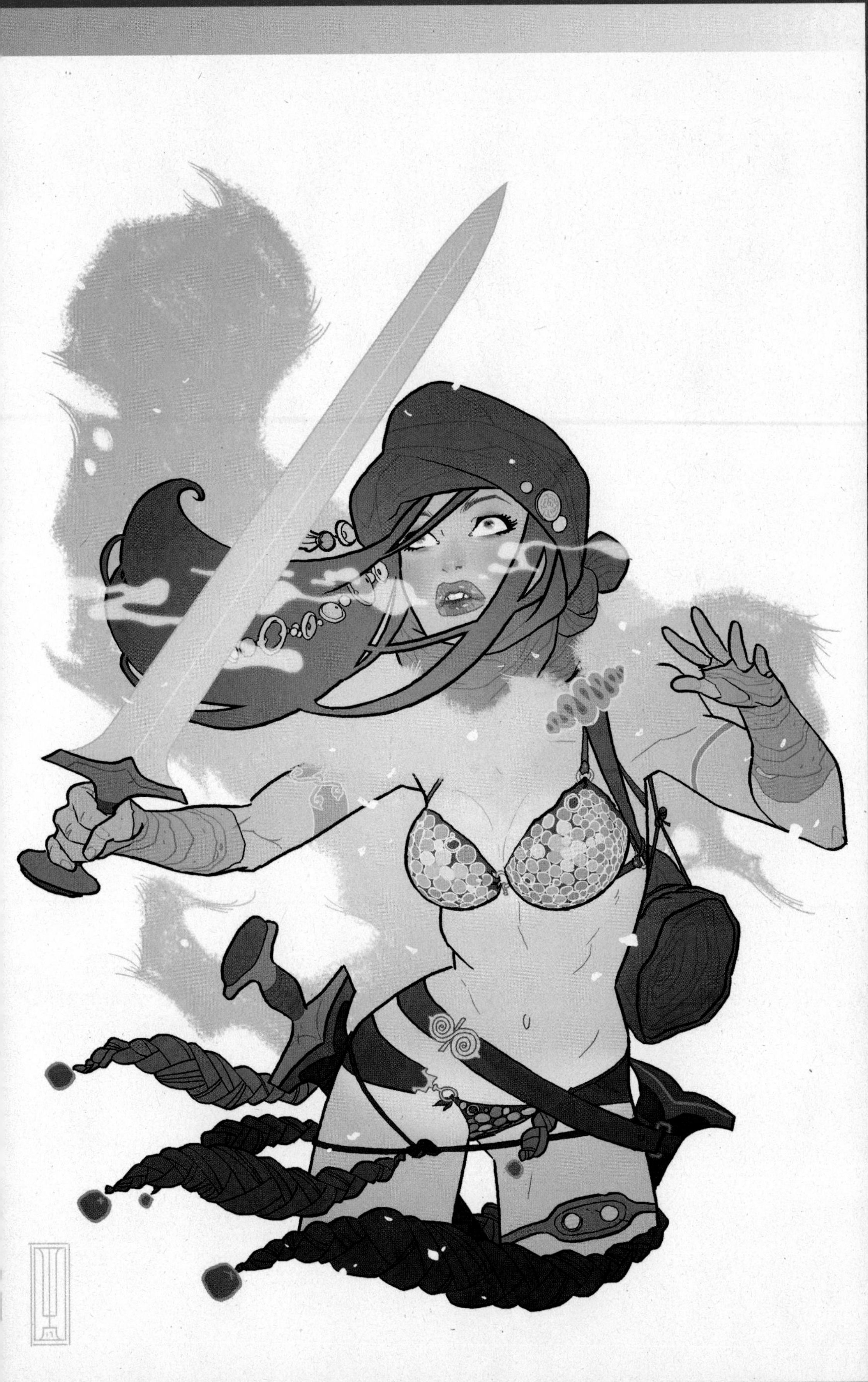

ISSUE #5: COVER ART BY BEN CALDWELL

COVER GALLERY

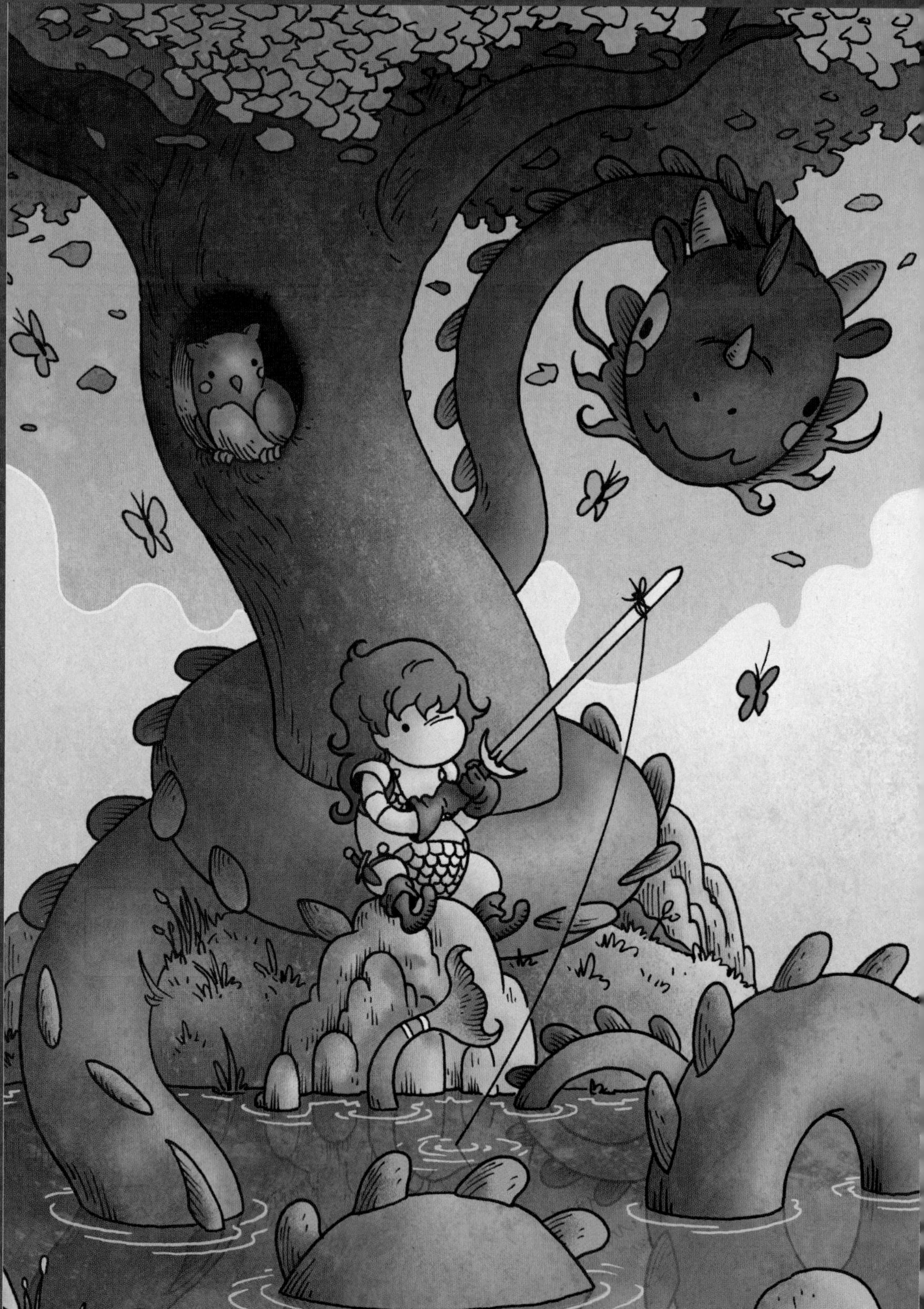
C.P. WILSON III

ISSUE #5: COVER ART BY CHARLES WILSON III

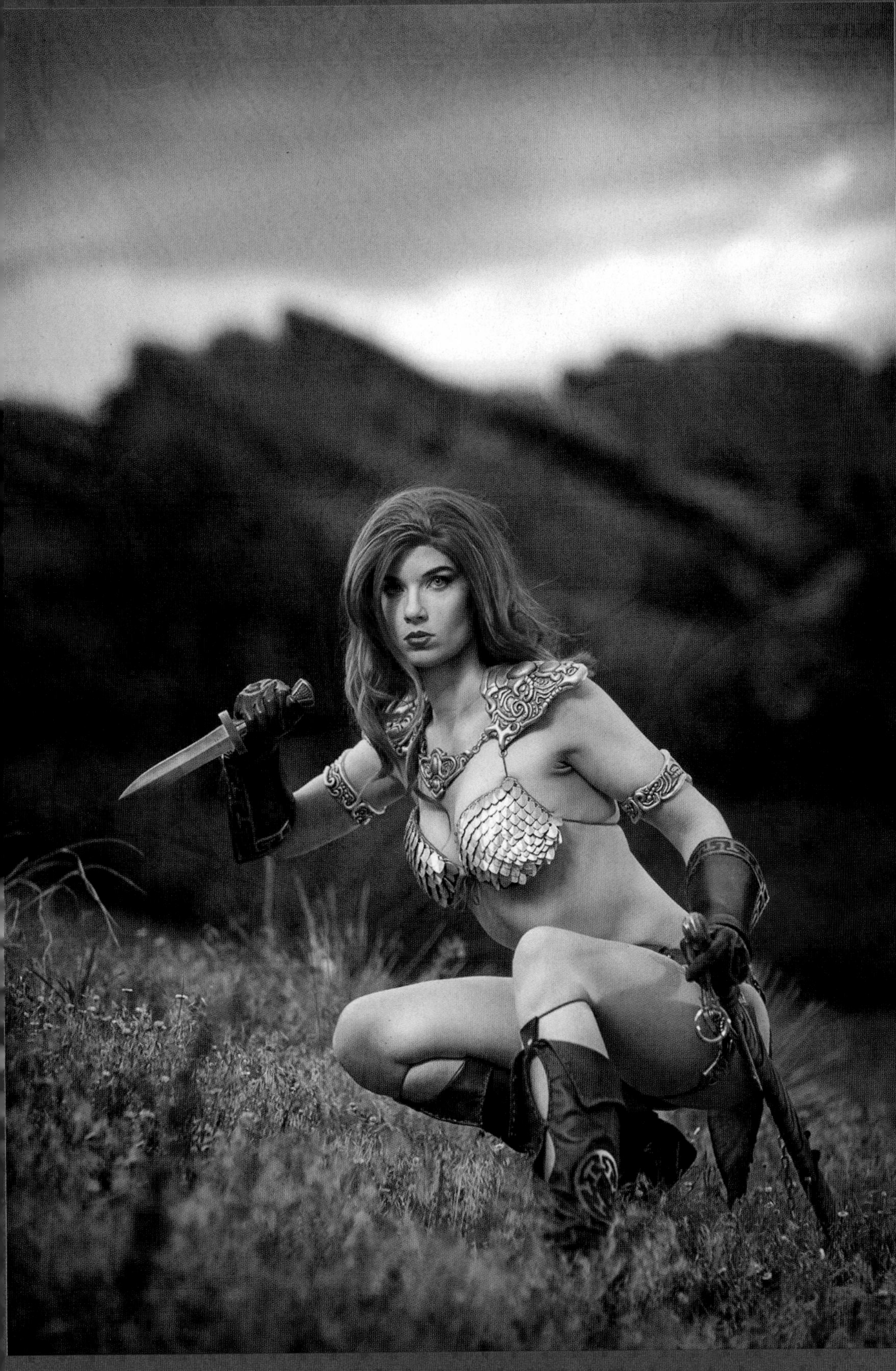

ISSUE #5: COSPLAY VARIANT
MODEL: JENNIFER ROSE aka JINGLEBOOBOO (TWITTER: @JINGLEBOOBOO), PHOTOGRAPHER: WeNeals

COVER GALLERY

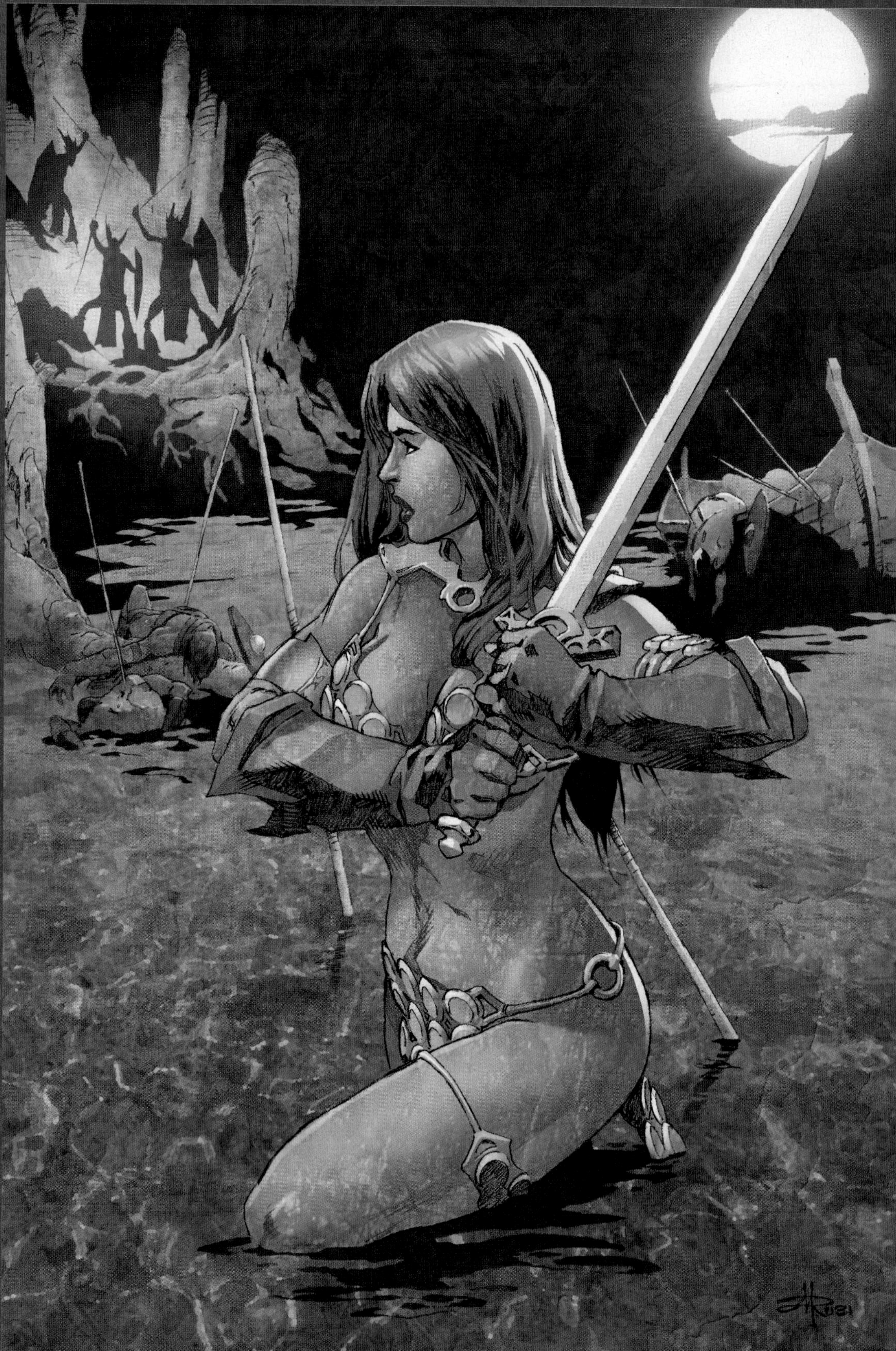

ISSUE #5: COVER ART BY **MEL RUBI**, COLORS BY **MOHAN**

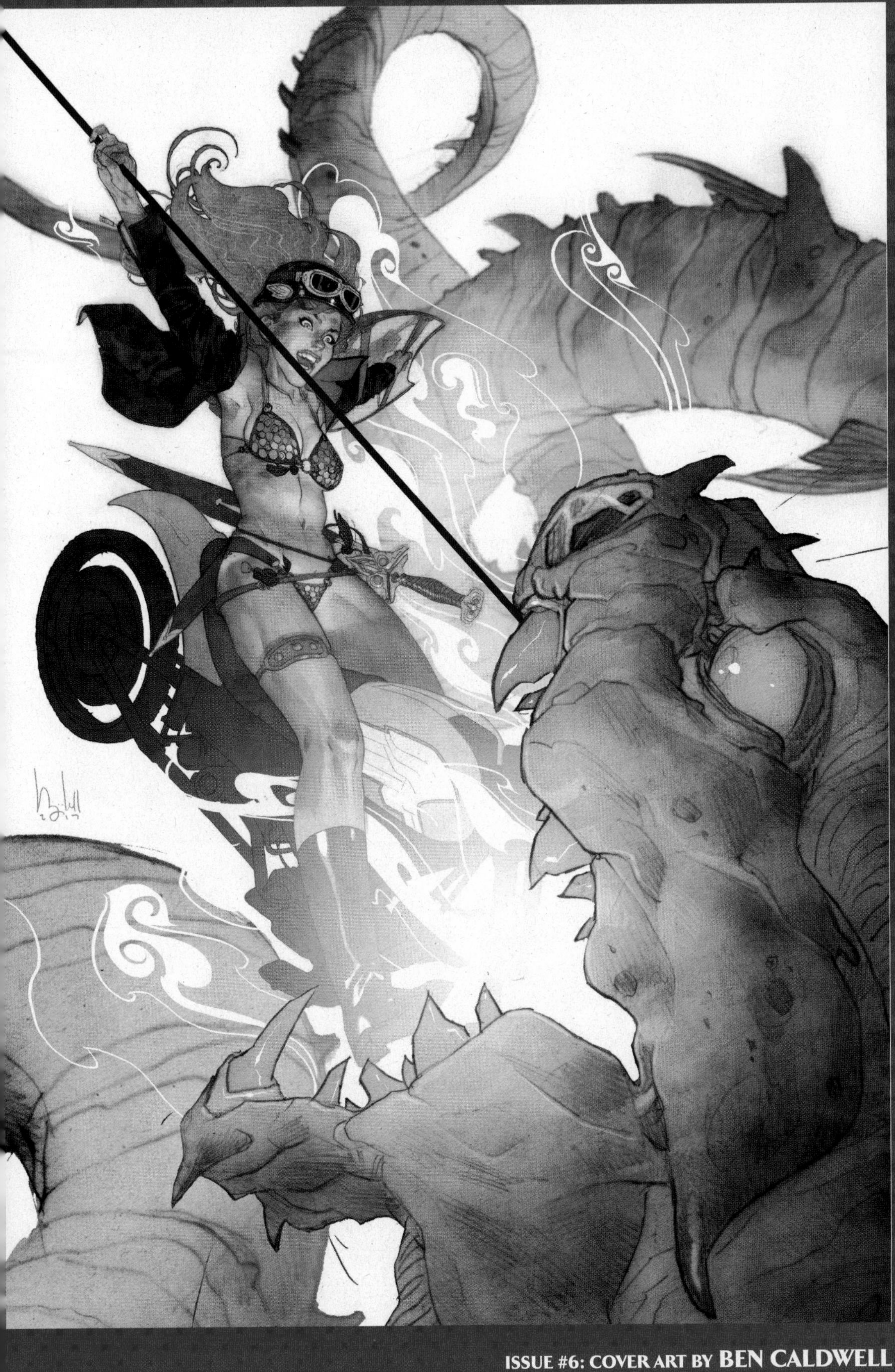

ISSUE #6: COVER ART BY BEN CALDWELL

COVER GALLERY

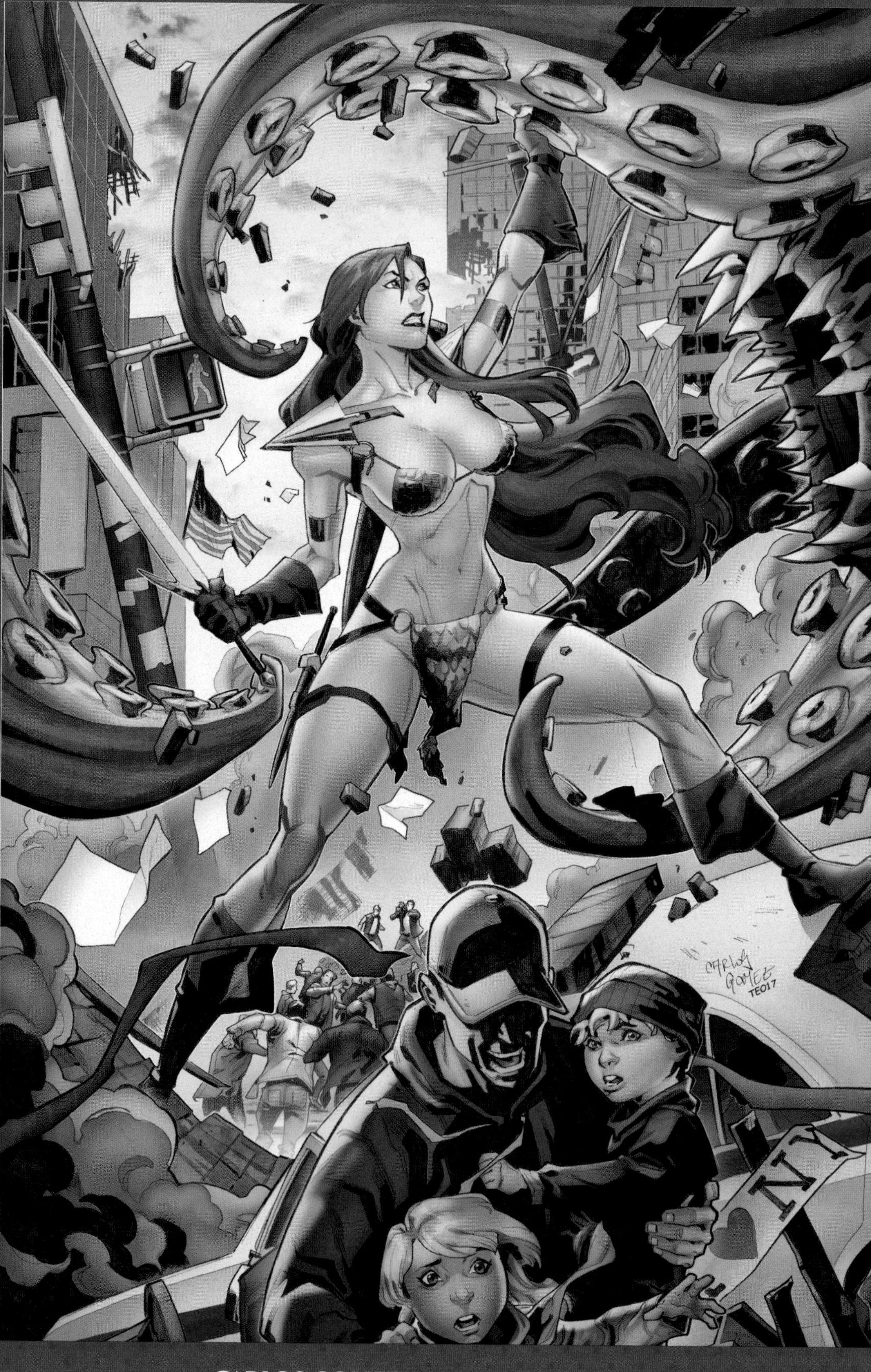
NY

ISSUE #6: COVER ART BY CARLOS GOMEZ, COLORS BY TEODORO GONZALEZ

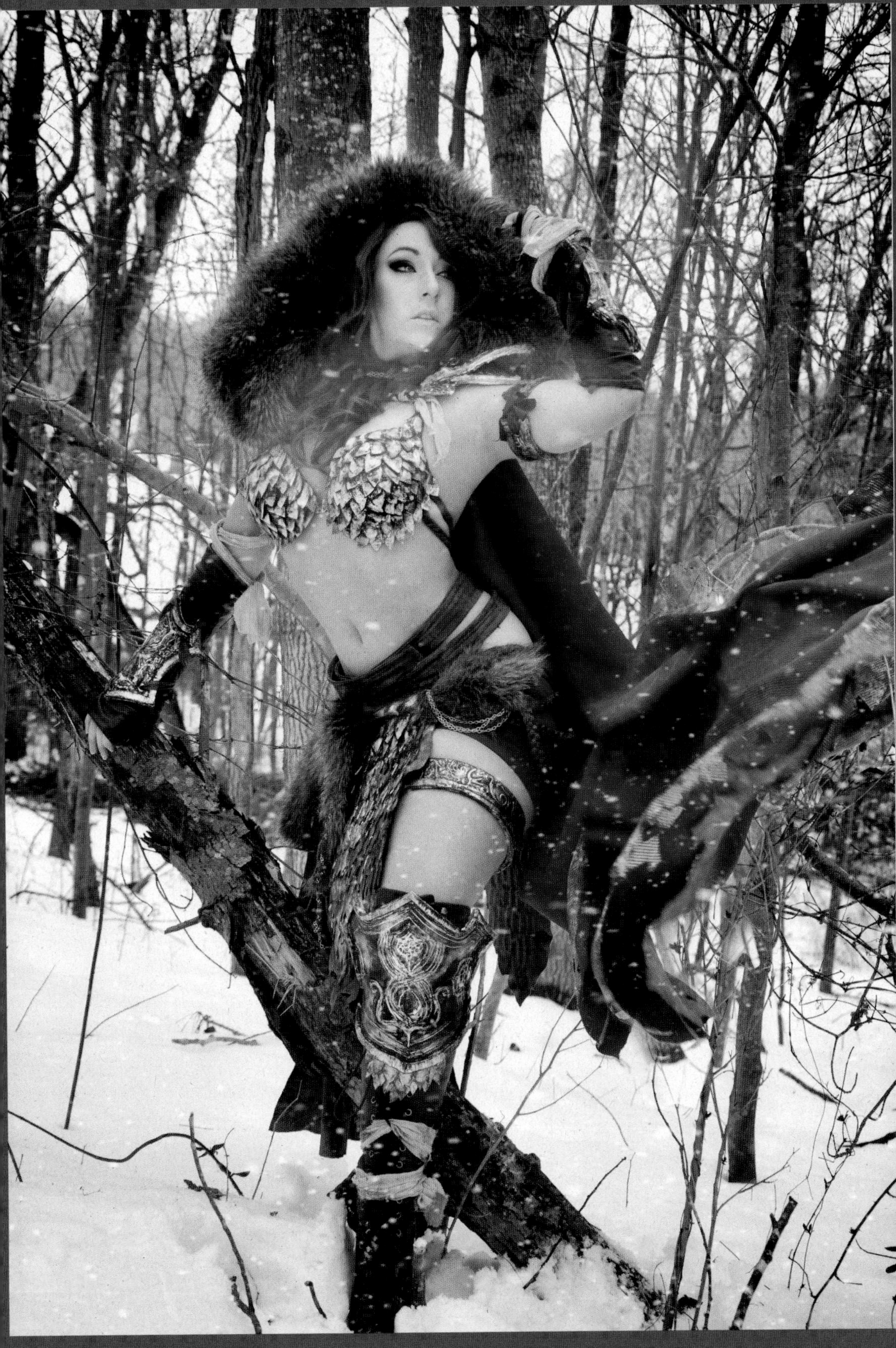

ISSUE #6: COSPLAY VARIANT
MODEL: DEANNA DAVIS (TWITTER: @ITSRAININGNEON, INSTAGRAM: @ITSRAININGNEON)

ISSUE #5: COVER ART BY MEL RUBI, COLORS BY MOHAN

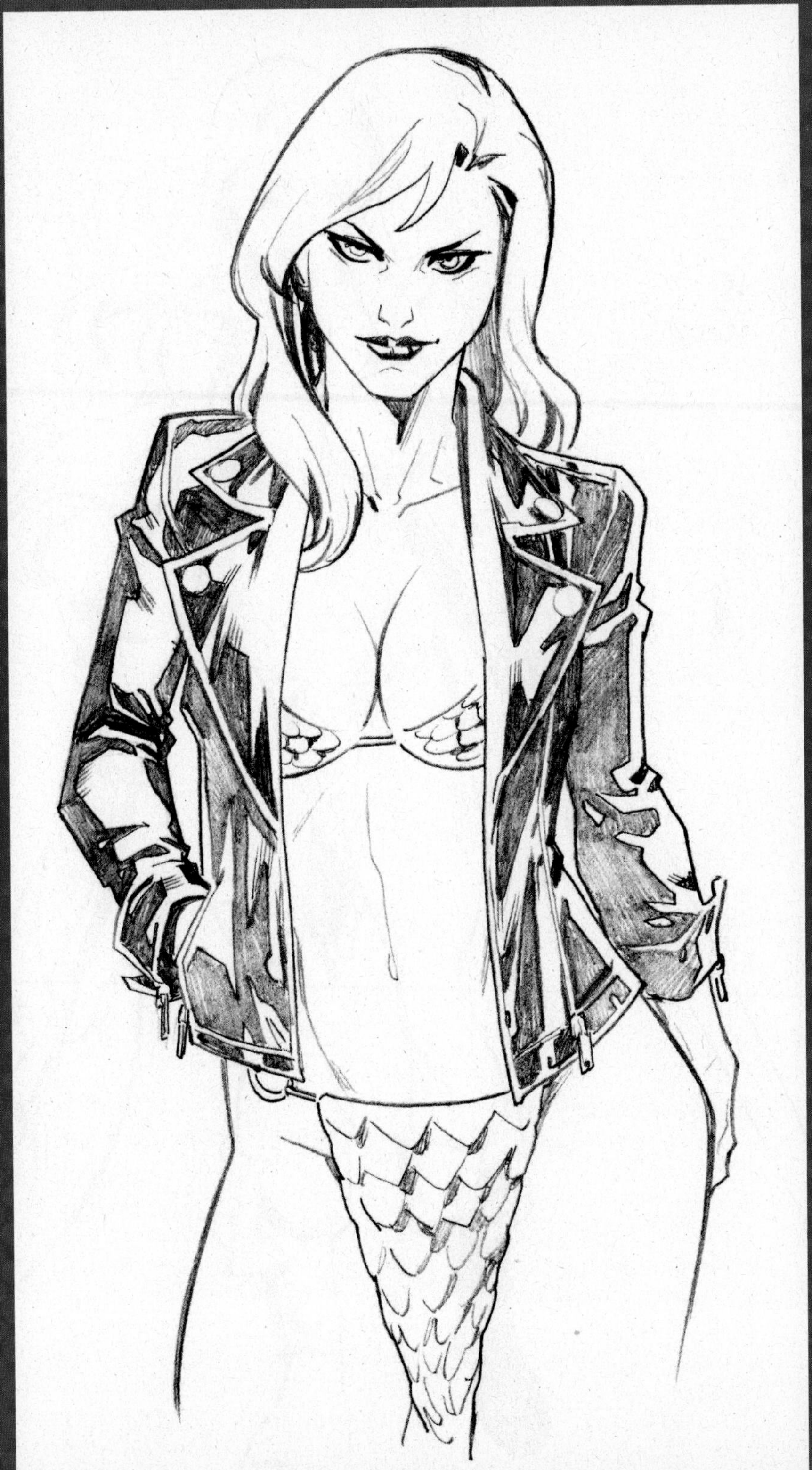

ART BY CARLOS GOMEZ

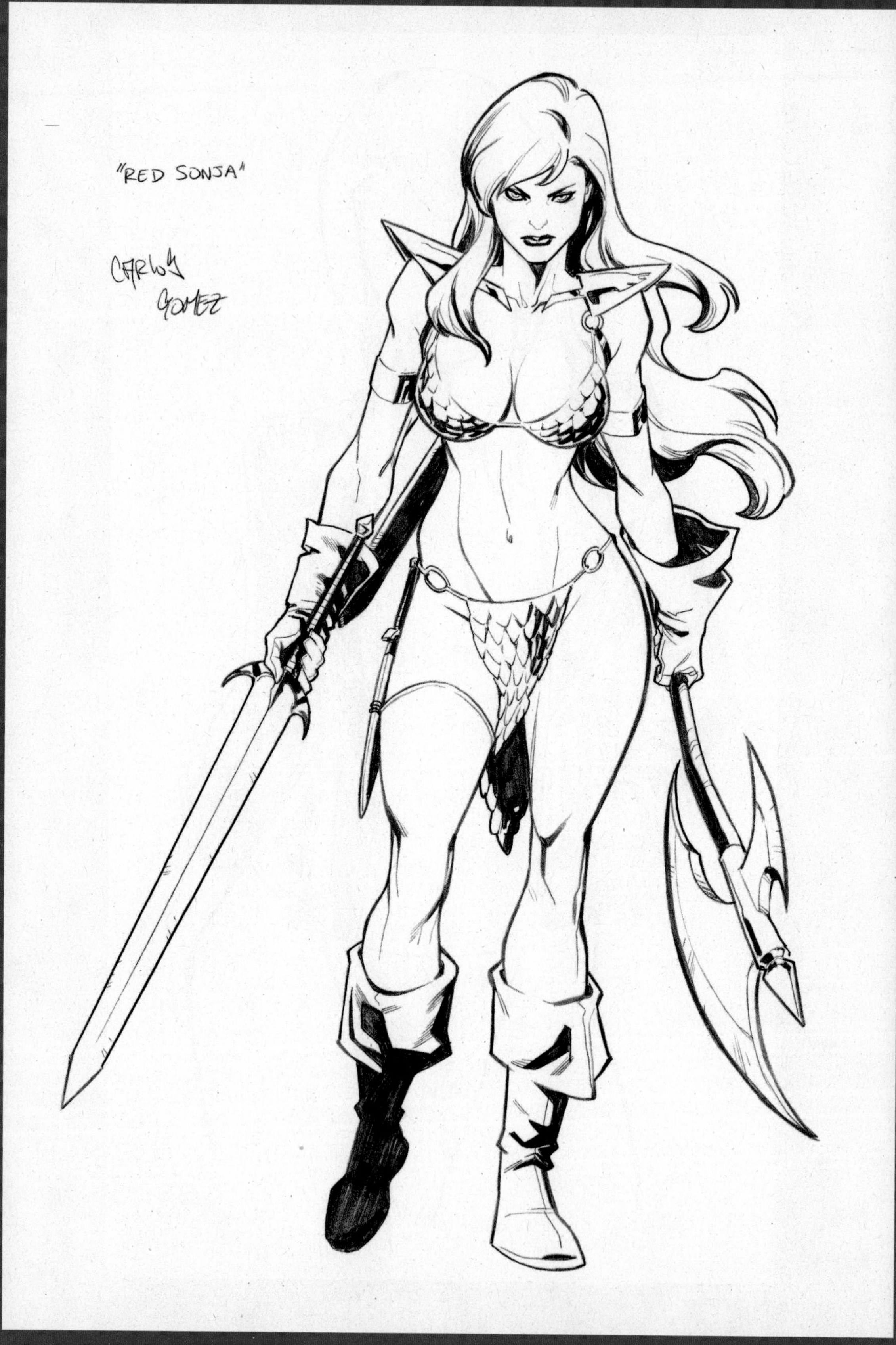
"RED SONJA"
CARLOS GOMEZ

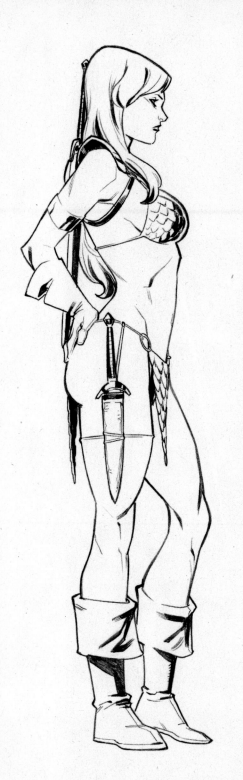

ART BY **CARLOS GOMEZ**

RED SONJA FAN ARTIST SPOTLIGHT

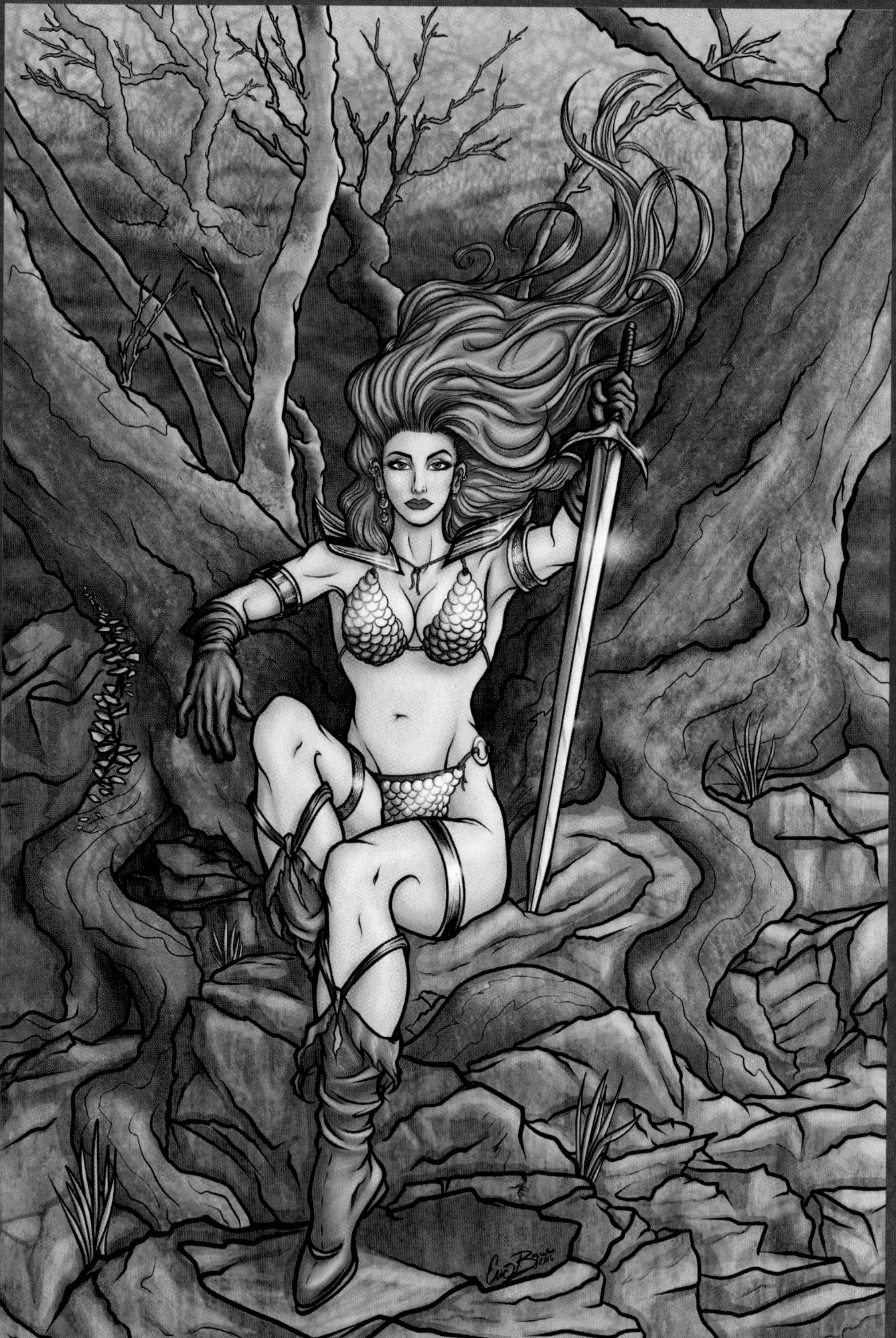

ART BY **ERIC BOGUE**

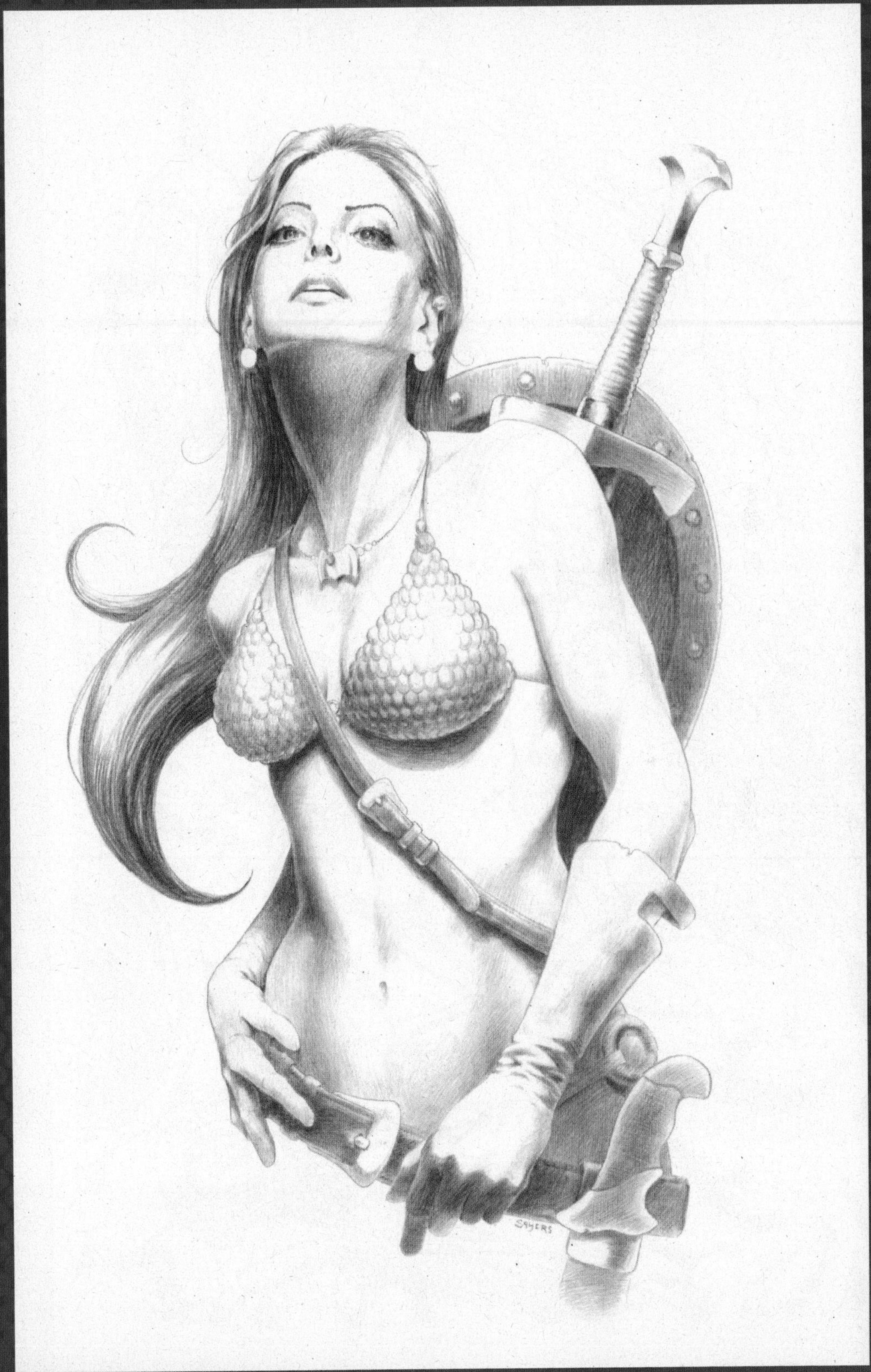

SAYERS

ART BY JEROME SAYERS

RED SONJA FAN ARTIST SPOTLIGHT

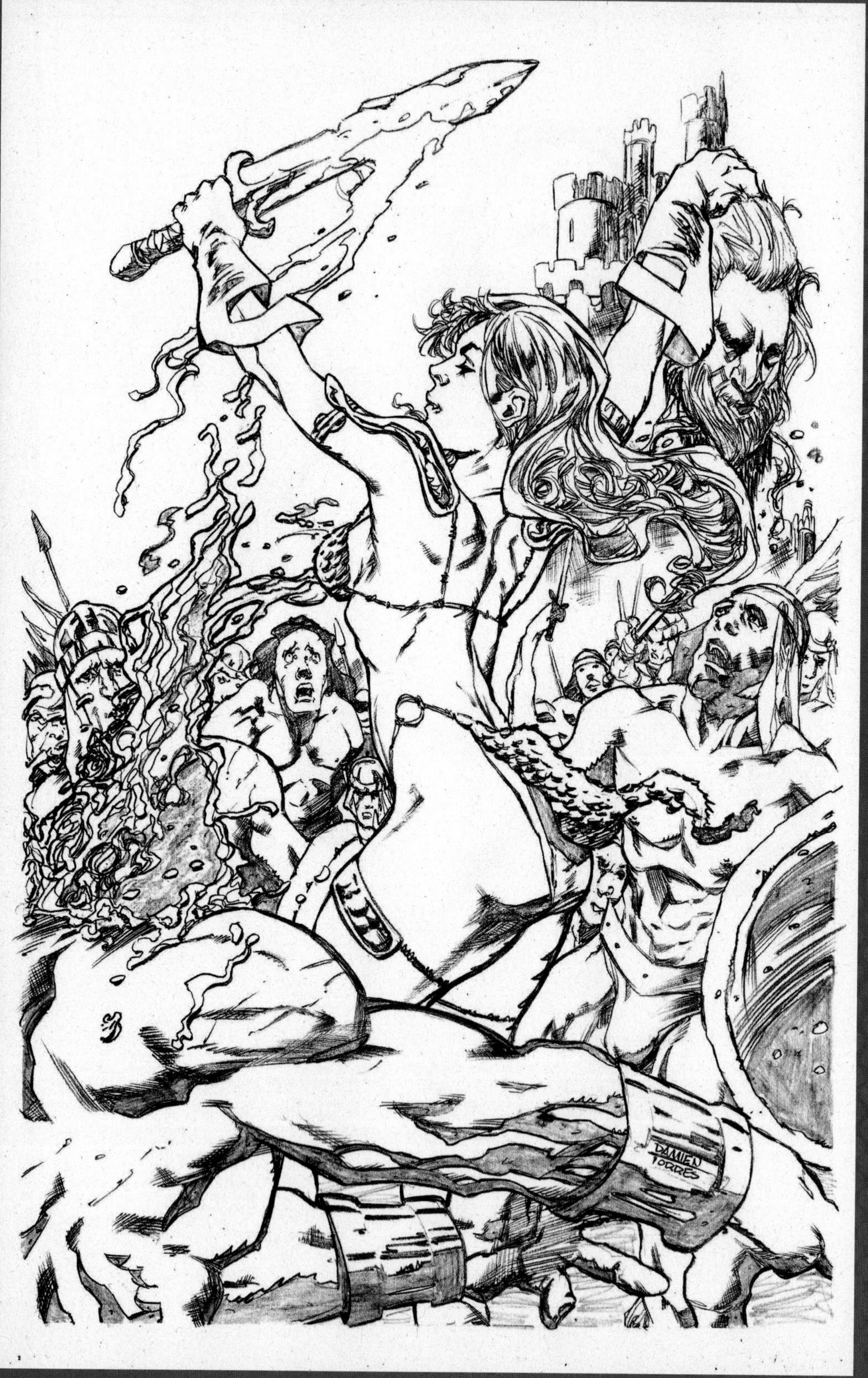
DAMIEN TORRES

ART BY DAMIEN TORRES

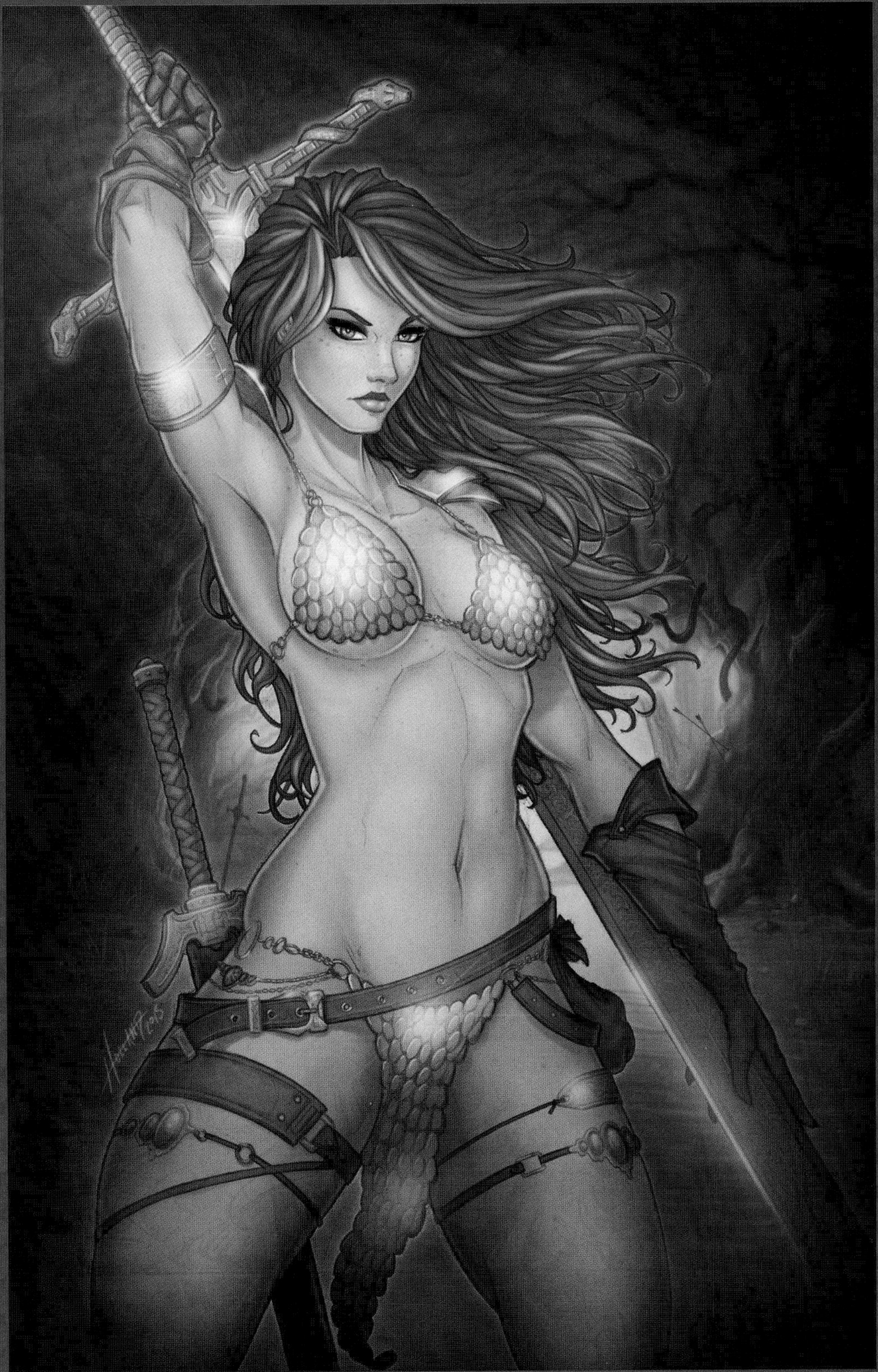

ART BY DUSTIN HOLLAND

RED SONJA FAN ARTIST SPOTLIGHT

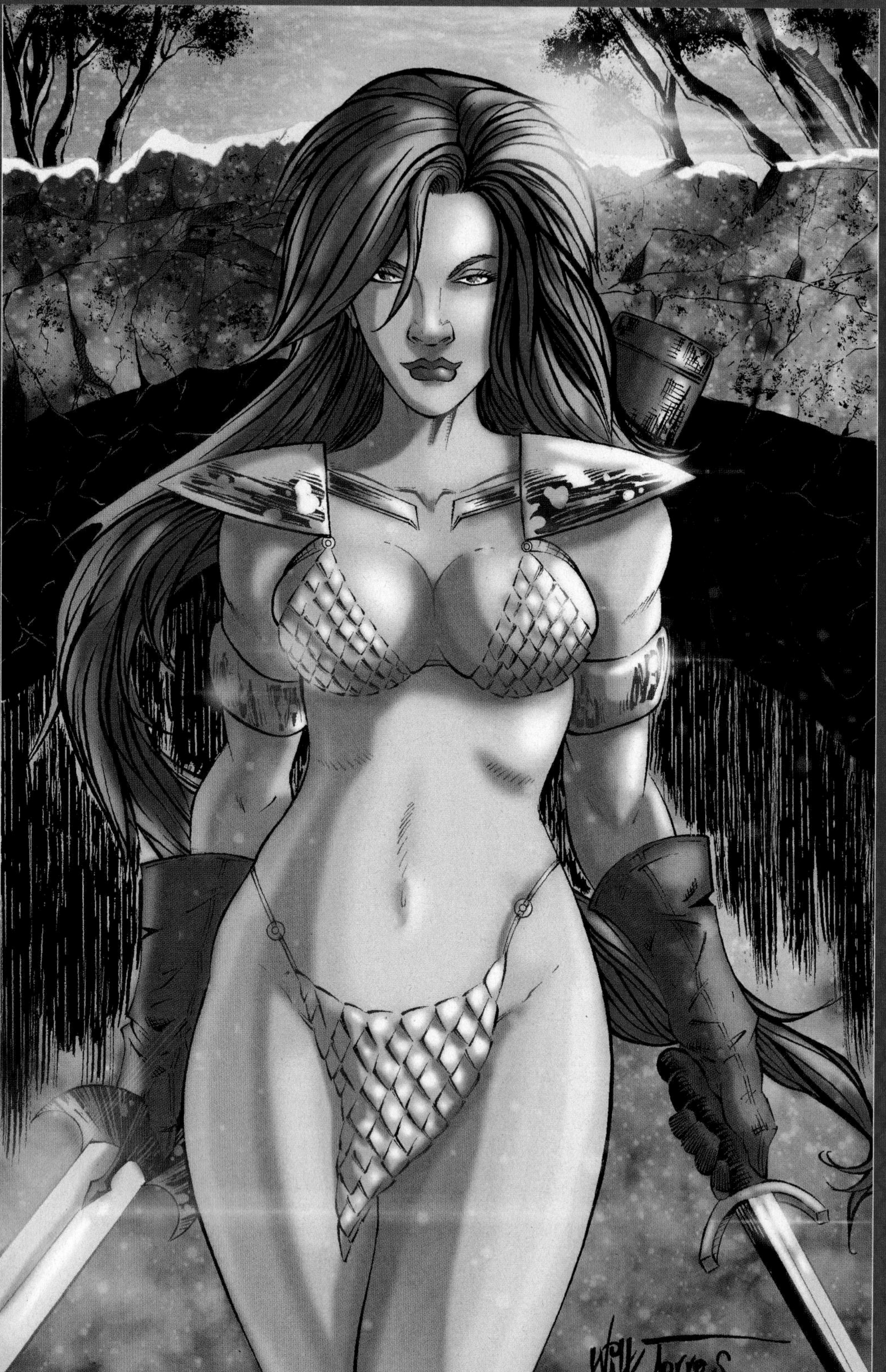
Will Torres

ART BY **WILL TORRES**

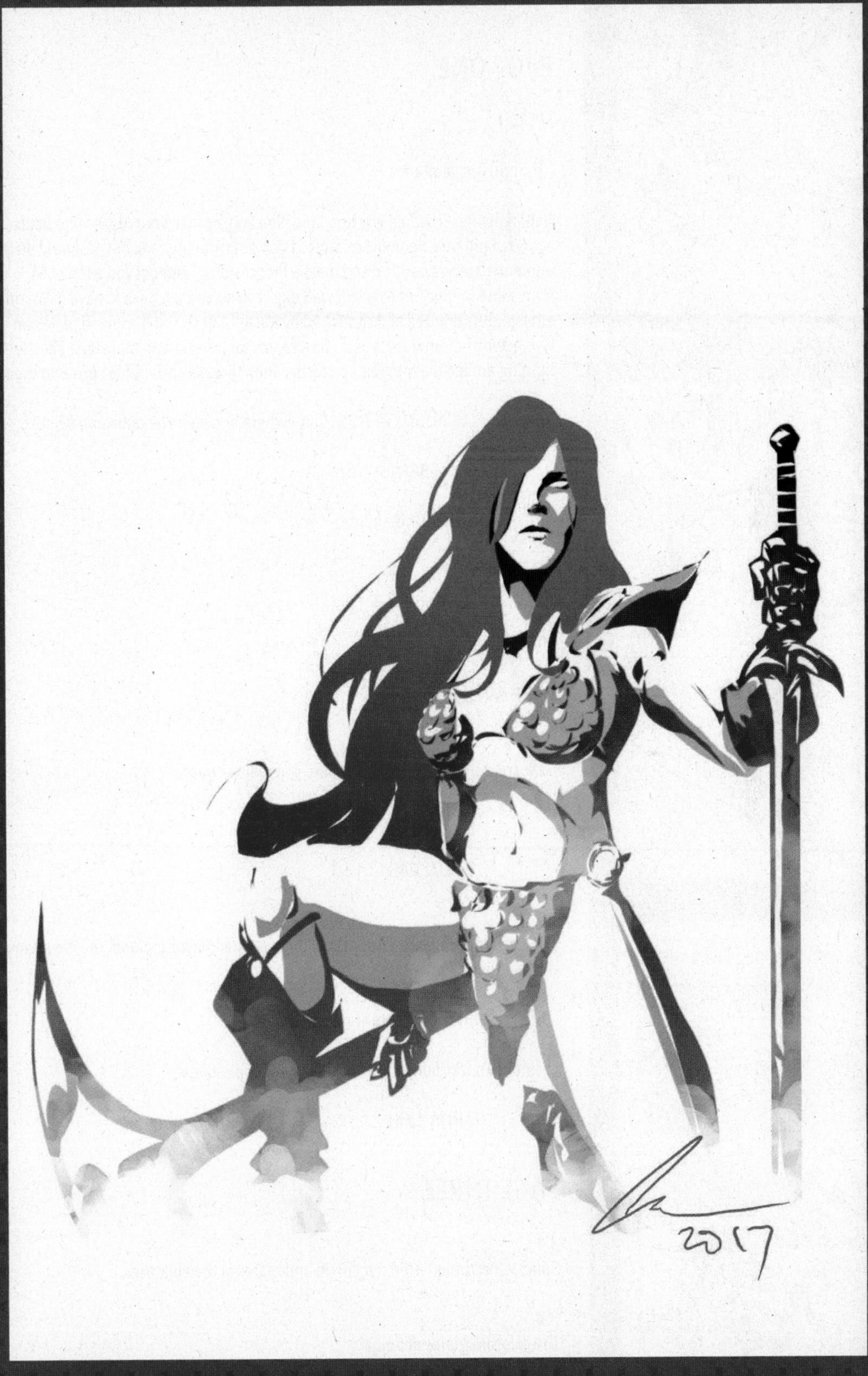
2017

ART BY CHRIS CHO

RED SONJA: WORLDS AWAY
ISSUE #0 SCRIPT

By Amy Chu
amywchu@gmail.com
9/6/16

PAGE ONE

SPLASH

- Start dream sequence -

Hyborian Age. Scorched war torn land. Red Sonja with sword rushes into battle against a gigantic demonic creature. I don't particularly care, but it should be immense, scary, awesome and maybe firebreathing, and get you a ton of $$ from some original art collector who digs it so much they have to have it. We find out later it's conjured and controlled by Kulan Gath so you may need to design it so maybe he can ride its back. Do a search for Lovecraftian monsters. They're fighting amidst the remains of a castle. Ruined walls and rubble surround them.

> LOCATION CAPTION: Somewhere between Hyrkania and Khitei...

> SFX: GRAAAHHHGH

> SONJA: <dialogue>

TITLE & CREDITS

PAGE TWO

THREE PANELS

2.1
Gath creature blasts Sonja with fire, she reels or ducks

> SFX:

> SONJA: GAH

2.2
Sonja charges forward underneath the creature, drawing blood, maybe slicing off an appendage.

> SFX: <creature shrieks>

2.3
Creature knocks Sonja down with a tail or appendage

> SONJA: UGH

PAGE THREE

3.1
Sonja wipes blood from her cut lip and glares at the creature.

3.2
The creature glares at Sonja.

3.3
Sonja rushes in again sword and dagger raised.

3.3
Sonja slashes the creature with force – she's making some decent headway.

3.4
The creature blasts Sonja with fire

SFX: <fire>

PAGE FOUR

THREE PANELS

4.1
Sonja emerges from the fire blast smoking, but unscathed, protected by some rubble.

4.2
A surprise blast comes from the opposite direction of the creature. Sonja looks surprised.

4.3
Sonja turns

PAGE FIVE

SPLASH

Kulan Gath swoops in, aiming a fiery blast straight at Sonja....

SONJA: KULAN GATH!

PAGE SIX

FIVE PANELS

- End dream sequence -

Now for some fun visual trickery - we need to show just enough but not reveal until the last few pages, so for the final page, it should all make sense that she's in the modern age. This may involve partial shots, silhouettes, shadows. Some people are already guessing that she's in the present, so I guess we just try to do what we can to throw them off ... From p.6 to 16 we progress from darkness to light, each panel and page getting lighter and lighter, revealing more and more.

6.1
Sonja awakens from her dream, almost completely in the dark. She's lying in a chamber somewhere underground.

SONJA: Aaahhh!

6.2
Close shot. Her hand is covered in rubble. Dirt and small rocks rain down on her.

SONJA: My sword. Where is my sword?

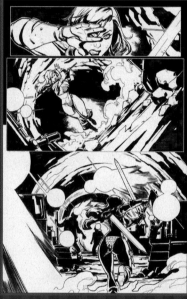

6.3
She sees the glint of her sword nearby.

>SONJA: There you are

6.4
She pulls her sword out from the dirt.

6.5
She kisses the blade.

PAGE SEVEN

FOUR PANELS

7.1
SONJA sits up. It's very dark.

>SONJA: Damn you, Gath. What kind of enchantment did you hit me with?

7.2
She stands up stiffly using her sword to help her.

>SONJA: Ow ow ow! Its hurts to move, worse than a hangover after a night of stygian fireballs. Why am I so sore? How long have I been out?

7.3
The ceiling starts collapsing, an opening appears in the wall...

>SFX: CRUMBLE

7.4
Sonja dashes through the opening ...

PAGE EIGHT

SPLASH

A large underground tunnel half constructed (subway tunnel). Lights shine on Sonja as she comes face to face with large yellow metal demons a tunnel borer- see photo ref, and (bulldozers- silhouetted in the foreground so we can't see exactly what they are). Her hair is tousled, she's covered in dirt. She's grimy from being asleep for decades.

>SONJA:

>DEMONS: ....! .....!

PAGE NINE

9.1
Covering her eyes with her left arm

>SONJA: Bring it on, demons!

9.2
She lunges at the demons

SONJA: HRAHHHH

9.3
The yellow demons grind to a halt. Their buckets lower to reveal a cab with the silhouette of a demon inside- a light shining from his forehead.

       SFX:

       DEMONS: ....! .....!

PAGE TEN

FIVE PANELS

10.1
The silhouettes of humanoid demons appear (construction workers in suits, also silhouetted so it's not immediately obvious what they are)

       DEMONS: ....,..!

10.2
Sonja blinded by the lights, swings her blade

10.3
SONJA charges forward, with her sword - the demons scatter

10.4
SONJA runs forward along a path upward.

       SONJA: Where are you Gath? I am coming for you.

10.5
SONJA looks around. She's in a rocky cave of some sort clearly manmade (it's a construction tunnel.)

PAGE ELEVEN

SIX PANELS

11.1
Sonja follows a tunnel. Sonja continues upwards until she sees light and hears thunder. Is it the dragon?

       SFX: ROARRRRRRRRRR

11.2
Inset panel- by her foot is a metal track.

11.3
She crouches down- it's a long straight metal track.

11.4
She touches her sword to it

       SFX: TINK

11.5
She puts her ear to the track. It's vibrating a little

SFX: HUMMMMM

11.6
She turns. A light shines on her grimy, face

SFX: ROOOAAAAARRRRRR

PAGE TWELVE

SPLASH

A huge silhouetted shape thunders down the tracks towards SONJA (it's a subway train). She adopts a fighting stance, sword ready, but the light is blinding her.

SFX: ROOOAAAAARRRRRR

PAGE THIRTEEN

THREE PANELS

13.1
SONJA jumps to the side.

SFX: <train noises>

13.2
Sonja rolls on the ground as the train roars past her (try to make it so it's not obvious that it's a subway train)

SFX: RUMBLE RUMBLE

13.3
SONJA gets up, shaken, looks at the back of the disappearing train, maybe hand up scratching her head questioning.

SONJA: What manner of beast was that?

SFX: SKRITCH SCKRITCH

PAGE FOURTEEN

FIVE PANELS

14.1
Sonja looks down at a large scruffy rat. It stands up on its hind legs and sniffs curiously at her without fear, as NY rats do...

SONJA: Finally a beast I recognize. Where am I, little creature?

14.2
Sonja look up with wonder at ice and icicles forming on the ceiling and sides of the tunnel. She shivers.

SONJA: This is too cold to be Hyrkania.

14.3
Pull back to show faded dirt encrusted graffiti art covering the tunnels. It's impossible to see the designs through the thick layers of grime.

> SONJA: What strange markings. No Khitei or Hyrkanian for sure.

14.4
Sonja wipes some of the dirt off to reveal strange colors she's never seen before- unnatural colors like dayglo orange

> SONJA: Magical to be sure. I've never seen such colors.

14.5
Sonja walks along the tunnel, towards a very slight ray of daylight, the rat trailing behind her.

> SONJA: Finally, some light. What lies ahead I know not, but it can't be worse than this tunnel.

PAGE FIFTEEN

FOUR PANELS

15.1
The daylight streaming from above reveals a metal ladder along
 the wall (make this a staircase if this makes more sense)

15.2
Sonja climbs up the ladder towards the light.

15.3
The light is coming from holes in a metal cover in the ceiling of
the tunnel (a manhole cover)

15.4
Sonja pushes the manhole cover off… daylight streams down
on her face....

PAGE SIXTEEN

SPLASH

A sunny day in winter. Construction site in present day
New York City, midtown Manhattan, maybe Rockefeller
Center since Times Square has been done so much, or
down by Wall Street and the Freedom Tower. Sonja emerges
from the ground, covered in dust and dirt like a devil. She is
shielding her eyes from the sun. Her sword and weapons are
sheathed.

Police surround her in NYPD gear (letters NYPD on their bulletproof
vests), shouting, guns aimed. Tourists and businesspeople in coats,
hats, winter gear, taking pics with their cellphones. A bulldozer,
construction workers like the ones underground gape. There are subway
station signs and an entrance nearby. Billboards, ads indicate it's
about to be New Year Countdown 2017

> SONJA: By Mitra!

> POLICE: ….. ….. ! ….. !

TO BE CONTINUED

SHE-DEVIL VOL. 1
9781933305110

SHE-DEVIL VOL. 2
9781933305543

SHE-DEVIL VOL. 3
9781933305523

SHE-DEVIL VOL. 4
9781933305639

SHE-DEVIL VOL. 5
9781933305837

SHE-DEVIL VOL. 6
9781933305905

SHE-DEVIL VOL. 13
9781606904565

QUEEN SONJA VOL. 1
9781606901823

QUEEN SONJA VOL. 2
9781606902158

QUEEN SONJA VOL. 3
9781606902660

QUEEN SONJA VOL. 4
9781606903391

QUEEN SONJA VOL. 5
9781606903780

WRATH OF THE GODS
9781606901441

REVENGE OF THE GODS
9781606902400

UNCHAINED
9781606904534

ADVENTURES OF VOL. 1
9781933305073

ADVENTURES OF VOL. 2
9781933305127

ADVENTURES OF VOL. 3
9781933305981

TRAVELS VOL. 2
9781606905845

WITCHBLADE/SONJA
9781606903889

PROPHECY
9781606903995

VOL. 1 (SIMONE)
9781606904817

VOL. 2 (SIMONE)
9781606905296

VOL. 3 (SIMONE)
9781606906019

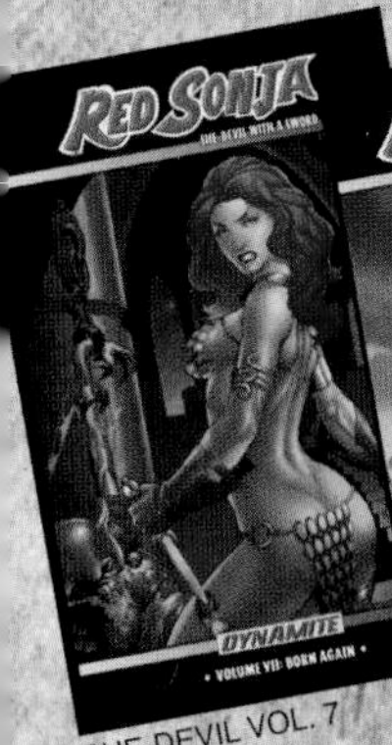
RED SONJA
SHE-DEVIL WITH A SWORD
DYNAMITE
VOLUME VII: BORN AGAIN
SHE-DEVIL VOL. 7
9781606900116

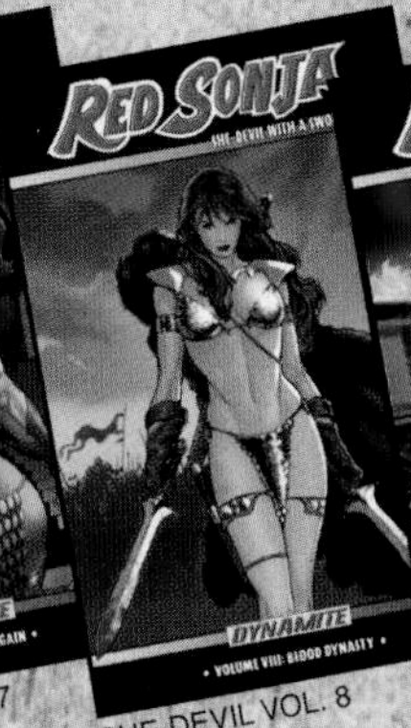
RED SONJA
SHE-DEVIL WITH A SWORD
DYNAMITE
VOLUME VIII: BLOOD DYNASTY
SHE-DEVIL VOL. 8
9781606900635

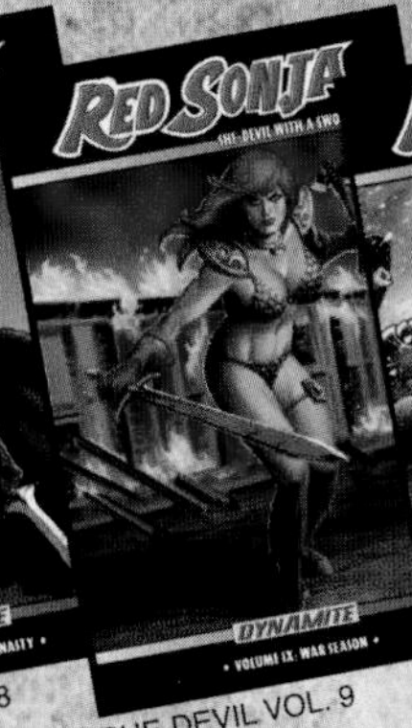
RED SONJA
DYNAMITE
VOLUME IX: WAR SEASON
SHE-DEVIL VOL. 9
9781606901120

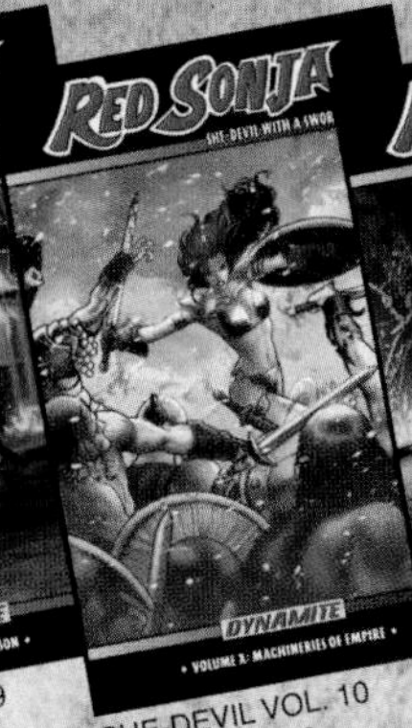
RED SONJA
SHE-DEVIL WITH A SWORD
DYNAMITE
VOLUME X: MACHINERIES OF EMPIRE
SHE-DEVIL VOL. 10
9781606903162

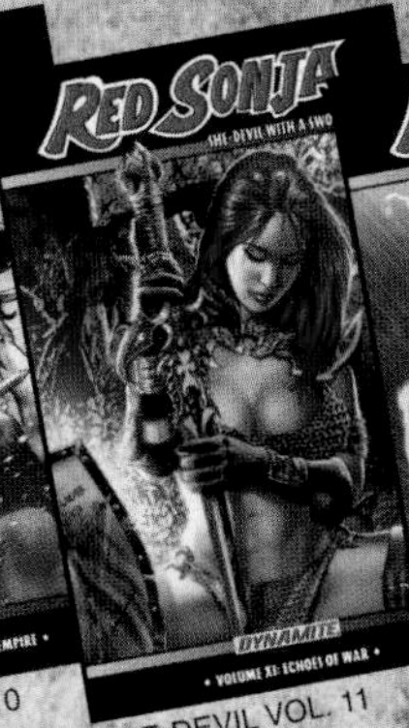
RED SONJA
DYNAMITE
VOLUME XI: ECHOES OF WAR
SHE-DEVIL VOL. 11
9781606904091

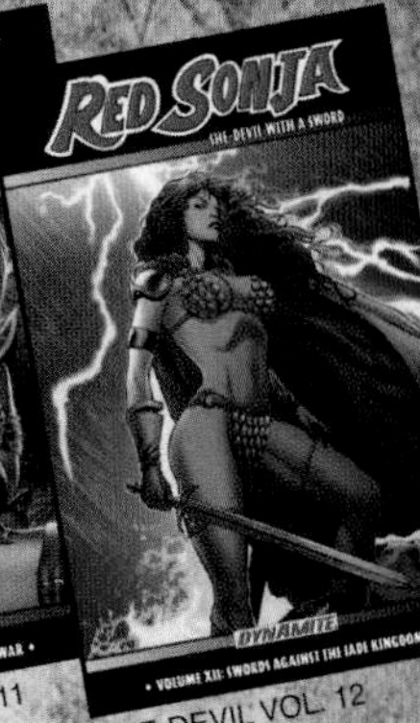
RED SONJA
SHE-DEVIL WITH A SWORD
DYNAMITE
VOLUME XII: SWORDS AGAINST THE JADE KINGDOM
SHE-DEVIL VOL. 12
9781606904428

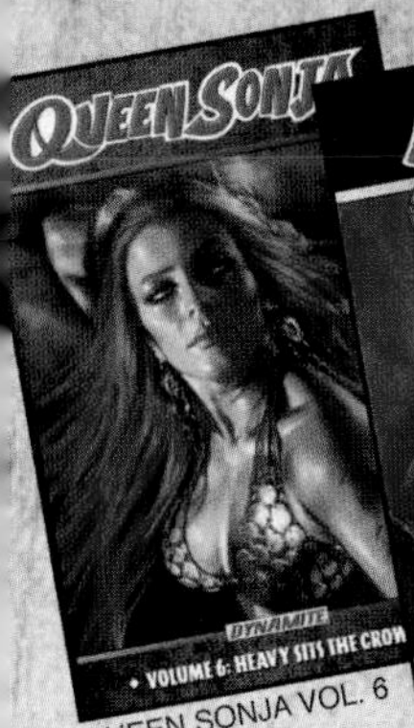
QUEEN SONJA
DYNAMITE
VOLUME 6: HEAVY SITS THE CROW
QUEEN SONJA VOL. 6
9781606904022

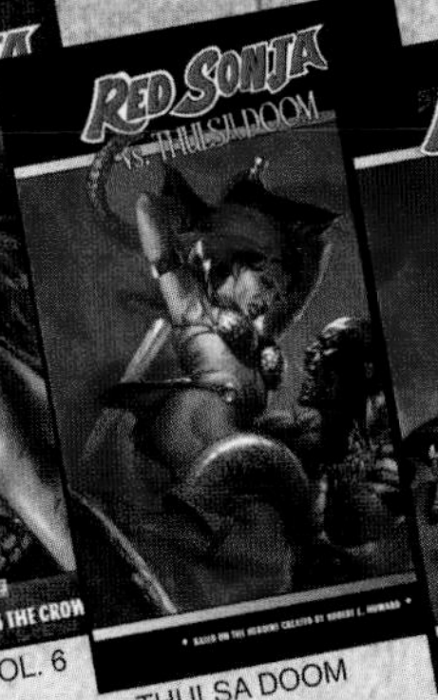
RED SONJA
vs THULSA DOOM
vs THULSA DOOM
9781933305967

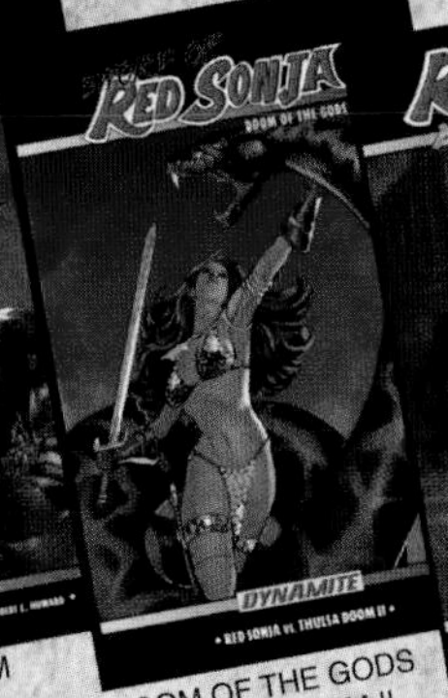
RED SONJA
DYNAMITE
RED SONJA vs. THULSA DOOM II
DOOM OF THE GODS
vs THULSA DOOM II
9781933305769

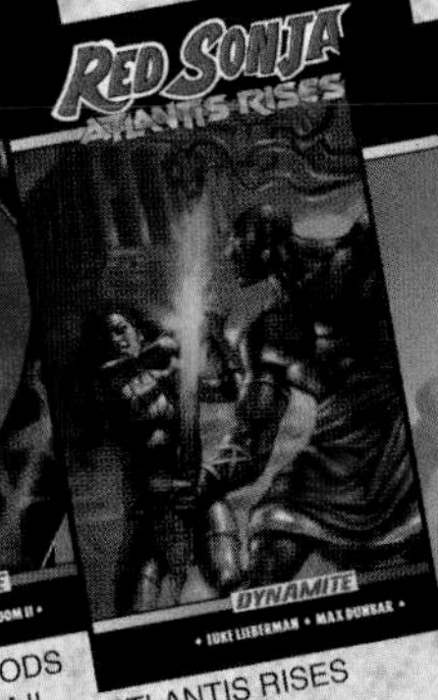
RED SONJA
ATLANTIS RISES
DYNAMITE
LUKE LIEBERMAN • MAX DUNBAR
ATLANTIS RISES
9781606903940

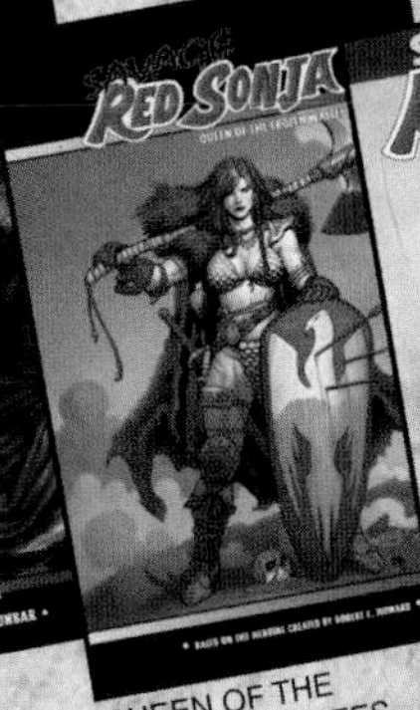
RED SONJA
QUEEN OF THE
FROZEN WASTES
9781933305387

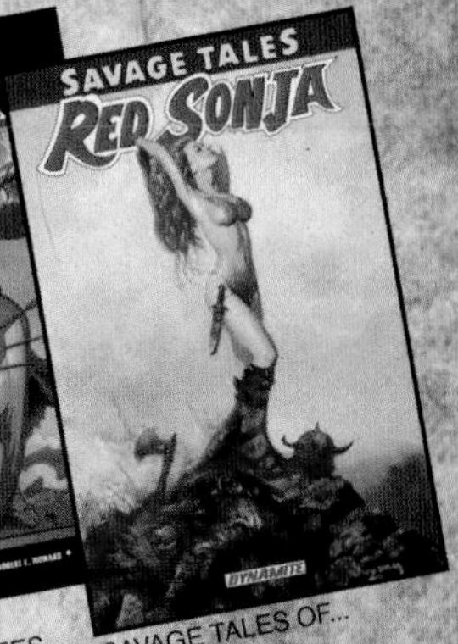
SAVAGE TALES
RED SONJA
DYNAMITE
SAVAGE TALES OF...
9781606900819

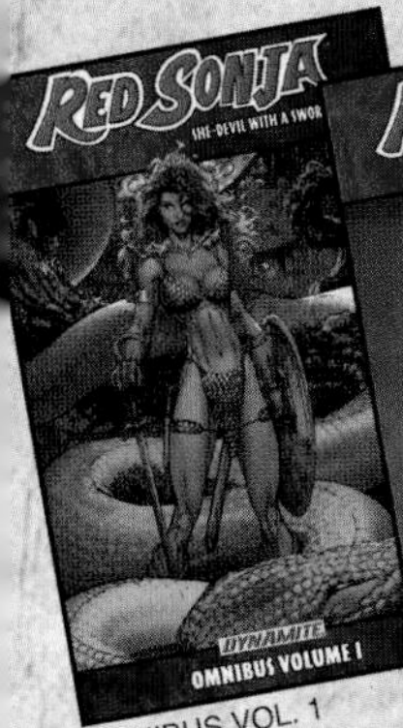
RED SONJA
DYNAMITE
OMNIBUS VOLUME 1
OMNIBUS VOL. 1
9781606901014

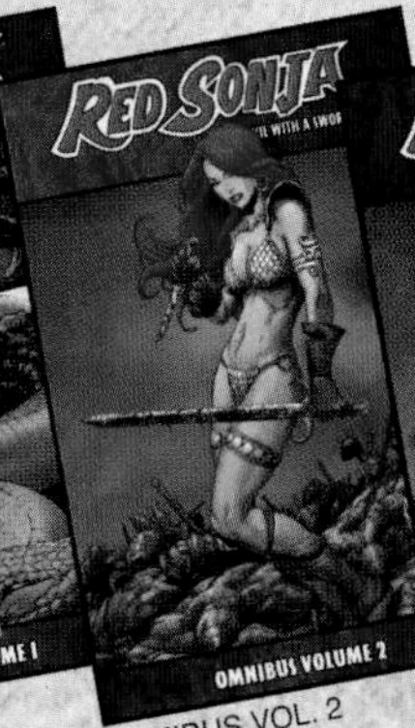
RED SONJA
OMNIBUS VOLUME 2
OMNIBUS VOL. 2
9781606902318

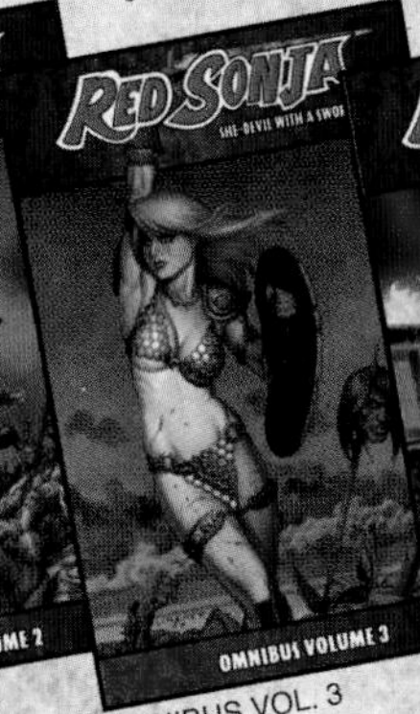
RED SONJA
OMNIBUS VOLUME 3
OMNIBUS VOL. 3
9781606903445

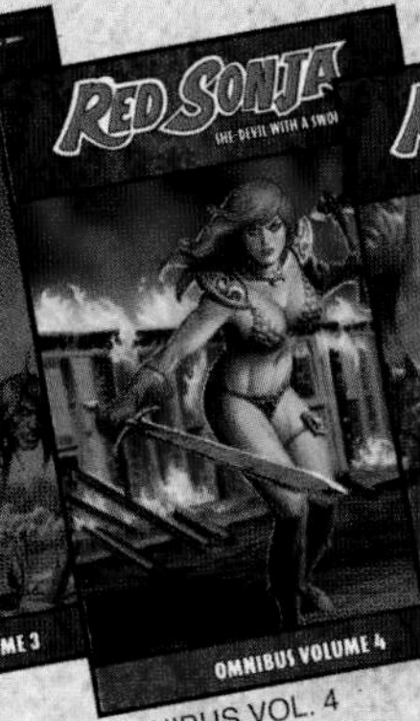
RED SONJA
OMNIBUS VOLUME 4
OMNIBUS VOL. 4
9781606904251

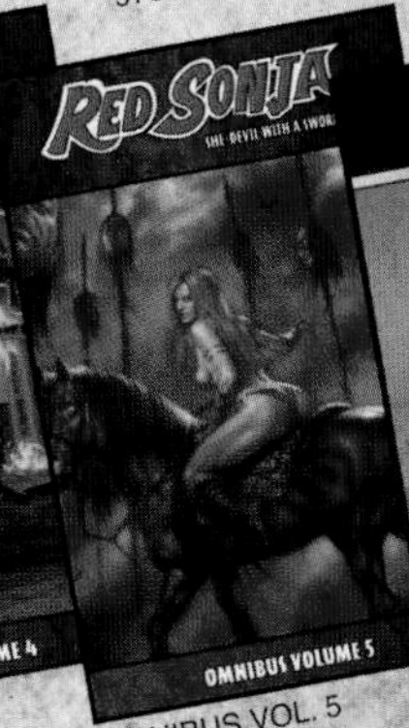
RED SONJA
OMNIBUS VOLUME 5
OMNIBUS VOL. 5
9781606904886

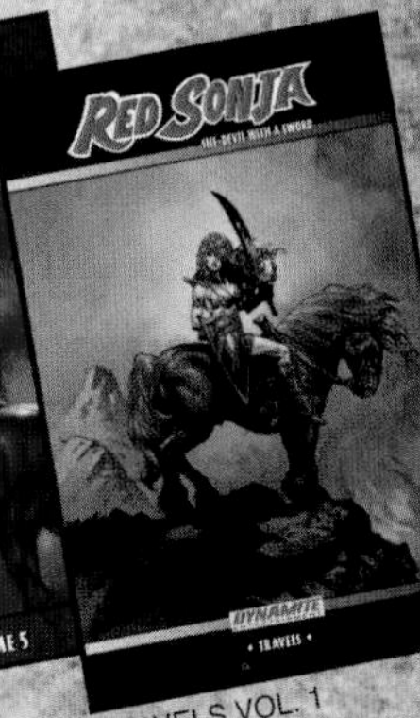
RED SONJA
SHE-DEVIL WITH A SWORD
DYNAMITE
TRAVELS
TRAVELS VOL. 1
9781933305202

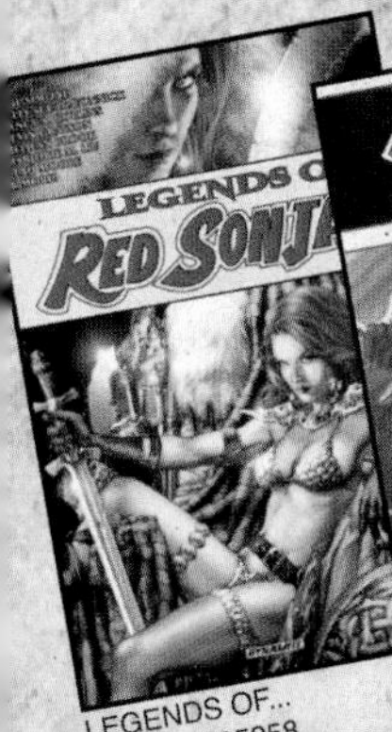
RED SONJA
LEGENDS OF...
9781606905258

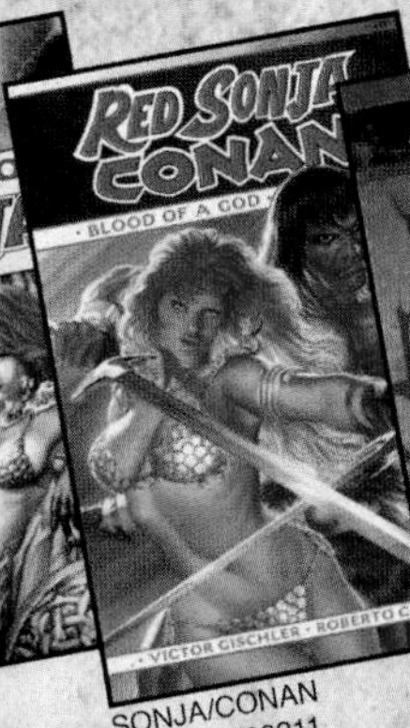
RED SONJA
CONAN
BLOOD OF A GOD
VICTOR GISCHLER
SONJA/CONAN
9781606908211

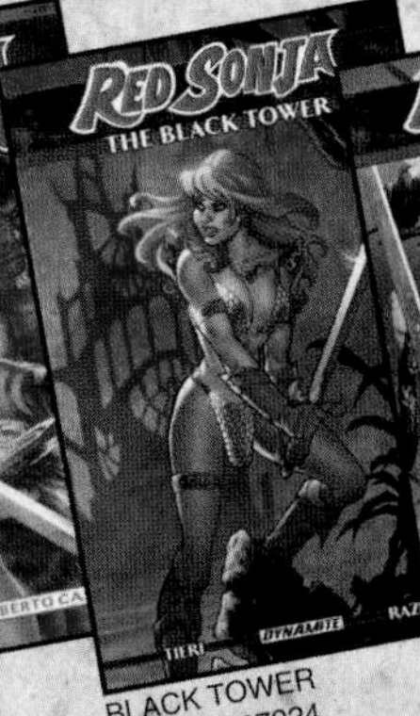
RED SONJA
THE BLACK TOWER
DYNAMITE
BLACK TOWER
9781606907924

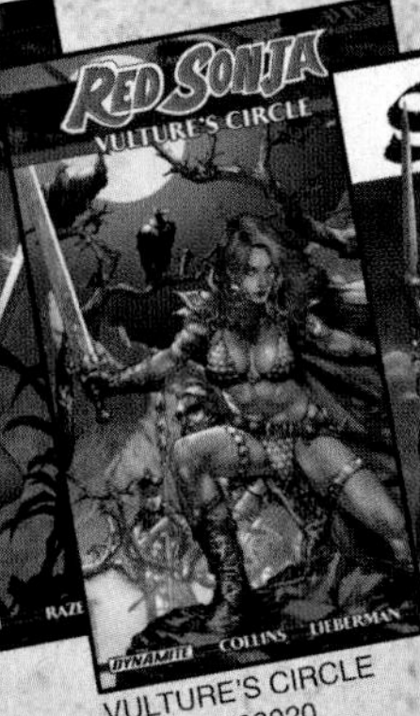
RED SONJA
VULTURE'S CIRCLE
DYNAMITE
COLLINS
LIEBERMAN
VULTURE'S CIRCLE
9781606908020

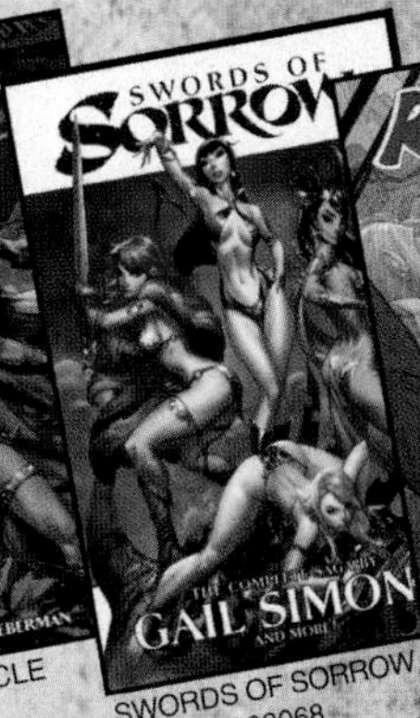
SWORDS OF
SORROW
GAIL SIMONE
AND MORE
SWORDS OF SORROW
9781606908068

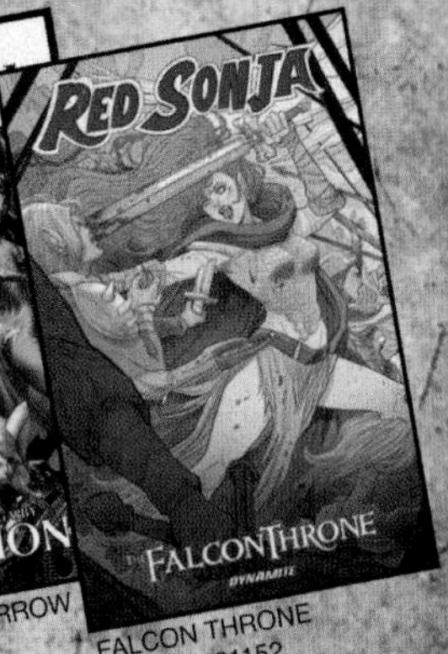
RED SONJA
FALCONTHRONE
DYNAMITE
FALCON THRONE
9781524101152

Online at **www.DYNAMITE.com**
Instragram **/Dynamitecomics**
On Twitter **@Dynamitecomics**

On Facebook **/Dynamitecomics**
On Tumblr **dynamitecomics.tumblr.com**
On YouTube **/Dynamitecomics**

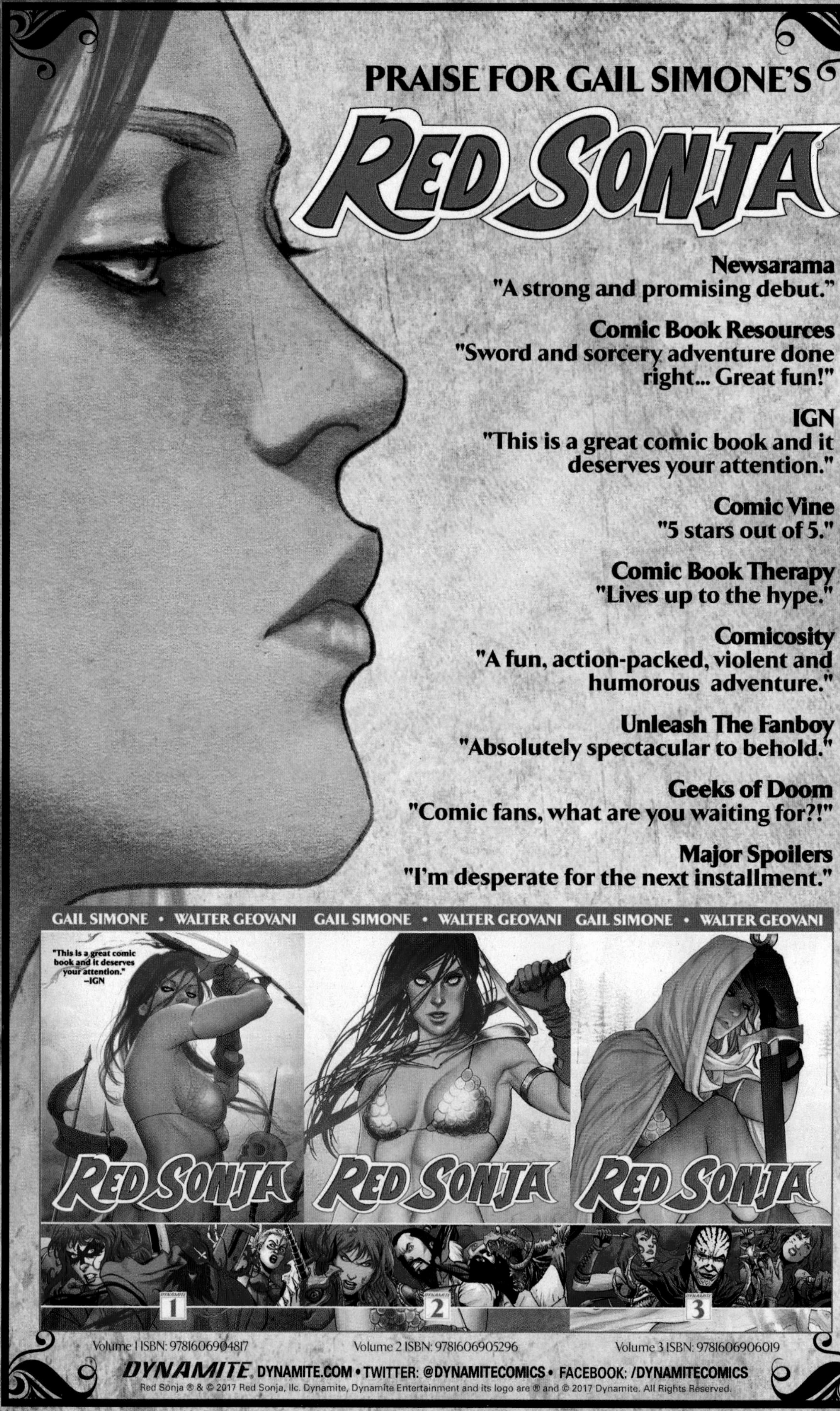
PRAISE FOR GAIL SIMONE'S
RED SONJA
Newsarama
"A strong and promising debut."
Comic Book Resources
"Sword and sorcery adventure done right... Great fun!"
IGN
"This is a great comic book and it deserves your attention."
Comic Vine
"5 stars out of 5."
Comic Book Therapy
"Lives up to the hype."
Comicosity
"A fun, action-packed, violent and humorous adventure."
Unleash The Fanboy
"Absolutely spectacular to behold."
Geeks of Doom
"Comic fans, what are you waiting for?!"
Major Spoilers
"I'm desperate for the next installment."
GAIL SIMONE • WALTER GEOVANI
GAIL SIMONE • WALTER GEOVANI
GAIL SIMONE • WALTER GEOVANI
"This is a great comic book and it deserves your attention." –IGN
RED SONJA
RED SONJA
RED SONJA
DYNAMITE 1
DYNAMITE 2
DYNAMITE 3
Volume 1 ISBN: 9781606904817
Volume 2 ISBN: 9781606905296
Volume 3 ISBN: 9781606906019
DYNAMITE. DYNAMITE.COM • TWITTER: @DYNAMITECOMICS • FACEBOOK: /DYNAMITECOMICS
Red Sonja ® & © 2017 Red Sonja, llc. Dynamite, Dynamite Entertainment and its logo are ® and © 2017 Dynamite. All Rights Reserved.